Ethnicity, Class, and Nationalism

Caribbean Studies

Lexington Books' Caribbean Studies Series is committed to publishing scholarship that either rethinks or imagines anew all aspects of Caribbean history, culture, politics, literature, and social organization. The Series will be interested in publishing studies and monographs that deal either with the Caribbean as a discrete geographical region or that treat the Caribbean and its diaspora collectively. Ever since it was brought into the orbit of Europe, the Caribbean has been defined by overlapping cultures of difference and similarity that are always in contest and conversation. This is the idea of creolization and syncretism that defines the Caribbean and its people, and that cannot be ignored in any attempt to understand the region and its diasporas. The Series's editors recognize the great insular and regional diversity that characterize the Caribbean and its diasporas and are most keen to highlight the multiplicity of theoretical and intellectual approaches needed to capture this most complex region, both historically and in contemporary times. To this extent they welcome manuscripts written from structuralist, poststructuralist, modernist, postmodernist, and even microinteractionist perspectives. The latter speaks in part to the question of psychology. For while there are many macro studies of the Caribbean from historical, sociological, political, economic, and literary points of view, there is precious little that has been done on a "Caribbean psychology" or something that seeks to capture the essence of the "Caribbean mind or psyche." In all of this one thing remains clear: the Caribbean cannot be subsumed beneath the banner of any one school or perspective. Nor can it be studied (1) independently of each state's own cultural and political situation and contemporary relationship to international capital, or (2) without taking into account the interrelationships among other Caribbean states. In other words, the Series seeks to promote a cross-disciplinary appreciation of the Caribbean that is just as intellectually robust as the Caribbean itself.

Titles in the Series

"Colón Man a Come": Mythographies of Panamá Canal Migration
    by Rhonda D. Frederick
Negotiating Caribbean Freedom: Peasants and the State in Development
    by Michaeline A. Crichlow
Ethnicity, Class, and Nationalism: Caribbean and Extra-Caribbean Dimensions
    edited by Anton L. Allahar

Ethnicity, Class, and Nationalism

Caribbean and Extra-Caribbean Dimensions

Edited by
Anton L. Allahar

LEXINGTON BOOKS
Lanham • *Boulder* • *New York* • *Toronto* • *Oxford*

LEXINGTON BOOKS

Published in the United States of America
by Lexington Books
An imprint of The Rowman & Littlefield Publishing Group, Inc.
4501 Forbes Boulevard, Suite 200, Lanham, Maryland 20706

PO Box 317
Oxford
OX2 9RU, UK

Copyright © 2005 by Lexington Books

British Library Cataloguing in Publication Information Available

Library of Congress Cataloging-in-Publication Data

Ethnicity, class, and nationalism : Caribbean and extra-Caribbean dimensions /
Anton L. Allahar [editor].
  p. cm. — (Caribbean studies)
  Includes bibliographical references and index.
  ISBN 0-7391-0887-5 (cloth : alk. paper) — ISBN 0-7391-0893-X (pbk. : alk. paper)
  1. Ethnicity—Caribbean Area. 2. Nationalism—Caribbean Area. 3. Group
identity—Caribbean Area. 4. Social classes—Caribbean Area—Cross-cultural
studies. 5. Caribbean Area—Race relations. 6. Globalization—Political aspects.
I. Allahar, Anton L. II. Series: Caribbean studies (Lanham, Md.)

GN564.C37E84 2005
305.8'009729—dc22

2004025436

Printed in the United States of America

⊚™ The paper used in this publication meets the minimum requirements of
American National Standard for Information Sciences—Permanence of Paper
for Printed Library Materials, ANSI/NISO Z39.48-1992.

Contents

Foreword

Selwyn Ryan

In the Caribbean and the rest of the decolonizing world, the years just prior to and following independence were marked by heated debates as to the role that ideas and concepts such as race, class, and ethnicity would or should play in the construction of the new nations, or in what today is called "nation building." Among both active political participants and bystanders there was a widespread expectation that in the wake of modernization and secularism, irrational considerations such as "race" or blind ethnic allegiance would give way to rational and universalist factors such as class and nationalism. Indeed, following Marx and Engels, many Third World politicians and social scientists were hostile to, and impatient with, ethnic discourse, insisting that preoccupation with race and other ethnic markers was a by-product of colonial expansion and the divide and rule policies that imperialist interests promoted as a means of cementing their hegemony.

Optimists and utopians held two general and related beliefs. According to the first, following independence and the inheriting of the political kingdom, properly organized political parties, led by ideologically conscious elites, would put in place plans, policies, and programs that would be scientifically constructed and ethnically neutral. The second belief was more cautious and provisional. It held that even if scientific construction and ethnic neutrality were not realizable, at least political leaders would implement policies that would privilege the have-nots and have-littles in the society, regardless of ethnicity, at the expense of the haves and have-mores who were the beneficiaries of the colonial order. In the process, the consciousness of the masses would be fertilized and developed. Some commentators went even further and assumed that the masses would ultimately opt for socialism in one or more of its many varieties as their social consciousness became heightened and less false.

There were, however, others who were less optimistic and who believed that ethnicity would not simply wither away or disappear, for the struggle for political independence and economic reordering of society would exacerbate ethnic conflicts. This was expected to result naturally from the competition for scarce resources as various interest groups sought to maintain, obtain, or regain space for their members in the newly emerging order. In sum, the struggle against the colonial establishment would be replaced by struggle on the part of opportunistic ethnic entrepreneurs to seize the new state and the symbols, rents, and resources that such control would make possible. Far from "withering away," then, the pessimistic view was that ethnic identity differences would persist in heightened form, and if not managed and accommodated in an inclusionary way, would lead either to the collapse of the nation-state or to a dictatorship of one ethnic group over the other.

The foregoing group, who considered themselves realists, believed that while nationalism would be seen as the essential political identity pole for many, others would resist such identification, either because they regarded the new political order as less valid than the colonial alternative that it was seeking to displace, or less emotionally satisfying and legitimate than the "mother" or "father" land from which their ancestors had come originally. To them, the injunction of Dr. Eric Williams, former prime minister of Trinidad and Tobago, was not very persuasive. For Williams there could be no Mother India for those who came from India, no Mother Africa for those of African origin, no Mother England, and no dual loyalties. Nor could there be a Mother China, even if one could agree as to which China is mother; and no Mother Syria or Mother Lebanon. For Eric Williams's conviction that "a nation, like an individual, can have only one mother" was not only unacceptable but difficult to understand.

On one hand, those who challenged Williams's doctrine were regarded as reactionaries or communalists who could not see that, like the owl of Minerva, the old order was already in flight, and that their children would inherit the new kingdom, notwithstanding the recalcitrance of their parents. On the other hand, those who challenged the modernizing elites were of two kinds: the old displaced elites and the more radical left-wing pretenders to leadership. Along with the inheritors of the postcolonial state, these challengers would come to play a central role in the political and economic fortunes of the newly independent states.

The old elites accused the new ruling groups of deliberately ignoring the reality of ethnicity or, more perversely, of surreptitiously aiming to privilege their own group. According to this view, the new ruling group was seen as rationalizing their actions by claiming that they were the logical successors of the old colonial elite and by claiming the latter's old prescriptive rights to defining the new nation. The displaced elites also charged their successors with romanticizing the nation-state, which, in their view, had no legitimacy. For their part, those on the left charged the new inheritors of state power with betraying the masses and manipulating national symbols and practices to mask their own bourgeois interests and comprador designs that were fated to deepen the economic dependence of the new states.

This book explores these and other related issues, drawing on the post-independence experiences of the Caribbean generally, and Guyana, Trinidad, Jamaica, and Puerto Rico in particular. But while its Caribbean empirical focus is clear, its strength lies in the generalizability of its insights beyond the Caribbean. Thus, the volume also ranges further afield geographically to explore ethnic political conflict in Fiji, where the native Fijians are locked in battle with Indo-Fijians for control of the postcolonial state, and also embraces the compellingly topical case of ethno-national politics in Turkey, where Kurds are seeking to establish an ethnic state or home that would bring together the Kurdish "nation" that now straddles three states—Turkey, Iran, and Iraq. The book is conceptually rich, the case material well illustrated, and the conclusions provocatively argued. The seven authors and the editor/contributor in particular deserve our plaudits and our commendations.

Preface

Anton L. Allahar

At a border crossing between Belize and Guatemala one day I looked through the open door of the Belizean immigration office and asked, "Is that Guatemala out there?" "No," said the officer, pointing to what I later learned was the Guatemalan immigration office, "Guatemala is just one hundred yards over there, beyond that grey building." "So," I persisted, "who are those people standing out there *between* this office and the Guatemalan immigration office?" "They are in no man's land," was the officer's casual reply. *No man's land*—the term is as imprecise as it is provocative. It suggests that no one really owns or has a claim on the land in question; hence, it has no clear identity apart from that which is embodied in its odd-sounding title. Those people in no man's land are in transit between clearly defined lands (Belize and Guatemala). For the moment they are an unnamed, ill-defined people occupying an unnamed, ill-defined space.

This concern with the land, with who owns it and who belongs on it or to it, has come to define a huge part of modern politics in the global age of physical displacement, diasporic identity, cultural uprooting, and the search for home. It is about a dual sense of identity and belonging: (1) the psychological or individual, and (2) the sociological or group sense. Of note, too, is the fact that in the countries of the so-called developing world there are amazing commonalities or parallels among seemingly disconnected populations. This in large part has to do with the facts of colonization and conquest and the specific use of race to divide and control colonized populations. For while colonialist styles of domination may have differed among the English, French, Spanish, Dutch, Portuguese, and so on, race did play a central role in defining power and separating the "in" group from the "out" group. And in today's world of globalization and neocolonialism, the political departure of the colonizers has been accompanied by the economic arrival of the neo-colonizers. What this has meant is that the scars or the legacies of race think-ing have remained, albeit in somewhat altered form, and the old questions of identity and belonging that persist have likewise been transformed.

But belonging also implies boundaries that separate those of the "in" group from those of the "out" group. What criteria, then, are employed in setting those boundaries? It seems to me that one of the clearest answers to this question is place of birth: where one is born is a vital part of who one is; of one's identity. Thus, the English term *nation* can be traced directly to the Latin verb *nasci* (to be born). As will be seen, however, given my focus on ethnic nationalism in the modern world, the matter is a great deal more com-plex than this. For example, whereas the Greeks have just one word to ex-press this combined or compound idea, *ethnos*, which means both "ethnic" and "nation," other societies make a definite distinction between the two. To elaborate, in Greek the notions of ethnicity and nationality are synonymous, and such terms as *ethnikos* (ethnic or national) and *ethnikotis* (ethnicity or nationality) would suggest that for them the concept of ethnic nationalism is somewhat redundant. This is so because the Greek conception of *ethnos* speaks to the idea of a nation-state or a state that comprises a single ethnic group. This is obviously very much at odds with most modern day multi-ethnic states such as those that characterize the Caribbean region, where the contested politics of national identity can and has assumed ethnic dimen-sions, and is often conducted in competitive and acrimonious terms.

To return to the idea of belonging, the basic social and gregarious make-up of human beings is seen to be bound up with their above-mentioned search for home. It is a search that is fuelled by a desire not to be left alone, for such aloneness is unnatural and leads to feelings of insecurity and vul-nerability (Allahar 1994:18–21). And this is why Benedict Anderson could write that "nationness and nationalism command such profound emotional legitimacy" (Anderson [1983b] 1991:13–14). Much like being the member of a family, to be rooted in one's own land implies an unquestioned acceptance by fellows and a sense of belonging that is both physically and emotionally reassuring. Speaking specifically about the individual in the group, Harold Isaacs wrote:

> He is not only not alone, but here, as long as he chooses to remain in and of it, he cannot be denied or rejected. It is an identity he might want to conceal, aban-don, or change, but it is the identity that no one can take away from him. It is *home* in the sense of Robert Frost's line, the place where, when you've got to go there, they've got to take you in. (Is 1975:43)

This said, the present volume proposes a study of the complex ways in which the categories of "national" and "ethnic" identity are intertwined in the drama that is the modern Caribbean. It is important to acknowledge at the outset, though, that no single volume on a region as differentiated and multi-textured as the Caribbean could ever be considered complete or exhaustive. Of this we are very mindful and hence the aim is to be more modest; it is to make a contribution to a sociological appreciation of identity politics in this vast region with comparative reference to two other countries that provide instructive parallels: Fiji and Turkey. The principal risk we run here is the same as faces any generalist, who lives in constant apprehension of the specialist. We feel, nevertheless, that there are certain broad similarities among the countries of the Caribbean that will permit informed generalization while not violating the uniqueness of any discrete country.

Furthermore, since comparative work is the sociological cement of understanding, along with references to several Caribbean countries, we have also included two other dimensions of comparative case studies. The first of these concerns the fact that no full understanding of the Caribbean can be undertaken without paying attention to the United States. The latter's geographical proximity to the countries of the Caribbean, and its obvious social, political, and economic impacts, whether positive or negative, are impossible to ignore. For this reason at least three of the chapters address the reciprocal influences between the countries of the Caribbean and the United States. The second set of comparisons will include two countries that are not even part of the Western hemisphere but whose social and political structures are also products of colonial and neocolonial domination, and whose struggles with defining their national identities are also compounded by considerations of ethnicity. They are thus highly suggestive of the Caribbean situation, and for this reason, are most instructive.

In chapter 1, I set the tone for the volume by proposing a schema for analyzing the contemporary politics of national and ethnic identity in post-colonial Caribbean states. To this end, my chapter seeks: (1) to provide a comprehensive operational definition of nationalism, (2) to qualify that definition by the addition of the adjective *ethnic*, and (3) to assess the extent to which the concept of ethnic nationalism can help us to understand some of the politics of ethnicity and national identity in a post-independence setting. The argument is situated within the broad theoretical framework of a non-reductionist, neo-Marxist class analysis, for it is my conviction that ethno-national consciousness and politics are better understood if one is able to trace the concrete class interests and motives of their promoters. In other words, whether as sentiment or as movement, nationalism cannot be divorced from the class interests of its leading promoters. To this end, the chapter provides a discussion of and seeks to clarify the distinctions between bourgeois nationalism, petty-bourgeois nationalism, and working-class nationalism. Recognizing the non-Marxist implications of the latter term, I problematize its definition and argue that instead of being dismissed simply as reactionary false consciousness, proletarian nationalism is but a stepping-stone to proletarian internationalism. I also warn against the error of absolutizing the class claim, for in the specific case of ethnic nationalism, for example, Robin Williams has noted that "to dismiss ethnicity as false consciousness ignores the clear evidence that *ethnies* often sacrifice economic interests in favor of symbolic gains" (1994:64–65), and even beyond this, as Ronaldo Munck reminds us, "nationalism matters because people die for it" (1986:2).

In chapter 2, Joshua Jelly-Schapiro extends the foregoing concerns and focuses on the case of Trinidad, where contemporary struggles to define the identity of the nation have assumed increasingly sharp ethnic dimensions. From its inception as an independent nation-state in 1962, Trinidad officially conceived of itself as a multicultural, multiracial nation. The 1956 "People's Charter" of the Afro-Creole dominated People's National Movement (PNM), which was to act as the leading party in creating and governing an independent Trinidad, emphasized the need for a progressive understanding of "West Indianness" that acknowledged the cultural contributions of all peoples of the Trinidadian mélange.

This rhetoric notwithstanding, it is only in the past fifteen years or so that Indians have gained an equitable presence in the political, economic, and civic spheres. For nearly three decades almost all components of the nation-building project were dominated by Afro-Trinbagonians. Whether tied to inertia and corruption, or justified by "plural society theories" stating that the segmentation was inevitable and ethnic domination of one group over another was unavoidable, the political and cultural history of Trinidad since independence has thus had as a central component the struggles of the Indian people to gain political power and cultural recognition.

Thus, where neither major group has a clear majority in numbers, conflicts over the cultural definition of the nation are as salient today as ever. Jelly-Schapiro also adds a unique dimension to the above conflicts by including the politics of Trinidad's diasporas in places like New York, London, and Toronto, and the complex ways in which those diasporas serve to define and inform the politics of home. Through his focus on popular music, he highlights the ways in which the ongoing creolization of cultural forms throughout Trinidad's diasporas paradoxically relates to the continued embrace of oppositional identities by Trinis of different heritages throughout the larger "nation-space." This investigation highlights some of the most fundamental questions surrounding the ways in which collective identities are formed and mobilized in our current moment; identities at once born of local circumstance and designed to function on a global scale.

Chapter 3 is a rich addition to the literature on national and ethnic identity, which until now has been largely the property of politics and political commentators. Diana Thorburn discusses the phenomenon of economic nationalism in Jamaica and Trinidad via the banking industry. Generally ignored in analyses of nationalism, she asks us to understand the economic movements for independence and national sovereignty in the postindependence Caribbean. At the beginning of the twenty-first century, the structure of banking markets in the English-speaking Caribbean reflected a shift from the 1970s of large, government-owned, commercial banks and some foreign-owned banks to a consolidated banking market dominated by private ownership, based primarily in Canada and Trinidad. In this context, Thorburn examines how changes in the ownership of banks reflect perceptions of national and regional identity in the English-speaking Caribbean, with a particular emphasis on Trinidad and Jamaica. In so doing she links the physical institution of banks and the political and economic decisions manifested in banking policy to the notions of nationalism and identity in the twenty-first century English-speaking Caribbean.

Perceptions and definitions of national identity are influenced and formed by political ideologies and political rhetoric. Once arrived at, these ideas of national identity are manifested in the symbolism of government policies, state institutions, and cultural events such as festivals and awards ceremonies. And just as ideas about national identity change with time and political trends, so does the context within which governments and political movements attempt to create symbols of national identity. For example, it may be the case that an external environment can change to the extent that extant notions of national identity are no longer feasible in the new context. This is the case with the banking sector in the Caribbean, where Thorburn argues that due to the recent changes in the ownership structure of the banking sector, banks are no longer used as political symbols at all. By focusing on the banking sector as a microcosm and material manifestation of political ideas, twenty-first century ideas of identity in the Caribbean continue to reflect an emphasis on island-specific notions of nationhood. This continuation of post-independence trends comes at the expense of the creation of a true regional identity, suggesting that even as global dynamics change, individual Caribbean states reshape their political rhetoric to maintain individualistic ideas of national identity.

In chapter 4, Shona Jackson adds a postmodern twist to the treatment of the contemporary crisis in Guyanese national identification. Via an engagement of Walter Rodney's work, she is intent on showing that the struggles over national identity and the cultural ownership of the nation have less to do with class than with ethnicity and race. For evidence Jackson selects articles, commentaries, and debates from the popular press, and uses these to construct her case for the ethnic coloring of the nation's politics.

In Guyana and in its diaspora, the social cohesion of the population is complicated by the struggles of a variety of ethnic groups not only to gain access to state power but also to reclaim their identities as formerly oppressed peoples in a way that allows state power to be disseminated through these identity struggles. The country is marked by bitter contests over who has both a historical and cultural right to rule it and which ethnic groups have the power to remake the nation in their own image. Shortly before independence, the two leading political black and East Indian figures for much of the twentieth century, Forbes Burnham and Cheddi Jagan, respectively, once shared the hope of a unified politico-cultural vision for the nation. As an expression of that vision, both hoped that the date of Guyana's independence from Britain could be the anniversary of the largest slave uprising in the country's history: the February 23, 1763, rebellion led by Cuffy (Daly [1966] 1975). But the unity was illusory.

The right to rule Guyana had been interpreted by the Burnham administration as a cultural right for blacks (Hintzen 1997) as decades of ethnic antagonism came to mark both People's National Congress (PNC) and People's Progressive Party (PPP) regimes. After the charged 1997–1998 election period and the racial violence that ensued, Guyanese again became more forcefully aware of how much the shared national vision of Cheddi Jagan and Forbes Burnham had evaporated as the single most significant black symbol of national unity (the statue of Cuffy) was routinely defaced by the dumping of trash at its base, which mirrors the problems associated with securing an agreed-upon national representation in the country. In this multiethnic, multiracial, postindependence society, there are several narratives and specific cultural discourses that encode the struggles of each group for national recognition and cultural survival, and it is the politics of such contentions that color the contemporary crisis of national belonging in Guyana.

Making the link with the U.S. influence on questions of Caribbean nationalisms and ethnicity, chapter 5 focuses on the question of black nationalism as a strategy for resisting racism and ultimately for liberating black people. Here I look at the United States in the 1960s and the experiences of black nationalists there with a view to assessing the relevance of black power and black nationalism as strategies for liberation in the countries of the Caribbean. In other words, given the loud echo of the U.S. civil rights and Black Power movements in the Caribbean, and because those movements were so tied to the philosophy and practice of black nationalism, I feel that contemporary black or cultural nationalist politics in the Caribbean are centrally informed by the struggles for liberation of black people in the United States during the 1960s and 1970s.

The U.S. connection is to be found in the long-standing relationship between American and Caribbean peoples. Whether through the institution of slavery, through travel and migration, through the presence of American military bases and multinational corporations on Caribbean soil, through general sporting and cultural exchanges, or through political and economic collaborations between the American and Caribbean elites, the peoples of the United States and the English-speaking Caribbean have a great deal of historical, social, economic, and political continuity. Thus, in the United States, where the civil rights struggles generally, and the Black Power movement specifically, are crucial chapters in that country's history, one cannot ignore the spillover effects in the Caribbean. Indeed, lest we forget, the very term *black power* was coined by Stokely Carmichael, a Trinidadian. The idea in chapter 5 is to look critically and analytically at the Black Power movement in the United States; to tease out the various internal, ideological strands and strains that characterized it; and to examine how that has served to inform the contemporary manifestation of black nationalism in the Caribbean.

In chapter 6, Jeffrey Ogbar extends the focus on the U.S. connection, but with a twist. He examines the phenomenon of Puerto Rican nationalism during the 1960s and 1970s as a nationalism from below; from the streets of cities like New York and Chicago. Given Puerto Rico's unique status within the American union, this study speaks to the ethno-national self-determination of a minority group within a larger alien culture. Ogbar's approach to nationalism is quite consistent with that defined in chapter 1. It speaks to nationalism as (1) a movement for independence or sovereignty over a territorial space and (2) a sentiment of ethnic distinctiveness and commonality that informs the movement in question. The sentiment is best expressed as a yearning for recognition or respect of minority ethnic rights, in this case Puerto Ricans in the United States. Given the history of Spanish colonialism and American neo-colonialism in Puerto Rico, and the fact that the United States today is arguably the most racially fractured country in the world, many Puerto Ricans have long struggled on two fronts. The first has been directed at securing the political independence of their homeland, while the second focuses on those Puerto Ricans who live in the United States and must also struggle for ethno-national recognition and social justice. The widespread racialization of public consciousness in American society has made for a complex challenge to independence-minded Puerto Ricans.

It was not until the late 1960s that Puerto Rican radical activism would develop around both mainland and island issues, while also generating a broader class appeal. Several factors precipitated the development of popular grassroots Puerto Rican nationalism, including larger anti-imperialist struggles, Cold War politics, and the black freedom movement in the United States. The new Puerto Rican nationalism of the late 1960s developed simultaneously among baby boomers in two different cities, converging and giving rise to the most celebrated Puerto Rican organization of the era, the Young Lords. This chapter tells the story of the Young Lords and their contributions to the definition of Puerto Rican identity in the United States.

Chapter 7 takes us outside of the Western hemisphere to Fiji in the South Pacific, where Steven Ratuva analyzes a social and political reality that bears striking similarities with both Trinidad and Guyana. This chapter is concerned with what Ratuva calls a post-colonial communal democracy in which political identity and ethnic identity exist side by side, define, and shape each other. It is a tense yet mutual relationship that has helped to maintain a fragile yet self-sustaining continuity in a country recently beset by major political instability.

Fiji became independent from Britain in 1970 after ninety-six years of colonial rule during which time British colonial policy dictated the formal and political separation and distinctive communal development of these ethnic groups through a series of legislations under the native policy. According to that policy, indigenous Fijians remained locked into a rigid communal and subsistence way of life, which kept them distant from mainstream national politics and economic development. Indo-Fijians, on the other hand, who were brought in as indentured laborers in the late 1800s and early 1900s, were confined to the regimented life of the sugar cane plantations, while Europeans largely ran the civil service, government, and business.

While previously there was minimal social interaction among the three ethnic groups, by the 1980s ethnic separation began to give way to ethnic strife as indigenous Fijians came to feel like third-class citizens in their own country (after securing the vote only in 1965 while the Indo-Fijians had done so as early as 1929). The result was a number of indigenous Fijian military coups in the 1980s and 1990s, aimed at the Indo-Fijian minority that dominated business and commerce. There was no mistaking the ethnic content of the coups as leaders on both sides played the race card in an attempt to win support for its respective ethnic definition of the Fiji nation. This is the backdrop against which an analysis of the dynamics of ethnic and national identity construction and reproduction in Fiji is undertaken.

Still outside of the Western hemisphere, chapter 8 takes us to Turkey and an analysis of the very timely and explosive question of Kurdish political and ethnic identity. While the empirical evidence for this chapter is derived from a context that is quite different from the rest of the volume, the theoretical focus is right on target. Following the argument laid out in chapter 1, Saraçoğlu is able to come to grips directly with the Marxist theory of ethnicity and nationalism. His is a non-orthodox approach, but one that is highly instructive and makes a compelling case for the retention of Marxist methodology in any study of class, ethnic, and national identity, particularly as these touch on the questions of bourgeois, civic, and ethnic nationalisms.

As the largest ethnic minority in the world, Cenk Saraçoğlu reminds us that the Kurds are scattered across a number of countries and especially in the post-9/11 world, they have served to define the shape and content of ethnic politics in all of those countries. Apart from Turkey, Kurdish regions include eastern and southeastern Anatolia, northeastern Syria, northern Iraq, northwestern Iran, southern Armenia, and Azerbaijan. Because the Kurds do not have a state of their own, they are subject to the external authority of other countries, most notably Turkey, Iran, and Iraq. However, because Kurdish groups in the various countries have developed distinctive features, the Kurdish question in Turkey can be analyzed independently of the Kurdish conflict in Iraq and Iran.

Because the social significance and power of ethnic identities in shaping group action and social activity may vary according to location and time, Saraçoğlu insists that any theoretical appreciation of ethnic politics must address the following questions: Under what social conditions do ethnic attachments become important? What kind of social factors are important in influencing the political behaviors of an ethnic group? How does a change in the political behaviors of a certain ethnic group affect the general organization of society?

Answers to these questions are pursued in the investigation of the relationship between ethnic identities and capitalist relations of production in Turkey. In this chapter, ethnic nationalism is viewed as an ideal that holds that a defined territory should be governed by a state whose structure is shaped according to values of one dominant ethnic group. This is to say that ethnic nationalism is a form of ethnic consciousness that is tied to the idea of a state. Thus, as will be seen, the notion of Turkish ethnic nationalism refers to the idea that all social and political relations in Turkey should be organized according to cultural values of Turkish ethnicity. Kurdish ethnic nationalism, on the other hand, implies that it is necessary to form a separate state in the Kurdish areas of Turkey, which is to be constituted on the basis of Kurdish ethnicity. For according to Saraçoğlu's argument, Kurdish and Turkish ethnic nationalism are necessarily irreconcilable sentiments.

In chapter 9, I seek to tie the project together with a discussion of identity politics, nationalism, and ethnicity. I elaborate the discussion of false consciousness and class consciousness that was begun in chapter 1 and introduce the questions of Afrocentricity and *Hindutva* (Hindu Nationalism), both of which have had significant echos in the Caribbean. The focus here will be largely on the impacts of these ideologies on Trinidad's political culture. For it is the bourgeois and petty-bourgeois nationalist intellectuals of the region who have come to serve as ethnic entrepreneurs and who seek deliberately to fashion myths of the nation with a view to mobilizing popular political support for one or another political project. Such intellectuals and ethnic entrepreneurs "select the historical memories and elaborate the myths of descent of the relevant *ethnie*" (Smith 1988:13), and are usually quite clear to name which elements of culture will be emphasized and which will be ignored in the mythical reconstruction of the nation. In other words, the aim is to present a clear and compelling history of the group, even if largely invented, with a view psychologically and emotionally to mobilizing coethnics for political ends.

1

Situating Ethnic Nationalism in the Caribbean

Anton L. Allahar

CLASS THEORIES OF ETHNICITY AND RACE

Since the 1960s, neo-Marxists who focus on the social constructedness of political identities, particularly class, have sought to reject fixed, biological, or primordial claims to identity. However, recognizing the limitations of class reductionism embodied in orthodox Marxism, and mindful of the contemporary struggles of peoples all around the world for self-determination, these theorists have also devoted a great deal of attention to studies that seek theoretically to incorporate considerations of ethnicity and nationalism with class analysis (Nairn 1977; Bonacich 1980; Hall 1980; Wolpe 1986; Hobsbawm 1990; Gilroy 2000; among many others). Like elsewhere, then, the articulation of ethnicity and nationalism with class is a central element in any neo-Marxist appreciation of the contemporary manifestation of identity politics in the Caribbean.

One set of these theories, known as split labor market theories (Bonacich 1972, 1976), places labor competition at the heart of capitalist exploitation. It envisions a single labor market marked by very keen competition among an ethnically differentiated labor force, and examines the ways that capital divides workers racially by rewarding (hiring, wages, promotions, security, etc.) one group more than the other. This serves to exacerbate perceived differences among workers, politicizes the competition over scarce jobs, and in the process prevents workers from developing a critical class awareness that transcends their ethnic, national, and racial differences. In countries like Trinidad and Tobago, Guyana, and Suriname, the political consequences of this ethnoracial division of the working classes are very evident (Allahar 2001b; Dupuy 1996). It is not the case, however, that race trumps class. Rather, the two are mutually reinforcing of one another. In the words of Stuart Hall: "Race is the modality in which class is lived. It is also the medium in which class relations are experienced" (1978:394). To this Harold Wolpe added, "The simple opposition between race and class must be rejected. Race may, under determinant conditions, become interiorised in the class struggle" (1986:123).

Along with split labor market theories, there is the dual labor market approach (Beck, Horan, and Tolbert 1978), which also sees class as fundamental, and which also problematizes the questions of race and ethnicity. Whereas the above approach spoke of a single labor market that was split between or among ethno-racial groups, the dual labor market approach speaks to the existence of more than one labor market, each characterized or dominated by a different ethno-national group, for instance, Italians in the North American construction industry, Chinese in the laundry and dry cleaning industry, or Caribbean blacks and Mexicans as migrant agricultural workers in Canada. In this approach (which was developed initially to analyze the situation of black and white workers in the United States), there is less interethnic contact, but class exploitation remains the central driving force of capital. In the case of Trinidad, in the years leading up to and following independence, one might be able fruitfully to apply this framework to an analysis of the two leading industries of the country: the Indians in sugar and the blacks in oil.

Another group of theorists sees ethnicity (race) and class as more or less co-terminous (Fanon 1963; Cox 1970; Wallerstein 1972). This approach lends itself to an understanding of situations such as South Africa under the system of apartheid, the U.S. South in the era of Jim Crow and after, and Trinidad and Guyana during indentureship and right into the immediate post-indentureship period (La Guerre 1974). The idea here is that one's station in life was ascribed and one's life chances were limited to achieving what was dictated by that ascribed status. Whether talking about jobs and income, place of residency, pool of potential spouses and friends, place and content of education, treatment before the law, or guarantees of the basic liberal freedoms, the most significant determining factor was a combination of color, ethnicity, and perceived race.

For those who work in this area, ethnicity and race are generally seen as good predictors of class and economic position, just as one's class and economic position could usually be used as a predictor of one's ethnicity or race. It is thus understandable that in these situations ethnic political entrepreneurs of all groups would be tempted to use the concepts of ethnicity and race as bases for political mobilization, just as the scholars in question might use them as shortcuts for class analysis. Frantz Fanon captures the essence of this thinking best when he says: "In the colonies the economic substructure is also a superstructure. The cause is the consequence; you are rich because you are white, you are white because you are rich" (1963:40).

Finally, there are those theorists who speak of the international division of labor, and who tend to be class reductionistic by virtually ignoring ethnonational divisions within countries. In this approach countries function as classes, and within the international division of labor, it is not uncommon for them to see entire blocs of countries referred to as the proletariat. The principal theorist here is Immanuel Wallerstein, whose definition of class is summarized by Daniel Chirot as comprising "a group of individuals, or a *group of social systems* united by a common economic interest" (1977:13 [my emphasis]). For his part, Wallerstein sees the capitalist world system and the international division of labor as stratified into core, semiperiphery, and periphery countries. Describing the process of capitalist accumulation on a world scale, Wallerstein even goes on to speak of the core countries as constituting an upper class, the semiperiphery as playing the role of a middle class, and the periphery as a lower class (1979:69–70). In this tradition too are the theorists of so-called *internal colonialism*, who gloss over class and ethnic differences among the oppressed and homogenize the struggles for national autonomy in the internal colonies as essentially proletarian struggles (Blauner 1972; Geschwender 1978; Wotherspoon and Satzewich 1993).

THE POINT OF DEPARTURE

This said, the present chapter will propose a schema for analyzing the contemporary politics of national and ethnic identity in postcolonial Caribbean states. To this end it will seek: (1) to provide a comprehensive operational definition of nationalism, (2) to qualify that definition by the addition of the adjective "ethnic," and (3) to assess the extent to which the concept ethnic nationalism can help us to understand some of the politics of ethnicity and national identity in a post-independence setting. My argument will be situated within the broad theoretical framework of a non-reductionist, neo-Marxist class analysis, for it is my conviction that ethno-national consciousness and politics are better understood if we are able to trace the concrete class interests and motives of their promoters.

To begin, there is so much disagreement over the definition and proper meaning of the concept that Ernst Haas (1986) has questioned, Why bother even to ask "what is nationalism and why should we study it?" At the very broadest of levels, nationalism can be seen as an ideology espoused by those who live in already established nations, complete with economic, political, legal, military, economic, and civic autonomy in a clearly demarcated territorial space. But as an ideology, the term *nationalism* can also be used to characterize a *sentiment*, a yearning or *movement* for independence and autonomy on the part of peoples, who, though sharing what Clifford Geertz calls "a corporate sentiment of oneness" and "a consciousness of kind"

(1973:260; 307), do not yet inhabit a clearly defined territorial space. As Daniel Chirot writes: "almost all the present nations would like to become nation-states, but many nations are actually parts of other states, and many states are not nation-states" (1977:11).

It is this latter phenomenon that interests me most. It brings to mind the intriguing challenge posed by the playwright Luigi Pirandello in his play *Six Characters in Search of an Author*, where he pioneered the technique of writing the play within the play. In the work in question, Pirandello created six complete characters but neglected to create roles for them, and this gave the play its central theme: the trials of the six characters as they embark on their quest for the author who would assign them their roles and thus complete the play.

With some poetic license I see this situation as quite suggestive of post-colonial social formations in areas such as the Caribbean, where multiethnic states like Trinidad and Tobago and Guyana house nations in search of homes. I am thinking of *nations* as ethnic groupings that share the above-mentioned "corporate sentiment of oneness," and of *homes* as places (territories) where the members of such groupings can feel a sense of unquestioned belonging and acceptance. My approach to the nation, then, deals as much with unwritten sentiment as with juridical meaning, and differs somewhat from Anthony Giddens' strictly state-centered view:

> By a nation I refer to a collectivity existing within a clearly demarcated territory, which is subject to a unitary administration, reflexively monitored both by the internal state apparatus and those of other states. A nation . . . only exists when a state has a unified administrative reach over the territory over which its sovereignty is claimed. (1984:116)

Colonies and those colonial subjects that inhabit them are by definition not independent or sovereign entities. It is possible, however, for colonial subjects to develop a sense of nationness and to agitate for independence and national self-determination while still under the colonizers' yoke. This was clearly the case in the English-speaking Caribbean on the eve of independence as Crown Colony government paved the way for the emergence of nationalist politics. However, it is after securing political independence, whether by war or by peaceful negotiation with the colonial master, that the *process of nation building* can be said to begin. But since no two countries are exactly alike in their historical experiences, their social class structure and composition, their natural resource endowment, their demographic make-up, or even in the specific values that their cultures embrace, the process of nation building can be expected to vary from country to country. It stands to reason, too, that in multiethnic states where two or more ethnic groups are more or less even in numbers, the process of nation building could be a very contentious one. And this is likely to be even more accentuated where the ethnic groups in question have a developed racialized consciousness (Trinidad and Guyana).

Furthermore, in order fully to understand the sentiment of nationalism one must look at its proponents and interrogate their motives. In other words, whether as sentiment or as movement, nationalism cannot be divorced from the class interests of its leading promoters. By this I mean that nationalism, along with the peculiar brands of ideological appeal that nationalists make, will most often be linked to the discrete economic and political interests of its champions. But one must be cautious in absolutizing the class claim, for in the specific case of ethnic nationalism, for example, Robin Williams has noted that "to dismiss ethnicity as false consciousness ignores the clear evidence that *ethnies* often sacrifice economic interests in favor of symbolic gains" (1994:64–65). Even beyond this, economic gain is not all that is sacrificed for as Ronaldo Munck reminds us, "Nationalism matters because people die for it." And "if people are prepared to die for their country, then this must be a phenomenon worth investigating" (1986:2). The class reductionism of orthodox Marxism must therefore be guarded against, for at different times some peoples and groups will value the symbolic and cultural aspects of group identity higher than the rationally calculated economic and political gains to be derived (or lost) from pursuing class interests.

On the other hand, as will be seen presently, while the concept of false consciousness generally is fraught with difficulty, it cannot be entirely ignored in any assessment of the political calculations of specific actors, especially when those calculations relate to claims of ethnic belonging. In other words, what to some may appear as false consciousness, to others will represent strategic, rational calculation. It all depends on the situation at hand, and the long-term and short-term goals and class interests of the leading actors. In what follows I will flesh out the concept of false consciousness as it speaks to social classes, with a view later to applying it to an understanding of ethnic and national consciousness. My goal is to show that not all working-class consciousness is tantamount to false consciousness. Because the working class is not a homogeneous political and economic entity, it is possible to identify (1) a fraction that is falsely conscious and given to a reactionary form of ethnic and cultural nationalism, and (2) another fraction that is more politically consciousness and capable of pursuing nationalist politics as a short-term strategy that leads ultimately to socialism and proletarian internationalism.

CLASS CONSCIOUSNESS AND FALSE CONSCIOUSNESS

When discussing class and class consciousness Marx was keen to point out that classes, and the proletariat in particular, are not always aware of their potential power. As the capitalist mode of production came to supplant feudal social relations in the countrysides of Europe, large masses of displaced and dispossessed rural dwellers came under the sway of capital, and the beginnings of a proletarian class could be detected. But lacking political organization and education, members of this class were not automatically or spontaneously united and conscious of their collective strength and possibilities. They amounted to what was basically a statistical aggregate, a group of workers brought together merely by the fact of their common subjugation by capital. For this reason they constituted what some have termed a *class in itself*.

In time, however, as greater exposure to capitalist exploitation sharpened the contradictions between this class and the owners of capital, as their organization and education grew, so too did their consciousness of themselves as a class that faced a set of common problems. In the process there also developed the awareness of the fact that they could do something to better their conditions of existence, but this necessitated the collective action of a *class for itself*. In Marx's words:

> The combination of capital has created for this mass a common situation, common interests. This mass is thus already a class as against capital, but not yet for itself. In the struggle . . . this mass becomes united, and constitutes itself as a *class for itself*. The interests it defends become class interests. (1963:173 [my emphasis])

This said, what is the definition of false consciousness, and how is it related to the themes that will be pursued in the following pages? Before answering this question I must underscore the point that in a class-reductionist sense, where actors are seen generally to lack agency, I find orthodox Marxism to be incomplete as an explanation for political behavior in modern society. However, though incomplete, the insights of the orthodox position cannot be entirely dismissed. What I will do, therefore, is to utilize those insights as they are relevant and, where necessary, I will provide a critique of them.

Although the specific term *false consciousness* was never used by Marx, there are many allusions to the term in Marx's work, and within the Marxist literature generally, it is quite commonly encountered in analyses of such phenomena as class consciousness, revolution, and ideology. As argued above, class consciousness or class awareness, for example, speaks to the notion that a social class is made up of individuals who share a set of common interests, are politically aware of this fact, and are indeed capable of acting together to promote and defend those common interests. False consciousness, conversely, describes a situation in which individuals who share that common class situation are not aware of the fact, and as a consequence are not able to conceive of acting in concert to pursue their interests. As George Ritzer has written:

The ideas of class consciousness and false consciousness are closely related in Marx's work. Both refer to idea systems shared by social classes. In capitalism both capitalists and workers have incorrect assessments of how the system works and of their role and interest in it (false consciousness). . . . What is characteristic of capitalism, for *both* the proletariat and the bourgeoisie, is false consciousness. (1992:172)

Though correct, Ritzer's contribution is not original, for given the structure and conditions of capitalist exploitation, Georg Lukács earlier had reminded us that both the bourgeoisie and the proletariat are subject to false consciousness. The main difference is that bourgeois class consciousness leads to false consciousness because the bourgeoisie is unable to see beyond capitalism as a system, and end up by creating the conditions for their own demise as a class: "the barrier which converts the class consciousness of the bourgeoisie into false consciousness is objective; the class situation itself" (Lukács 1971:54). To which might be added Marx and Engels' forecast that "what the bourgeoisie therefore produces, above all, are its own gravediggers. Its fall and the victory of the proletariat are equally inevitable" (1955:22). Stated differently, the bourgeoisie is incapable of solving the crises of capitalism for it is locked into a logic of exploitation and accumulation that produces increasingly unmanageable economic crises (e.g., overproduction and underconsumption), that in turn condition the development of opposition political consciousness within the proletariat. The vision of the bourgeoisie thus "becomes obscured as soon as it is called upon to face problems that remain within its jurisdiction but which point beyond the limits of capitalism" (Lukács 1971:54).

On the other hand, the sheer survival of the proletariat as a class presents us with an interesting contradiction whereby it is compelled to envision an alternative to capitalism. And that alternative, which is supposedly socialism, will see the disappearance of the proletariat qua proletariat. This notwithstanding, Lukács writes that "the protracted death struggle of the bourgeoisie" is dialectically related to the fact that "only the consciousness of the proletariat can point to the way that leads out of the impasse of capitalism" (Ibid:68, 76). Following this logic, Ritzer is able to claim that "the bourgeoisie can never transform its false consciousness into true class consciousness; this is possible only for the proletariat" (1992:173). The idea here is that, in calling the proletariat into existence, the bourgeoisie unwittingly sows the seeds of its own destruction; but the dilemma is systemic and lies beyond the reach of individual actors or the capitalist class as a whole.

But what about proletarian false consciousness? In *The German Ideology*, Marx and Engels acknowledged the limitations of reductionism and mechanical thinking when they wrote that "man also possesses consciousness," but owing to the dominance of bourgeois ideology and the vicissitudes of daily living, it is "not inherent, not pure consciousness" (1947:19). In other words, rather than romanticizing the worker as an always-conscious and informed revolutionary actor, Marx and Engels understood the power and pervasiveness of bourgeois ideology and the practical difficulties that militated against effective proletarian political education and the development of class consciousness.

Given the exploitive, oppressive, and alienating conditions under which the worker is forced to live and work, and speaking specifically of the relationship between ideology, consciousness, and political action, Engels was led to write the following in a letter to Franz Mehring in 1893: "Ideology is a process accomplished by the so-called thinker consciously, it is true, but with a false consciousness. The real motive forces compelling him remain unknown to him; otherwise it simply would not be an ideological process" (1977:496). What Engels is suggesting is that workers, who are often steeped in the bourgeois ideologies of individualism and materialism, are not to be expected automatically to develop a critical class understanding their difficult life circumstances. And such workers may be duped into accepting a bourgeois definition of nationalism as a political goal that is consistent with their proletarian interests. This could be an example of proletarian national consciousness as false consciousness. Viewed in more micro terms, what objectively might be in the best long-term interests of the worker (e.g., joining a labor union) might be resisted out of fear of losing his or her job or rejected in favor of a course of individual action (e.g., snitching to the boss) that is tailored more to his or her immediate or short-term interests: job security. This example of what is supposedly false consciousness points up the question of rationality and the fact that what may be seen as an appropriate and rational decision in the short-term may just turn out to have been wrong in the fullness of time.

Because human beings are subjective beings who are subjectively involved in their worlds, their apprehensions of those worlds are understandably ideologically formed. This means that any talk about the existence of objectivity or an objective reality is bound to be itself ideological. So, to speak of consciousness as somehow false begs the question of what true consciousness is, and how one might go about discovering it. This means that class consciousness and false consciousness are matters of *subjective imputation,* which led Georg Lukács to observe that:

> It must not be thought, however, that all classes ripe for hegemony have a class consciousness with the same inner structure. Everything hinges on the extent to which they can become conscious of the actions they need to perform in order to obtain and organize power. The question then becomes: how far does the class concerned perform the actions that history has imposed on it "consciously" or "unconsciously"? And is that consciousness "true" or "false?" (1971:53)

CONSCIOUSNESS IS CREATED, NOT GIVEN

Although he was roughly of the same mind as Marx and Engels on the question of false consciousness, Lenin was even less inclined to romanticize the revolutionary potential of the proletariat. Indeed, talking about ideology and political action, he was opposed to seeing the working class as specially endowed with a spontaneous, proletarian, revolutionary consciousness. For him, consciousness was created, not given. It was the culmination of a period of education and struggle, for the working class was so dominated by bourgeois ideology that it could not be expected automatically, naturally, or spontaneously to develop a revolutionary consciousness. Equating working-class revolutionary consciousness with socialist consciousness, Lenin was in full agreement with Karl Kautsky, whom he quotes as follows in *What Is to Be Done?*

> Socialist consciousness is something introduced into the proletarian class struggle from without and not something that arose within it spontaneously. . . . The task of Social Democracy is to imbue the proletariat [literally: saturate the proletariat] with the consciousness of its position and the consciousness of its task. (1969:40)

Then Lenin goes on to add his own views to the effect that trade union consciousness amounted to false consciousness. For what trade unions encouraged was a narrow *economism* according to which workers focused entirely on their local, individual, material interests and in the process lost sight totally of the wider class struggle for socialism and *proletarian internationalism*. Thus, he writes: "Since there can be no talk of an independent ideology formulated by the working masses themselves. . . . The only choice is— either bourgeois or socialist ideology. . . . Trade unionism means the ideological enslavement of the workers by the bourgeoisie" (1969:40–41). In sum, then, false consciousness is a thorny term but, if carefully nuanced, will nevertheless prove useful for analyzing ethnic nationalism, the motives that impel ethnic entrepreneurs, and the class interests that underlie "the activism of Third World leaders bent on inventing nations where they do not exist, and engaged in the project of constructing the nation-to-be" (Smith 1988:6).

ETHNIC NATIONALISM

My definition of the term *ethnic* includes the notion of identity and is borrowed in part from Anthony Smith, for whom an ethnic community, or *ethnie,* is "a named human population possessing a myth of common descent, common historical memories, elements of shared culture, an association with a particular territory, and a sense of solidarity" (1988:9). I add to this the idea of situational ethnicity, which sees ethnic identity as "incipient, problematic, and situationally determined" (Nagel and Olzak 1982:129), and which implies that since not all ethnic groups are politically mobilized at all times, ethnic mobilization is a calculated, rational response to the challenges faced by some ethnic groups at historically specific times. As will be suggested, the recent concerns among cultural nationalists with establishing purity of African and Indian roots among various Caribbean populations are cases in point (see chapter 9). This said, I will understand (ethnic) nationalism as an ideological claim, or a movement seeking to make such a claim, of self-determination and sovereignty. Integral to this statement is (1) the existence of some bounded territory or nation over which nationalists already have jurisdiction and are able to maintain it, or (2) in the case of a nationalist *movement*, some bounded territory over which members wish to claim jurisdiction.

A WORKING DEFINITION

In an attempt to deal analytically with the density of the concept of nationalism, scholars have spoken of two broad types: (1) modern civic or territorial nationalism, where the nation is legally or juridically defined and contains clear class elements; and (2) a more traditional ethnic or genealogical nationalism, where the nation is more ethnically and culturally defined (Calhoun 1993:221). The civic definition sees territory as central but adds a common economy, common laws that apply equally to all citizens, a public mass educational system, shared administrative and military institutions, and a single civic ideology (Smith 1988:9). The latter will include such charged political symbols as a national flag, a national anthem, a national coat of arms, and a set of national holidays. Deciding on which of these will represent the nation is potentially a matter of intense and continuing political debate among co-nationals, especially in the case of a multiethnic nation-state, whether already formed or in the process of formation. As a mode of political being, civic nationalism is more prevalent in those modern states such as are encountered in the post-colonial Caribbean. And it is the fact of their multi-ethnic make-up that renders the debate over ethnonational identity so intense and at times so acrimonious, for, masked by emotive claims of ethnic entrepreneurs, the class dimensions of civic nationalism often shade into and become complicated by the reawakened ethnic consciousness so characteristic of modern society. In other words, while not always grasping the class nature of the situation, parties to the debate view such identity in terms of ethnic competition for material and symbolic resources and as contested terrain. And in the specific case of cultural nationalism as articulated by middle-class ethnic entrepreneurs and embraced by working-class activists, one can see just how false consciousness can be created in an economically vulnerable working class, where keen competition for scarce resources is defined ethnically or racially.

The other approach to nationalism is more traditional and more culturally and ethnically exclusive. I am referring to those cases, both historically and today, where ethnic groups assert themselves as nations (e.g., the Nation of Islam in the United States or the First Nations in Canada) or else where they are in the process of asserting national status. In other words, similar to the Greek usage described earlier, this understanding of the term *ethnic* is closely bound up with that of *nation*. Thus, "ethnic" is meant to designate those groups that experience a distinct sense of *we-ness,* or what can be called *nationness,* that claim a common history, a common line of ancestral descent, and a common culture complete with a set of common customs and unifying myths. While it is generally felt that civic nationalism is more modern and grew out of this earlier form of ethno-cultural nationalism, the contemporary politics of ethnic nationalism in the Caribbean suggests, if not the reverse, at least a return to the earlier form of group identification.

Ethnic nationalism, then, is to be found in situations where a discrete ethnic group lays claim to a national identity and patrimony that (1) separates it from other groups, ethnic or nonethnic; and (2) has in mind a clear territorial base. Given the above discussion of civic nationalism, it goes without saying that not all nationalism is ethnically driven, for there are numerous examples of multiethnic nations or multiethnic states in which class forms the basis for nationalist appeals. Therefore, any comprehensive definition of nationalism will have to include both the civic and ethnic dimensions of the phenomenon. Caught up in the dislocating economics and politics of globalization, certain countries in the contemporary Caribbean evince a fluid back-and-forth movement between the two approaches to nationalism, as various ethnic entrepreneurs attempt to capitalize on the peoples' general sense of cultural uprootedness and dislocation. As will be seen presently, the entrepreneurs in question are not averse to excavating (their invented version of) history with a view to mobilizing specific ethnic groups for political ends, and this is where nationalist sentiments can be manipulated by skilful ethnic entrepreneurs who appoint themselves as spokespersons of the working class:

> The aim is to present a vivid, archaeologically faithful and comprehensive record of the nation from the dawn of its existence until the present in a convincing and dramatic narrative form, which will inspire members of the *ethnie* to return to ancestral ways and ideals, and mobilise them to create on its basis a modern nation, or, in nationalist language, "reawaken the nation." (Smith 1988:13)

Viewed in this way, the overall process of mobilization involves a reciprocity between the two approaches to nationalism whereby both appear to be mutually reinforcing as ethnic groups compete for the right to (re)name or (re)define the juridical nation. And when parties to the competition are of roughly equal power and resources, refusal to yield or compromise will tend to result in separatism or ethnic strife.

The foregoing is related to one additional matter that concerns the idea of territory or the "home" in homeland. As Harold Isaacs charges: "Territory has a critical role to play in maintaining group separateness; without it a nationality has difficulty becoming a nation and a nation cannot become a state" (1975:53). This is particularly important in the modern age of globalization, diasporas, long-distance travel, and mass migrations, and is intimately bound up with the politics of identity and belonging. For whether one is driven out of one's homeland as a slave, as an indentured worker, as a political refugee, for reasons of economic hardship, or simply for purposes of family reunification, diasporic politics and the nostalgic imaginings of home from abroad are crucial elements in the territorial aspects of identity and belonging to a homeland. One of the important questions that comes to mind here is whether those Caribbean countries such as Trinidad and Guyana may be considered as African and Indian diasporas, or whether the processes of creolization have rendered them neither. What we do know, however, is that even those communities that have lost their homelands through colonial or imperial conquest, war, migration, and so on will continue to root themselves in the world by reference, even spiritually, to that (imagined) homeland.

MARXISM AND NATIONALISM

Of the various attempts to deal analytically with the vexing question of nationalism, I have found the work of neo-Marxists to be the most sophisticated and instructive. Among them, however, there is no automatic, agreed-upon consensus. Thus, as a neo-Marxist, when Tom Nairn wrote: "The theory of nationalism represents Marxism's great historical failure" (1975:3), he was echoing the sentiments of many like-minded others who were caught off guard by the persistence of nationalist and ethnic identity allegiance right into the modern era of global capitalism. But Marxists were not the only ones guilty of this shortcoming, for functionalists, modernization and dependency theorists, among many others, were convinced that the social identities of clan, tribe, village, ethnicity, and nation would not survive into the modern period. The exigencies of modern living, industrialization, secularization, urbanization, the destruction of traditional community, and the freeing of the individual were all expected to dictate a more rational approach to identity and survival. Life in a thriving and bustling metropolitan setting, it was felt, would be based more on one's occupational and economic position than one's membership in a tribe, clan, family, or ethnic group. Indeed, all the other non-class forms of identity and awareness, particularly the ethnic and nationalist ones, were felt by Marxists to constitute epiphenomena—a *false consciousness*—to be distractions from the *true realization* of the roots of class (economic) exploitation and political disenfranchisement (Campbell 1972:5–6).

Given Marx and Engels' political and ideological commitment to socialism and the politics of class struggle, it is not difficult to understand why they would have downplayed the questions of ethnic and national consciousness. But as the historical record demonstrates, even if the above-noted expectations may have been warranted in their time, world events over the past one hundred years have proven them wrong. Benedict Anderson says it well: "The 'end of the era of nationalism,' so long prophesied, is not remotely in sight. Indeed, nationness is the most universally legitimate value in the political life of our time" ([1983] 1991:12). As we know, the processes of colonization, slavery, imperialism, and globalization have done more to keep global ethnic and national consciousness alive than Marx and Engels ever could have predicted. Furthermore, because their political vision was internationalist (Munck 1986:3), it is understandable that Marx and Engels would have been opposed to nationalism. The final sentence of *The Communist Manifesto* is clear in its exhortation: "Workingmen of *all* countries, unite!" (1955:46 [my emphasis]).

This exhortation was based on their view that the development of capitalism would internationalize exploitation and thereby eliminate the national differences among the proletariats of various countries. On this basis they claimed that "the workingmen have no country," for "national differences and antagonisms between peoples are vanishing . . . owing to the development of the bourgeoisie, to freedom of commerce, to the world market, to uniformity in the mode of production" (1955:29). Their point was not so much that working men (and women) had lost their countries to the forces of capitalism and imperialism, but rather that the historic role of the proletariat was one of international solidarity against the forces of imperialism.

NATIONALIST CONSCIOUSNESS AS TRUE CONSCIOUSNESS

In the estimation of Marx and Engels, the proletarian struggle was aimed at securing world socialism, not at the national liberation of a single country or group of countries. For this reason nationalist consciousness appeared to them as divisive of the international proletarian solidarity in struggle, as false consciousness, and they tended to ignore it. As V. G. Kiernan has noted,

"Nationality in itself was not a theme that greatly interested them; they looked forward to its speedy demise, and in the meantime were far more concerned with its component elements, social classes." And "nationalism is a subject on which Marx and Engels are commonly felt to have gone astray, most markedly in their earlier years, by greatly underestimating a force which was about to grow explosively" (1983:344 and 346).

This point was picked up by Marxists like Lenin and Stalin and those neo-Marxists who followed them. For by the turn of the twentieth century, when imperialism, as the highest stage of capitalism, became manifest, movements for national liberation in Europe showed that "where a straightforward struggle against imperialism was being waged, fusion or linkage of socialism with nationalism won many successes" (Kiernan 1983:349). Thus, throughout the remainder of that century there was an uneasy, very tenuous alliance between those nationalist movements that waged wars of national liberation and those Marxist movements that struggled for socialism. But the standoff was not as black and white as many have made it out to be; for despite their internationalist politics, Marx and Engels did acknowledge that the struggle for socialism is more practically waged in the first instance at the national level: "the struggle of the proletariat with the bourgeoisie is at first a national struggle. The proletariat of each country must, of course, first of all settle matters with its own bourgeoisie" (1955:21). This is a very important point to underscore, particularly because ideological opponents of Marxism are so quick to distort the record and claim, as Ronaldo Munck does, that "essentially, Marxism has no theory of nationalism" (1986:2). Hence, though aware of the limitations and distractions of nationalist consciousness, Marx and Engels recognized the need to incorporate some consideration of that consciousness as part of the process of the larger struggle for socialism. How, then, does the so-called national question become articulated with the ethnic dimension of the struggle for emancipation in multiethnic, post-colonial settings such as the Caribbean?

CLASS AND NATIONALISM

Regarding the class aspects of nationalism, and in the specific context of the Caribbean, I want to offer some more theoretical observations and suggest three ideal types of class-bound nationalism: (1) bourgeois nationalism, (2) petty-bourgeois nationalism, and (3) popular or working-class nationalism. The key questions in each of these is, which class gets to name or define the nation? and Which class's vision and values will prevail in that definition?

The first example of nationalism, *bourgeois nationalism*, is the type with which we are most familiar. It encompasses the kind of appeal that the capitalist class in Europe made early in the development and consolidation of national economies and the identification of national boundaries. This type of nationalism is very effective in fostering false consciousness and distracting the middle and working classes from a clear understanding of their economic and political exploitation and disenfranchisement. It suggests that national allegiance and devotion, from which the bourgeoisie stands to benefit, are paramount and represent the only viable route to sovereignty, security, national unity, and prosperity.

As a political ideology, bourgeois nationalism works hand in hand with capitalism and liberalism, which seek to portray the private concerns of the bourgeoisie, rationalization of business practices, bureaucratic efficiency, and the securing of huge profits as benefiting the nation as a whole. The class vision of bourgeois nationalists is one that understands the nation and its wealth as belonging to the bourgeoisie, and although some concessions have to be made to other social class fractions and groups along the way, in the final analysis the lion's share of the political and economic spoils belongs to their class. Thus conceived, bourgeois nationalism sprang from European capitalism and the various wars of the eighteenth and nineteenth centuries that were aimed at nation building on that continent. In the process, as European capitalism spread across national boundaries to encompass new lands and continents, especially the Americas, it consolidated itself in the practices of colonialism, imperialism, and globalization, giving birth to today's *imperialist bourgeoisie*, which has such a direct hand in the molding of nationalisms in the rest of the (developing) world. Curiously, with the world as its economic playground, the imperialist bourgeoisie is more internationalist than nationalist, for internationalism today is a defining feature of globalization and neoliberalism. Thus, whereas Marx and Engels clearly favored the idea of internationalism as it spoke to the proletariat, they clearly opposed the bourgeois version of such internationalism.

The second type of nationalism, *petty-bourgeois nationalism*, is as the name suggests. It is a form of bourgeois nationalism, albeit on a somewhat smaller (petit or petty) scale. Of course it is not possible to quantify nationalism per se, so what do I mean by smaller scale? Quite simply, petty-bourgeois nationalism in this usage speaks to the scale of surplus value appropriation of the petty-bourgeoisie relative to the scale of bourgeois appropriation. For example, whereas in economic matters one fraction of the bourgeoisie will favor policies of *free trade* in those areas where it has comparative advantage, the petty-bourgeoisie is more traditionally in favor of *protectionism*. Unable to compete internationally, the petty-bourgeoisie's scale of operations is restricted to the local market, and to the extent that they make nationalist appeals, those are aimed at promoting and protecting their specific spheres of operation: local industry, local manufacturing, and the exchange of locally produced goods and services. To this end the petty-bourgeoisie is also keen, to the extent it is possible, to have control of or input into the post-colonial state, where decisions governing the operations of the local economy are taken.

Note, however, that while there exists a petty-bourgeoisie in the countries of advanced capitalism, I wish to call attention to the petty-bourgeoisie in the so-called third world or developing countries, and the attempts of the latter to define the nation politically and economically. Understanding the position of the third world petty-bourgeoisie is very complex owing to the fact that some scholars use the term *petty-bourgeoisie* to refer to the class fraction that has *political control* of the post-colonial political order and the state (Fanon 1963; Sudama 1983; Dupuy 1991), while others focus on the third world petty-bourgeoisie as a class that is *economically subordinated* to the imperialist bourgeoisie (Frank 1972; Chirot 1977, 1986). In the present context I will treat the petty-bourgeoisie as a single class with distinct economic and political fractions that are also given to intra-bourgeois conflicts at specific moments. I am thus in agreement with Trevor Sudama, when he wrote that "the petty-bourgeoisie emerged as a class in the pursuit of control over the post colonial state apparatus" (1983:77), but at the same time this class was limited to the role of junior partner of the imperialist bourgeoisie.

For this reason, whether in its political or economic guise, petty-bourgeois nationalism contains no critique of capitalism, is generally reformist, and seeks mainly to accommodate the interests of the imperialist bourgeoisie. This means that petty-bourgeois nationalism is guided by the clear class goal of securing a space for its own economic and political maneuvers in between the imperialist bourgeoisie and the working classes. To this extent the petty-bourgeoisie is a class that has had different names, some of which are not too flattering. André Gunder Frank (1972) called it the *lumpenbourgeoisie*, while Frantz Fanon, who saw it as a "national bourgeoisie," felt nevertheless that its behavior was that "of a traditional bourgeoisie, of a bourgeoisie which is stupidly, contemptibly, cynically bourgeois" (1963:150).

Alex Dupuy has dubbed the political fraction of this class a *managerial bourgeoisie* given the fact of its control of the post-colonial state, and that in exercising state control it is answerable to the will of the *international corporate bourgeoisie* (Dupuy 1991:75). Because the economic wealth of third world countries is largely owned and controlled by the international corporate (imperialist) bourgeoisie, access to power and privilege among local classes is seen to come from control of the state, for this is the most promising avenue to power, prestige, personal enrichment, and privilege via graft, corruption, and other less-than-legal means. On penalty of removal from power, and as junior partners of the imperialist bourgeoisie, members of this class are obliged to do the bidding of the latter.

Understood in this way, the third world petty-bourgeoisie can be seen to comprise two separate class fractions. The first fraction discussed above can be described not as national but as *anti*national, in that its policies are geared to servicing the interests of the imperialist bourgeoisie and are not designed to promote truly national or indigenous development of local industry and manufacturing and the infrastructure that accompanies such processes. Writing about post-independence Trinidad and Tobago, Sudama notes that this class fraction "hardly ever took an independent position on any question." It contented itself with "the knowledge that the chosen path of capitalist development and the dominant influence of the international bourgeoisie guaranteed conditions for the pursuit of its economic interests" (1983:80).

The second take on the third world petty-bourgeoisie is related to the presence of another important set of local economic actors. I am referring to what Chilcote and Edelstein (1974:735) label the *comprador bourgeoisie*. Compared to the other fraction of this class, the comprador bourgeoisie is smaller and weaker and has a clear interest not in cooperating with the imperialist bourgeoisie but in lessening the country's degree of dependence on the latter. Therefore, following the logic of my argument, I dub this fraction the *patriotic* national bourgeoisie. For whether as large landowners, local manufacturers, merchants and traders, or even financiers, this fraction of the bourgeoisie is one that is said to pursue policies that, though bourgeois, are more concerned with harnessing the indigenous resources for local industrial growth and development. The activities of this class, which, in strictly local-national terms "owns the means of production of industrial goods, and whose interests are, as a consequence, opposed to those of foreign capital" (Torres Rivas 1977:39), are also concentrated in the areas of small business, banking, transportation, insurance, real estate, legal, and accounting services. Its industrial policies are largely those of *protectionism*, which serve to shelter locally nascent industrial, manufacturing, and service operations from ruinous foreign competition.

Compared to the *anti*national bourgeoisie, which benefits from the partial freeing of trade and which is primarily interested in the export of non-processed or unfinished raw materials, this latter fraction is seen to act more as a national, in the *patriotic* sense of the word, bourgeoisie (Allahar 1990:227–35). It is not that this *patriotic petty-bourgeoisie* is somehow more virtuous than the anti-national or even the imperialist bourgeoisie. It just so happens that its class interests do not go as clearly and as immediately counter to the interests of the third world nation in question. Given its structurally antagonistic position vis-à-vis the imperialist and anti-national bourgeoisies, the patriotic petty-bourgeoisie is likely to be more progressive than its local counterpart but can be expected to stop short of calling for socialism and the genuine nationalization of the country's means of production. Analytically, then, it is important to make a distinction between the political and economic arms of lumpendevelopment. The class fraction that has political control of the state in the post-colonial order is separate from the local economic actors who control commerce and the entire agro-export industry, but who are subject to the laws enacted by the former fraction of the petty-bourgeoisie in control of the state.

In a region such as the post-independence, English-speaking Caribbean, the political fraction of the petty-bourgeoisie is composed of the intellectuals, who were groomed by the colonizers and later by the imperialist bourgeoisie to assume state power after the latter's departure from the colony. They were often educated in the universities of the colonizers and former colonizers, steeped in the latter's political culture and values, and as a consequence their political campaigns were and continue to be funded, both directly and indirectly, by foreign interests. Writing on the eve of independence in 1961, C. L. R. James referred to this group collectively as "the West Indian middle classes" and as "political *nouveaux-riches*," whose "ignorance and disregard of economic development is profound and deeply rooted in their past and present situation. They do not even seem to be aware of it. . . . I do not know of any social class which lives so completely without ideas any kind" (1980:131–34). And half a century later not much has changed. For once elected, this petty-bourgeois class of political leaders, the ones who are put in power to carry on the business of the colonialist and imperialist bourgeoisies, are also able to call upon politically and ideologically sympathetic foreign states to provide military support and protection whenever threats to their continued rule, actual or perceived, might arise locally. On this score James's critique of this class, though more than forty years ago, is still generally applicable: "They seem to aim at nothing more than being second-rate American citizens. . . . They are dying to find some communists against whom they can thunder and so make an easier road to American pockets" (1980:134). This is the soil that proves particularly fertile for the growth of ethnic political entrepreneurs who target the masses of exploited and alienated workers with their cultural nationalist appeals.

This fraction of the petty bourgeoisie is also described by Frantz Fanon variously as "the national bourgeoisie" or "the national middle class" (1963). And speaking of this class, one of Fanon's foremost interpreters, Irene Gendzier, writes of "the inability of the bourgeoisie to act in the national interests" and as exhibiting "a total indifference to the needs of the mass of the population; and worst of all, an economically ineffectual and pretentious minority" (1973:218). Generally speaking, neither the political nor the economic fractions of the local petty-bourgeoisies in the post-independence Caribbean countries is either revolutionary or nationalist in the genuine sense of the term, for their principal mandate is to preserve the conditions for the expanded reproduction and accumulation of capital. And capitalism has not shown itself to have the interests of the masses of any single country, let alone the masses of the world, at heart (Allahar 1995:127). In other words, because the leaders of these countries are committed to the retention of capitalism, and even if at times they have been known to espouse a populist rhetoric aimed at national mobilization, the fact remains that each passing day bears testimony to their inability to deliver the goods to the people.

Finally, there is *working-class nationalism*, one manifestation of which, in my estimation, comes closest to a true or genuine nationalism. As the largest class in terms of sheer numbers, its policies have the potential, if only statistically, of taking into account what is in the best interests of the majority of the nation. On this basis I will argue that a genuine working-class nationalism, as opposed to a working-class nationalism based on *false consciousness*, is a stepping stone to socialism!

In the same way that the bourgeoisie and the petty-bourgeoisie of different countries are able to promote and pursue class-bound nationalist strategies, one may also conceive of popular or working-class nationalism. Just as one may speak of a capitalist state that serves principally the interests of the capitalist class(es), I am speaking here of nationalism as an ideology that informs a worker's movement bent on creating a nation, whose policies and programs are more in tune with its interests. Because the interests of the bourgeoisie and the petty-bourgeoisie do not coincide exactly with those of the working class or the wider masses, it is possible to envisage a nationalist claim on the part of workers that goes against that of the various petty-bourgeois fractions. But to the extent that the working class is not homogeneous and workers do not all share the same politics, how is it possible to speak of a workers' state that will pursue the interests of the working class?

As hinted above, this is a serious issue, for it begs the question of whether nationalist consciousness among the working class is false consciousness. The answer has to begin with the acknowledgement that while not all the members of the bourgeoisie or the petty-bourgeoisie as a whole will have identical political interests, so, too, within the working class it is to be expected that there will be political differences. And this is where the thorny issue of *false consciousness* comes into play. Those members of the working class who, for whatever reasons, are not interested in challenging bourgeois or petty-bourgeois definitions of what is in the best interest of the nation, who are most susceptible to the appeals of opportunistic ethnic entrepreneurs, and whose political stance does not include a critique of capitalism may well be said to be suffering from false consciousness. For as I have argued, throughout its history capitalism has shown itself to be inimical to the interests of working people everywhere.

On the other hand, as long as a significant proportion of the class is organized, educated, united, and conscious, and as long as they agitate for a nation in which the broad interests of workers are protected and promoted, we are able to speak either of a genuine working-class nationalism or a genuine working-class nationalist *movement*. The latter is relevant in the context of territory, for nations that are in search of homes are understandably concerned with the establishment of a physical homeland or space that they can call theirs: "Possession of territory is, after all, a *sine qua non* of statehood and an essential goal of every nationalism" (Smith 1983b:xiii).

In sum, therefore, *true* working-class nationalism is a step toward socialism or, stated differently, a step toward working-class internationalism! For it is only when the proletariat "wins the battle of democracy" (Marx and Engels 1955:31) and establishes a socialist state that the interests of the working class as a whole can begin *genuinely* to be addressed. This is precisely the sentiment of Marx and Engels as expressed in *The Communist Manifesto*: "In the national struggles of the proletarians of the different countries, they point out and bring to the front the common interests of the entire proletariat, *independently of all nationality*" (1955:23 [my emphasis]). This is also consistent with the argument of Anthony Smith, who affirms that "nationalism is typically a political argument, a tool for seizing the state by mobilizing, coordinating and legitimating the movement of the masses" (1988:5).

My argument, then, is that a working-class nationalism that is not based on false consciousness must in effect be internationalist in its vision, and this is synonymous with socialism. The specifics of such a working-class movement, however, will understandably have to take into consideration the practical conditions facing the working class or proletariat in a given country, be it advanced industrial or Third World, and the specific socialist content of the policies to be implemented once that movement is successful. However, since the main focus here is the Caribbean, my thoughts are mainly on the Third World, post-colonial context, and the racialization of the struggle or movement for national liberation.

CONCLUSION: LEADERSHIP, CLASS, AND ETHNIC NATIONALISM

At this point, the question of the leadership of such a movement is relevant. While the working class is quite capable of generating its own nationalist (and revolutionary) leaders, and in fact has done so with regularity over the years and all over the world, one also has to be aware of the political influence of conscious, non-proletarian individuals on the proletarian movement. A compelling case in point is that of Marx and Engels themselves, who were decidedly not from the working class; yet they were very cognizant of the potential for change inherent in a politicized and class-conscious proletariat that contained radical elements of bourgeois or petty-bourgeois sympathizers: "In times when the class struggler nears the decisive hour, the process of dissolution going on within the ruling class . . . assumes a violent, glaring character," and it is precisely at this time that "a small section of the ruling class cuts itself adrift and joins the revolutionary class, the class that holds the future in its hands." In other words, "a portion of the bourgeoisie goes over to the proletariat and, in particular, a portion of the bourgeois ideologists, who have raised themselves to the level of comprehending theoretically the historical movement as a whole" (Marx and Engels 1955:20).

Lenin is in full agreement and is very clear not to romanticize the revolutionary potential of the working class as something that is either automatic or spontaneous. Indeed, while making the case for scientific socialism, he was keen to underscore the central role of theory, criticism, and reflection in the process: "Without revolutionary theory there can be no revolutionary movement" (1969:25). And speaking of theory and its relationship to the process of scientific analysis and understanding, once more he cites approvingly Karl Kautsky, who argued that socialist consciousness can arise only on the basis of profound scientific knowledge:

> The vehicle of science is not the proletariat, but the bourgeois intelligentsia: it was in the minds of individual members of this stratum that modern socialism originated, and it was they who communicated it to the more intellectually developed proletarians who, in their turn, introduce it into the proletarian class struggle. . . . Thus, socialist consciousness is something introduced into the proletarian class struggle from without and not something that arose within it spontaneously. (1969:40)

In the Caribbean context this brings to mind the potential leadership role of middle-class or petty-bourgeois intellectuals in a working-class nationalist movement (Allahar 2001a, 2001d). It also brings to mind Tom Nairn's provocative charge in the European context that "the new middle-class intelligentsia of nationalism had to invite the masses into history" (1977: 340). For what I want to suggest is that, depending on the circumstances at hand, such bourgeois or petty-bourgeois intellectuals may be able either to hijack the working-class movement and harness its energies for their own purposes or to provide genuine internationalist leadership. In other words, depending on the movement's leadership and its general degree of class consciousness and political action, working-class nationalism can be channeled in either a reactionary bourgeois or a progressive socialist direction. The former, as is often the case, may witness the emergence of politically skilled, petty-bourgeois ethnic entrepreneurs who use appeals to race and ethnic solidarity as distractions, and who also exploit false consciousness by tapping into the emotions of the workers and commanding their allegiance. The latter, on the other hand, will look beyond race and ethnic differences and attempt to retain its class character. This will speak to true class consciousness and the attempts by both the leadership and the rank and file of the movement to promote a socialist alternative to dependent capitalism and to create possibilities for the triumph of humanism and communalism over materialism, consumerism, and individualism.

To elaborate, as an example of the first (false consciousness) I want to suggest a critical look at the politics of *négritude* and Afrocentrism, as well as the politics of *Hindutva* and Hindu nationalism. Both sets of politics will be seen as promoting false consciousness. My point of departure is a comment made by Paul Gilroy and directed specifically at Afrocentrism, but is equally applicable to *Hindutva*. Gilroy writes that such (Afrocentric) politics lack "even the possibility of imagining an alternative to capitalism" (2000:210), thus tying their fate to the fortunes of capital, and relatedly, their spokespersons are responsible for promoting a politics of distraction (race) within the working classes. Stated differently, my charge is that Afrocentrism and Hindu nationalism are political appeals made by ethnic entrepreneurs who have very clear and narrow class and power interests at heart, but who, in order to realize those interests, will mask them by emotional appeals to race, hoping thus to gain the support of as broad a base as possible. To secure their goal of mobilizing politically and emotionally a given population, such ethnic entrepreneurs play on an assumed ethnoracial commonality, which distracts members of the target population from a class understanding of their situation. In the process, the latter are prevented from coming to see that the so-called harmony of ethno-racial interests may well mask serious class divisions *within* the ethno-racial group in question.

On the other hand, for my example of genuine working-class consciousness and proletarian internationalism, I refer the reader to socialist Cuba, complete with all its notable triumphs and glaring failures. I would also invite the reader here to separate the genuine problems of socialism in Cuba from those problems of socialism induced by imperialist aggression (Allahar 2001b). Because human beings are imperfect (that's what makes them human), the social and political systems they create will reflect those imperfections. The challenge, then, is to establish priorities based on humanistic ideals, to assess the potential costs or consequences of achieving those ideals, and to strive to minimize the latter. To this I suggest that the imperfections of socialism are to be preferred over those of (dependent) capitalism in the Caribbean and elsewhere.

2

"Are We All Creoles Now?" Ethnicity and Nation in a Heterogeneous Caribbean Diaspora

Joshua Jelly-Schapiro

Culture abhors simplification.

—Frantz Fanon

In Trinidad and Tobago, the lack of a clear ethnic majority has made for a nation-building project fraught with complexity and conflict. The emergence of a significant new diaspora in recent decades has only further complicated the questions of race, power, and representation already so central to national political and cultural discourse. As such, examining processes of ethnic and national identity formation for Trinidadians, both those who reside in the physical territory of the nation-state and those who reside far outside it, can serve as a useful lens through which to approach some very important issues. Among these are questions relating to the continual human search for affirmative, rooted identity, and those relating to the larger trajectory of nationalist projects in the formerly colonized world as well.[1] Such an investigation will show how the negotiation of the structural realities of life in global North Atlantic cities necessitates a reexamination of identity with profound implications, not only for the émigrés who undertake it but for the larger nation as well.

Though there are many mediums through which to examine the evolution of a third world nationalism in the current moment—inclusive of literature, politics, and sport, to name but a few—in this chapter I will focus largely on Trinidadian music; its evolution, its circumstances of reception, its implication within transnational structures, and its linkage to sensibilities of national belonging (or alienation). This highlights a central point of my argument here: that even as cultural forms within the diaspora become more and more creolized, the multiple identities associated with them become increasingly particular and oppositional. With an eye to this apparent truth, and with implications far beyond the scope of this current study, examining the hows and whys of such processes of identity formation will be crucial to understanding identity-mediated ethnic conflict in our ever-more globalized world, and to the forging of a new planetary humanism that moves beyond it.

Before delving fully into such weighty issues, though, it is important first to glance at the historical context of Trinidad as Caribbean nation, to comment on the utility and shortcomings alike of theoretical models presently brought to bear on these problems, and to explicate the contentious and highly significant terms by which identities, cultures, and nations are defined in the present context.

PREMISES: THE CARIBBEAN AND THE INTERNATIONAL NATION

Anthony D. Smith has written that "if anything, nation-building is the basic Third World ideology and project" (1983a:232). Insofar as the cultural, intellectual, and political history of the third world over the past century has been defined by processes of decolonization, it is inarguable that the discourse on nation and nation-building has predominated in all spheres. And yet, though theorists of nationalism and ethnic relations generally agree on the inevitable centrality of the idea of the nation to recent history, the complexity of the nationalist discourse in a multicultural, multiracial third world and New World nation such as Trinidad and Tobago challenges the applicability and flexibility of the best of these theories (Harney 1996:6).

C. L. R. James, perhaps the greatest of Trinidadian and West Indian intellectuals, likewise recognized the difficulty in pinning Trinidad down as any particular kind of nation. He emphasized the degree to which its history had always featured an *inter*national element that prevented the development of ideologies of bounded culture so indelibly tied to many other nationalisms the world over. He wrote:

> Trinidad is at once a western nation, an immigrant nation and a Third World nation. . . . It has little in common in its cultural development structurally or ideologically with Pakistan or Iran. . . . In the Caribbean, the national culture has always been international because the economy has always been international. . . . There is no way to remove the international from the national in the Caribbean. (cited by Harney 1996:163–64; recited by Ryan 1999b:18)

The fractured popular histories of displacement and genocide, the constant outward orientation of its economy, the fact that for the disappearance of the native population *all* the diverse peoples have roots elsewhere—all contribute to the sense of Trinidad as lacking the homogeneity; the stable, rooted culture; and the ancestral history crucial to normative (Western European) paradigms of nation-building. Nation-building is always at least in part an ethnically mediated process, and in an ethnically heterogeneous nation like Trinidad, it is a process imbued with great complexity. From the first tentative agitations for decolonization and self-determination in the middle 1800s to today's debates about neo-colonial dependence on foreign capital, questions of race and the challenges of heterogeneity have necessarily been central to the national political discourse. The perception of Trinidad as possessed of a racial heterogeneity problematic to effective and/or just governance has remained a constant feature even as the racialized groups in question have changed dramatically and as the political problem in question has shifted from colonial administration to the assertion of independence.[2] In recent years, this perception has been well evidenced in the fallout from the crippling crises of a party political system still framed almost exclusively around ethnic opposition (see chapter 9).[3]

The contemporary ethnic mix that is primarily the historical legacy of the two great influxes of humanity brought to work in the cane fields over centuries of British colonial rule, first African slaves and later Indian indentured laborers, means that from its inception as an independent nation-state in 1962 Trinidad officially conceived of itself as a multicultural, multiracial nation.[4] The 1956 "People's Charter" of the Afro-Creole dominated People's National Movement (PNM), which was to act as the leading party in creating and governing an independent Trinidad, emphasized the need for a progressive understanding of "West Indianness" that acknowledged the cultural contributions of all peoples of the Trinidadian mélange. The document also professed belief in a nationalism that forwarded the interracial "spirit of Bandung," and stated the aim that decolonization not be allowed to lead to the creation of new forms of dominance by the black majority (Ryan 1972:122).

This rhetoric notwithstanding, it is only in the past fifteen years or so that Indians have gained an equitable presence in the political, economic, and civic spheres. For nearly three decades almost all components of the nation-building project were dominated by Afro-Trinbagonians. Whether tied to inertia and corruption or justified by "plural society theories" stating that the segmentation was inevitable and ethnic domination of one group over another was unavoidable and even necessary as a safeguard against a descent into chaos, this domination persisted (La Guerre 1975; Smith 1965; Yelvington 1993). The political and cultural history of Trinidad since independence has thus had as a central component the struggles of the Indian people to gain political power and cultural recognition (Ryan 1996).

As such, in Trinidad, where neither major group has a clear majority in numbers, conflicts over cultural recognition take place between two contending and more or less equal parties, one having been more centrally involved, until very recently, in the nation-building project. The most recent available numbers place "Africans" at 39.6 percent of the population, "East Indians" at 40.3 percent, and the ambiguous and probably much larger category of "Mixed" at 18.5 percent (Central Statistical Office, *1990–91 Population and Housing Census*). In a nation where carnival, calypso, and steel drum—presumably "African" cultural forms, though of course never purely that, as I will discuss below—have long been seen as the emblems of the national culture, ongoing debates such as that over the wisdom of establishing and funding a "Centre for Indian Culture" have occupied a prominent place. In that instance, representative public citizens of both ethnicities have alternately argued that the centre harmfully resigns "Indian culture" to a static, marginal place outside of the "national culture." This, they claim, discounts the dynamic and historical presence of Indian forms in that culture, or else it is viewed as a necessary institutional bulwark against the historical dominance of Africans in both the cultural and political realms. The tenor of such polemics would no doubt be very familiar to citizens of North Atlantic nations who have followed recent debates about whether cultural rights need most essentially to be viewed as collective or individual rights (Taylor et al. 1994; Habermas 1994).

Though much scholarship exists on the myriad issues facing heterogeneous societies in the global south, the specific discourse around "multiculturalism" in recent decades has generally focused its attention on the first-world nation-states from which it originates. In Canada, the United States, Germany, France, and Great Britain, the discourse on multiculturalism has come to function as a necessary corrective to the troubling rise of xenophobia and neo-fascist politics that have accompanied increased immigration from Asia, Africa, Latin America, and elsewhere to such countries. As such, this discourse has tended also to direct much of its analytic focus on first-world nation-states such as these, possessed as they are of strong, historically ingrained imaginings of the nation as territorially and culturally bounded, especially in Europe. For such nations the transgression of set borders, both physical and cultural, by "foreign" elements can easily be construed as threatening. Thus, applying competing theories of multiculturalism to a nation such as Trinidad presents a number of challenges, and demands that we concurrently engage other theoretical idioms. Such an open, interdisciplinary approach is necessitated by the particularities of a more fluid nationalism as it exists in a small, relatively new, increasingly diasporically imagined nation such as Trinidad.

Indeed, questions of the heterogeneous multiethnic nation aside, Eric Hobsbawm has recently questioned whether nationalism itself is even an appropriate term for the process of identity formation in post-colonial, multiethnic states (1990:160). He sees little similarity between the creation of the Trinidadian nation and the great upheavals and realignments of Europe in the previous century that produced its modern nation-states.

EMIGRATION AND THE (TRANS-)NATION

Acknowledging the many unique particulars of Trinidad as a heterogeneous nation, and the various national imaginaries and modes of thought this heterogeneity has produced, we can see emigration as yet another complicating factor. From its early history through much of the twentieth century, relatively wealthy Trinidad functioned more as a destination—for free blacks and others from neighboring islands looking for work—than point of departure (Williams 1970:337). Even in the postwar years, when massive numbers of West Indians left the islands, Trinidad saw a much smaller portion of its population emigrate to Britain or the United States than peer Commonwealth nations such as Jamaica and Barbados (Oxaal 1971:6; Davison 1962). Recent decades have brought something of a change, however. The contemporary post–oil-bust period (approximately 1980 to the present) has brought mass migration to the north and created a significant new diaspora in Miami, Toronto, Brooklyn, and London.

Considering Hobsbawm's observation about the tenuous applicability of theories of nationalism to the Trinidadian case, in relation to the ways it is impacted by emigration, we might look to the various models of *transnationalism* toward which numerous scholars have moved in recent years (e.g., Appadurai and Breckenridge 1989; Basch, Glick Schiller, and Blanc-Szanton 1992, 1994; Gupta 1992; Kearney 1991; Ong 1999). The analytic of the "transnational" has proved very useful as a mode of examining social fields associated with migration in an age of ever-expanding technologies that facilitate instantaneous global communication and rapid travel. In the words of Basch, Glick Schiller and Blanc-Szanton:

> We define "transnationalism" as the processes by which immigrants forge and sustain multistranded social relations that link together their societies of origin and settlement. We call these processes transnationalism to emphasize that many immigrants today build social fields that cross geographic, cultural, and political borders. . . . Transmigrants take actions, make decisions, and develop subjectivities and identities embedded in networks that connect them simultaneously to two or more nation-states. (1994:7)

Such a conceptualization of transnationalism does much to acknowledge the ways the lived experiences of "transmigrants" challenge normative historical conflations of geographic space and social identity (1994:8). Yet the sort of in-betweenness with which transnational experience is associated has not readily led to individuals, communities, or even states identifying as transnational. Indeed, it can be argued that it is only in the realm of some contemporary postcolonial fiction that such a state of in-betweenness has gained substantive voice (the work of some of Trinidad's greatest writers like Samuel Selvon and V. S. Naipaul, discussed below, stand as primary examples) (1994:8). As Basch,

Glick Schiller and Blanc-Szanton write, "Living in a world in which discourses about identity continue to be framed in terms of loyalty to nations and nation-states, most transmigrants have neither fully conceptualized nor articulated a form of transnational identity" (1994:8).

It has become an increasingly popular position among some theorists that the nation-state is on its way out as a definitive social formation (Appadurai 1996:18–21). However, as Akhil Gupta rightly argues, the nation-state nevertheless remains the "hegemonic representation of . . . spatial identity" and continues to be primary in "an increasingly postmodern world" (1992:75). As such, identities of migrant populations continue to be rooted in nation-states, however deterritorialized such nations may be. Many nation-states of the global south that have seen substantial portions of their populations emigrate have adopted official policies that reinforce this new notion of the nation-state as something other than a people possessed of a certain common history bounded within a finite territory. In many cases, these policies have taken the form of acknowledging as "citizens" those peoples physically dispersed within the boundaries of multiple other states, who remain socially, politically, culturally, and economically a part of the nation-state from which they or their forebears came.[5]

This is the context in which discourses concerning *diaspora* have attained a resurgent currency. The influential work of James Clifford (1992), Paul Gilroy (1993), and Avtar Brah (1996) stands as testament to this trend, as does the appearance in the past decade of a number of scholarly journals explicitly focused on diaspora and the cultural logics of transnational movement. Due in part to its very etymology—from the Greek *dia*, "through," and *speiren,* "to scatter"—diaspora refers to the scattering of peoples from a prescriptive center or home (Brah 1996:181). Though the Jewish diaspora has long functioned as the paradigmatic example of a population scattered across many locales (again, significantly to Zionist thought, scattered *from* a presumed site of "homeland"), recent decades have seen the advent of discourses concerning the African, South Asian, Irish, Palestinian, Chinese, and Caribbean diasporas, among many others.

For my purposes here the prescriptive though broad definition Brah gives for her concept of *diaspora space* is very useful. The conceptual space of diaspora is understood by her to be "inhabited not only by those who have migrated and their descendants but equally by those who are constructed and represented as indigenous" (Ibid.:181). Such a definition of diaspora (or, more accurately, of *diaspora space*) necessitates an examination of the relationships between those who still inhabit the physical territory of a nation-state such as Trinidad and those who live abroad. It also demands an examination of the ways both groups inform—or don't inform—the construction of the "nation," both as normatively termed and in the new, deterritorialized versions of the current moment.

Much of the scholarship on transnationalism and popular figurings of diaspora tend to presume a stable, homogeneous, or bounded "culture" and "nation" at the center/home. Though perhaps more applicable to third world states with largely uniform ethnic composition, the fluidity and heterogeneous composition of Trinidadian "national culture" makes much of this literature only partially applicable to the forms the development of a Trinidadian diasporic and/or transnational imaginary has taken. Acknowledging the unique complexity of preexisting Trinidadian nationhood, so inflected by questions of race, power, and representation as it is, can be immensely instructive in deepening our understanding of nationalism and cultural identity more generally in the contemporary moment.

NEGOTIATING MEDIUMS AND TERMS

In the present discussion, beyond basic cultural and political contestations over what defines that which is "Trinidadian," the body of terminologies of identity are of great significance. Words like "West Indian," "East Indian," "Creole," "black," and even "Caribbean" are fraught with ambiguities stemming from the fragmented histories from which they come. Under the British colonial system, indentured laborers from India were described as "East Indians" to distinguish them from the indigenous peoples of the Americas whom Columbus had given the misnomer "Indians." At the same time, all people living in the Caribbean were called "West Indians" to differentiate them first from the native "Indians" and later from the East Indians. Given the great majority of African-descended persons in the islands, the term "West Indian" became largely synonymous with "Afro-Caribbean." This association of course discounted the Indian population of the West Indies, seemingly implying such cumbersome and patently absurd terms as "East Indian West Indian" and "West Indian East Indian." For this reason many Indo-Caribbeans still call themselves "East Indian" (Birbalsingh 1997:xi).

As I will explain below, these appellations are particularly significant in the diaspora, where in cities like New York and Toronto, the regional/racial term "West Indian" often becomes the chief self-identification for (black) Trinidadians. The descriptor "black," though, is itself a contested and subjective term in the context of Trinidad itself. Especially in the two decades following independence when black nationalism and Black Power were powerful discursive currents, the question of who qualified as "black" was very much at issue. In Trinidad, this was especially prominent given the nearly successful Black Power revolution in 1970 (Pantin 1990; Oxaal 1971; Ryan and Stewart 1995). Add to this complexity the differing racial standards in the two English-speaking nations vying for cultural hegemony in Trinidad (in Britain, South Asians are "black," not so in the United States) and one begins to get a sense of the potential for conflict. Claims to blackness are naturally tied to recurrent debates over what group has suffered most at the hands of white colonialism and racism. In Trinidad, accusations—most particularly in the Indian community—of "black on black" racism have been recurrent (Figueroa 2000).

The term *creole*, though, may be the most complex, as well the most important to explicate. *Creole* holds and has held many different meanings in different locations and times, and claims to "creoleness" and debates over the true meaning of the term are quite prominent in the Trinidadian diaspora. As a noun, in its strictest definition it can denote the end product of processes of creolization, meaning cultural mixing. Finding its origin in the Spanish New World, the term (from the Spanish *criollo*) was first used to describe subjects of the crown born in the colonies, differentiated from those *peninsulares* born in Iberia. Later, in Louisiana, "creole" came to describe all those of French or Spanish ancestry after the Anglo–United States took over political control of the territory. In the British Caribbean, "creole" evolved to mean all those African slaves born in the New World rather than across the sea. In times of decolonization, it was used to describe the black elite of the anti-colonial struggle, who were analogous to the great criollo figures of Latin American independence, like Simón Bolívar.

This sense of *creole*, as descriptor of the urban Afro-Trinidadian civil servants of Port of Spain, or even all Afro-Trinbagonians, still persists in Trinidad. Yet for decades this definition has been accompanied by the other sense of the word, as inclusive of all those belonging to the heavily mixed *creole* culture. The Indians of the diverse neighborhood of St. James, Port of Spain, who unmistakably identify as *creole*, serve to exemplify this usage. Posing the question, "Are we all creoles now?" as many are wont to do in Trinidad today, prompts a none too straightforward debate. It is a question whose complex answer follows its own indeterminate meaning, as a question that could possibly refer to an individual or group's relative Africanity, to their relative urbanity, to their self-understanding as a nation-builder, to their acknowledgment of cultural mixing.

In the cultural realm, questions of appellation are further complicated as words like "Caribbean" and "West Indian" no longer simply refer to culture that is produced in the geographic area of the Caribbean, or the West Indies, if they ever did. Histories of constant movement—both forced and voluntary, to the Caribbean and away from it, by various groups in various eras, in a region whose history-bearing aboriginal people (at least in the islands) have vanished—combine to make the Caribbean what Antonio Benítez-Rojo has aptly called a "meta-archipelago" with "the virtue of having neither boundary nor center," that is, an idea more than a geographic place, that along with its people "flows outward past the limits of its own sea with a vengeance" (1996:4). This dynamic becomes ever more apparent in our present post-colonial moment. Contemporary migration patterns have created new diasporas stretching far beyond the Caribbean basin. As a result, it is increasingly the case that that which is termed "Caribbean culture" is formed, altered, and contested at least as importantly in a few North Atlantic cities as it is in the geographic territory of the sea and its lands themselves.

This being the case for the culture of the larger Caribbean or West Indies, it follows that the national culture of a country like Trinidad is similarly implicated within such processes. The nation, perhaps even more than the sea and its lands, is an idea before it is a geographic place. "West Indian" and "Trinidadian" (not to mention "East Indian") culture is constantly formed and reformed in many locations across the globe—reified in sports, individually narrated in literature, expressed and celebrated in music. Examining the historical and present content and reception of these cultural forms is crucial to understanding the ways in which individuals and peoples throughout the diaspora space, both in Trinidad and in North Atlantic cities, formulate and act upon their political subjectivities and cultural identities.

SPORT AND LITERATURE

As mentioned above, my principal focus here will be music and the ways that musical traditions lend themselves to various discourses surrounding nationalism and identity in the Trinidadian diaspora. Yet before moving to that sphere, it is important to glance at both sport and literature, and the ways that both narration and play relate to the nation. This highlights major issues surrounding the ways in which both individual artistic expression and collective cultural experience impact on the nation-building project. Such a glance will do much to contextualize these themes as they relate to other mediums and traditions.

To first take the example of sport, keen commentators have long noted the prominent role it has played in popular history in the West Indies. Many such observers have made use of sport as a highly nuanced lens through which to view the sociological development of the region, from anti-colonial struggles through to post-colonial nation-building projects (James 1969; Patterson 1973; Beckles and Stoddart 1995). Some have argued that the West Indies success in international cricket particularly has not merely reflected but actively fomented the rise of nationalist (and racial) self-consciousness, that is, that watching their cricket team united against the English masters has played a huge role in West Indians from different territories understanding themselves to have a common history, culture, and destiny, and has allowed them to transcend the insularity and inter-island rivalry that many observers hold to be among the most infamous legacies of colonialism. Given the standing of cricket as a primary means by which West Indian national identities and cultures are displayed and reified on a global scale, in Trinidad, the role of Indo-Caribbean cricketers, their presence or absence in the West Indies side, and the way they have alternately been included or excluded from larger narratives of individual and collective redemption so often tied to cricket tests, has been the source of much contention and played a prominent role in some of the more infamous moments of racial discord on the island.[6]

In the current transnational moment, following teams and athletes can play a central role in strengthening self-identifications with national (along with ethnic and/or regional) identities, and in maintaining ties to the internal affairs of home islands. The recent example of the 1998 Jamaican World Cup soccer team and the frenzy of renewed national pride and reconnection to an ancestral home that their success prompted among Jamaicans in North Atlantic cities evidences this truth. The fact that some of the most globally prominent Trinidadians are black athletes such as the cricketer Brian Lara, the sprinter Ado Boldon, and the footballer Dwight Yorke (the latter two living abroad), along with the predominance of blacks in national teams and the all-important West Indies cricket team, may be seen as emblematic of the ways in which Indo-Caribbeans are marginalized from the national (and transnational) imaginary. However, the historical and now resurgent presence of Indo-Caribbeans in the West Indies team is a key way in which a common narrative of redemption from indenture along with slavery can be reified, and a more inclusive sense of West Indianness can be forwarded—a fact of even more consequence in a diasporic location like New York, where the West Indian identity becomes even more important and is more fraught with contestation than it ever is in the national territory of Trinidad itself.

Perhaps in both its production and reception, literature is in many ways not imbued with the noisy popular democracy of crowds at cricket tests. The place of the written word in nation building projects, though, is likewise absolutely central, as many theorists of nationalism have recently reminded us. As with any social idea, the nation exists only in the telling, and particularly in the former colonies, where "from the 1940s . . . the empowering image for many Third World intellectuals has been the nation," the creation of a national literature has long been viewed as tantamount to the creation of the nation (Brennan 1989:1, cited by Harney 1996:6). Trinidad has always seemed to possess a wealth of novelists beyond its share, who have imagined and reimagined (or, in certain cases, wholly rejected) the nation a great many times over the years.

Though the first efforts at the creation of self-consciously Trinidadian national literature were made in 1930s Port of Spain, it was probably not until some two decades later that a self-consciously West Indian literature prominently surfaced. In 1950s London, the sophisticated work of such writers as (the Guyanese) Wilson Harris and (Barbadian) George Lamming emerged in the years immediately preceding independence, amid a groundswell of discussions concerning what it meant to be West Indian. Of this group, the Indo-Trinidadian Samuel Selvon was an important figure. His great novels of the Afro-Trinidadian immigrant experience in post-war London powerfully exemplify C. L. R. James's belief that in diaspora "the East Indian becomes as West Indian as all the other expatriates" ([1962] 1992:313). Selvon exhibits in his work the Jamesian conceptualization of a holistic West Indian identity and nationalism not limited to one ethnicity or language group. He is further significant in the context of other Indo-Trinidadian novelists, for the fact that he prevents seeing the alienation of many subsequent writers from their birthland as fairly representative of the sentiments of all diasporic Indo-Trinidadians toward Trinidadian or West Indian nationalism.

In more contemporary times, "native and national" authors residing full time on the island have created works consciously grounded in the particulars of Trinidadian life and cultural traditions. Novelists of this group, such as Michael Anthony, Willi Chen, and Earl Lovelace, though, remain committed nationalists even as they subtly critique the dominant nationalist discourse, joining assertions of a peoplehood that preexists the nation to an abiding love for the nation and its people.

Others, such as V. S. Naipaul, perhaps the most famous literary product of all the Caribbean, have used the figure of flight from the intolerable island milieu to point to the absurdity of all nation-building projects in the third world—Naipaul from the vantage point of an adopted home in Britain. The massively talented prose stylist and creator of what many regard as *the* great West Indian novel (1961's *A House for Mr. Biswas*) has moved on in more recent years to create works that heap scorn not only on the land of his birth but on many other cultures and national traditions across the globe. Yet as Trinidad's other Nobel winner (of St. Lucian birth), the great poet and playwright Derek Walcott, has said, "Despite themselves, West Indians claim Naipaul, and Naipaul cannot shake the West Indies" (cited by Harney 1996:139).

Today, one of the diasporic Trinidadian writers, Toronto's Neil Bissoondath, adopts a similar approach to that of his uncle Naipaul, choosing to contest the bounds of nationalism, as well as the limits and expectations placed on third world authors, by articulating a profound disconnection not only from the nation-state of Trinidad but also from its people, its land, and its culture.[7] In the work of Bissoondath, the sense of alienation from the very idea of Trinidad holds that the island can only ever be a "stopover" for the Indian who has no place there. Such an approach is expressive of a larger current of younger authors for whom the sense of homelessness so famously first elucidated by Naipaul becomes the dominant mode of imagining identity for the post-modern migrant. For Bissoondath and some contemporaries, whose work, in the words of Stefano Harney, "can be read as a kind of personal liberation from either migrant communities or home countries . . . a liberation that always, ironically, imagines the nation in order to run from it," the diaspora is decidedly *not* a location where a unified and plural national identity in the Jamesian vision is articulated (1996:120). Though this view is by no means shared by all diasporic writers working today, its prevalence cannot be viewed as purely accidental.

The reading of novels by authors such as those I have noted here, and many others besides, provides a crucial means for understanding diverse narrative imaginings of (or sensibilities of disconnection from) the Trinidadian nationalist project. Yet since such nationalisms are often formulated not only in opposition to official statist forms but also in collectivist contradistinction to the still rarefied—and solitudinous—sphere of literature, I turn now to the cultural forms that in many ways amount to the popular literatures of the Trinidadian diaspora: the musical traditions that have enjoyed state support as explicit components of the nation-building project yet also evolve and change according to the organic logic of collective experience in the streets. James once wrote, "In dance, in the innovation in musical instruments, in popular ballad singing unrivalled anywhere in the world, the mass of the people are not seeking a national identity, they are expressing one" ([1962] 1992:314). And though perhaps it is in the published writings of West Indian authors that a West Indian national identity is sought and individually narrated, it is to the popular musical forms of the streets that I now turn. Tracing current trends in the form, dissemination, and social function of popular musics by peoples throughout the Trinidadian diaspora space does much to illustrate the paradox at the center of my argument here: that creolization of cultural forms and the creolization of the identities associated with them are not parallel processes.

CARNIVAL AND THE SYMBOLS OF POPULAR NATIONALISM

Some decades ago, calypsonian The Mighty Power posed the question in song: "Why neglect your culture? Calypso and steelband is the culture of Trinidad!" He was of course addressing himself primarily to those Indo-Trinidadians who felt marginalized by the forwarding of calypso, steelband, and associated cultural forms, all normatively termed "African," as *the* cultural emblems of Trinidad and Tobago. Though developed much earlier, it was during the process of attaining independence that the prominent place of steelband and calypso was solidified, along with its legendary practitioners such as Mighty Sparrow, Black Stalin, and Lord Kitchener. Due to the central, state-supported place in the nation-building project these musics have played, the character ascribed to the nation and its people in such landmark songs as "Model Nation" and "Caribbean Man" have played major roles in debates over the ethnic/cultural identity of Trinidad and Tobago, as I will discuss below.[8] Likewise, the marginal presence of Indian calypsonians, as well as the somewhat more prominent role played by mixed-race "Douglas," have been significant in complicating such debates.[9]

At present, though, it is carnival above all that has come to be seen as the prime embodiment of all that is Trinidadian (Allahar 2003:38–44). The popularization of this notion has been helped by the state, which, from independence in 1962, has provided institutional support to carnival as an expression of national culture and lucrative tourist attraction. In the current transnational moment, Trinidadian carnival is significant as a draw not only to foreigners traveling to the island but also to nationals living abroad, who make eagerly awaited annual or semiannual return trips at carnival time (Ho 1991:124). Beyond this, massive Trinidad-style carnivals are today held in cosmopolitan North Atlantic cities like London, Toronto, and New York, and in recent years have come to act as the prime signifiers of West Indianness in the countries where they take place.

In Trinidad, carnival had its roots in pre-Emancipation Lenten celebrations of African slaves condoned by the white plantocracy and developed in its present form in the historically African-dominated city Port of Spain. More recently, though, it has come to be something of an all-inclusive national party (Hill 1972). In the postindependence years, as it grew in size and renown, and as more and more Indians moved to Port of Spain to join those already residing in long-mixed neighborhoods such as St. James, carnival has grown to its current collective state. The anthropologist Daniel Miller (1997) even argues that today the love of "bachannal"—or *jhanjhat* in Hindi—has come to be a common unifying principle for Trinidadians of all ethnicities (cited by Ryan 1997b:17). He states that "bachannal" has come to be the single most common word used by Trinidadians to describe the particular character of their society in Trinidad, and that "the concept most succinctly defines the specificity of Trinidadian cultural formations. . . . Looking for bachannal is something like a national hobby" (Miller 1997:227–28; 239).

For a celebration that in its New World origins was characterized by slaves being allowed to playfully imitate the dress and manners of their colonial masters, and in places like Brazil is still characterized by such practices, the suspension of everyday roles for the duration of carnival time has a long historical pedigree. Discussion of this sort of turnabout is ubiquitous to the work of theorists who have written of carnival and its rituals. Mikael Bakhtin (1968), for example, develops an argument, very much applicable to current cases, that medieval carnival acted as a time of liberation from the established order, a suspension of hierarchical rank, a space free from any rules or norms imposed from outside or above its own natural, basal flow. Carnival, for Bakhtin, is about playful (rather than serious or negative) "turnabout" of all existing logic and order, making the high the low, the front the rear, and so on; carnival exists outside of bureaucratic order, and in so doing, playfully contests that order. Furthermore, Bakhtin holds that the basic truth of carnival time lies in the fact that its activities ideally do not engender any kind of divide between spectator and performer but instead create the festive laughter of a communal *lived* experience, as opposed to experience observed or performed—a line followed by anthropologists like Victor Turner (1986) in examining modern carnivals in Brazil, Trinidad, and elsewhere. Particularly in light of much recent work that has expanded on Walter Benjamin's ([1936] 1968) early observations about the place of spectacle in the fomenting of nationalist sentiment, it is highly significant that the national cultural symbol of Trinidad is a mass activity that has little in common with the vulgarities of fascist nationalism (Gilroy 2000:137–76).

In the modern Trinidadian carnival, the Bakhtinian principles of a "folk culture that does not know footlights" surely holds up—carnival as neither art nor spectacle but as lived, participatory reality that embraces all the people, with life itself during carnival time subject only to carnival's own laws of free play (Bakhtin 1968:7). The extravagantly costumed thousands "playing mas" on j'ouvert Morning in Port of Spain powerfully exhibit these principles, all simultaneously filling the roles of performer, participant, and spectator. During carnival, the streets of Port of Spain are a prime embodiment of a truly creole cultural formation. The mud-coated bodies of the people in the streets, stripped of racial identity, symbolize the degree to which persons of different ethnicities and cultural heritages all contribute to the singular reality of carnival time. The streets of the ever-more-diverse capital become a genuine melting pot of creolization wherein the cultural mores of all involved are subsumed under a common form.

Though to an extent the heterogeneous crowd of revelers does affirm the unique breakdown of opposition during carnival time, much of the music that accompanies those in the streets, both for its content and for the context and form of performance and dissemination, does hold up the opposition of performer/spectator. As such, the origins, form, evolution, and lyrical content of the music, along with the ethnic identities of the performers themselves—not to mention the judges and administrators of carnival and its associated competitions—are of great importance. Likewise, records, existing outside of momentary time, as transportable commodities, hold a different and unique importance throughout the diaspora. Given these truths, it is important to look more closely at the historical form and function of Trinidadian popular musics and their intrinsic relation to discourses surrounding the development of ethnic and national identities.

ROOTS MUSIC: ORIGIN MYTHS AND
THE CREOLIZATION OF SOUND

"But what are roots? Music is shapeless, colorless."

—George Oban

The popular myths of origins surrounding the birth of calypso and steelband on the streets and docks of early to mid-twentieth-century Port of Spain, ascribing both to be of more or less "pure" Afro-Trinidadian origins, map onto the regional discourse holding that "Africans" have been the primary creators of all culture in the Caribbean (Stuempfle 1995). As Earl Lovelace (1988) writes,

> It is the Africans who have laid the groundwork of a Caribbean culture—those Africans who struggled against enslavement and continued their struggle against colonialism—and the reason they did so was because they had to. They had no choice but to become Caribbean and address the Caribbean landscape and reality. (cited by Ryan 1999:30–31)

This version is echoed by Indo-Trinidadians like the cultural activist Ravi-Ji, who states that "Afro-Trinidadians are mostly creators of culture because the experience of slavery left them culturally denuded. Hindus and Indians are basically carriers of culture and have inherited their culture, albeit uprooted and severely hegemonised" (*Guardian*, October 24, 1998, cited by Ryan 1999:31).

The common version forwarded by such commentators, however, upholds a conception of cultural purity that does not sufficiently recognize the ways in which the cultural histories of *all* the peoples of the Caribbean are marked by instances of both continuity and fracture—not to mention harmfully homogenizes the cultural histories of persons from every part of the vast and variegated continent of Africa (see chapter 1). Furthermore, as many prominent scholars of the Black Atlantic attest, though the Triangle Trade and African slavery did indeed place a massive damper on the ability of persons brutalized and thrown together in a strange land often without a common language to retain their ancestral cultures, the musics, languages, and religious practices of the New World are full of West African forms (Thompson 1983). And though some Hindu traditionalists may argue otherwise, "Indian culture," like any other, was and is inevitably forced to adapt and recreate itself in the New World context. Creolization truly is an inescapable process, and myths about the "purity" of any cultural form, in its association with any particular group, especially in a place so heterogeneous as Trinidad, are bound to be overstated. In Trinidad, the lived "Caribbean reality" confronted by both dominant groups has, for nearly two centuries, been profoundly impacted by both "African" and "Indian" cultural practices.

Whereas in the past it was perhaps easier to cling to popular versions about the ethnically pure origins of traditional musical forms, at present the more overtly creolized sources of newer musics has made such stories impossible. Soca, the "soul-calypso" offspring of calypso proper and dominant carnival music of the past two decades or so, is widely acknowledged to be a melding of calypso and Indian forms. The birth of soca during the oil-boom period is most often traced to Lord Shorty, a calypsonian from the predominantly Indian south of Trinidad—the central component of his innovation being to add Indian rhythms and instruments to the sped-up mix (Regis 1999:121).

Furthermore, since the Indian cultural revival of the 1990s, soca has been joined by the much more self-consciously Indian form of "soca chutney," which exploded onto the carnival scene in 1996. The development of soca chutney came soon on the heels of *pitchakaree*, which emerged in 1990, attached to the important springtime *phagwa* festival, and according to some observers represented a kind of Indo-calypso. In early years pitchakaree used many Hindi and bhojpuri words, yet soon most lyrics were sung in English, and like calypso the music took social commentary as its major theme, with singers/culture warriors soon claiming, "This Pitchakaree gun is we only weapon to voice we opinion" (Mohip Poonswasie, "The Sheriff in Town," cited by Ryan 1999b:174). The advent of soca chutney also came not long after the establishment of the first all-Indian national radio station in 1994, Radio Masala, before the establishment of which "Indian music," whether classic folk, ragas, or chutney, was often relegated to "ethnic music" slots on popular radio (Ryan 1999b:170).

Chutney itself is said to have traditional beginning in the pelvis gyrating "*Lawa*" dance, performed by Hindi women for friends and relatives before weddings as a kind of sexual education for the bride to be (Ryan 1999b:175). This basing in the sexual body, of course, lent chutney well to the commonly profane tenor of carnival and soca lyrics, and the soca chutney that developed has become wildly popular, with the "Chutney Soca Monarch" competition, begun in 1998, becoming one of the biggest events of the carnival season. With these formal contests especially, discussions about the distinguishing characteristics of "soca chutney" have been recurrent, with the stock answer of "soca rhythm with chutney melodies" by no means excluding many of the most popular "soca" tracks of recent years.[10] This confusion surrounding the fluid lines between contemporary Trinidadian musical genres is exemplified by the fact that one performer recently sang the same song at the calypso monarch, the soca monarch, and the chutney soca monarch competitions in the same year (Ryan 1999b:178).

Still, the soca chutney boom can in many ways be seen as emblematic of the ever-increasing creolization of Indo-Trinidadian social habitus. One opinion-page commentator observed in 1993 that "in those bawdy, wild chutney shows, grassroots Indians are creating their own Indo-creole cultural and physical space in which to get on bad." And while the same commentator notes that such unrestrained debauchery in the tradition of (lower class, African) carnival feting offends his middle-class Hindu sensibilities, he has the grace to admit that "that fact holds no currency—chutney is very popular, very West Indian syncretism. . . . Indians have created these chutney shows where they can go and wine (dance erotically, with much close contact) without having all the Africans you'd find in a calypso tent" (Brinsely Samaroo, *Sunday Express*, May 16, 1993, cited by Ryan 1999b:177). In the years since, chutney shows have come not only to closely mirror the rowdy carnival fetes of soca but have come to be an integral part of the larger carnival season itself.

Predictably, as this growth in popularity has occurred, some have argued that the Tourism and Industrial Development Corporation (TIDCO) has been lacking in promoting the new form and giving it musical marketplace recognition. It is also argued that chutney is not only a vital part of the musical culture of Trinidad and Tobago but, what is more, has greater potential as an export than either calypso or soca. As a spokesman for the National Association of Chutney Artistes of Trinidad and Tobago stated,

> Chutney music is the only entertainment activity that goes on every weekend, every month in Trinidad. It has developed its market in U.S.A., Canada, Holland, England, and is now moving to Asia, Africa, and Latin America. Yet it is the only entertainment activity that was never assisted by the state. (cited by Ryan 1999b:187)

This concern over state funding and legitimization is of course among other things tied to the prominent place calypso/steelband has played in the statist nation-building project—particularly in its use by the PNM. Add to this that both calypso and pan, unlike Jamaican reggae, have never been particularly commercially viable—pan performed by large ensembles mostly at seasonal events, calypso disseminated mostly through radio and never capturing a substantial record-buying international audience—and one sees why state support is so crucial. Yet though calypso has of course held this formal statist function, and especially around Independence time has played a well-delineated role in celebrating the virtues and promise of the new nation, it has also functioned as an invaluable space for popular dissent, satire, and political commentary. Familiarly, debates about the right to dissent—and the regularization of the form that dissent takes—stands as a crucial litmus test of the health of the state, and in Trinidad, the state of relations between the two major ethnic groups.

SINGING THE "MODEL NATION" AND ITS DISCONTENTS

As mentioned previously, calypsonians such as the Mighty Sparrow famously lent the clout of their name and words to celebrating the "Model Nation," and to celebrating the leaders of that nation. Concurrently, early governments were very conscious of the value of attaining support and using steelbands and calypsonians in campaigns and to solidify power. As such, it can be argued that the contemporaneous rise of the PNM, steelband, and calypso in the years surrounding Independence were reciprocally mediated processes (Stuempfle 1995:116–18). In any event, calypsonians played a major role in those years carrying out the cultural work of the nation-building project. In Gramscian terms, calypsonians can be viewed as true organic intellectuals (Allahar 2001d:23), in counterdistinction to the traditional intellectuals at the helm of the PNM, in their music both fomenting and voicing the nationalist consciousness of the masses that the party sought to create. Viewed in relation to the "new class" of the elite Afro-Trinidadian nationalists who made up the leadership of the Independence Movement, calypsonians were indeed:

> the "organic" intellectuals which every new class creates alongside itself and elaborates in the course of its development . . . for the most part "specializations" of partial aspects of the primitive activity of the new social type which the new class has brought into prominence. (Gramsci [1991] 1997:6)

The "new social type" to which Gramsci refers can here be thought of as the proud Trinidadian national, the empowered citizen of the postcolonial nation whom its leaders seek to create and control, the proud citizen whose aspirations the calypsonian expresses. In Independence time, the "primitive activity" of that new national is his or her cultural practice, his or her gaining a sense of that cultural practice as unique, his or her gaining a sense of membership in a "model nation." In Trinidad, wherein the cultural practice of music was to occupy such a prominent place in the nation, the "specialization" of the calypsonian in that facet of the "primitive activity" naturally lent his work a central role in the creation of a nation of proud citizens.

In their function of lending voice to popular sentiment, however, calypsonians have of course also played a historical role far different from cultural handmaiden for the state and its heads. From the years immediately following independence, as inevitable instances of state malfeasance gave rise to perceptions of government/people divides, calypsos came to reflect those views. As Bro Valentino sang in 1980, "As sure as Calypso is the culture of this Land, the calypsonian is the only true opposition" ("True Opposition" cited by Regis 1999). And indeed, notwithstanding their more establishment-oriented role in the post-Independence time, prominent calypsonians, as organic intellectuals, have long boasted that they have the power to both make *and* break political leaders (Allahar 1997:18). The great majority of calypsonians have come from the urban black population that is the prime constituency of the PNM, and as such have historically lent their support to the party during moments of crisis, such as the 1970 Black Power uprising and the post–oil-boom recession of the early 1980s that led to its being swept from power in 1986. Yet still, over the past decades infamous schisms and lyrical battles over the proper course of government have sprung up between iconic calypso figures like Lord Kitchener, Mighty Sparrow, and Black Stalin.[11]

The satirical function of calypso predictably reached a new, controversial head in recent years with the first-time ascension to power of an "Indian government" in 1995. As Selwyn Ryan notes in his perceptive study of the period, the electoral "defeat" of the PNM and the anticipated marginalization of the black community led many calypsonians to feel that it was their job to function as spokesmen for their endangered tribe and the political party that represented it (Ryan 1999b:137). Prime Minister Basdeo Panday came in for savage criticism by calypsonians, with one 1997 hit, "Mr. Panday Needs His Glasses," portraying Panday as a "drunkin old man" and a pedophile.[12] Panday's rejoinder was to declare that such songs were "ethnically venomous" and that it was the duty of his government to hold together a "plural and fragile" society by preventing people from using national occasions to spread racism and denigrate innocent citizens. He insisted that the government "would not sit idly by and allow the practice to continue. The government must insure that it does not happen again" (*Trinidad Guardian*, February 4, 1997, cited by Ryan 1999b:132). The thrust of his comments was that state funds would be withdrawn from the nationally televised precarnival *Dimanche Gras* if calypsos maintained their objectionable characteristics.

His threat provoked a justifiably indignant reaction from musicians and commentators alike, who noted that PNM Prime Ministers—including most principally the revered "Doctor" Eric Williams—had come in for savage lampooning in the past, never with any discussion of banning such criticism, which was viewed as a part of the creole tradition.[13] Panday, it was said, could not take "fatigue" (jokes) and as such was not a "true Trini."[14] Dennis Hall (a.k.a. "Sprangalang"), the President of the Trinbago Union of Calypso Organizations (TUCO), likewise responded quite negatively to the prospect of this form of state censorship, and warned of unanticipated negative consequences if any such steps were taken. He commented, "You can't pass a law to decide what is a nation building song. At what point will the song be banned, at the time of writing, in the tent, or at Dimanche Gras?" (*Newsday*, February 27, 1997, cited by Ryan 1999b:134).

During this period, however, many of both ethnic groups did feel that the critiques were moving beyond satire to vicious generalization (Allahar

1998a:28), again perhaps due to what some have called "the extremely vulnerable position of the Afro-Trinidadian in the postcreole time" (Cudjoe
2001a; Ryan 1999b:142). Where previously the presence of Indians in calypsos was limited to objectification and exoticism (the sexy Indian woman),
some felt that Indians were occupying a more prominent, and negatively
racist, place in calypsos, mirroring the tenseness of a time which saw any
criticism of a public figure of one ethnic group by a member of the other often as provoking a storm of charges and countercharges of racism.

A particularly interesting element of the reception to the music of this period is commentary holding that its many "attack songs" were in part dictated
by the perceived marketability of such tunes in the diaspora (Ryan 1999b:165).
Whether true or not, this version latches on to the popular perception that in
the diaspora individuals of both groups, due in large part to a segregated social life, develop more militant ethnic identities, a key current that I will explore further below. As calypso, soca, and soca chutney music have developed a year-round market in Caribbean, European, and North American cities
at the various carnivals held therein, the economy of the record business is a
major way in which music is embroiled in transnational mechanisms. Along
with the export business, much music today is first recorded in New York or
elsewhere, disseminated and popularized in Trinidad, and then reimported to
the diaspora market. In this realm, it is worth noting that while a majority of
the persons who sing calypsos professionally are still black creoles, many
Indo-Trinidadians on the island and abroad are well represented in the business side and benefit financially from the music business, particularly as
traders of instruments and recording equipment.

CREOLIZATION AND MILITATED IDENTITY, HERE AND THERE

Yet aside from significant considerations both economic and lyrical, on a
purely formal level what is important here is that what we term "Trinidadian
music" has inevitably become more and more creolized in form. As fluid expression of the street, Trinidadian musical traditions increasingly reflect the
constant and ever-increasing mixing of populations and cultures in Trinidad.
However, along with the aforementioned perceptions of differing commercial viability of the different forms, the popular segregation of life in the diaspora helps to create a crucial paradox. For even as the respective musics
of the two groups become more and more indistinguishable, the dichotomous ethnic militancy of life abroad means that people of both African and
Indian descent base their vociferous claims to authentic and singular cultural
identities on these musical forms of ever-lessening differentiation.

The endpoint is that cultural forms and musical traditions in Trinidad, both
hegemonic and suppressed, which have never been as pure as some would

like to think, are every year more fully creolized. As such, though the labels and ascriptions of relative Africanness and Indianness may persist, the aesthetic sensibilities and cultural forms embraced by persons of African and Indian descent are ever-more congruent. As the anthropologist Morton Klass (1991:59) observed upon recently returning to an Indian village in Trinidad where he had conducted fieldwork some decades ago, the sense of "Indianness" and religious practice had only increased, even as the people were more "westernized" than ever: "As the educational and professional levels of Indo-Trinidadians has improved, Indian ethnicity has become more visible, although its representatives are evidently more strongly creolized than ever as regards their actual representations and practices" (Ryan 1999b:19–21). The Old World tradition-based habitus of the rural Indians that Klass once observed has been replaced by a creolized New World Indianness heavily influenced by Afro-Caribbean forms and the imperial popular cultures of Great Britain and the United States.

Though the musical cultures of Trinidad have grown ever more expressive of the integrated mélange of cultures that its streets have become, during carnival time and year round, these developments have not precipitated a decrease in culturally mediated ethnic conflict. This apparent truth can be traced to a great many factors, including the formal structures of record distribution, electoral politics, and largely separate emigration networks. And yet popular music, for its very *popular* nature, for its association with the unique national cultural emblem that is carnival in the Trinidadian case, for its implication within transnational structures of communication and economic linkage, make it an exceedingly rich lens through which to examine evolving national and/or ethnic imaginaries throughout the larger nation. In ascribing such a central place to the medium, it is my contention that the segregated use and dissemination of such musics away from the island both reflects and informs the development of more militated stances around opposed "West Indian" and "East Indian" cultural identities. Such stances, no matter if they originate in the specificities of social life in one particular locality, bear great consequences on processes of identity formation for persons *throughout* the diaspora space—no matter how congruent the creolized cultural texts through which that identity is celebrated and proclaimed.

Examining the form in which the Trinidad carnival tradition presently manifests itself in one diasporic city, along with the causes, implications, and consequences of that form, sheds much light on the ways in which the realities of diasporic life in particular locations impact imaginings of the nation more generally. Namely, it shows how the identities designed to negotiate the social, racial, and economic realities of life in cosmopolitan North Atlantic cities have a profound impact on imaginings of Trinidad as a nation *throughout* the diaspora space.[15]

ETHNIC OPPOSITION AND THE NORTHERN METROPOLIS

Identity is always plainly situational. The formulation of identities is always a process profoundly impacted by the given context in which such identities are to be utilized. Both self-conscious assertions of belonging and bureaucratic regimes of categorization always rest on definite economic and political bases and are delineated according to those bases. It follows logically that the identities (ethnic, racial, religious, regional, national) available to, and utilized by, persons living in Trinidad and those living abroad are different in many ways. Yet given the existence of the diasporically imagined nation and the transnational social fields that sustain it, identities designed to function in particular contexts inevitably find their way to other contexts and impact imaginings of identity throughout the nation as a whole.

Just as identities differ and change according to context, so do local cultural traditions evolve abroad, coming to at once reflect and foment the new collective identities they express. In the cosmopolitan cities that are the adopted homes of Trinidadian émigrés, the various significations and ethnic and racial identities attached to the carnival tradition illuminate much about processes of identity formation for transmigrants more generally. For even if in Trinidad itself the carnival tradition is now (at least in part) attached to pluralist Trinidadian nationalism, in diaspora that tradition is attached to identities that emphasize historical commonalities quite divergent from those upon which such an inclusive nationalism is attached. In diaspora, carnival is attached to identities that emphasize shared histories of grander scope than that of one particular nation-state—Trinidad or any other. The formulation of these new identities of connection in Northern metropolises are highly complex processes impacted by a great many factors. They are processes impacted at least as significantly by the structural realities of racial and economic segregation in the first world city as they are by the new connections and forms of consciousness presented by its worldliness.

In New York, one of the great cosmopolitan cities of the world and home to one of the largest Trinidadian populations anywhere, the tradition of Trinidadian carnival manifests itself in the West Indian Labor Day Parade. As mentioned above, along with Caribana in Toronto and Notting Hill Carnival in London, Labor Day is the most spectacular and best-known Caribbean-style carnival in the world outside of Trinidad, and today attracts upwards of 3 million people. Its present form, though, serves to exemplify the lack of cultural contact between members of the two major ethnic groups in the Trinidadian diaspora—and bears on a great many other facets of race and identity in the diaspora besides. Though the carnival in New York had its start in the days of the Harlem Renaissance, as uptown Caribbean émigrés held masquerade dances in houses and ballrooms, it was moved to Brooklyn in 1965 by an Afro-Trinidadian man named Rufus

Gorin, inaugurated in its present form and location in 1967, and grown in size and sophistication since then (Henke 2001:107–9). Today, the essentially leaderless carnival/parade, though based in Trinidadian tradition, is an expression of a certain kind of pan-Caribbean identity, and incorporates much Jamaican music and some Haitian elements as well. Taking place primarily in an area of the borough dominated by Afro-Caribbeans and Afro-Americans, it has come to function as a prime rallying point for the often-exclusive racially coded version of (Afro-Anglophone) West Indianness that is dominant in New York.

In a city not lacking for parade days set aside for its many proud ethnic groups, Holger Henke has opined that "more than any other minority, West Indians use their parade to proclaim and celebrate their difference rather than . . . to claim their recognition as a legitimate part of U.S. society" (2001:109). Whether or not it is fair to make such a differentiation from other parades, in the present context the important point about this celebratory assertion of militated ethnic identity is that Indo-Caribbeans are largely excluded from it— if not from actually participating in the event, then certainly from its larger, racially coded significations. And in New York, where Indo-Trinidadians reside mostly in Queens, as a part of the quite sizable Indo-Caribbean community there (rather than in Brooklyn, where the majority of Afro-Trinidadians live, along with many other Afro-Caribbeans) they and their even more numerous Indo-Guyanese nieghbors carry out their own carnival-like celebration in March of every year.

Begun in 1986, the Queens *phagwa* parade and celebration in the Richmond Hill neighborhood itself attracts 50,000 persons and has come to be a major yearly event in the borough (Henke 2001:109). Though phagwa exists in Trinidad, the new emphasis and inflection placed on it in New York can be tied to the desire for communal celebration of *Indian* West Indianness not found in Brooklyn. Likewise, the relative religiosity of the festival can be tied to the generally acknowledged current of Indo-Caribbeans living abroad growing more militant and dedicated to a religious and cultural heritage often taken for granted in familiar surroundings. Many have noted how the embrace of traditional Hindi culture even by young Indo-Caribbeans is done proactively, in the process of seeking an affirmative identity through which to negotiate a complex new society, in the process of figuring out how to define themselves within diverse peer groups in the United States (Henke 2001:81).

Yet even with the heightened embrace of traditional faith and Indian popular culture by Indo-Caribbeans in the North, theirs is a population often shunned by the South Asian Indian community, prone to be viewed as a sort of cultural oddity contaminated by their New World experience. As such, what is especially significant about the Queens phagwa festivities is that many South Asian Hindus admire it and take part, seemingly the one time in the year when they affirm a common heritage with their Caribbean relatives (Henke 2001:110).[16] This fact can be seen to exemplify the ways in which the experience of living abroad in a hostile cultural environment often prompts peoples to reexamine—and passionately embrace, in this case—some component of their historical identity that had been suppressed in the previous context. In the northern metropolis, where this critical examination of identity takes place at the same time as unprecedented contact is made with peoples of the same ancestral origin as one's own, new diasporic imaginaries and connections are formulated; new identities present themselves.

RACE, RESIDENCE, AND IMMIGRANT IDENTITY

First among the set of realities met by immigrants in the northern metropolis that contribute to the necessary formulation of such new identities are the racial structures confronted therein that so heavily impact all elements of social life, from housing and job opportunities to education and recreation. Though other contexts may present contrasting pictures, the United States, and more specifically New York, represents a crucial site of analysis in this regard, for its status as an entry point and as a center of population and culture for Caribbean émigrés, and for its hypersegregated residential structure so endemic to American metropolises.[17]

The importance of a city like New York to the imagining of the Trinidadian nation is exemplified by the statement of an Afro-Trinidadian who recently left it: "Brooklyn is in many respects more Trinidadian than Trinidad. Brooklyn is so much like the Trinidad I know, for the simple reason that you have the food, the music, and a lot of my friends from back home" (cited by Ho 1991:112). This sentiment attests to the density of cultural activity in Brooklyn that makes it a center of global West Indianness, a place that for this immigrant does not offer the freedom from the suffocating culture of his home island that he desires. Yet when this statement is unpacked it takes on an even greater importance, as the Brooklyn that this man refers to is not the area of the city where Trinidadians of all ethnicities reside, but rather the place where the vast majority of Afro-Trinidadians settle (Crowder and Tedrow 2001). Viewing the statement in light of this fact points both to the ways in which Afro-Trinidadians are understood to be prime bearers of West Indian/Trinidadian culture and to the racial segregation of housing in New York. The reason that Afro-Trinidadians—along with other, more numerous groups of West Indian immigrants—have historically moved into areas such as Brooklyn (and before that Harlem) has largely been due to the formal and de facto segregation of American housing which has prescriptively delineated the spaces of black residence to which Afro-Caribbeans have necessarily gravitated.

As Mary Waters (1999) elucidates in her important study of New York's West Indians, the terms of the assimilation process for many new immigrants to the United States have changed a great deal over the years. Though once the dominant paradigm for European arrivals to this country was that "becoming American" was a process conjoined to gaining economic integration into the society, today that version has changed: in many scenarios it seems that remaining immigrant or ethnic identified is advantageous in easing economic and even social incorporation into the United States. Many new immigrant incorporation studies show how "the social capital immigrants bring with them, and the racial and ethnic definitions of nonwhite immigrants as minorities, combine to create a situation where becoming American in terms of culture and identity and achieving economic success are decoupled" (Waters 1999:4). Black West Indians (along with Africans and others) fit this model very well, as becoming American, for them, also means becoming black American, and thereby assimilating into a discriminated-against, impoverished, and downwardly mobile stratum of society.

As such, many Afro-Caribbean immigrants initially do quite well in the American labor market, equipped with human capital, positive attitudes toward employment, often higher levels of professional training, and expectations of race relations formed in their "home societies" that are distinctly different from those of American blacks who have internalized the racialist social mores of the United States (Waters 1999:6–7). Ultimately, though, as Waters notes, the structural realities of American race relations often swamp the cultural advantages of Afro-Caribbeans. Particularly in the second and third generation, frustration at persistent discrimination and the consequences of living in neighborhoods with substandard city services, poor schools, concentrated poverty, and high levels of violence begin to take their toll (Waters 1999:7–8; Massey and Denton 1993). Many young Afro-Caribbeans, possessed of an embittered view of American race relations and lacking the expectations of achievement held by their parents who grew up in societies where blacks held positions of power, develop oppositional identities in line with those held by American blacks. Many react to blocked mobility and derogatory images by what John Ogbu (1990) has called "cultural inversion," coming to view certain symbols or forms of behavior (like going to school) as inappropriate, for their association with the dominant class (cited by Waters 1999:198).

This said, the density of Afro-Caribbean populations and cultures—and more particular Jamaican, Trinidadian, Haitian cultures—in neighborhoods of Brooklyn in particular exemplifies the fact that Afro-Caribbeans do not simply shrug off their ethnic heritage and "become black." The affirmative West Indian identity fomented in Brooklyn is itself an oppositional identity of considerable currency, as exemplified in the Labor Day carnival discussed previously, as well as in the political organizations formed around this sense of West Indianness.[18] What is important to note is that due largely to segregated housing patterns, this West Indianness is not of the holistic, plural nature of James's conception, but rather is racially coded black and has a complex interrelationship with the Afro-American cultural forms of the neighborhoods where it grows, as cross pollination between the two traditions has been massively important to the development of both.[19]

Indo-Trinidadians, by contrast, fit a different place in the American racial structure and exhibit concordant differences in the pattern of settlement and collective identity formation in the diaspora. Unlike Afro-Caribbeans, who map onto a very low rung of United States's social order, the physiognomy of Indo-Trinidadians places them in the "model minority" status of persons of South Asian descent, a role that has historically entailed a very different relation to the dominant class (and to other minorities) than that held by blacks (Prashad 2000). Indo-Trinidadians have largely settled in sections of Queens and northern New Jersey, where many Hindu and Muslim South Asian immigrants have historically resided. Indo-Caribbeans, though in certain ways caught between the "West Indian" social and cultural networks of Brooklyn and the "Indian" or "Hindu" networks of their continental relatives, are so numerous and densely settled in the New York area that they have developed their own sophisticated community with its own organizations and traditions, numbering in the hundreds of thousands in Queens alone (Melwani 1995).

The building of such communities (and the identities associated with them) is both dictated by the structural realities of the Northern city and proactively designed to function in the chaos of its cosmopolitanism. Like the transmogrification of local cultural traditions abroad, the evolution of sensibilities of ethnic and national belonging in the diaspora is closely linked to the creation of identities not limited in their utility to the particular context of one small island, to the creation of identities designed to function in a global city, on a global scale.

CONCLUSIONS: CARIBBEAN DIASPORAS, NEW IDENTITIES, AND HYPERGLOBALIZATION

"Identity is not in the past to be found, but in the future to be constructed."

—Stuart Hall

The Caribbean is a place where the idea of culture as bounded and self-contained has been deemed anachronistic only recently, has in much of the world has been plainly evident for centuries. The processes of creolization facilitated by movement and integration that are viewed as endemic to our current global moment have long been features of Caribbean life—especially in a place like Trinidad, the most ethnically complex of the all Caribbean territories. Many other immigrant groups encounter a feeling of uprootedness for the first time on leaving their ancestral homes, but not so for Caribbean emigrants. The peoples of the Caribbean have always felt alienated from the historical privileging of a "sedentarist metaphysics" that has meant that connections of peoples, cultures, and nations to place, connections normatively discussed in terms of *roots*, have been the most essential determinant of identity (Malkki 1992). In the Caribbean, the yearning for roots grows out of the sense of uprootedness that permeates the historical being of all its peoples, who due to forced migration and genocide live in a region whose indigenous inhabitants have long since disappeared. It can be argued that all manner of Caribbean cultural production has thus been centrally concerned with the search for and articulation of roots. The second migration, away from the Caribbean itself, while fomenting a new sense of rootlessness also prompts a reexamination of the imagined loci of historical roots. Globalization, circular migration, instantaneous communication, and ever-increasing interaction and social equity among the contending ethnic groups in Trinidad have all facilitated the development of new and different creolized forms of these cultures.

Yet the central paradox around current processes of creolization is that, while throughout the Trinidad diaspora space the respective cultural representations of both Afro- and Indo-Trinidadianess are increasingly congruent, the ethnic identities associated with these forms have become increasingly visible and distinct. In Trinidad itself, the creolization of the daily habitus of diverse peoples is facilitated by the integration of residence throughout the island—and especially in the cosmopolitan capital of Port of Spain. My contention, however, is that the cultural politics of opposition witnessed throughout the nation's diaspora space are exacerbated and even created by recent large-scale emigration and the social realities of life in northern cities.

In the political realm, the fact that ethnic antagonisms have only increased in recent years can in many ways be attributed to hyper-segregated residential patterns abroad and to the related and consequent formulation of militated and oppositional ethnic identities. As historically marginalized East Indians have gained political power in Trinidad, such sensibilities have only increased, as transnational activity in the diaspora largely takes the form of Indo-Trinidadian émigrés acting to support the party that is protecting "their interests" on the island. In sport, a crucial site for the celebratory codification of identity, particularly for emigrants living abroad seeking to maintain connections to their homes, the "West Indies" tag of the cricket team, along with its dominance by Afro-Caribbean cricketers, reifies the racially prescriptive version of "West Indianness" so important in the northern cities of the diaspora—a pattern somewhat mitigated by the historical and now resurgent presence of Indo-Caribbean cricketers in the side (Allahar 2001d:17–20).

Much contemporary literature emerging from the diaspora, in contradistinction to sport, undercuts the dominant discourse on a plural nationalism, and in some cases even articulates a disconnection from the nation itself. And in the popular musical cultures of the streets that I have discussed here, new creolized forms evocatively express the free play of identities during carnival. The organic integration of forms and styles—and of Trinidad carnival itself—has resulted in a near indistinguishability of "African" and "Indian" musics from Trinidad. Yet in the diaspora, as carnival has come to signify the *Afro*-Caribbean culture of West Indians from diverse islands, the distinct ethnic identities associated with these ever-more congruent musics are accentuated and inevitably find their way back to Trinidad.

In this era of hyper-globalization, when many citizens of the global south necessarily migrate to the North Atlantic in search of work, it is in the interest of building globally visible collectivities that the identities associated with small, new nation-states are foregone in favor of broader regional or even historical identities. It is this second migration, away from the Caribbean and to these rich states, that enables the idea of the islands as merely a "stopover." More than ever, India or Africa—and their racially coded New World transmogrifications as "West Indian" and "East Indian"—come to be seen as the important loci of rooted identity. Yet even as these identities are forwarded, their representative cultures are more strongly creolized than ever before in terms of their form and actual practices. Indeed, in all senses of the word, we are all creoles. Yet even as cultures have become more and more hybrid and creole, discourses surrounding cultural identities have only become more exacting and oppositional.

In this regard, however, it is important to remember that racial, ethnic, and even national identities are not zero-sum entities. It is possible to hold several at one time, and they are always plainly situational (Waters 1999:147). Even under the dichotomous Trinidadian framework, multiple, particular identities are available to nationals in the diaspora. In the American context, Trinidadian emigrants have a wide variety of appellations of identity to choose from according to the given scenario—West Indian, Caribbean, black, Trinidadian, East Indian, Indian, Hindu, South Asian—and all are used in different ways by different people in different contexts for varying purposes.[20] Cultural identity, like culture itself, is a diffuse proposition, and is always in flux. Yet cultural identity is not amorphous or free from categorization; instead, it moves through a great number of specific and bounded versions of itself.

Appadurai has recently suggested that "set theory, fractals, polyethnic classifications, and chaos theory" may be necessary to revamp social theory sufficiently for the purpose of coping with what he calls the disjunctures of the "ethnoscapes, financscapes, technoscapes, mediascapes, and ideoscapes" that stream and flow as cultural material across ethnic and national boundaries (1990:19). Though he himself doesn't venture to undertake such a project, his appeal comes out of an understanding that political and cultural identities today are characterized by a great many overlapping diasporic connections and imagined communities, often contradictory and tied to multiple nation-states, religions, brands, cultural groups, and racial identifications.

Cultural identity must not be vulgarized by oversimplification. Many of the theoretical models of transnationalism and diaspora that have held sway up to now do not sufficiently recognize the complexities inherent to the ways in which we formulate cultural identities. Even as the cultural logic of corporate globalization, instantaneous communication, and movement and integration of the world's peoples have contributed to a universal creolization, militated new ethnic identities have been on the rise in recent years, perhaps as a defense against this overwhelming creolization. It should thus come as no surprise that such processes are exceptionally prevalent in the cultural identities of peoples from the Caribbean, who come from a region where the two features we think of as postmodern in their effects on identity—the mixing of cultures and peoples from different continents and migration and displacement as a fact of life—have been a feature of popular histories for centuries (Waters 1999:23).

The nation-building projects that have dominated political and cultural discourse in the third world over the past half century are profoundly impacted by the cultural identities formulated by emigrants residing in first world metropolises. The ways that such émigrés maintain and articulate connections to their home nations, to each other, and to larger diasporic and regional imaginaries are of utmost importance to the development of deterritorialized nationalisms—and identity formation more generally for third world people. The formulation of affirmative identities designed to function on the global scale or in the cosmopolitan world cities of the North Atlantic by such émigrés likewise affects the course of ethnic relations and political discourse within their nation-states of origin.

Identity, like culture, is a many-splendored thing, and the ways in which we all formulate political and cultural subjectivities are impacted by a great many factors. Today, even if the nation-state and nationalism continue to be the prime determinants of identity, the historical narratives of shared experience across national boundaries—particularly around shared uprootedness and oppression—are becoming increasingly important. Global racialist discourses and social structures, the disappointments of third world nation-building projects, and the universal encroachment of hegemonic corporate culture are central to the enduring and resurgent importance of the globally imagined collective identities through which all people celebrate their cultures and seek to construct their futures.

NOTES

1. It should be noted that herein I often use "Trinidad" as shorthand for the nation-state "Trinidad and Tobago," inclusive of Trinidad and its smaller neighbor. Though this is done for convenience, it also denotes a privileging of the larger, heterogeneous island Trinidad, and the specifically Trinidadian diaspora, as my site of analysis. Though conjoined together as a nation-state, and thus sharing many cultural mores, the two islands have distinct colonial histories and ethnic compositions—Trinidad being the place of residence of many of Indian descent and Tobago being populated almost entirely by those of African ancestry. It is important to note that the history and cultural and political opposition between the two islands (especially around Tobagonian desires for autonomy) are significant and deserve attention, though they are largely beyond the scope of this essay.

2. As Eric Williams notes, even before explicit demands for national independence, the imagining of Trinidad as fundamentally—and problematically—multiracial in nature were prominent. After expelling the Spaniards from the island in 1797, the British crown was met with Trinidad's perplexing racial makeup in debating whether to institute a sort of planter democracy on the island as they were wont to do in other colonies, in contrast to Spanish autocracy, confronted with the question of whether the structure of popular government instituted elsewhere was applicable to Trinidad—where not only did the free people of color outnumber the whites, unlike anywhere else, but where also existed the unique situation among the whites that the French, Spaniards, Corsicans, and Germans outnumbered the British. The British Secretary of State noted these troubling facts in an 1810 memo to the Governor of Trinidad, opining that "the greater part of them must be wholly ignorant of the British Constitution and unaccustomed to any frame of government which bears any analogy to it," and stating, "The circumstances on the Island of Trinidad are in many respects so materially different from those of all the West India Colonies, that supposing the system of Government established in those colonies to be the best could be afforded them in their situation, it would not follow that the same system could be rendered applicable either in justice or in policy to the Island of Trinidad" (Williams 1970:395).

3. The most recent crisis I refer to here began in December 2001, when Trinidad and Tobago's general elections ended in the two dominant parties, the United National Congress (UNC) and the People's National Movement (PNM) winning eighteen seats apiece in the nation's parliament. With nothing in the constitution providing for what is to happen in the event of such a tie, President A. N. R. Robinson appointed PNM leader Patrick Manning to be Prime Minister. Without a popular mandate, Manning's term started in chaos: debates over constitutional semantics predominate in the papers and in Woodford Square, the parliament not to meet for months, protests over the lack of diversity and size of Manning's cabinet, and a loud revival of charges and countercharges of corruption and racism between the two parties. Though this state of affairs prompted something of a resurgence of racial/political antagonisms, with the UNC calling for new elections and protesting the ethnic composition of Manning's new cabinet, it is safe to say that the mess—since resolved—deepened a growing suspicion of government in general among all Trinidadians, tired as they are of scandal and corruption.

4. African slavery was outlawed in the British colonies in 1835. Soon after, in 1845, the first Indian indentured laborers were imported to take the place of the slaves on the sugar plantations, an influx that was to continue until the outlawing of indenture in 1916 (see Klass 1961).

5. Examples of such new policies include the formal advent of the Haitian "10th department" (in addition to the nine that exist on the island) constituted of migrants living abroad, and the recent adoption in Mexico of laws granting transmigrants residing in the United States expanded citizenship and voting rights in their birth country.

6. Perhaps the most famous such incident of ethnic conflict tied to sport took place in the midst of the national elections of 1976, when Team India came to play a series of tests in Port of Spain. After defeating the West Indies on the final day, the Indian side left the oval to the cheers of watching Indo-Trinidadians, prompting renewed debate on the part of contending politicians on the place of Indians in the nation. For a general history of Indian involvement in Caribbean cricket, see Birbalsingh and Shiwcharan (1988).

7. The most famous particular "restriction" placed on the individual third world writer to which I refer and against which Bissoondath may recoil is Fredric Jameson's (1986) assertion that writers in the third world always produce novels that are "national allegories," novels in which the self-realization of the narrative reproduces that of the nation. It should be noted here as well that there of course are a great many other younger diasporic Trinidadian writers (the vast majority of whom interestingly happen to be of Indian descent) who are currently producing work that is quite likely of higher quality that that of Bissoondath, and who are also in many cases possessed of a quite different view of their birth island. I choose to mention Bissoondath here though not only for his alienation, his outspokenness, or his often reactionary politics, but for the simple fact that for all the media exposure he gets he is a representative figure, for better or worse, and may in fact be *the most* visible of the younger generation. In recent years, he has been held up as a representative face of the "New Canadian writer," has appeared frequently on Canadian television to pontificate on (his problems with) multiculturalism, and had one of his short stories selected to lead off the new *Faber Book of Contemporary Caribbean Short Stories* (Morris 1990).

8. The Mighty Sparrow's euphoric "Model Nation" (1962) extolled the virtues and racial harmony of the new nation as follows: "The whole population of this little nation/ is not a lot/ But oh! what a mixture of races and culture/ That's what we've got/ Still no major indifference/ Of race, color, religion or finance/ It's amazing to you I'm sure/ We didn't get independence before. . . . (chorus) Trinidad and Tobago will always live on/ Colonialism gone, our Nation is born . . . everybody/ We go follow our leaders/ They always do their best, oh yes/ we want to achieve, we going to aspire/ We bound to be a success" (as cited by Regis 1999:17). A later example of a prize-winning calypso that gives a different racial picture is Black Stalin's "Caribbean Unity" (1979): "Is one race/ The Caribbean Man/ From the same place/ The Caribbean Man/ That make the same trip/ The Caribbean Man/ On the same ship/ The Caribbean Man." Though the lyrics themselves may not seem so divisive, when Stalin clarified on television that by "Caribbean Man" he meant "Afro-Caribbean Man," he caused quite a stir (as cited by Regis 1999:198).

9. An early example of this is Dougla's 1961 tune "Split Me in Two," "cut me in half," in which he asks what would happen to him, a mixed race "dougla," if for some reason they decide that "everybody got to find their country/ According to your race originally." He thinks perhaps they will shoot him into space, because he can't rightly go back to Africa or India. He concludes, "I am neither one or the other/ Six o' one, half a dozen of the other/ Well if they serious 'bout sending back people for true/ They bound to split me in two" (as cited by Regis 1999:11).

10. An example of this type of song is Preacher's 2002 hit, "Mi dulahin," which features a Hindi melody and Indian background singers singing about roti and curry, as a black calypsonian tells of checking out a pretty Indian girl at a party.

11. One early example of calypsonians engaging in debates over the proper course of government occurred in the very early years of independence, when C. L. R. James split with his former pupil Eric Williams, and many calypsonians urged a place for him in the government. A more recent example of this occurred in 1981, when the Mighty Sparrow took the radical step of lending his support to the Organization for National Reconstruction (ONR), which subsequently lost the election. In the aftermath, prominent calypsonians like Lord Kitchener, a staunch defender of the PNM, took Sparrow to task for his "defection," and a mighty war of musical jibes followed (Regis 1999:157–62).

12. Watchman was the 1997 author of "Mr. Panday Needs His Glasses." Other calypsonians who offended Panday's government in 1997 included Cro-Cro and Sugar Aloes (see Ryan 1999b:130–32).

13. Eric Williams once summated his approach to calypsonians (whose continued support was crucial to his remaining in power, it must be stated): "let donkey bray, but listen attentively to what donkey say."

14. An editorial in *The Independent* (February 13, 1997) summed up this common reaction to Panday's approach to the offending calypsos: "Irreverence and mockery have been essential elements of both the carnival and calypso, the most effective tools available to a people who lacked political power, the legal status or the material means to promote their interests otherwise. . . . The satirical, undeferential cast of mind and the cultural forms that express it are not easily understood by those outside the tradition. What Trinidadians call 'fatigue' is something not taken lightly by their West Indian cousins. . . . In Trinidad and Tobago, however, officialdom has been the butt of calypsonians ridicule from colonial times to this. . . . Now it is Mr. Panday's turn and, apparently, he doesn't like the treatment at all" (cited by Ryan 1999b:133).

15. In a discussion closely related to Brah's definition of "diaspora space," Homi Bhabha's (1990a) conceptualization of "nation-space" includes much on how identities and subjectivities designed to negotiate social contexts far outside of the physical territory of the nation impact imaginings of it.

16. As the well-known "Bollywood" Indian film maker Ajay Sharma put it in his message to the cheering crowd gathered for the 1991 parade: "When I left Bombay a few days ago I thought I would miss Holi, but today, playing Phagwa with you I feel totally at home" (Sharma quoted in *Global Times*, 1991:19, as cited by Henke 2001:110).

17. Forty-nine percent of the approximately 140,000 Trinidadian-born persons in the United States first came to and lived in New York. In addition to this number, around 80,000 people in the United States claim Trinidadian ancestry (these are projections based on the 1990 census numbers). It is impossible to know what the eth-

nic breakdown of these populations is, as such records are not kept. And though some popular myths exist about the preferred historical destination of "Indians" (Canada) versus "Africans" (United States), contradictory stories exist as well, and all surface indications show that there is not really a major difference in terms of numbers or destinations between the two ethnic groups. It is appropriate to note as well, though, that due in large part to more liberal immigration laws, Canada has become a slightly more popular destination for Trinidadian immigrants in general than the United States—and that Toronto, the principal destination in Canada, is a city noted for its integration in housing and may present a different picture from that in New York discussed here.

18. In recent years, efforts by such "West Indian American" organizations to incorporate Haitians (who often live in the same areas), though not Hispano-phone Caribbeans, signifies the degree to which the "West Indian" identity is, in the New York context, at least as much about race as it is about language or anything else.

19. The advent of hip-hop in the 1970s South Bronx stands as a strong example of this sort of cross fertilization. Most commentators believe that hip-hop music grew out of Jamaican DJ culture, the crucial feature of which was the practice of "toasting," talking in rhythm over "dub" or instrumental versions of other artist's records.

20. As Waters (1999:53–60) notes, Afro-Trinidadian immigrants may use different appellations of identity: "Trinidadian" when in the context of other West Indians to emphasize national identity, "West Indian" when among other blacks to emphasize a certain cultural/historical commonality, and "black" for the purpose of confronting discrimination with other dark-skinned peoples, to name just a few.

3

Nationalism, Identity, and the Banking Sector: The English-Speaking Caribbean in the Era of Financial Globalization

Diana Thorburn

At the beginning of the twenty-first century, the structure of banking markets in the English-speaking Caribbean reflected a shift from the 1970s of large, government-owned commercial banks and some foreign-owned banks to a consolidated banking market dominated by private ownership, based primarily in Canada and Trinidad. In this chapter I examine how changes in the ownership of banks reflect perceptions of national and regional identity in the English-speaking Caribbean, with a particular focus on Trinidad and Jamaica. In so doing I link the physical institution of banks and the political and economic decisions manifested in banking policy to the notions of nationalism and identity in the twenty-first century English-speaking Caribbean.

Perceptions and definitions of national identity are influenced and formed by political ideologies and political rhetoric. Once arrived at, these ideas of national identity are manifested in symbols such as government policies, state institutions, and cultural events such as festivals and awards ceremonies (see the discussion of civic nationalism in chapter 1). Just as ideas about national identity change with time and political trends, so does the context within which governments and political movements attempt to create symbols of national identity. For example, it may be the case that an external environment may change to the extent that extant notions of national identity are no longer feasible in the new context. This is the case with the banking sector in the Caribbean. Recent changes in the ownership structure of the banking sector in the Caribbean have augured for a context in which banks are no longer suitable as symbols of national identity at the individual island level. However, rather than shift the identification with the banks as a symbol of nationalism to one of regionalism, banks are no longer used as political symbols at all.

Analyzing the changes in the use of banks as symbols of national identity reveals subtle but important dimensions of how political leaders attempt to construct concepts of identity. This is particularly interesting in the contemporary context, where the dynamics of traditional symbols of national identity, such as banks, are as (if not more) influenced by external forces as they are by domestic or internal factors. By focusing on the banking sector as a microcosm and material manifestation of political ideas, twenty-first century ideas of identity in the Caribbean continue to reflect an emphasis on island-specific notions of nationhood. This continuation of postindependence trends comes at the expense of the creation of a true regional identity, suggesting that even as global dynamics change, individual Caribbean states reshape their political rhetoric to maintain particular ideas of national identity.

GLOBALIZATION AND BANKING IN THE CARIBBEAN

The late twentieth and the beginning of the twenty-first century are overwhelmingly characterized by political and economic shifts and accommodations to continued globalization. We can understand globalization in the present context as a continuing process of economic and political restructuring on a global scale that directly and indirectly brings about political and economic realignments on a national scale, the same as those national-level realignments dynamically influence change at the global level. In practice, contemporary globalization can be understood as comprising neoliberal policy applications and the multifaceted occurrences of multinationalization and internationalization.

Neoliberalism as a policy framework comprises financial antiinflation measures, trade and capital market liberalization, and the reduction of government intervention at the domestic level (Milner and Keohane 1996:20). Contemporary neoliberal policy responses to globalization in developed and developing countries generally comprise the deregulation of economic activity, privatization of government enterprises, openness to foreign investment and trade, and the rationalization of the fiscal account. Neoliberalism assumes that markets are free and fair, and that left to the market, the economy and society will realize the optimal outcomes of efficient resource allocation. Neoliberalism further proposes that all economies obey certain universal laws of economics, rather than the opposing view that economic processes are embedded in specific social and political contexts (Girvan 2000:70).

At the global level, neoliberalism's advocates argue that countries will perform those productive functions to which the global market "freely and fairly" deems them best suited, thus achieving global competitiveness where their national endowments (whether of land, labor, or intellectual capital) allow them. Norman Girvan argues, however, that "competitiveness achieved at the cost of increasing unemployment, social exclusion, poverty and in-equality is not acceptable" (2000:70).

Yet another challenge to neo-liberalism's opposition is its endorsement by the global power elite. For example, neo-liberalism has been the main ideo-logical influence behind global trade agreements, specifically as embodied in the World Trade Organization agreements, and including the Free Trade Area of the Americas and European Union agreements. These international regimes have not come about as a result of a democratic process in which all global citizens are equally represented, and the rule makers of these trade regimes correspond to those countries that are globally politically and mili-tarily dominant. The implication is that developing countries have little say in these rules but appear to be much more subject to severe economic and political pressures should they break those rules (Block 1994:704).

Multinationalization, or transnationalization, implies the integration of production and service provision across national borders, often via foreign direct investment abroad, under the rubric of one large corporation, whose home base is usually in a developed country. In its twentieth-century incar-nation, this process of global sourcing began in the 1960s. Global sourcing is "the use of multiple sources in different countries for the components of a particular product that is assembled elsewhere" (Knox and Agnew 1998:282). In some cases, newly independent countries that sought to par-ticipate in the global economy attempted to capitalize on their perceived comparative advantage of surplus labor and primary products, and thus in-corporated themselves into the global production chain of multinational (or transnational) corporations. Other developing countries incorporated them-selves into the global production chain upon the realization of the limitations of autonomous import substitution industrialization strategies. As early as the mid-1950s, in Asia and Latin America, companies with the technology and capital were invited in to broaden the range of local production to include more consumer goods, as well as to build up local manufacture of capital and intermediate goods that were still imported and which drained foreign reserves (Gereffi and Evans 1995:211).

Internationalization is akin to multinationalization, except that it implies a more spontaneous set of actions and activities that emerge out of the open-ings created by the revolution in information technology and the neo-liberal policies that precede, facilitate, and accompany globalization. International-ization is that set of "processes generated by underlying shifts in transaction costs that produce observable flows of goods, services and capital." What this means is that "internationalization affects the opportunities and constraints facing social and economic actors, and therefore their policy preferences." Furthermore, "as incentives change through internationalization, we expect to observe changes in economic policies and in political institutions" (Milner and Keohane 1996:4). Thus, internationalization could be considered the precursor to increased multinationalization, while both are the outcomes of globalization.

Since the end of the cold war and the concomitant sea change in the global economy, access to new and cheaper sources of labor and raw materials has increased with increased communication and transportation technology. The realization of these new opportunities is made possible by trade and economic opening on the part of those countries, many of whom have formulated and implemented neo-liberal economic policies. Together with the changes in global politics, these new patterns of industrial organization in the world economy imply that a nation's development prospects "are dependent on how it is inserted into global commodity chains" (Gereffi 1994:225).

While an evaluation of the results of these processes of globalization, neo-liberalism, multinationalization, and internationalization is beyond the scope of this chapter, I can state that in most developing countries in the twenty-first century, including in the Caribbean, economic and social problems are unwieldy and increasing. The state in developing countries has less control over both its internal and external environments. Whether this is a direct result of globalization, or of forces and trends related to globalization that are simultaneously producing these phenomena, or an outcome of an entirely discrete set of dynamics coincidental to globalization, remains the subject of debate.

In the midst of this, at the state decision-making level, there is a broad agreement on a few general assumptions regarding any short- and medium-term economic development strategy:

1. The Caribbean as a whole cannot disengage from the international economy or avoid its trading/production position in relation to the world economy; its most viable option is to attempt to maximize its "inevitable" position in the international economy.
2. The Caribbean region is dependent on foreign capital and trade, especially in services such as tourism, for economic growth.
3. Both of these mean that the Caribbean countries must also play by political rules and norms that might not be of their own choosing, were all else equal. These political rules include:
   a. A foreign policy that at best pleases and at worst does not offend the regional and world hegemon, the United States of America.
   b. Domestic economic policies in line with those promoted by the United States and by multilateral financial institutions, mainly involving fiscal cutbacks, privatization of state enterprises, and lowering of barriers to trade.
   c. The practice of U.S.-style liberal democracy, or at least the appearance of such, even where it is not compatible with traditional political configurations, or it has been so corrupted as to be a farce.

d. Agreement to the implementation of policies and programs, usually designed and funded by the United States, intended to stem the supply and passage of drugs illegal in the United States Even where these policies and programs breach international law, such as the jurisdiction of territorial waters, or go against local traditions, such as the growing of non-cocaine-intended coca, the pressure to accept them is enormous.

This leaves Caribbean countries with little room to maneuver and it would appear that their best option, at this point, is to optimize their options within these strictures, while attempting to maintain domestic political and social consensus, as well as some measure of political control at the domestic level. This is indeed a formidable challenge, akin to being painted in the proverbial corner. As Haggard and Maxfield (1996:210) have written:

> Given the common trend in policy across a large number of developing countries, there are good reasons to think that international systemic pressures are at work and that the developing countries' growing integration with the world economy has constrained government choices with respect to international financial policy.

As will be clear from the above, the process of globalization creates openings for shifts in political dynamics, which may also lead to struggles for power and control in a new environment. The question then arises with regard to the financial sector: Does the globalization of financial services also lead to realignments or shifts in the political status quo ante? It is safe to say that where power connotes privilege and control, no holder of power is likely to want to give it up or share it, and will therefore attempt to maintain its position (Coleman 1996:19). This chapter explores how, in the Caribbean, the changing power dynamics in the financial sector have manifested themselves in relation to nationalism, regionalism, and identity.

THE POLITICAL ECONOMY OF THE
FINANCIAL SECTOR: GLOBAL CONSIDERATIONS

There is a process of consolidation under way in the banking industry throughout the world. The multinationalization of retail banking in the late twentieth century is a global phenomenon (IMF 2000:152). The internationalization of financial services must be understood as an interplay of the domestic situation within the country—what can be called "pull factors"—and a number of "push" factors on the part of the banks themselves. Since the 1990s, these two sets of factors have created a sort of inevitability as the global banking industry follows certain trends and patterns. Starting in the early 1990s, throughout the world most national regulations regarding banks had been significantly liberalized. With increasing levels of deregulation, domestic banks lose their monopoly position over retail banking activities as barriers to entry fall (Pomerleano and Vojta 2001). At the same time, individuals' financial behavior has grown more varied, complex, and sophisticated, with a greater demand for more, and more efficient, financial products and services. Along with this must be considered the rapid developments in technology that have been developed and applied to the financial industry, just in the decade of the 1990s, many entailing significant front-end investment requirements (Smith and Walter 1997:102). This global scenario is entirely relevant to the consideration of the Caribbean financial sector in the twenty-first century.

In sum, there are five major aspects of the multinationalization of retail banking:

1. The domestic political economy vis-à-vis the banking sector and entry barriers to foreign banks ("pull factors")
2. Motivation of banks to expand beyond their home country (push factor)[1]
3. Global trends towards deregulation of the banking sector (push factor)
4. Global trends towards consolidation in the banking industry (push factor)
5. Increased consumer demand for more and more sophisticated financial services at the same time as such services are for the most part delivered via new and expensive technology, investments which can be offset by economies of scale (pull factor)

There is synergy among many of these five factors. The demand for new and expensive technology offset by economies of scale promotes greater consolidation. Similarly, as countries follow the "trend" of deregulation, foreign banks are presented with opportunities for expansion that did not previously exist. For example, in an analysis of the Spanish banks in Latin America, Guillén and Tschoegl (1999) conclude that the Spanish expansion resulted from a saturation of the Spanish market, and a lack of market opportunity in Europe and Asia, at the same time as Latin American banking markets were being deregulated and liberalized in the early 1990s. The Spanish banks, having recently experienced radical market liberalization themselves, sought to use their market know-how and implement new information and telecommunications technologies in culturally and linguistically comfortable environments.

Thus, the changes in the composition of the banking sector in the Caribbean are representative of a broader global trend. Indeed, most policy changes with regard to the financial sector in the Caribbean have been common to other developing countries, era by era, trend by trend. Most developing countries had enacted some sort of legislation during the 1960s and 1970s that either barred or restricted foreign banks from entering their countries. As well, some developing countries undertook the nationalization of foreign banks that had been present in the region for decades. In many sub-Saharan African countries in the 1960s, the banking sectors were largely controlled by private foreign banks that remained after independence. The foreign banks' risk-averse lending objectives, and the absence of a priority on their part towards local entrepreneurs, often led to nationalization of the foreign banks. By the 1980s most of these banks were insolvent, and by the 1990s they were reprivatized and resold to foreign owners once again (Murinde 2001).

In Colombia, prior to 1967, foreign investment was not restricted as it fit into the general outward-oriented development model. By 1967, however, the state reassigned itself as the director of investment and production, and no new foreign investment, including in the banking sector, was approved. After Colombia had joined the Andean Pact, further restrictions were placed on investment in the financial sector in 1970, as the Andean Pact reserved the financial sector only for domestic investors, or investors from member countries (Barajas, Steiner, and Salazar 2000).[2] That same year in Chile, the banking system was nationalized by the Allende administration with the direct aim of gaining control of the commanding heights of the Chilean economy. The ostensible aim was to cut off control of the resource allocation mechanism from the business and middle class groups that had held it for the previous fifty years (Bosworth, Dornbusch, and Labán 1994:31). Shortly after Allende was overthrown, the economic reforms included reprivatization of banks. In December 1974, Chile abandoned the Andean Pact so as to allow foreign banks to open subsidiaries and branches and to allow direct foreign investment in commercial banks (Ibid.:155). Today, even in India, where banking institutions and the social content of lending are still considered legitimate instruments of social and economic change, the rules governing the entry of foreign banks changed significantly in the 1990s. There continue to be restrictions on the percentage of equity foreign entities can own in domestic banks, but by 2002 there were twenty-eight banks operating in India, with another twenty maintaining representative offices (Arun and Turner 2002).

What is different about the Caribbean is the way in which domestic political dynamics, as created by history and specific interpretations of history, accommodate these global trends. Throughout the developing world, and the developed world, too, the internationalization of the financial sector under globalization has taken place. But the paths that individual countries have taken to arrive at their distinct national consequences depend on the structure of the national financial system. As John Zysman's seminal study on the political economy of financial systems argues, domestic issues are worth focusing on exclusively, "not because the dramatic changes in international monetary and banking systems are unimportant, but because one can isolate

the dominant domestic structural elements that determine the domestic ramifications of an international economic development" (1983:56).

Examining the Caribbean financial sector in the era of financial globalization is not only worthwhile as an academic exercise. In the context of developing countries' experiences in the contemporary global financial polity,
the English-speaking Caribbean is virtually unique in being one of the only
regional grouping of countries that has emerged in the twenty-first century
with strong indigenous banking institutions. Indeed, the Caribbean is one of
the few developing regions with "national champions."[3] This alone is worth
exploring as a complete anomaly in the literature and experience of the
globalization of the financial sector.

ECONOMIC NATIONALISM AND THE BANKING SECTOR

The study of banks and banking is usually assumed to be the purview of
economists; however, banks are important symbols of national identity, and
are fulcrums for political and economic power. In economic theory banks
are considered key intermediaries by which money is created, distributed,
and stored (Mizruchi and Brewster Stearns 1994), but banks are not simply
mechanistic economic institutions that operate in financial market vacuums.
Banks, and who controls them, are both potential sources and explanations
of power in a society, as well as key symbols in economic nationalism. It is
well established that domestic political influence and private financiers influence financial sector reform.[4] Thus, political power is an essential concept
for the study of the politics of financial services (Coleman 1996).

As a historical phenomenon, nationalism constantly changes (Wright
1974). Economic nationalism in the twentieth century has its own dynamics,
quite different from those of nineteenth-century mercantilism. Modern economic nationalism can be dated to the post–World War II era, as the wave of
independence and national autonomy spread throughout the developing
world. As Samir Amin (1987:594) puts it, achieving political independence
augured for a national bourgeois project to bring certain processes under
control through the state and by the hegemonic national bourgeois class.
These processes included control over natural resources, markets, and "financial circuits thus enabling the centralization of surplus and the orientation
of its productive use." Thus, control over the banking sector is germane to
economic nationalism.

More specific, as part of a political ideology, economic nationalism opti-
mistically promises a better material future for a nation's citizens. As Winthrop
Wright has argued convincingly, economic nationalism has two main objectives. First, "it seeks an amorphous goal of achieving as much economic self-
sufficiency for a nation as possible," and the second, which relates to the first,

"encompasses the attempts of developing states to pattern their economies after those of recognized world powers." Both objectives are premised on the assumption that a nation can safeguard the well-being of the individual citizen if it is able to control its own economic resources. Thus, economic nationalists are convinced that a nation's greatness depends both upon its economic strength and its political independence, which hinges upon economic power: "Thus the fight for freedom is translated into a fight against outside economic penetration" (Wright 1974:7). This approach to economic nationalism falls squarely within the parameters of the Caribbean historical experience, and speaks to the notions of bourgeois and petty bourgeois nationalism discussed in chapter 1.

The role of the banking sector—insofar as it channels savings to credits and participates in the system of payments—in economic development has always been preeminent, regardless of the ideological basis of the economic development strategy or the composition of the productive sector. This is because the banking system is the main arbiter of channeling savings to credit for investment, and because it controls the system of payments. Even private banks may be vulnerable to being leaned on by governments to direct and manage the flows of capital within their countries: "they can be influenced quietly and privately to favour certain industries, firms, projects, or regions" (Beim and Calomiris 2001:256). Therefore, the banking sector is central to ongoing political debates involving governments, financial and industrial elites, developmental ideologies, and the role of market forces. Accordingly, banks are important institutions for economic nationalists.

First, financial institutions are central to economic development, especially in market economies, which most Caribbean countries ostensibly are or aim to become. Banks are at the center of economic and financial activity, and are distinct from other economic or financial institutions as primary providers of payments services and as a fulcrum for monetary policy implementation. Financial institutions and markets rely on the payment system to mobilize, allocate, and transform domestic and international savings into productive investments. A country's payment system is essential to the development of money and capital markets and the implementation of monetary policy. Retail banks play a number of functions in a market economy, primarily as conduits for information, instruments for the payment of goods and services, and repositories for savings and investment.[5] The retail banking sector is also important as a growth sector in and of itself: as economies become more market driven and individuals become more aware of their choices as consumers, the sector is an increasingly important provider of goods and services whose profit-making potential expands exponentially with the liberalization of an economy.

Second, bank fragility is of critical concern to policy makers because of the negative externalities associated with bank failures and the contagion and domino effects that bank failure can have on other banks and the economy, not to mention on the national psyche. Public policy is also especially concerned with banks because of the public goods that banks provide vis-à-vis payment services and savings mobilization; virtually no government will permit widespread bank failures. Decisions regarding the payment system are policy matters and not merely a technological or technical project. Such public involvement has political as well as economic determinants (Lindgren, Garcia, and Saal 1996:6).

Third, economic nationalists consider that the banking system is an inherent part of sovereignty. In an era of financial globalization, there may be fears that domestic groups will lose access to financial services, as well as concerns that the country could lose control over the course of development if the domestic banking system is taken over by nonnationally owned banks (Pomerleano and Vojta 2001:3). In this vein, Makler and Ness (2002) have explored how changes in financial intermediation, particularly the ownership of banks by non-nationals, challenge sovereignty in developing countries. They argue that the globalization of financial institutions and markets combine with domestic financial structure powerfully to challenge national sovereignty by weakening the state's ability to make and enforce domestic policies, and ultimately eroding a country's capability to project and maintain power.

Finally, at the micro level, individual banks operate based on access to private, usually quite sensitive information from debtors, and in accordance or response to the broader investment and political climate in which they are situated. The control and management of that type of information is critical, especially where members of a standing government are themselves entrepreneurs or debtors in some way to financial institutions. The identification of debtors in the aftermath of the Jamaican financial crisis of the 1990s was a contentious issue for exactly this reason. The Minister of Finance argued that while public money had bailed out the banks, the identification of the benefactors of taxpayers' dollars would risk serious social and political cleavages. This makes for an interesting dynamic where ownership changes from nationals to nonnationals, with regard to preexisting and sometimes longstanding bank-client (whether government or private individual) relationships that were not entirely based on rational economic decision making.

BANKS, FINANCE, AND IDENTITY IN THE CARIBBEAN

Simply put, money is power. Money—how much of it there is and how it is allocated—is fundamental to a country's political, economic, and social relations. Money may not be the entirety of an economy and a society, but it affects most of what happens in one way or another (Hoffman 2001:20). Money is also an important symbol of identity. Nowhere is this more evident than in newly independent countries, for whom an "own" currency, bearing a nationally relevant name and/or images of national icons, was among the first order of business, along with a national anthem and a flag. After the failure of the West Indies Federation, and subsequently individual independence in the 1960s, a number of steps were taken to establish separate national island identities. One of these steps involved the creation of a national currency for each island, abandoning the West Indian dollar that had acted as a regional currency since 1951. For example, in Jamaica the front of each bank note bears the portrait of either a Jamaican national hero or a former prime minister, while local scenes and popular landmarks appear on the back. In sub-Saharan Africa, the names of the currencies range from the Zambian *kwacha* and the Angolan *kwanza*, to the Botswana *pula* and the Ghanaian *cedi*, all reflecting the names of traditional, precolonial means of exchange.

The creation and existence of a Central Bank is also an important symbol of identity and status as a sovereign state, beyond its practical function as an institution in the national monetary and financial system. Central banks were established as real symbols of nationhood and a major aspect of the effort to "shed the yoke of colonialism" (Danns 1996:5). Jamaica's creation of its own Central Bank in 1960 was one of the first signs that Jamaica was contemplating withdrawal from the West Indies Federation (Brown 1989:164). Ironically, in the twenty-first century context of Caribbean politics, where the idea of a monetary union is held as the ultimate symbol of regional integration, those steps taken in the early 1960s meant the demise of what was the first true regional financial institution (Danns 1996:3).

Beyond the Central Bank, retail and commercial banks are also used as symbols of national pride and identity. In the Caribbean, commercial banks have been used as symbols of national identity and as political focal points for decades. The banking sector as a symbol of national identity has many different and sometimes contradictory aspects, however. The ownership of the bank may or may not affect where the average retail customer—the working person with a checking and a savings account, for example—takes his business. In countries where the national banks have been weak, retail customers tend to prefer to take their business to a foreign bank, with the expectation that they are more stable and trustworthy. This was the case in Argentina, where in 1995 deposits moved from domestic to foreign institutions in the wake of the Mexico "Tequila Crisis." After decades of government intervention in private deposits, the general idea was that foreign banks would not be subject to the vicissitudes of Argentine government bank policy.

Nevertheless, banks are used as symbols of identity when the conditions surrounding the banks are perceived as favorable. For example, in Mexico after the near complete takeover of the domestic banking sector by foreign banks, there was one remaining Mexican-owned bank, Banorte. Banorte, based on consumer and market surveys, carefully manipulated its ownership status in its public relations and advertisements. In Argentina, the one remaining Argentine-owned bank, Banco Galicia, capitalized on its foreign-sounding name when depositors were transferring their deposits from local institutions. However, when the financial crisis broke in 2001 and public resentment was directed towards the foreign banks, Banco Galicia changed its public relations strategy to emphasize its "Argentineness." While banks may not capture the rousing sentiments of a national sports team, or even a strong foreign policy position such as the Jamaican government's strong opposition to the United States's proposed Ship Rider Agreement in 1997, there is a strong basis for arguing that the ownership of a bank is relevant to a sense of national identity and national pride. There are two distinct periods in recent Caribbean history that further support this argument.

BANKS AND THE SYMBOLIC POLITICS OF COLOR

According to Raymond Forrest (1991), in Jamaica during the highly nationalist administration of the People's National Party (1970s), the Worker's Savings and Loan Bank (WSLB) was founded (1973) in an attempt, practically and symbolically, to garner popular support:

> The WSLB was born during the 1970s, a time when the ruling government moved the public sector in the direction of taking over the "commanding heights of the economy." Greater local financing of the powerful banking sector was the objective of this drive as the then banking sector was not believed to be doing enough to support and facilitate local development, especially in new areas of growth.[6]

Following this, the Jamaican government also nationalized Barclays in 1977, and changed its name to the National Commercial Bank (NCB). NCB had started out as the Colonial Bank of London and began operating in Kingston, Jamaica, in 1837. In 1925 the eleven branches of the Colonial Bank were acquired by Barclays Bank of London and in 1975, Barclays Bank transferred its Jamaican operation to a wholly owned subsidiary, Barclays Bank of Jamaica Limited. The NCB takeover in many ways epitomized the struggle against colonialism, as well as a manifestation of both nationalism and nationalization.[7]

In similar vein, the Black Power movement in Trinidad expressed its frustrations with the failure of the promises of independence and focused much of its energy on the Canadian commercial banks that dominated the banking system. For the political activists of the day, the banking sector provided a clear example of imperial domination and control in Trinidad. It may also be argued that the storied preference of the banks for "fair-skinned" employees was a key factor in the choice of the banks as a Black Power target. Deryck Brown (1989) argues that it was the events of 1970 that precipitated what became the "localization" of the foreign banks in Trinidad and Tobago. In responding to the sentiments expressed by the Black Power movement, the government's agenda was to increase national participation in "important sectors of the economy" (1989:181). What followed was a decades-long process of legislation geared toward forcing the foreign banks to issue local share offers. This process culminated in a near-complete "indigenization" of the Trinidadian banking sector by the beginning of the twenty-first century, and, perhaps surprising from the viewpoint of the early 1970s, Trinidadian bank expansion throughout the English-speaking Caribbean.

The second clear episode where we can identify images and issues of national identity in the banking sector was in Jamaica in the early 1990s. As a result of the privatization and liberalization policies carried out, a number of nationally owned private banks entered the market and by 1994 there were many "indigenous" private financial institutions of many different types, including a number of retail banks. It was widely noted at the time that the bulk of government assets appear to have gone to young black professionals or small to medium entrepreneurs. Workers Bank was sold, not to interest in the twenty-one families[8] but to a relatively inexperienced group of black entrepreneurs.[9] Again, one might be able to see hints of the resentment against the colonial and early postindependence days' preference for light-skinned bank workers resurfacing here.

It can be argued that this comprised the People's National Party's (PNP's) larger effort to create a black entrepreneurial class and black economic elite. At the time, the new "indigenous" banks were held up by the government and the media as nationalistic examples of Jamaicanness, and often too of black entrepreneurship—images that were key to the implicit identity of the governing party and its political rhetoric, particularly during the 1993 election in which P. J. Patterson is widely held to have played the "race card." These banks invested widely in real estate, tourism, and agriculture. And while these extrabanking forays were retrospectively seen as a major cause of the later fallout, these investments were undertaken "in the mood of the 1980s and the early 1990s, when there was official government policy support for the expansion of the domestic financial sector into the productive sector" (Chen-Young in Franklyn 2001:39).

An in-depth study of the "noneconomic" factors of race and identity behind the Jamaican financial sector debacle has yet to be undertaken. There are, however, some widely held perceptions, including on the part of the PNP itself, as to what transpired:

Dr. [Omar] Davies (PNP Member of Parliament and Jamaican Minister of Finance) in a bold speech in the preelection period, admitted to two errors. One, that he indulged in some amount of social engineering by encouraging indigenous participation in the ownership and control of major banking institutions. Two, that in his zealousness to achieve a sociological (as opposed to an economic) objective, he stepped over the line in giving "blys" (I take that to mean unmerited favours) to individuals who would be proved by subsequent developments to be either unworthy of such considerations or incapable of making good on them.

The admission is innocuous enough in that it points to a fault or weakness in the minister that almost any progressive or nationalistic-minded Jamaican would forgive.[10]

The indigenous bankers that headed these banks were, as it is phrased in Jamaica, "visibly black," and were feted in the media, by the political elite, and by the wider community. The cases of Century National Bank and of the Worker's Bank epitomize this phenomenon, though virtually all of the "indigenous" bankers of the early 1990s fit this general trajectory. The charismatic head of Century started out as a teller at the Bank of Nova Scotia (BNS) in the mid-1960s, rising to the position of Senior Assistant Manager of the BNS head office, only to be later recruited to run the Girod Bank in Jamaica.[11] He eventually gained a controlling interest in the bank, and it was renamed the Century National Bank.

The government divested the Worker's Bank in the early 1990s. Five financial groups, three of whose roots were inarguably in some of Jamaica's leading entrepreneurial (and fairer skinned) families, bid to take control of the bank. The winning bid was a surprise to many. The new CEO revolutionized the banking industry, introducing new banking products and services, investing beyond the banking sector, establishing scholarships, and winning an award for business personality of the year in 1991. This CEO was seen as "one of the new-breed Jamaican businessmen aggressive with against-the-odds confidence . . . not so long ago, he was, by his own admission, just another ordinary Jamaican with a big dream."[12] Other "stars" at Worker's Bank were lionized in the media:

Cooly [*sic*] confident, [this banker] is unruffled by the late hours and heavy demands of his job. After all, he is only digging his teeth into what he does, and likes best: making money. With a business savvy that has earned him the reputation of a hard-nose financial dealer, [this banker] is himself the product of a competitive, result oriented corporate culture which has already spawned a host of young, rising stars in Jamaica's financial industry.[13]

This type of press was typical of the coverage given these high-profile bankers.

The consequences of this "experiment" were disastrous for the banking system, the economy, and the individuals involved. A summary of the condition of the banks that were taken over by the Financial Sector Adjustment Company (FINSAC), including the Worker's Bank, found a litany of woes, including unreliable financial statements, inaccurate Bank of Jamaica reporting, nonexistent investments recorded on bank accounts, loans diverted to subsidiary companies to avoid reporting as past due, and mis-stating financial statements and inflating balances, among many, many other findings (FINSAC 1999). Except for a very brief prison stay for one banker, none has yet been prosecuted, but they are all either living outside of Jamaica, or in much humbler circumstances just a decade after being held up as splendid models of entrepreneurship, success, and possibility. For some, too, it is lamentable that "the country has returned to the days when Jamaicans of a darker hue would be hard-pressed to recall names and count off on one hand, people in 'big' business who look like them. There is an unintended but inestimable cost to all of this."[14]

Interestingly, and adding further weight to the argument that banks reflect perceptions of national identity, is the presence of two Indian banks in the two CARICOM (Caribbean Community and Common Markrt) countries that have significant Indian populations. The Bank of Baroda operates in Guyana and the Intercommercial Bank operates in Trinidad and Tobago. The role and operations of these banks, and their relationship to Indian identity in Guyana and Trinidad, merit further research. Their presence, however, points to some of the underlying "fault lines" of a prospective Caribbean regional identity, with regard to the question of the possibility of creating a Caribbean identity where "Indians in the Caribbean have had a somewhat ambivalent relationship with the other peoples of the region and to proposals for its political unification" (Ryan 1999a:151). This theme is picked up and further amplified in chapter 9.

Beyond the use of currency and financial institutions as political symbols of national identity, governments are concerned with bank ownership for less direct reasons of power and control. Banks and other financial services firms possess economic power in market economies through their control over the allocation of credit, the behavior of financial markets, and as well through their relationships with the productive sector and their customer base. This economic power provides these firms with a considerable potential to shape what become matters for political consideration and to influence the outcomes of the public policy process. Governments, therefore, have multiple interests in maintaining, at best, control over and, at worst, a mutually beneficial relationship with those banks operating in their domestic system. At the same time, financial services firms seek to protect and further their interests through obtaining special access to political leaders, either through personal contacts or via institutional government relations divisions that monitor the policy-making process (Coleman 1996).

BANKS, OWNERSHIP, AND NATIONAL IDENTITY

The history of banking in the Caribbean explicates this argument. During the nineteenth century, up until independence in the 1960s, the banking sector

was primarily geared towards financing and facilitating trading relations between the colony and the metropole. There was virtually no investment in
production or consumer credit. This de facto established the identity of the
then-Caribbean colonies as exporters of primary products and consumers of
manufactured goods. The main banks present in the region were the British
Barclays, which had grown out of the original Colonial Bank that was established in the 1820s and 1830s throughout the region, and three Canadian
banks, BNS, the Canadian Imperial Bank of Commerce (CIBC), and the Royal
Bank of Canada. Canadian banks began establishing themselves in the
Caribbean in 1910 and by World War I "could be described as major financial institutions in the Caribbean" (Baum 1974:21).

In the politically charged decade after independence, the foreign-owned
banks were negatively viewed and were to become a chief target of rising
economic nationalism. Advocates of the economic nationalism of the 1960s
considered foreign ownership of strategic sectors a barrier to economic development and, ultimately, to political independence. Public ownership and
control of key economic sectors became a primary goal as the generally socialist orientation of the government became more pronounced. Thus, decisions about the banking sector would have been made in the context of dependency theory, which had become something of the reigning economic
orthodoxy in many developing countries in the 1970s. Dependency theory
broadly prescribed economic policies that were intended to insulate the domestic economy from international shocks. As Clive Thomas (1974:156)
stated:

> We are satellite economies integrated to each other and to the U.K. and U.S.A.
> by a pervasive system of branches of financial institutions with Head Offices in
> these metropolitan countries. These institutions are neither exclusively con-
> cerned with developments within our economy or with promoting the sort of
> regional integration we may desire. Their exclusive interest is to make profits on
> *all* their operations, no matter where they may be located. Ultimately the only
> effective reform is the development of indigenous institutions and the imposi-
> tion of controls on the movement of all funds outside the region.

Through the 1970s and 1980s, the larger CARICOM countries moved from
branch banking operations owned and run by British and Canadian banks to
full or part nationalization by governments.

> Localisation occurred first in Jamaica and almost immediately afterward in
> Trinidad and Tobago, following a wave of structuralist economic thought of the
> 1960s and 1970s. Some economists, among them [George] Beckford, explicitly
> recommended the nationalization of commercial banks, and by the mid-1970s
> most banks in both Jamaica and Trinidad and Tobago were either locally or gov-
> ernment owned. (Williams 1996:68)

The newly independent countries felt it necessary to have banks that would be more responsive to the needs of the local economy and to nationally determined developmental objectives. The thinking was that the "banking arrangements of the preindependence era did not favour economic and social progress in the colonies," owing, among other things, to the persistence of racism, and the fact that "the mechanics of the [colonial] banking system, as Clive Thomas wrote, favoured the transfer of resources to overseas, and not to the host country" (July 1995:91). Commercial banks were seen to hold "the key to resource allocation and had the collective institutional capacity to determine lasting outcomes in the [Caribbean] economies" (Danns 1996:21). By 1974 the situation was such that a Canadian analyst wrote:

> For a number of reasons, both rational and irrational, there is a Commonwealth Caribbean sense of being exploited, and an answer is found for many in what must be described as *black nationalism*. Not infrequently, Canadian banks as holders of money find themselves the object of blame. After all, so the argument might run, the banks hold the money; if the banks used their deposits in the interests of the people, then the people would prosper. (Baum 1974:6 [emphasis added])

According to Baum, growing nationalism "nudged" the Canadian banks to offer stock and, in some cases, control to nationals of the islands in which they operated. Where the "nudging" was not heeded, a government might have intervened, expropriated, and reformed a locally owned bank, as happened with the Bank of Montreal in Trinidad. It was actions such as these that further "nudged" Canadian banks to "localize" ownership and, ostensibly, control (Baum 1974:26).

Throughout the Caribbean there were moves towards ownership and localization in one form or another. Danns (1996) chronicles the various actions taken in Guyana, Trinidad, Jamaica, and Barbados. Where Caribbean governments did not nationalize foreign banks, regulations were designed so that loan requests were directed to sectors that had been targeted based on overall development goals. Many of these regulations brought about conditions of financial repression, where government intervention to set interest rates and direct the flow of credit, combined with price inflation, was detrimental to the deposit base for domestic bank lending (McKinnon 1973).[15]

These trends were not limited to the Caribbean. As but one example, in Colombia, prior to 1967, foreign investment was not restricted as it fit into the general outward-oriented development model. Foreign investment in the financial system dated to 1912, and the first financial legislation of 1923 did not restrict foreign banks. In 1967 a new foreign exchange and trade regime based on strict foreign exchange controls was adopted. The state reassigned itself as the director of investment and production, and no new foreign investment, including in the banking sector, was approved, though it was not explicitly restricted by law. After 1970, the Andean Pact (to which Colombia was signatory) reserved the financial sector only for domestic investors, or investors from member countries.[16] Branches of foreign banks had to convert themselves into domestic firms. No new direct foreign investment in the financial system was allowed. In the early 1990s the laws were changed, the system became fully open, and foreign banks entered Colombia once again (Barajas, Steiner, and Salazar 2000).

In sub-Saharan Africa, where the history of the financial sector was more similar to the Caribbean than that of Latin America, there was also a similar pattern of events in the banking sector. In African countries in the 1960s the banking sectors were largely controlled by private foreign banks that remained after independence. Their risk-averse lending objectives and the absence of a priority on their part towards local entrepreneurs often led to nationalization of the now-foreign banks. By the 1980s most of these banks were insolvent, and by the 1990s they were reprivatized and resold to foreign owners once again (Murinde 2001).

Those policies that aimed to fulfill the nationalist aspirations of newly independent countries, such as those in the Caribbean, were in many ways attempts to replicate similar processes and policies under way in the developed world. Particularly with regard to the financial sector, most developed countries in the post–World War II era placed stringent controls on cross-border capital movements and on the ownership of domestic financial institutions. The liberalized trading relations envisioned by the United States and the United Kingdom were limited to commodities and, to some extent, services. The financial sector, however, was to remain under the control of national governments. The main intellectual framers of the post–World War II economic order "concluded that a liberal international financial order would undermine the new state role emerging at the domestic level" (Coleman 1996). The irony of the economic nationalism of the 1960s and 1970s, in many developing countries, is that it set out, as a populist measure, to give control of the country's economic resources to the "people." The result, in many cases, however, was a consolidation of economic power in the bourgeois political elite and their private-sector elite constituents. As an economic strategy it was entirely bourgeois (see chapter 1), and it failed the "people."

STRUCTURAL ADJUSTMENT AND
CHANGING DYNAMICS OF BANKS AND IDENTITY

Beginning in the late 1970s, there was the realization (whether conscious or forced) that, due to the changing international economy, nationalist economic plans would not produce the expected growth and development. Following this, in the 1980s, "structural adjustment" policies were implemented in most Caribbean countries, with their general prescriptions of diminishing state regulation, ownership, and control over the economy. Structural adjustment resulted in the "freeing up of the region's financial sector from strangling exchange and other controls and regulations" (Danns 1996:4). And to this Marion Williams added: "Policy makers were forced to accept the deficiencies of the structuralist approach." Today, however, "it is ironic that those Caribbean countries which were most wedded to the structuralist approaches have abandoned those views and now adhere to the more monetarist prescriptions prescribed by the international financial institutions" (Williams 1996:231).

Whether due to the divestment of government holdings of publicly owned banks, gradual divestment via public share offers of foreign banks over many decades, or new startups by Caribbean nationals, the ownership structure in the banking sector shifted to nearly complete private ownership, both national and foreign. After a decade of what could be considered "settling into" the new realities of private ownership, an open market economy, and further openness to the international economy, by the beginning of the twenty-first century the number of banks owned by Caribbean nationals was lower in 2003 than it was at the beginning of the 1990s. This is especially so because of the fallout in Jamaica in the mid-1990s and the closure or takeover of virtually all the indigenous banks there. After a brief heyday in the early 1990s of Jamaican-owned commercial and merchant banks that for a short time promised to become regional financial giants, the banking sector in the Caribbean has consolidated. The Caribbean-owned banks that remain, in large part, particularly those in Trinidad and Tobago, are strong and are successfully expanding throughout the Caribbean (Bissember 2003).

As noted, one of the casualties of the 1990s was the Jamaican banking sector, due in part to internal mismanagement and poor investment decisions, and in part due to an exceptionally harsh macroeconomic policy environment, which saw virtually all of the banks failing in the midst of a financial sector crisis that began in 1996. Jamaica's financial sector crisis is proportionally one of the costliest in the world, costing more than ten times that of the Mexican "Tequila Crisis" of 1994–1995, in terms of the amount the government had to put out to prevent widespread bank closures and stabilize the banking system.

One of the principal outcomes of the Jamaican financial crisis was a remapping of the ownership of Jamaican retail banks. Many of the failed banks were taken over by the government, through FINSAC, while most of the assets of the smaller ones were merged and sold together to the Trinidadian RBTT Financial Holdings. At present there are four principal retail banks in Jamaica: BNS, a majority Canadian-owned bank; First Caribbean International Bank, formerly Canadian Imperial Bank of Commerce,[17] also majority-Canadian owned; NCB, which was sold by the Jamaican government to a Canadian company, AIC;[18] and the Royal Bank of Trinidad and Tobago (RBTT). There is no nationally owned retail bank in Jamaica today. Interestingly, given these developments in the financial sector, banks are no longer used as symbols of identity, at least not in the political dialectic. The banks themselves, however, continue to play the identity card.

The case of NCB is very interesting in this regard. In 1986 and 1991 two public share offerings gradually sold shares to the public, with the government eventually giving over controlling interest in the bank to the shareholders of the Jamaica Mutual Life Assurance Society and Jamaica National Building Society. In the early 1990s, in keeping with the nationalist fervor of the financial sector, NCB considered itself "bankers to the nation" or the "nation's bank." Internally, the bank thrived on idealistic notions and plans to "build Jamaica" and ventured into investments in tourism and agriculture. In 1993 NCB acquired another large bank before going into severe fiscal problems that nearly forced its closure; it was taken over by FINSAC until its sale in 2002.

NCB was bought by AIC, which is owned by a Jamaican who emigrated to Canada in the 1970s and who built a successful business in Canada in mutual funds. While the bank was bought and restructured using entirely Canadian capital, it heavily promotes itself as a "Jamaican bank," and one of its principal public relations strategies is to capitalize on nationalist sentiment, emphasizing the Jamaican birth of its owner and of its CEO, a Jamaican who built his banking career in the Middle East. Its slogan since its purchase by AIC is "come back home." It has launched a number of initiatives, such as announcing the repatriation of all of its profits in Jamaica for at least five years, and establishing an education fund based on a fixed percentage of its credit card receipts.

While Jamaica's nationally owned banking sector melted down in the 1990s, Trinidad and Tobago's stabilized and strengthened. Trinidad and Tobago was one of the more "aggressive" countries in the Caribbean to nationalize its banking sector in the 1970s, and it did not suffer the fallout of the Guyanese or the Jamaicans. This itself warrants further in-depth research, as an inquiry into the nature of Caribbean entrepreneurship. By 1994 five of the six retail banks in Trinidad and Tobago were fully or majority owned by nationals (Danns 1996:21). For example, the Republic Bank in Trinidad and Tobago grew out of Barclay's gradual divestment and sale of shares to government and private interests. Similarly, RBTT was created from the assets of the former Royal Bank of Canada.

The Trinidadian RBTT influence in Jamaica, as one of only four major banks in the country, is replicated throughout the Caribbean region. Today it is the Trinidadian banks that are the dominant regional players. Republic Bank in 2000 acquired majority shares of Grenada's NCB, and Guyana's National Bank of Industry and Commerce. By 2001 RBTT had branches throughout the English-speaking Caribbean, and even in Suriname and the Netherlands Antilles.[19] The other dominant force in the Caribbean banking sector is Canada. The Canadian banks are Barclays merged with CIBC in 2002 to create the First Caribbean bank, and with their combined operations, First Caribbean operates in virtually every CARICOM member state. The Canadian Bank of Nova Scotia has branches in ten CARICOM member states.

There are still a few, albeit small, private and public "indigenous" banks in the Caribbean, but there is a general agreement that they will soon give way to the inevitable consolidation already in process. Despite this reality, regionalization does not appear wholeheartedly to have been accepted. Certainly the political rhetoric at the popular level does not reflect this. For example, in the case of Dominica, according to the head of Republic Bank, one of the Trinidadian banks that is expanding throughout the Caribbean, and thereby stands to gain from any bank privatizations:

> There is really no good reason why the government should still be holding on to [the National Commercial Bank of Dominica]. But it sees the bank as being a partner, with the state, in effecting government policy. The governments feel comfortable dealing with a local bank.[20]

It would appear that these nationally owned banks, however small, are perceived to represent one of the last holds these governments have over their countries.

BEYOND NATIONALISM: BANKING AND THE CREATION OF A CARIBBEAN REGIONAL IDENTITY

Beyond structural adjustment, economic liberalization, and a reduced role for the government in developmental-type activities and enterprises, one of the main issues for the Caribbean in a globalized world polity is regional integration. The Caribbean integration movement has gone from CARICOM's 1973 objectives of closer political, economic, and social union among the former West Indies Federation members, to a "wider and deeper" Association of Caribbean States that include all the countries whose shores are washed by the Caribbean Sea. Ostensibly responding to the West Indian Commission's admonition to "integrate or die," CARICOM members meet more and more often and continue to sign agreements for the creation of regional institutions. Central to the success of CARICOM, however, is the creation of a regional identity that goes beyond Heads of Government summits.

Integration theory has long held that regional integration is successful when ordinary citizens come to identify themselves as part of that regional entity at which the integration effort aims. Ian Boxill has convincingly argued that successful regional integration must be guided by an ideology that promotes regionalism. That ideology can "only be said to exist if a common perception of the region or a regional identity" is present (1993:29). Boxill concluded that the Caribbean regional integration movement is weak precisely because "it is not based upon nor is it guided by an ideology of regionalism" (Ibid.:109). In previous work on Caribbean integration,[21] I found that the processes of integration and development of a regional identity tended to occur in sectors or programs where CARICOM governments had relatively little intention of this as an objective. The Caribbean banking sector would appear to be yet another example of this phenomenon. Referring specifically to the banking sector, in a 1993 address to the BNS management meeting Terrence Farrell noted this very fact:

> It is not the case that economic integration is being driven by the CARICOM political process. Rather it is being driven by a Caribbean private sector which has moved out front of their governments in achieving Caribbean economic integration at the level where it really matters. The end result of this process is likely to be a financial sector characterized by larger, stronger institutions, with a regional presence and a hemispheric reach. (Farrell 1993:unpublished)

In the Caribbean, many (if not the majority of) ordinary citizens are aware of the presence and activities of banks. Banks have been used as symbols of national identity throughout our post-independence history. We have today, without any deliberate intention or effort of CARICOM or of individual Caribbean governments, an already regional and "regionalizing" institution that could serve as a symbol of a regional identity, just as it has served as a symbol of national identity at different times over the past decades.

Relative to the rest of the developing world, the Caribbean banking sector is one of the few in which there are remaining "indigenous" banks that are strong and have the potential to become stronger. In the political rhetoric of symbols of national identity, the Caribbean banks ought to be a cause for celebration and pride. They were important symbols of independence and autonomy throughout the Caribbean in the 1970s. In Jamaica at the beginning of the 1990s they were potent symbols of black nationalist identity. Yet the emphasis on banks and the financial sector as symbols of development and of a regional identity has yet to be made in today's Caribbean political rhetoric, either at the regional or the national level.

OBSTACLES TO REGIONAL IDENTITY

The question, then, is why hasn't this opportunity been grasped? I argue that there are three main reasons:

1. There is the continued emphasis on national-level ideologies of identity, as opposed to a true commitment to the creation of a regional identity. This tendency can be attributed to two discrete but parallel national-level factors. In the case of Jamaica, for example, regionalism is not perceived as a viable populist symbol of identity, and thus it is not emphasized. In other CARICOM member states, primarily Trinidad and Guyana, there are strong, what we might call "Indocentric," sentiments that reject what they perceive as the dominant Afro- or Creole-centric identity of the regional integration movement (see chapter 2). Those who hold these perceptions and attitudes tend to be suspicious that the regional integration movement is one in which their own Indo-Caribbean identity is at best subsumed and at worst eradicated (Ryan 1999a). Hence, at the national level there is ambivalence about regional integration, despite the plethora of summits, agreements, and commitments to regionalism.

2. There is the persistence of an interisland rivalry among the Caribbean business elite that dates back to the 1960s and 1970s. This is an area for which more research must be undertaken, but there is a popular sentiment, certainly in Jamaica, that the situation of Trinidadian and Barbadian business expansion in the late 1990s and early 2000s is "unfair" given the closure of those economies to Jamaicans in previous decades. This thus leads to a rejection of the Trinidadian banks as "regional" banks. The extent to which this perception is held at the level of the political elite is also an area of further research.

3. There has been a change in the perception of a bank as a symbol of national identity in those countries where the banks are no longer under national control. It is debatable why this change has come about. Is it because the banks have escaped national control and there is no realistic prospect of them returning to national control, and thus it is a pragmatic change in attitude? Or has there been a shift in ideology that no longer sees banks as nationalist institutions but as necessary service providers whose owners' nationality should be of no concern?

ANALYSIS

By examining the banking sector in the English-speaking Caribbean over the past fifty years, one can discern three main features:

1. Banks in the Caribbean have been used as symbols of national identity, sovereignty, and control over a nation's development.

2. Ownership of banks in most Caribbean countries has gone from post-independence nationalization and individual national, usually government

ownership, with some foreign ownership, to a general trend of Canadian and Trinidadian ownership, with only a few small nationally owned banks.

3. The more recent changes, to the present scenario as just described, have taken place without government direction, but rather have been market driven.

From the experience and trajectory of the banking sector in the Caribbean, I argue that the construction of identity, both national and regional, is subject to the vagaries of individual CARICOM members' political rhetoric regarding national identity at the local level. Nationalistic symbols that were once apt for political manipulation are discarded once those symbols change as a result of external forces, or forces that are beyond the control of the national government. However, while external conditions may change, the core post-independence emphasis on national identity does not change; it only adapts to the new environment by abandoning old symbols and focusing on new ones.

At the beginning of the twenty-first century, that powerful symbol of identity of the past, the banking sector, has become one of the most regionalized businesses in the Caribbean, without the input or impetus of Caribbean governments. Further regionalization and expansion of regional financial services and institutions, not only banks, are impeded by national laws and prudential regulations of individual countries. These impediments include obstacles to the free movement of capital, to the right of enterprises to establish outside their home base, and to the ownership of real property under the Alien Landholdings Act. All of these issues are on the agenda for Caribbean governments to address (Bissember 2003). There is also an important barrier that continues to be discussed among regional decisionmakers but that has not yet been materially altered on a regional basis, despite over a decade of discussion and promises, which is the free movement of labor. It is difficult to take CARICOM governments' promises seriously when the first real move towards truly liberalizing the movement of persons within the region only came in 2003 when it became clear that this would be necessary to facilitate the smooth running of the 2007 Cricket World Cup.

The complete liberalization of the banking sector would appear inevitable given global and regional trends. The initial stage of liberalization, since the mid-1980s, has led to increased competition and profitability in the financial sector in the Caribbean (Williams 1996). One might also argue that it has led to greater transparency, particularly in the case of Jamaica after the 1996 crisis. There may be the concern that with the further relaxation of barriers to entry, Caribbean countries will then be open to the true financial giants that have swept much of Latin America, including the Dominican Republic. Yet here the Caribbean presents an unusual case in the current global context.

The English-speaking Caribbean banking market, however enormously profitable it may be for the Canadian banks that are already here, is too small and too saturated to be worthwhile for any of the current expansionist giants, such as Banco Santander Central Hispano or Citibank North America. As Bissember points out, given the pattern of the banking sector in the past few years, the removal of both financial and nonfinancial sector restrictions could likely "see the creation of a truly CARICOM transnational corporation financed by regional financial resources" (2003).

There of course remains the fact that, as well as the new Trinidadian banking powers are doing, the Caribbean banking sector remains heavily dominated by Canadian banks. According to CARICOM's figures, without distinction for type of bank, in 2002 there were ninety-four banks in the region of which thirty-nine were locally owned and ten CARICOM (i.e., Trinidadian) owned. The remaining banks were owned by foreign entities mainly from Canada, and, to a much lesser extent, the United States, via Citibank. Many of these Canadian banks, however, are partially owned by Caribbean people, as a result of the localization programs of the 1970s. Including shareholders' stakes, local and regional ownership ranges from 56 percent of the banks in Barbados and Guyana, to 62 percent in Jamaica, and close to 85 percent in Trinidad and Tobago (Bissember 2003).

Regardless of nationality, however, it is inarguably the case that all privately owned banks have the same main objective: increased profits for shareholders. That they are profit oriented does not mean, however, that they cease to be civic minded or to invest in "developmental" projects that do not promise a worthwhile return on capital, whether on their own initiative or with prodding from the government. Furthermore, financial institutions have many incentives beyond profit to need to maintain good relations with the government, for their own benefit. They also need to be seen as good corporate citizens by their customers, and thus are unlikely to ignore the public relations benefits of their involvement in certain projects. Finally, it is in the bank's long-term interest to invest in low-yield development projects, as the overall health and stability of the economy only redounds to their own benefit. Indeed, many banks, at least in Jamaica, factor nonprofitable loans and investments in public works–type projects into their cost structure, as a part of the cost of doing business in a heavily politicized environment.

CONCLUSION

In the Caribbean, the banking sector has consolidated, as it has throughout the world. In the late 1960s and early 1970s the bank market structure was virtually controlled by British and Canadian banks. By the mid-1980s the banking sectors of many Caribbean countries showed significant market share by nationally owned, mostly public, banks. In the early 1990s, especially in Jamaica and Trinidad, there was a strong presence of nationally owned, private retail banks. By the late 1990s and into the early 2000s, the ownership pattern of banks in the Caribbean had changed significantly, so that today the largest market share in the English-speaking Caribbean is held by Canadian and Trinidadian majority-owned and controlled banks.

While the current ownership structure of the banking sector would suggest that English-speaking Caribbean countries are moving towards a consolidated regional financial sector, these facts have not been incorporated into the political rhetoric at the national or regional level. This examination of the banking sector in the Caribbean supports the proposition that the construction of a Caribbean regional identity will not come about if left to Caribbean governments. CARICOM governments have yet to make good on their repeated commitments to regional integration and the construction of a regional identity, even where opportunities to capitalize on existing regional institutions, such as banks, exist. They are still too concerned with island-specific definitions of and debates over national identity, despite the ever-tightening noose around the possibilities to promote these ideas. Nationalism and identity, after all, provide one last tool with which governments and political movements can rally public support and capture the people's imagination in a global political and economic context where little else is available for this purpose.

NOTES

1. This factor is especially significant after the mid-1990s, as even in countries like Chile and Argentina where the banking sector had been relatively open for a decade or more, foreign banks only went there as part of a general Latin America expansion.

2. This meant that branches of foreign banks had to convert themselves into domestic firms, and new direct foreign investment was prohibited. Due to loopholes in the law, however, control of the joint-ownership banks that were permitted ended up in foreign hands.

3. "National champions" are those large, regionally or even internationally competitive, private banks that are still owned by nationals of the developing country in which the bank is operating. In some developing countries where foreign banks have begun to dominate the retail banking market, there is a "national champion" that is still managing to hold its own. In some cases, the national champion is even expanding, making acquisitions alongside the foreign banks' acquisitions.

4. For Latin America, for example, see Kessler (1999); Neiman Auerbach (2001); and Marichal (1997). For Asia, see Lukauskas (2002) and Claessens and Glaessner (1999). For Spain and the former Eastern European socialist bloc, see Pérez (1997), and Blejer and Škreb (1999), respectively.

5. Retail banking is that part of commercial banking concerned with the activities of individual customers, generally in large numbers (Smith and Walter 1997:101). Retail banks are those which provide services such as checking accounts (demand deposits) and consumer debit and credit cards.

6. Raymond Forrest, "No Requiem for Workers Bank," *The Financial Gleaner,* January 18, 1991.

7. "Big Bank Merger in Offing," *Insight* IX (2), December 1–15, 1992, p. 8.

8. The "21 families" refers to a commonly held perception that in Jamaica a handful of people, commonly called the oligarchy of the 21 families, are able to command and control the resources of the country for their exclusive use because of their wealth and access to the corridors of power.

9. Neville Spike, "The Oligarchy and Privatization," *The Gleaner,* February 2, 1992, p. 20.

10. Henley Morgan, "Dr Davies' Mea Culpa," *Jamaica Observer,* October 25, 2002.

11. Girod Bank was established by a Puerto Rican entrepreneur in Jamaica in the mid-1980s.

12. Paget deFreitas, "The Making of an Empire," *The Gleaner,* March 20, 1992, p. 2.

13. *The Financial Gleaner,* October 16, 1992, p. 7

14. Henley Morgan, "Dr Davies' Mea Culpa," *Jamaica Observer,* October 25, 2002.

15. True to McKinnon's hypothesis, Marion Williams's comprehensive study later found that a liberalized banking system in the Caribbean meant increased competitiveness, greater profitability, and more availability of bank credit (1996).

16. Foreign ownership of more than 20 percent of local banks was prohibited under Andean Pact rules during 1971–1987.

17. Up until 2001, British Barclays still retained branches in fourteen Caribbean countries. They are expected to rebrand under the First Caribbean name since the merger with CIBC.

18. AIC originally stood for Advantage Investment Counsel, but is now known solely by its acronym.

19. See Bissember (2003) for a detailed account of the Royal Bank of Trinadad and Tobago (RBTT) and Republic Bank's recent regional expansion.

20. Robert Norstrom, cited in David Renwick, "Unsettled Waters in the Caribbean," *The Banker,* October 1,, 2002.

21. I examined the work of the CARICOM Women's Desk (1997), and of the Master in International Business degree program between CARICOM, the Dominican Republic, and Haiti (2000).

4

The Contemporary Crisis in Guyanese National Identification

Shona N. Jackson

INTRODUCTION

On his website, Ian Chambers, a Guyanese residing in the United States, offers "a walk through Georgetown," the country's capital. Framing the pictures that dominate the site, Chambers explains,

> I took a walk through Georgetown during the past Christmas holidays (1996) and so many memories came back that I had to put into practice what I had promised (to take pictures) so long ago. . . . For those of you who are from Guyana, I hope this brings back memories of the country I know you love. For those of you who are not Guyanese, I hope this gives you an insight into our small but beautiful country.[1]

A search on the World Wide Web for information about the Republic of Guyana will produce a variety of images, like those found on Chambers's site. The images collectively represent the nation in this global space known for its deterritorialization and respatialization of otherwise bounded geographies and cultures. One is likely to encounter a map of the country across which its flora, fauna, and export industries like sugar, rice, and bauxite are identified by region. The placement of these products on the Web is in fact a (symbolic) recommoditization of these national products in the global market. Not only are they produced for consumption in international markets, but in a kind of visual metonymy, their placement on a virtual map for visual consumption produces a new product for export—national culture. Despite the diversified nature of cyberspace, Chambers is able to secure the integrity of the nation for himself and others in the diaspora, seeking cultural connection. His recreation of the nation through visual images relies on what Homi K. Bhabha calls "the power of the eye to naturalize the rhetoric of national affiliation" (1990a:295).[2] The pictures of the Town Hall, Parliament Building, Stabroek Market, St George's Cathedral, and of course the country's flag are the "nation's visual presence" (Bhabha 1990b). Chambers's pictures signify the nation they simultaneously reconstruct, making *it* visible through the constant deferral to some whole that, presumably, refers back.

In Guyana and in its diaspora, however, the "social cohesion" and national space of Chambers's homage are complicated by the struggles of a variety of ethnic groups not only to gain access to government power but also to reclaim their identities as formerly oppressed peoples in a way that allows state power to be "disseminated" through these identities. "The country I know you love," to which Chambers directs us, is marked by bitter contests over who has both a historical and cultural right to rule that country. The monuments and historic places represented on his website are sources of pride for every Guyanese, but the national culture they gesture toward is fragmented by the struggles of different ethnic groups, since independence, to remake the "nation" in their own image and thus secure their right to portions of the "national pie."

THE DISAPPEARED NATIONAL VISION

At one point in Guyana's history, shortly before independence, the two leading political black and East Indian figures for much of the twentieth century, Forbes Burnham and Cheddi Jagan, respectively, once shared the hope of a unified politicocultural vision for the nation. As an expression of that vision, both hoped that the date of Guyana's independence from Britain could be the anniversary of the largest slave uprising in the country's history, the February 23, 1763, rebellion led by Cuffy (Daly [1966] 1975). However, independence was not granted until May 1966 and the anniversary of the Cuffy rebellion instead came to mark the establishment of the Cooperative Republic of Guyana a few years later. The eventual erection of the statue of in Cuffy's honor became not just a symbol of the country's long history of anticolonial struggles. It also symbolized the consolidation of Afro-Creole nationalism in the country. The right to rule Guyana had been interpreted by the Burnham administration as a cultural right for blacks (Hintzen 1997). Decades of ethnic antagonism, primarily between blacks and East Indians, and at times violent, have marked both People's National Congress (PNC) and People's Progressive Party (PPP) regimes since independence.

After the charged 1997–1998 election period and the racial violence that ensued, Guyanese again became more forcefully aware of how much the shared national vision of Cheddi Jagan and Forbes Burnham had evaporated in the years since independence as what would have been its most significant, single symbol, the statue of Cuffy, was routinely defamed by the dumping of trash at its base by unknown persons. The defamation of Cuffy, a black symbol for a nation that is not, reflects the problem for unified national representation in the country. This popular query was writ large on the national level when the Indian-led PPP first came to power. At that time, it chose to celebrate the country's independence on its original date of May 26, not on the date elected by the PNC, February 23, the anniversary of the Cuffy rebellion and the establishment of the Cooperative.[3] Now, in this multiethnic, multiracial, postindependence society, these formerly subaltern groups (blacks, East Indians, Chinese) and subalterns (Aboriginals, hereafter Amerindians) compete in order to establish their right to govern a land that some claim *none*[4] is native to by recapturing moments of the Republic's "history" into ethnonationalist narratives.[5] These narratives are the particular cultural discourses that encode the individual struggles of groups throughout history to articulate their belonging to the territory. To satisfy diasporic longing for "home" and the need for a sense of national "belonging," Chambers's website must eclipse this contest as he unwittingly recreates the political, economic, and even geographic discrimination within the nation that relegates some groups and their query of the nation—read the defamation of Cuffy—to the base or margins of the national destiny.[6]

The discussion in this chapter is figured at a contentious moment in recent history, which has set a variety of discourses into play and reveals the competing images of the nation that, in fact, undergird Chambers's image of Guyanese cultural nationalism. On December 15, 1997, Guyana held presidential elections following the death of President Cheddi Jagan. The party in power at the time of Jagan's death, the PPP, retained its political majority with Jagan's wife, Janet Jagan, becoming the new president.[7] The PPP/Civic coalition maintained that it supported the working class and that it was committed to unity and equality for all Guyanese.[8] However, Janet Jagan's presidency met with sustained opposition from the PNC. Open violence by those who invoked the party name was directed toward East Indians in general, as well. To no avail, the PNC leveled charges of election fraud and of discrimination in housing and employment, among others, at the new government. Then PNC leader, the late Desmond Hoyte, refused to accept the position as Minority Leader in the Parliament in order to contest the legitimacy of Janet Jagan's presidency, despite an independent audit by the Caribbean Community (CARICOM), which found that the election was fair. Under the Hermandston Accord, both parties were required to meet to reevaluate the 1980 constitution but Hoyte initially stalled these discussions, principally because they would force him to recognize Jagan as the new president. As a result, the decades-old struggle between blacks and Indians in the country flared, and an ethnic relations committee was formed by the PPP to address these concerns. The situation did not improve with the holding of fresh presidential elections in the 1999–2000 election period. Months after, the "dialogue" between the then PNC/Reform opposition leader Desmond Hoyte and the current President Bharrat Jagdeo's PPP administration was still in trouble, even though that election was not accompanied by the political acrimony and ethnic violence of the 1997 presidential election.[9] For weeks, the crisis of the 1997–1998 election period produced a wave of racial and cultural claims by blacks, East Indians, and, to a lesser extent, Amerindians in the nation's newspapers. While some argued that there were "no racial problems in Guyana," others cited "racial distrust" among "ethnic" groups and still others called for marches against racism. Each ethno-political group sought to find solutions to the national crisis and reaffirm their cultural identity as Guyanese and the political rights that citizenship affords. They did this in editorials and in letters to the editor in the metropolitan paper, the *Stabroek News,* and in other papers.

This chapter reads those letters published in the *Stabroek News* and examines the difficulty they convey of representing group claims.[10] It argues that ethnic or racial politics in Guyana is not strictly a function of class or culture but, in the contemporary period, also rests on claims to history and how each ethnic/cultural group represents itself and its role as it revisits the colonial and postcolonial history of the former colony. It further argues that in these letters and in other writings, Guyanese history is in fact being rewritten in a manner that solidifies ethno-political power. My reading of the letters also demonstrates that the "nation" is being remade incessantly as groups seek the cultural imagery necessary to secure political power by negotiating the "language" of racial politics and national representation that the Forbes Burnham/PNC regime solidified as the medium for political expression and power in the late 1960s and early 1970s. The "nation," which was once an orienting point of political resistance to colonial power, for most groups, still codes the collective histories of dispersal, disappearance, slavery, and indenture of the Guyanese people. And, in the post-colonial period, it fails to bring them together.

While the chapter shares this volume's premise that ethno-national identity in the Caribbean is bound to and lived through class identity, it does not undertake a formal class analysis. Nor does it make claims about the actual class positions or interests of the majority of blacks and East Indians in Guyana.[11] In re-examining the origins of current class conflict, it instead relies on the a priori identity for current class formations in Guyana, the "working people" of Walter Rodney's socialist thought. It is in Rodney's work that we first see a Guyanese working class take shape across racial and ethnic divisions created by the plantation labor demands. However, it is also here that we truly see the divisive element of that plantation labor as it inhibits this working-class solidarity from eclipsing ethnic and racial division in later decades.[12] The chapter argues that the struggle over history that the letters reveal is contingent upon the identity as laborers—during the plantation era—that each group in the territory holds. Furthermore, it rests on the ability of groups to re-imagine a new identity to the land via the manner in which their own labor shaped it. It is these labor identities that come in and out of focus as the governing element of all claims to power. They allow groups to claim that each has in fact "made" the nation both culturally and economically, and even in terms of giving it its physical (topography) shape. For example, there are the tons of polder enslaved blacks moved to develop the plantations and the present coastline (Rodney 1981). On the other hand, there is the tremendous part East Indians played in developing the rice industry which help fortify Guyana's economy after sugar markets declined. It is these identities that give power to some group claims and which at the same time prove problematic for others as Guyanese debate whether sugar or rice is the greater national symbol.

CLASS HISTORY AND CONTEMPORARY POLITICS

In Guyana, the undercurrent of social and political discourse is the constant message of unity and racial harmony. In the debate, no one wants to be labeled anti-Indian or anti-black, but most Indo and black Guyanese credit each other with initiating the racial and ethnic conflict that heightened in the 1950s when it became politicized. Many of the educated elite in Guyana avoid the "race" question altogether in order to limit the problem to class antagonism, despite evidence that they are intertwined. Indeed, the elite have long manipulated the racial division in order to secure their own interests and, at the same time, prevented working-class Guyanese from achieving cultural solidarity.[13] The conflict between blacks and East Indians has led to arguments that East Indian cultural allegiance to India undermines loyalty to Guyana. It has led to the questioning of black allegiance, by East Indians, to pan-Africanist discourses of culture, especially those that originated outside of the region itself (see chapter 9).

A recent book which offers its own explanation for the ethnic antagonism and violence of the 1997–1998 election period has instead only served to exacerbate the culture of blame in Guyana.[14] In her work, Kean Gibson suggests that Hinduism is akin to Zionism and Nazism and, as such, promotes black inferiority (2003). She, therefore, blames Hinduism for the racial problems in the country, specifically black antagonism. Ignoring the significance of Hinduism in maintaining diasporic cultural and religious connection with India, Gibson claims that East Indian hatred and their attempts to destroy blacks are worse than anything blacks have done to East Indians. Her work thereby remains trapped in the circular or closed logic of partisan, ethnic politics. The current conflict really took shape in the 1950s with the failure of the shared cultural and political platform of Burnham and Jagan when Burnham left the PPP due to ideological disagreement with Jagan. Burnham formed the PNC and, with independence an inevitability, each party became the focal point of political expression that solidified around the ethnic background of its leader (Gomes [1979] 1998).

After the party split and Burnham's rise to power, political representation became irreversibly linked to cultural identification. The threat of domination by a single group fueled Burnham's desire to wed state power to racial and cultural identification, after independence. This tactic by Burnham worked because of the entrenched fear of political power being consolidated by any one group, a fear that continues to undermine political solidarity today. Writer Sydney King (later Eusi Kwayana), a staunch PNC supporter in the 1950s and 1960s, advocated early on for black and Indian segregation in Guyana[15] (Manley 1979). As a then member of the Society for Racial Equality, Sidney King is quoted as calling for "partition of the country into an African Zone, an East Indian Zone, and a *free* Zone" (Ibid.:8 [emphasis added]). At the other end of the spectrum, there was the deep fear of "Negro rule" on the part of East Indians (Ibid.). These sentiments were reinforced on either side initially by the electoral system. The old system of election (popularly called "first past the post") was considered favorable to East Indians, allowing Jagan to come to power in the 1962 election. However, it was replaced by the current system of proportional representation without which, many agree, Burnham could not have become Prime Minister.[16]

While the problem is historical and emerges from the color, class, and caste stratification in the plantation era, there is the tendency to see it as strictly an unavoidable consequence of the racial and ethnic tension prevalent in plural societies.[17] The social and political problem in Guyana, however, is not the racial or ethnic tension and class conflict of blacks and East Indians alone, or what happened in the 1950s to change the political landscape of the nation. While it does originate with what Antonio Benítez-Rojo has termed the "plantation machine" (1996), it cannot be adequately explained by most studies that trace its development in the class, caste stratification of the plantation era. What remains to be further elaborated is its origin in the historical dimension of these sociocultural bodies (blacks and East Indians) whose existence is justified in different cultural systems that are not moored in the colonial era but precede it. These "systems" are black cultural origins in pre-colonial Africa and East Indian cultural origin in pre-colonial and colonial India. They encode what it means to *be* black and what it means to *be* East Indian.[18] Upon arriving in the New World, each group therefore needed to find a way to maintain these modes of being and did so adequately.

In the New World, Indian and African cultural systems became moored to a labor identity, prior to the transformation of blacks and East Indians into political subjects and citizens. As East Indians and blacks interact today, these reinvented systems and modes of being in the world also come into play. While the importance of the cultural connection has been underscored poignantly in works like Derek Walcott's Nobel Prize lecture (1992) and by Brackette Williams (see note 17), it and its larger significance are often ignored in contemporary writing on politics, race, and class in Guyana. In addition to creating the present social stratification, the plantation was also the place where, in order to preserve these ancient modes of being in the world that had guaranteed their psychic, spiritual, and cultural existence for centuries, under the thumb of British colonialism blacks and East Indians imagined a new relationship to the Guyanese landscape, through their own labor. And they succeeded. Their ability to recreate their identity in the land lies at the core of their contemporary ethno-political challenges to each other and consequently this is what is at stake in those challenges. The ability to have this newly imagined ontological and geo-cultural identity represented within the pre-colonial and colonial cultural terms of each group underscores current struggles and racialized class identity.

Moreover, blacks created this new identity, for themselves, as a more essential, native identity than any other group, including Amerindians. They did so because, unlike all subsequent groups that entered the country—Portuguese, Chinese, and others—they could not rely on a possibility of return to Africa. What happened in Guyana is similar to what José Louis González astutely observed in the case of blacks in Puerto Rico at the time of the U.S. invasion.[19] In identifying blacks as the "first" Puerto Ricans, González wrote, "it was the blacks, the people bound most closely to the territory which they inhabited (they were after all slaves), who had the greatest difficulty in imagining any other place to live" (1990:10). Blacks were the first to see themselves as Puerto Ricans and, following González, I argue that blacks in Guyana were the first to see themselves as Guyanese, even before a working class emerged. Later, East Indians also came to imagine themselves as Guyanese and both groups marginalized or, better yet, usurped Amerindian claims of belonging in the process.[20] Nowhere is this clearer than in Walter Rodney's analysis of early class formation among plantation workers.

After emancipation, black labor was controlled by the introduction of "bound," indentured Indian, Chinese, and Portuguese labor. In the decades immediately after slavery, the planters actively sought to control the ability of former slave labor to realize itself as a proletariat (Williams 1970). East Indians, the largest groups of indentured labor to enter the colony, found in slavery a comparison to their own situation and in the first decades of immigration were also bound by slavery, though never having been slaves (Lamming 1981; Ruhomon [1947] 1988; Mangru 1999). Because of the long history of unfree labor in the colony and the initial function of indenture to curb free black labor, in his proto socialist history of Guyana's working classes, Walter Rodney suggests that the working class in Guyana did not begin to constitute itself as such until the period of 1881–1905, "through its own activities" (1981:220). According to Rodney's *A History of the Guyanese Working People, 1881–1905*, the fluctuation in world sugar prices during the 1880s helped to speed the decline of the planter class and greatly influenced the struggle by blacks and East Indians for control over their own labor. Rodney defines the Guyanese "working class" during this period as one that was constituted as working classes have been since the sixteenth century, by the labor market and by transformations of global capital. However, Rodney writes, "care has been taken to avoid imparting to the various social classes greater precision than they had achieved within the evolving social formation of the nineteenth century and the early twentieth century. If classes are to be defined in their mutual opposition . . . then the differentiation of working class, peasantry, and middle class was incomplete" (Ibid.: 218). With the decline of the planter class, blacks and East Indians consolidated their identity as a class with interests distinct from those of the planters. Those interests, however, were still bound by culture since the plantation system had effectively kept blacks and East Indians apart. Blacks, after slavery, left the plantation and moved into towns, while East Indian livelihood and identity took shape around it, as had happened with blacks earlier.[21]

Early in his study, Rodney connects the land to the black laboring body by referring to the immense effort by enslaved blacks to create the current coastline by moving "100 million tons of soil" (Ibid.: 3). He describes enslaved blacks as "working people" who made a "tremendous contribution to the humanization of the Guyanese coast environment" (Ibid.). He later connects East Indian indentured labor to the land as well, saying, "They too had to face up to the steady work diet of mud and water" (Ibid.). Of significance is Rodney's use of the term *working people* to describe slaves, especially when, at a later moment in his analysis, he writes, "It is my contention that slaves became plantation workers immediately *after* slavery" (Ibid.: 218 [emphasis added]). The deliberate use of the word *working* to describe slave labor prior to emancipation and after, to describe indentured labor as well, has two functions. It provides a rubric within capital, or the economic discourse of capital, in which East Indians and blacks coexist as laborers, regardless of the *way* in which they entered the colony or the identities that they held when they did. "Working people" is also a revalued category to define those who were denied humanity and others who were at its edge.[22] Rodney is well aware that the labor category of "worker," as it existed to define free, white labor, was not available to black enslaved labor. His use of that term to describe a "plantation labor force" comprising blacks and East Indians provides both groups with a singular shared identity based on labor and humanity in the colonial period; an identity that precedes the realization of shared class interest.

In creating this shared labor identity, Rodney simultaneously redefines the initial product of that labor as the "humanization" of the landscape. Colonial markets could not strictly measure this type of productivity and it can be considered to belong to them, that is, they were not entirely "alienated" from their labor or from the product of that labor.[23] There is an attitude toward and identification with the land itself that, though both groups did now own it, nonetheless, belonged to them. But, Rodney credits enslaved peoples (blacks), not East Indians or Amerindians, with the humanization of the landscape. In describing the product of black enslaved labor in this manner, what Rodney establishes is an initial connection to the land that blacks have long cherished, and what blacks feel makes Guyana, in the post-colonial period, theirs. Historian Vere T. Daly has said that, at the time East Indians arrived in the colony, blacks considered the territory a home (1975). With this statement, Daly not only strategically eclipses Amerindian belonging and identification with the landscape but his writing shows the extent to which blacks reinvented themselves as a native population. This economic and cultural attitude is confirmed when Rodney writes, "Since Amerindians were excluded from the coastal political economy, African descendants portrayed themselves as the indigenous section of the work force" (1981:174). Blacks realized that their occupation of and labor on land that had such huge significance for the planters and the British Crown meant that it could be considered to belong to them. They literally "made" the nation. Both the experience of slavery and the containment of Amerindians by British policies and within colonial cultural narrative factored greatly into the ability of blacks to claim that they are the "first" Guyanese.[24] Today, when East Indians assert that, after slavery, they rescued the failing economy and hence saved the colony postslavery, they come forcefully against this prior labor identity of blacks and the historical claims to power it provides. Having established a prior, more essential belonging and deeper transformation of the land and the economy, blacks reject East Indian attempts like this to show that Guyana is equally their "home" because blacks saw themselves as having made it, not just the marketable products of their labor. More significantly, at the moment blacks began to recognize this ownership in the mid nineteenth century, East Indians still had the possibility of return. Blacks considered their stay temporary because East Indians had the "choice," however illusory or false, to return to India after their period of indenture expired.[25] As such, India remained a "home" in the immigrant imagination because of a possibility of return that could not develop on a grand scale in the Afro-Creole imagination.[26] Clem Seecharan has written, "Wherever Indo-Guyanese live today—in derelict Guyana or in the second diaspora: New York, Toronto, London, etc.—visions of India will not leave them. . . . To Indo-Guyanese, this India of the imagination is real; it instructs, inspires, and sustains them" (1993:60). For Seecharan, it was an image of India that helped Indians to claim a Guyanese identity. East Indian identity discourse was therefore not a nativist one as that of blacks was. Black perception of newly arrived Indian immigrants was based on and served to confirm the "prior" identity that they had "made" for themselves. Blacks retained cultural connection with Africa but, at the time East Indians entered the colony, it was already a Creole cultural connection. The image of Africa had already been transformed into a mode of existence in the New World that reflected their inability to return to a motherland. East Indians had yet to make this change and went about it differently. This did so with an image of India that now came into conflict with the Afro-Creole, neo-nativist discourse that, through Burnham, established itself as the standard for historical and cultural belonging in Guyana.

Rodney writes of the early encounter between blacks and East Indians: "The perception of race in nineteenth-century British Guiana was almost inseparable from the distinction made between Creoles and immigrants." "With Indian immigrants constituting such an overwhelming numerical majority, the term 'immigrant' came to be synonymous with 'Indian' (and was so used in official documentation)" (Ibid.: 174).[27] The way in which East Indians entered the colony against a Creole cultural backdrop, which they eventually shaped and became a part of, allowed blacks to use their difference or otherness against them. Rodney, however, is careful to note that groups adopted the racial attitudes toward each other that were held by the planter class. He then suggests that Creoles objected not to East Indians themselves but rather to the practice of indenture because of the unfair wage competition that it introduced. Blacks also objected, in this stage, to indenture, and consequently to the way in which East Indians entered the colony, because they saw it as means to control black labor power (Ibid.: 175). In countering later arguments to the contrary, Rodney notes that pro-Creole and pro-Indian sentiment were not mutually exclusive and at times even lacked the racial antagonism to which they are often reduced. However, Rodney cannot ignore that blacks and East Indians came in greater conflict. He writes that having adopted the views of the planter class, blacks begun to claim that they "deserved more" than East Indians because they were more "civilized," among other claims (Ibid.: 180). East Indians later countered with a view, also adopted from the planters, which held that blacks would have "starved" without indentured labor. The planters manipulated black and East Indian relationships, deliberately ensuring their separate evolution, by having the races "police each other," a practice begun when Amerindians were used to capture runaway slaves (Ibid.: 187). East Indians had been used to break strikes on estates by blacks and were, according to Rodney, offered land "postindenture," while blacks' claims were virtually ignored. Rodney suggests that despite cultural difference, in this period there was burgeoning, if not inchoate, class solidarity among East Indians and blacks. This prompted Rodney to write, "The coming together of Indians and Africans was delayed until a date more recent than the period under discussion" (Ibid.: 187).[28] He closes his study with the widespread and bloody riots of 1905, which saw agitation by blacks and East Indians against the colonial economic system and writes that race in the contemporary period was, in fact, "overemphasized."

The class solidarity, however, which Rodney sees in this period, was not a cross-cultural one. In suggesting that class is and should be seen as the larger factor, Rodney downplays the way in which racial and ethnic differences overshadowed the ability of groups to achieve a cross-cultural class solidarity. He also underestimates the significance of black and Indian labor achievements with the land; the ontocultural transformation of it and of themselves. Rodney is right in suggesting that it is not the plantation that kept blacks and East Indians apart, rather the class interest of the planters. However, race has become *the* factor in the contemporary period because of how each group needed to reinvent itself in the New World. This was necessarily going to happen differently for each group because of when and how they were brought to the colony and the way in which they were able to preserve their cultural connection to the past. Class identity, beyond that as laborers, cemented the reinvention of their cultural connection to the land. Furthermore, the views of the planters that blacks and East Indians adopted, separately, were those that preserved this new identity and relationship with the land. What Rodney does not realize is that in realizing the collective class interest, which is the focus of his study, blacks and East Indians were also consolidating the identities that they had already reinvented for themselves through their own labor. While the plantation is the locus for their initial labor and for their shared identity as "workers," it could not allow them to achieve class solidarity and that solidarity, which they exhibited in the 1880s, could not last. As blacks and East Indians performed the labor that eventually allowed them to begin to see themselves as a class in the plantation era, they were also imagining separate relationships to the land that were necessarily different and at odds with each other. Each was still able to imagine the land as a new *Eden*, and their connection became cemented in ethnic, and later political, discourse.[29] Furthermore, these relationships have been preserved through time and provide the cultural legitimacy for the ethno-nationalist discourse of both groups that establishes for blacks and East Indians a right to rule the post-colonial state.

Rodney's study is unique in that it locates an origin for contemporary class interests in anticolonial struggle among blacks, East Indians, and Amerindians. It also reminds us that those interests were fragmented at times by the different forms each group's resistance took toward the colonial state. Furthermore, we can argue from Rodney that the "views" blacks and East Indians held, and which persist today, were those shared and shaped by the planters. In the contemporary period, the initial way in which blacks and Indians used the racialized and hierachized language of the planters to view each other also structures the language of racial antagonism and class interest. Today, however, racial and ethnic antagonism prevents poor and middle-class blacks and East Indians from imagining solidarity with each other. Class interests were consolidated in the competition for resources and are inextricably linked to their identity as laborers, which in turn gave them a unique relationship to the land. It is this relationship that has allowed them to craft ethno-nationalist narratives of belonging and which resurfaces as the singular element that gives validity to ethnic politics. While class interest motivates the various ethno-political groupings and positions in play at the national level, "class" can only be understood by looking at the colonial period and the antiplanter position that allowed blacks and East Indians to organize together. To understand how and why race became "overemphasized" in the contemporary period, we must look at how Burnham interpreted the legacy of belonging (to the land) for blacks. Burnham and his administration realized that elite class interests would best be preserved and that he could hold onto the power falsely secured for him by British and American intervention in the political process by tying the right to rule to cultural nationalism.[30] With this, the possibly for the "working people" achieving a class-based and cross-cultural solidarity failed again.

NATION IN QUESTION: THE BURNHAM LEGACY

In Guyana, both pan-African nationalist discourse and the discourse of Indian nationalism since the 1940s have served as potential stakes with which to bind black and East Indian identity to the state. The nation is composed of symbols that have been deployed through the rearticulation of the myth of El Dorado inside the cooperative discourse, and which does not allow each group to actualize its political identity in its own "cultural logic," because of the narration by Burnham and the PNC of the transfer of colonial power. Burnham used the El Dorado myth to secure the narrative of black origin and inheritance in the New World, which historian Vere T. Daly then articulated as historical narrative, giving Guyana its first post-independence "history"; one which clearly historicized and legitimated black rule. Burnham also limited for blacks, East Indians, Amerindians, and others the possibility for dynamic cultural identity by tying cultural origin to state power. Each group was forced to act within a cultural logic that is filtered through a reductive, multicultural discourse, which, tied to the state and championed by the cultural elite, cannot recognize the historical dynamism of these cultures; a dynamic, to reiterate, which stems from their engagement with the land and the ability for them to find in it a new genesis for ancient cultural identities. Furthermore, in 1976, when Jagan offered his "critical support" to Burnham's PNC and both he and Jagan appeared together to stand for the nation, the fantasy that cultures could reconcile in this way, with the state providing the background, was solidified and continues to be sought after.[31]

In a presentation given at the August 1969 National Assembly debate on the motion to declare Guyana a Republic, Shirley Patterson, then PNC Minister of Education, stated: "We shall cull from the experiences of other countries . . .

but the model for Guyana's Cooperative Republic will come from the people themselves. It has been *pushed up from below*. . . . The significant thing about this Cooperative Republic is that there is a people and a Government who share the same philosophy. . . . This Cooperative Republic, having come from the heart of the people itself is merely *finding organizational expression through* the Government" (cited in Manley 1979:108–9 [emphasis added]). Patterson's statement reveals that the genius of Burnham's cooperative movement was not simply to collapse the "people" of the anti-colonial period with the "people" of the new nation, but through various strategies, like the manipulation of the Venezuela-Guyana border dispute and the call for creative writers and artists to image the nation (claiming often that he was just a "politician"), Burnham made Guyanese aware that the nation-state as a politico-cultural entity was the only viable expression of not only their cultural will but their political and economic will as well. Burnham established the Cooperative Republic as the cultural expression of the nation and simultaneously made culture a productive resource of the state. Guyanese culture was not in fact "pushed up from below"; it was being invented at that moment by the middle-class elites, by those Burnham had chosen to "identify the sources of culture" for Guyanese (Searwar 1970). The vision of Guyanese national cultural that emerged was not popular and it coincided with his administration's class and cultural interests. The working classes, which once realized their collective interests across the lines of race, were not called upon at that moment to put forward their image of the national culture, one that might have begun to both shape and reflect a real solidarity.

The independent state for Burnham becomes the justification for this culture that emerges from the past. What we see with Burnham, as with most post-colonial regimes, is that nationalism becomes a discourse of aggregates that can articulate with state structures of power to produce symbols, which work strategically and unevenly in the populace. There was a shift in the discourse as the "middle-class elite" sought to gain power and the "people," still holding onto the anti-colonial nationalism that was used to articulate their position of self-determination via the colonial state, were locked out of the new discourse of power and national belonging that emerged as the cultural apparatus of the new, cooperative, economic reform plan. In the years immediately following independence, Burnham used the form of the colonial state with its inherited borders to create a territorial nationalism that was so worked through with an idea of culture, as both historical excess and nationalist capital, that it allowed the "state" to be understood not just as a political inheritance but as a cultural one (for a specific group) as well, one that was integral to the discourse of Afro-Creole nationalism in the commonwealth Caribbean. Percy Hintzen has written cogently of the taking up of pan-Africanist discourse by the regime in order to establish its cultural legitimacy, saying, "Images of the national community came to incorporate only

those whose identities were located in memories of an African past"
(1997:62). Burnham's Afro-Creole nationalism is the logical future of pan-
African nationalist discourse which, in stressing the need to reject European
culture, puts in its place "the claim to a national culture in the past," a past
that is made to secure the rule of a particular ethnic and class grouping
which usurps the colonizers role (Fanon 1963). For the Caribbean, this culture must be re-imagined/re-invented as a prior national one which Burnham did using black status as first arrivants after the Amerindians to do
so. As stated earlier, the Burnham administration usurped the place of
Amerindians to make blacks the "new indigenes," to borrow from Sylvia
Wynter. Now, whether the "shift" in the discourse of anti-colonial struggle
that Burnham exploited for its meaning to the new Republic could be characterized as singularly "post-colonial" is less important than the fact that it
set up an idea of the nation that all subsequent regimes in Guyana and those
struggling for power must negotiate with.

According to Robert H. Manley, in his study of Guyana in the first decade
after independence, *Guyana Emergent*, Burnham rejected communism and
instead chose a socialist cooperative system because (and in opposition to
the Jagan PPP Marxist/communist rhetoric) the "solution" to Guyana's problems should be found "at home" (1979:17).[32] Not only could East Indian cultural and political identity not represent itself in the ways black identity
could, through a legitimizing pan-Africanist discourse, but East Indian political identification, at that time, could not articulate with neo-imperial interests because Jagan did not share Burnham's understanding of economic de-
terminism and cultural identification. In looking within Guyanese society for
solutions to achieve economic self-sufficiency, Burnham found the threads
of a democratic discourse of development that could articulate with former
colonial and neo-imperial interests well enough to secure his own position.
However, the problem was not that of finding what would "best" represent
the nation per se (which Burnham did easily), as Franklin Knight understands it, but the nation as a mode of representation for diverse peoples,
each with their own past and cultural logic, and which prevents the symbols
from ever being truly representative (Knight 1990).

Eventually, with Burnham's cooperative plan, the worker, whom he
termed "the small man," is not only endowed with a sense of culture by the
nation's creative writers, but his masculinity is restored through the socialist
elements of the discourse of pan-Africanism as he becomes "a real man."[33]
Burnham linked class interest to ethnic identity and sought to consolidate/
validate them by making ethnic identity, properly constituted, a necessity in
securing state power. However, this new man was, principally, the Afro-
Creole man and this *new* man's image is still trapped in the rationalist discourse of Western humanism and its conception of what it means to be human at particular historical junctures, even if he is temporarily liberated from

his image of the long-suffering proletariat under colonialism.[34] Burnham did not allow East Indian or Amerindian identity to be realized in this way, and Amerindian culture in fact served as the "unique" element on which a national culture could emerge to secure black power and cultural identity.[35] Burnham's legacy to Guyana includes the following: (1) a nation that does not come from the people and which co-opts popular culture in service of a liberal multiculturalism that secures the economic base for various regimes, and (2) a language or racialized politics with which every subsequent group that has come into power must struggle with in order to establish not just the political but also the cultural validity of their regime. It is this "language" and how it allows claims to be made within it that dominates the letters to the editor considered in the following section.

It is widely understood by Guyanese at home and abroad that the public discussion going on in the nation's papers is a key site for gauging the tenor of national debates. The editorial pages of local papers function as a negotiative medium where national subjects write in to voice their opinions on the present political situation and also to protest various discriminatory practices. However, the letters also serve as a figurative space where one can witness the threads of nationalist narratives by different ethnic groups, narratives that are being torn from and re-threaded into a shared historical fabric of conquest, resistance, and the lingering color-class hierarchy that emerged out of plantation society.[36] These narratives contest and complicate the identities of Guyanese citizens. Selected for both their reasoned and/or extreme engagement with the issues of race, ethnicity, and history that inform the present state of Guyanese politics, the letters that I discuss are by East Indian, Amerindian, and black Guyanese representing themselves individually and collectively, and arguing the facts of history upon which their current struggles and claims are based.

While some might argue that the letters considered are not "public opinion," they indicate the way in which the "nation" continues to exist as a negotiative/ed medium for self-actualization in the polity, on different levels.[37] The tension over the 1997–1998 election period and its lingering effects on the 2000–2001 election suggest that the way in which Guyanese have conceived of themselves as a nation, since the late 1960s, is no longer sufficient. The "nation," imagined by then Prime Minister Forbes Burnham as a single, collective expression of belonging to the state, is in crisis and it is being reconstituted through the imaginings of specific groups. Although one letter argues that Guyana has never been a nation-state, precisely because of the racial and cultural division, I argue that, at strategic moments, it has been represented as such. Since groups fight not only for separate, state rights, but also for national rights and recognition, its flag, national anthem, and currency are more than symbolic structures. Nevertheless, the competing gestures toward the nation made by specific cultural groups today constitute, I

argue, a shared understanding of "nation" among Guyanese, which is somewhat different that the one put forward at and in the years following independence. Indeed, it leads us to question what in fact was put forward at independence and how individual groups understood it.

The letters are a sustained engagement with the idea of the "nation" as
something to be claimed, located in, and identified through and with. In each
letter, the nation as a shared and contested cultural space is invoked differently. The letters reference and refute a view of the pre-independence past
often seen as a single national past simply because it is filtered through the
moment of independence and the solidarity among cultural groups on which
that independence rests. The "nation" then has no "History" other than that
of competing ethnic groups who place national history in a contested position and use it to validate group claims. One could even argue that this contest of voices is itself the national history. The problem is exemplified by Jagan's and Burnham's shared desire to have the date of independence in
Guyana be the anniversary of the 1763 slave rebellion. This collective desire
could only have emerged at independence in support of the concept of nation as solidarity. Outside of that moment, however, as the present discussions indicate, the slave rebellion and its memorialization in the Cuffy statue
forever speaks to the place of blacks in Guyana as prior arrivants to East Indians who, after decades of seeking to make Indian Arrival Day a national
holiday, have succeeded in doing so only in the past few months, though not
without controversy.[38] While celebrating Indian Arrival Day means greater
recognition for East Indians, their arrival coincided with attempts curb to
black labor power and a public recognition of it by the Indian-led PPP government comes as a slap in the face to blacks.[39] Efforts to establish an
Amerindian Day are still going on, but that, too, could be contentious. The
"nation," as it is understood and used by Guyanese today, becomes both a
figure invoked by specific groups and a place on which to articulate various
claims. I argue that the "cultural construction of nationness" by particular
groups therefore constitute a national dialogue. The nation is constituted in
the editorial pages of the local newspapers and in the editorial pages of those
published abroad through the transnational practices of its citizens at home
and in the diaspora.

The idea of "nation" as a "discursive formation"[40] is central in understanding how its "history" has become that of specific groups at particular historical moments and junctures in Guyana. In the introduction to *Nation and
Narration*, Homi K. Bhabha writes that the emergence of the nation as a
"form of narrative—textual strategies, metaphoric displacements, subtexts,
and figurative stratagems—has its own history" (Bhabha 1990:2). He continues, "to encounter the nation *as it is written* displays a temporality of culture
and social consciousness more in tune with the partial, overdetermined

process by which textual meaning is produced through the articulation of difference in language." For Bhabha, the nation "holds culture at its most productive position"[41] and "this cultural construction of nationness" is in fact "a form of social and textual affiliation" (292). "What I am attempting to formulate," he asserts, "are the complex strategies of cultural identification and discursive address that function in the name of the people or the nation and make them immanent subjects and objects of a range of social and literary narratives."

It is these "strategies of cultural identification" and the ways in which they reproduce the nation that is the main concern of this chapter: specifically, I am concerned with how cultural nationalist discourses function in a plural, post-colonial, and democratic cooperative republic, to "claim" the subordinated histories of particular ethnic groups. In Guyanese newspapers and other texts, the "nation," as it was envisioned by Forbes Burnham, is now being challenged through a recapture of historical material into new paradigms of ethnicity. The recapture is the attempt by groups to more firmly anchor those labor identities (identities produced exclusively from the body's own work physicality) and the reinvention of cultural heritage in the Guyanese landscape. In doing this, not only is the "nation" contested but also groups envision a new relationship to it. Unfortunately, it is one that puts them in conflict with others. The nationalist narrative strategies employed allow some historical material to be categorized as flawed memory by various groups, and thereby open a space for strategic revisions of that history. The nation becomes a discursive field onto which individuals and groups put forth particular "histories." It is within this discursive space that groups achieve empowered "voices," conditioned by their particular social locations and the convergence of race and class in the colonial history that produced them. Aware of how they have been misrepresented in the dominant nationalist narrative, the challenge now faced by groups is to recover elements of a historical past from this narrative in order to represent them in a new one.

I use Bhabha to argue that the cultural nationalist strategies include but are not limited to: a redefinition of "ethnicity" and its role through the revisionary experiences of specific groups, the necessary reordering of everyone's history that the rewriting of one group's history compels, and the establishment of new essentials which fix "race." To rewrite the nation is to restructure its components, and that explains why "ethnicity" and "race" are subject to innumerable textual slippages. What the letters ultimately show is that in Guyana, there is still no truly shared history, conception of history, or national culture, despite the shared, popular Creole culture. National culture continues to be fractured at the political level because it does not truly originate with "the people."

LETTERS TO THE EDITOR:
INDIANNESS, AFRICANNESS, AND PRIOR RIGHTS

In a June 1998 letter to the editor of the *Stabroek News*, Ravi Dev writes about the "semantic hurdle" imposed by the Western concept of "nation" Guyana adopted at independence.[42] Often dismissed as an extremist by Guyanese, Dev's visibility in ethno-political debate is undeniable. The letter is his response to two earlier letters titled, "The Core of Indianness Is Hinduness" and "Pan-Africanists Hail Mandela's Visit to the Region." According to Dev, the "jus soil" (right of soil) or territorial concept of nation that arose during colonial times and which defines nationality through territory or place of birth has been "foisted" on Guyana. In contradistinction, he refers to a "precolonial," ethnic concept of nation, prevalent in Eastern Europe, which defined citizenship both through birth and origin and through heritage and culture. He cites the different nationalities of the former Soviet Union as an example of how the Eastern concept of nation allowed for thirteen different "nationals" to coexist within the territory. Guyana has, of course, not achieved this "idealistic" coexistence with its six ethnic groups. In addressing the Guyanese predicament, Dev points to the fact that the ethnic groups that comprise Guyana have been "splintered" from their "original" nations. While these national "origins" are debatable, what troubles Dev is that while Guyanese are willing to challenge the colonial stereotypes of each other that were left by colonizers (Dutch and British), they refuse to "abandon" what he claims is the "outmoded" concept of nation under which they are governed. Dev's frustration with this method of citizenship, which identifies Guyanese primarily through physical and cultural belonging to the nation-state, stems from his desire to reclaim an Indian identity, one even more firmly rooted in Indian culture and which as such will not conflict with the Indo-Guyanese identity necessary for citizenship.[43] For Dev, the true achievement and test of multiculturalism would be the acceptance of other diasporic and sovereign cultural attachments outside the territory. This would allow Indians in Guyana and other ethnic groups as well to claim prior sovereignty and cultural allegiance. It would also allow a plurality of ethnicities to signify on and lay claim to the nation-state, equally. Ignoring India's own cultural rejection of those who left in the 1800s as indentured laborers, Dev places the blame squarely on Guyanese nationalism and offers, as an alternative, a concept of "Indianness."

As an "Indian" in the diaspora, Dev defines "Indianness" as a more inclusive, anti-essential category that "transcends" the limits of, he claims, Western concepts like "religion" and "culture."[44] Dev offers "Indianness" as a dynamic identity, which transcends and incorporates the differences among Indian groups throughout the world. "Indianness" becomes a diasporic rather than a continental, national, local, or compartmentalized cultural identity, which marks a discursive shift in the way "Indianness" has traditionally been imagined.[45] Presuming to speak for all Indians with this category, Dev says that Indians "dream" of the time when nations like Pakistan, Bangladesh, Sri Lanka, Nepal, and others will escape the division among them created by the British, to acknowledge a "common nationality." In viewing this extra-territorial vision as a mode of re-entry into a prior national and hence sovereign cultural identity, he adds, "and so too for the Indians in diaspora." Dev marks his distance from the geo-cultural "center" of Indian Nations mentioned above in a move which strategically allows him to achieve greater cultural proximity to that center, via his definition of "Indianness"; a definition of community that he hopes will supplant the center itself. In support of this concept, he remarks that, from his "limited reading of African philosophy," Africans share a "similar perspective" and that Africans and Indians in Guyana should reject the "western paradigm of 'unity as uniformity'" to focus instead on and embrace difference. He suggests this new point of social and structural organization, even though he admits that the "idea of various nations within a given state is fissiparous."

Dev's letter stems from a cultural anxiety on the part of East Indians about having and retaining a distinctly Indian identity within Creole culture. Informing that anxiety must, to some extent, be the fact that the "Indianness" of Indo-Guyanese has not allowed them to establish the same cultural legitimacy necessary for control of the state, in the way that Burnham did with Afro-Creole identity. In making the link between his concept of "Indianness" and African identity, what Dev fails to note is the way the colonization process affected blacks and East Indians differently. Blacks in Guyana do not experience African identity in the same way that East Indians experience Indian identity. This again is a large problem of Creole culture, which was first shaped not by East Indians but by black interaction with white British culture. On the arrival of indentured Indians in the colony, Lee Drummond has written, "East Indian indentured laborers were brought to British Guyana after the Christianization process had begun among Africans . . . they entered a society in which both the dominant minority and the subordinate majority shared a set of religious values that excluded the pagan beliefs of Hindus and Islam" ([1980] 1996:196). In addition, when former President Forbes Burnham opted not to mark independence day as the national even of primordial importance but instead the anniversary of the 1763 slave rebellion, it marked a moment in which the political power of a particular racial/ethnic group was writ large in a national context and it secured their cultural identity and teleology of historical progress.

Despite assimilation into and transformation of the Creole culture that had already begun to emerge when they entered the colony, the extent to which East Indians are in fact considered "Creole" also determines the extent to which they are in fact Indian. Indo-Creole identity does not signify on the nation in the way that Afro-Creole identity does, with blacks having imagined themselves as prior natives to East Indians. This is true in Guyana and especially in diaspora where celebrations like the annual Caribbean carnival in Brooklyn is overwhelmingly identified with blacks. Not only has this affected the legitimacy of Indian-led government in Guyana, but also it leaves Indo-Guyanese in a precarious position from which they must find and secure greater belonging. Dev essentially criticizes the "nation" as an expression of Afro-Creole cultural legitimacy in order to claim a "heritage" and "origin" for Indians in Guyana as a prior national one. For Dev, a national culture that allows Indians to reestablish cultural connection to India could give them an authentic identity that would enhance, not undermine, identification with the Guyanese state and allow them to escape the in-authenticating discourse of Afro-Creole nationalism with regard to Indo-Creole identity; a discourse that undermines the way in which East Indians have reinvented Indian culture in the land. He achieves this through the semantic malleability of "nation" as a discursive structure, apart from the real geographic and social spaces that it signifies on. Dev is therefore able to assert a "national" identity and claim to distant lands *through* "diaspora" (India, Pakistan, etc.), which can extend national sovereignty to those strewn about *in* diaspora. "Indianness" undergoes a change in the diaspora and is here, in Dev's formulation, reconstituted through a "desire" for nation that prefigures territorial attachment or detachment and relies on the power of cultural nationalist narratives. Since the currency for national power is minted in the diaspora, Indian diaspora currency is kept "current" by means of India, as a geo-political cultural signifier, and the construction of an Indian culture in Guyana that it continues to foster. This becomes a self-generating discourse that continuously provides more cultural material or capital. "India" functions here as an actual geo-political space that centralizes a philosophical conception of "Indianness."

After redefining "Indianness," Dev then equates it with a concept of pan-Africanism, which he imagines works in a similar fashion to unify blacks. He, however, fails to mention that pan-Africanism emerged as a diasporic point of entry into a black nationalist identity. While the more radical forms of black identity do work in the way of Dev's "Indianness," they have not taken hold in Guyana or been embraced by black leadership. The problem with Dev's concepts is that he invokes an "Indianness" and "Africanness" devoid of internal differences, forcing them to operate through a number of inconsistencies. For example, he ignores caste differences among Indians and does not speak to the ability of "Indianness" to transcend those. For Dev, "Indianness" becomes a spiritual and national concept devoid of political, economic, and territorial significance. Furthermore, he employs a homogenized idea of "Africa" to support this "transcendent" concept of Indian identity. This reduction may be due to the way in which "Africa" functions as a trope for "home" in various diasporic imaginings, or to a misreading on Dev's part.

In either case, Dev avoids addressing how different groups have been affected in particular ways by the colonization process. Finally, while he seeks to replace what he sees as a homogenous concept of "nation," through which Guyana and its citizenry are produced, in favor of a more "transcendent" one, Dev does not consider abandoning the concept altogether, and the structural inequality that it supports.[46]

I begin with Dev's letter for several reasons. It delimits the central tension in Guyana as one surrounding the issue of the ideology of nationalism, while simultaneously showing the roots of that tension in British colonialism. It demonstrates the ways in which the nation has become the filter for the attempts of various ethnic groups to create an identity that has social and political currency. The letter also maintains that, while there are other groups in Guyana, the key figures in the struggle, the ones who must redefine the "nation," are the majority groups: blacks and Indians. In both what it discusses and omits, the letter lays bare the fact that the nation envisioned by Burnham has left little room for East Indian cultural legitimacy and almost none for Amerindians or others who still could not benefit from the present or proposed nationalism because of both political marginalization and cultural containment. It reveals the way in which groups struggle to lay claim to the "nation" and to challenge colonial and postcolonial identities that limit their sense of belonging. In contradistinction to Dev's thinking, others like Ramesh Gampat firmly believe that individual, extraterritorial identity must not be emphasized in the political sphere but must be subordinated to a cohesive nationalism that integrates all cultures and lends validity to the state's representative capacity, much like the Burnham regime did.[47] Both Gampat and Dev demonstrate how difficult it is, given the present political and economic situation, to offer an alternative to racialized politics where control of the state is at stake and has been historically tied to national culture.

Creole Society, Cultural Visibility, and Cultural Politics

In order to understand the cultural dilemma that informs Dev and Gampat's statements, Creole culture and how it works in Guyana must be examined. Creole culture is that shared culture that all groups in Caribbean countries have shaped and which has evolved in each society to reflect the specific contributions of its inhabitants. It can be understood as "a culture formed out of an eclectic borrowing that it acknowledges, values and privileges" (King 2001:10). While Creole culture does reflect "the cultures of the Caribbean 'in play' before the arrival of the Europeans," many have argued that Creole culture evolved primarily from African slave culture as it was transformed and preserved in the New World (Ibid.: 10).[48] This culture is the basis for Guyanese society. As other groups, including indentured Indians, Portuguese, and Chinese, entered the society, they were presumed to be incorporated into what over centuries has become the social and "cultural" norm which they too transformed. But while these groups are wholly a part of Creole culture, they are often made visible *against* it as ethnic, not racial groups. Blacks located within this Creole culture are often then strategically eclipsed within it, appearing to have a culture that is less distinct than those of other groups, which make "cultural" not "racial" claims. Some historians have even argued that blacks only borrowed from the British. Roy Arthur Glasgow writes of the "perceived lack of defensible culture" by blacks against the greater sense of culture and cultural solidarity East Indians maintained (1970:83). He says that while Guyanese society was held together by a "combination of ideology" which "stressed" "Christianity, Education and moral uplift," East Indians wanted to maintain an "original cultural pattern of life" (Ibid.: 89).[49] By treating Creole society as an undifferentiated entity against which Indian culture could be viewed, Glasgow links the aims of British civil society with Creole (slave) culture created by encounters with the British. He supports the belief that Creole culture, before East Indians came to Guyana, was in fact the adoption of British culture by blacks, not an active transformation of British culture that preserved many aspects of African culture.

While Glasgow's analysis is flawed, it points to the ways in which Indian culture has been, historically, made visible within *and* against Creole culture, a central motivation for Dev's letter. His analysis also provides a way of interpreting how claims of racial and ethnic discrimination are differentially read by blacks and East Indians in Guyana. While Indo-Guyanese can mark their cultural origins, using India and point to immigration to show either rupture or continuity, black allegiance to Africa is seen as a racial, not a cultural, experience. Blacks have "racial" capital, while Indians have "cultural" capital. "India" and "Indianness," as Dev constructs them, become material with which to create a cultural history that can be mobilized as a tool of political power. Blacks are part of the dominant social form (Creole culture), which has incorporated elements from all areas of society. Thus, how can the dominant or hegemonic culture be discriminated against? If Creole culture is hegemonic by historical fact, then all attempts at a cultural politic are going to have to be written outside of it. For groups that have no original claim to Creole or slave culture, this creates a historical and cultural disjunction that necessarily evolves into political contention. The claims made by blacks that they are being racially discriminated against by East Indians continue to go unrecognized because they remain firmly tied to this cultural "backdrop."

Blacks occupy what can be considered a somewhat ambiguous position in Guyana as a group that is primarily identified as a racial one and secondarily as a cultural one. Blacks make claims based on racial discrimination, relying on race as it was used in colonial times. However, since there are no signs that say "no Blacks allowed," as one letter writer notes, there is no "racial" discrimination. However, Indo-Guyanese can claim "ethnic" discrimination when attacked by blacks on the streets. The result is that there is no "language" in which to speak of the structural racism that has been visited upon Guyanese society by British rule. No single group can take responsibility or be made responsible, and so a cycle of blame is initiated that facilitates the historical reinterpretation or revisions of particular groups. The positions that Guyanese occupy as national subjects are constantly reproduced through the racialization of ethnicity. Ethnic groups, historically differentiated in a structuring language of racial inequality, attain power through the new significances of that language. When in power, they reshape the terms of the debate, continuing the historic discrimination against those who are not in power. As in the colonial period, where a dominant group, in this case the planters, would invalidate the claims/rights of others, blacks and East Indians continue to do the same in order to achieve superiority over each other. While Guyanese have questioned the stereotypes, as Dev points out, which were used in the colonial period to demean and segregate them, they have not abandoned them entirely. Instead, they are rearticulated as part of various ethnonationalist discourses of power.

There is a dual tension in cultural nationalist attempts at resistance in postcolonial societies. A letter by Babur M. Khan suggests that in a plural, postcolonial society, the "nation" must in fact be "passed over" for the claims of individual groups. However, while Khan sees such an occurrence as one part of the changes a newly democratic society must undergo, he does not fault Western democracy and the structuring language of the party system which, in Guyana, forces ethnic/racial groups to represent themselves as whole contingencies whose politics benefit the particular ethnic group.

Babur M. Khan's borrowed declaration that "ethnicity is here to challenge the nation-state" opens his December letter to the editor, in which he quotes Ali Mazrui writing, "All in all, the world paradigm of the nation state was so committed to the principle of cultural homogeneity that ethnicity often retreated in shame."[50] Khan then asserts, "Guyana never was a nation-state. Neither ambiguous ideologies nor nationalist politics could have put ethnicity in bondage. . . . Ethnic loyalties . . . cannot be wished away—either by the ideology of the nation state or by the relentless erosion caused by western culture." Khan finds that while the "allegiance" of ethnic groups to other countries of origin is considered unpatriotic, it is natural and important in the formation and maintenance of ethnic identities and is, in fact, part of their "cultural capital" (his term), which ensures the survival of successive generations. He writes, "The two major parties have tried to bring ethnic and religious organizations under their control. However, it is political suicide when ethnic organizations in Guyana choose to live under the skin of the PNC and the PPP." Again quoting Mazrui, Khan continues, "Ethnic identification allows politicians to capture the hearts and minds of their constituents. Their entering politics and eventual place in Parliament/State reassures their constituents of representation and fosters racial stability." Khan suggests that both the PPP and PNC should no longer be umbrella organizations for ethnic groups. While the parties seek to control various "ethnic" and "religious" groups, a challenge could come for these same groups. Khan complicates Ravi Dev's argument about the role of plurality in challenging the "Nation" and further makes clear the ways in which state power continues to be consolidated through ethnicity.

In addition to the redefinition of nation that Khan and Dev point to, ethnicity is also debated and is appropriated always within the context of the historical location of particular groups or, more crucial, how groups choose to articulate those locations. Somewhat similarly to Ravi Dev, in Khan's letter ethnicity and its reservoir of cultural capital are tied to the particular homelands of groups of people and obtain currency from this affiliation. This is how "Indianness" must be conceived. However, for other letter writers like Rooplall Monar, this idea of an ethnic "Indianness" is itself "fissiparous."[51] For Monar, Indian culture is in the "past." It is tied to India and, for Indians in Guyana, it remains there. He writes that while he does not deny his past, which he identifies by listing the "Indian" music he listens to, "It would be false to act as an East Indian burdened with the trappings of a past, which to my mind, has no bearing on my conscious awareness as a Guyanese." Monar locates the origins of an Indo-Guyanese culture in the cultural practices of his Indo-Guyanese ancestors indentured on sugar plantations and rice growing villages. But for Monar, there is a huge difference between this cultural past and what Indian culture has become in Guyana. More important, he suggests that those who doubt him should turn to (Indian) Guyanese elders to help them distinguishing between "Indian" culture and Indo-Guyanese culture. In his view, to claim that what is being represented in Guyana is "Indian" culture would put Guyanese Indians in the habit of always mimicking that culture. He ends his letter by adding, "We have been tribalised and Creolised and those who claim kinship with their brothers in India ought to be awakened. . . . We are Guyanese."

Unlike Dev and Khan, Monar points to the way in which creolization has fundamentally changed Indian culture. For Monar, the appropriation of May 5 marks a rupture from that home society (India) that Khan finds essential to Indian ethnic identity in Guyana; it also marks the moment of origin for a distinctive Indo-Guyanese culture.[52] Monar's letter focuses on the integration of Guyanese society on a cultural level without, however, paying strict attention to the fact that the abilities of various ethnic groups to capitalize on a severely marked cultural difference is what allows these groups to secure state power. Monar's piece claims a definitive space in Guyanese culture for Indians.

The tension around ethnicity is twofold and inherently contradictory. On one hand, there is the attempt to resist integration into a single national identity, and on the other hand, to achieve the former without perpetuating the divisiveness that has already lead to violence. In December 2001, M. L. Kersting wrote to the *Stabroek News* saying that there is "no true racism" in Guyana, since no "ethnic" groups are prevented from participating in the (cultural) activities of another.[53] He offers South Africa under apartheid as an example of what Guyana is not, saying, "During the dark days of apartheid . . . there were signs in some stores that read 'no Blacks or dogs allowed here.' Now that is racism." The PNC continues to make claims of racial discrimination, but what M. L. Kersting's identifies as the "so-called 'racism'" reminds us that there is no valid language for some groups to articulate the structural racism of Guyana's government. Blacks are even further prevented from voicing racial discrimination because the idea of structural racism was previously exploited by Burnham's "dictatorship," and Kersting's letter cannot identify the racism at work here because of the way that culture is thought to function in a plural, cautiously integrative society.

In an editorial response to Kersting's letter, the *Stabroek News* call him "blinkered" and the situation in Guyana "a paradox."[54] In the editorial titled "One People," the editors maintain that "since 1957 politics have been dominated by ethnic voting patterns" which have "polarized the nation into ethnic groups."[55] For them, the "root of the problem" is that ethnicity has become the "rationale" for political division in the country. Before declaring that the country needs a "political vision" like that of the Mandela–de Klerk and Trimble-Adams pairings, they note:

> The results of the consequent negative, beggar-my-neighbor politics have been disastrous. Backwardness, underdevelopment, emigration and despair. And the syndrome reinforces itself as the struggle continues over an ever decreasing pie. The often reckless and malicious allegations of bias and discrimination fill one with despair. . . . Insofar as the government seeks not to portray itself as an ethnic party and to resist overtly taking on the concerns of its supporters it comes under increasing attack from Indian groups and analysts who see it as betraying their cause.

The warning and historical example offered by the editorial come at a time when the country is considering constitutional review and reform as mandated by the Hermandston Accord.[56] While the editorial shows the degree to which ethnic conflict is wedded to political conflict and how the former is actually a structuring element of the latter, as the Accord makes clear and the Kersting article underscores, there is a textual-semantic slippage between race and ethnicity in Guyana, which groups manipulate as they vie for power and rewrite the history of the nation. As the final section of this chapter demonstrates, one group in particular has been consistently left out of this process of rewriting. Having been positioned by Burnham as the "original" element of Guyanese culture, the elements from which are to be manipulated in the production of a national culture that limits and controls the ways in which they can in fact be present in it, Amerindians, in an even more profound manner, continue to suffer the structural inequality carried over from the colonial period.[57]

Prior Arrival Rights: Amerindian Struggles for Political Representation

The current debate about the "nation" occurs primarily between the majority groups, blacks and East Indians. Ethno-nationalist discourse by both groups strategically eclipses Amerindian articulations of belonging and reveal the historic inability of groups to voice certain claims and to challenge their representation in the nation. The debate surrounding "prior arrival theory" is a prime example. This theory, simply put, holds that as the first occupants of Guyana, Amerindians have sovereign rights that other groups do not. The "theory" is used by the politically, economically, and geographically marginalized native peoples of Guyana to argue that their prior occupation gives them essential rights to power. It is instrumental as Amerindians seek greater voice in a political process in which "proportional representation" strategically disenfranchises them. Ironically, "prior arrival theory" may in fact function as a key means of addressing the absence of a common vocabulary among the multiethnic groups in present-day Guyana. Writing against "prior arrival theory," which has reentered public discourse, letter writer M. L. Hackett warns that "if put into practice in any country, [it] will become a 'race' superiority doctrine."[58] He says that application of the theory would "lead to . . . dislocation" for those it excludes. Hackett maintains that today's Guyana is the result of the contributions of each group of inhabitants and that no court would give the territory to the only group that prior arrival rights theory would really benefit, the Amerindians. He says that there is also no way to define or assign prior arrival rights since blacks, too, have literally "built the coast land" that has made "our so-called modern Guyanese civilization." He goes on to propose that "the only legitimacy that the prior arrival/superior land rights theory has is: it gives those who are propagating it an equal share in Guyana—the same share that all of us have . . . not superiority." "Guyana," he says, "belongs to all of us equally and we must learn to live peacefully together." In his letter, Hackett quotes heavily from various UN documents on race relations essentially to say that the theory is racist. He provides Adolf Hitler's Nazi Germany as an example of its manifest racism. Most important, he chooses to quote from the 1967 UNESCO "Statement on Race and Racial Prejudice," which claims that the "racialist practices" employed in the liberation attempts of groups who have been subject to racism are a "secondary phenomenon, a reaction stemming from men's search for an identity which prior racist theory and racialist practices denied them. Nonetheless, the new forms of racist ideology, resulting from this prior exploitation, have no justification in biology."

For Hackett, "prior arrival theory" is a racial essentialist theory or functions as though it were. In seeking to have it thrown out, he points to the very problem that keeps it in race discourse in Guyana. As the UNESCO quote points out, one of the ways previously dispossessed peoples sought to reclaim power was through recapturing of and reinvestment in their formerly maligned racial identities. It fails to mention that this investment was at times the only one available to secure the claims of that group. Hackett's egalitarian pronouncement that all Guyanese must learn to live together and that all of them have equal shares of and stakes in the land also sweeps aside the colonial history he mentions and fails to address the issue of governance. Who will rule the "peaceful" populace, and how will that be decided? For groups who invoke "prior arrival (rights) theory," it provides an important counter to prevent the disinheritance that has been structured into the present political systems through colonial racialist ideology. Hackett can only focus on the way the theory seems to be valid only for "Amerindians" and fails to recognize that for a group so thoroughly marginalized, "prior arrival (rights) theory" is one of the only modes in which to seek recognition and power.

A letter, written in response to Hackett's letter, points to that fact that "prior arrival theory" continues to be misinterpreted by other Guyanese as a racial, essentialist doctrine. In the unsigned letter, an "observer" makes clear the impetus for Hackett's letter, which is, according to the observer, the recent lawsuit filed by the "Captains of six Akawaio and Arecuna communities of the Upper Mazaruni, which seeks . . . judicial recognition of the doctrine of aboriginal title ('prior arrival title') as an enforceable part of the common law of Guyana."[59] The observer writes that not only has Hackett misrepresented the UN data to readers, but that he has also misrepresented prior arrival theory since "the doctrine of aboriginal title has nothing to do with preferential treatment or race superiority." The observer cites the colonization of "our" (Amerindian) lands by Europeans and other groups according to racist doctrines that held one culture superior to another. The observer expresses bewilderment at the fact that Amerindians are the most disenfranchised group and yet are never mentioned in "discussions of racial discrimination." Finally, the observer maintains that Amerindians have been subject to "arbitrary definitions" of what their lands are and that contrary to what Hackett and history hold, when the Europeans came, they did have a concept of land "ownership" but one that was different to the European one of titles that persists today.

Of significance in this letter is the statement by the UN Committee on the Elimination of Racial Discrimination (CERD) in 1997 which, according to the observer, says that "indigenous people" continue to be deprived of their human rights and land; the committee calls upon various "parties" to "recognize and protect the rights of indigenous people to own, develop, control, and use their communal lands." Only when land cannot be returned, the document notes, should other forms of restitution be considered. The observer then remarks that while Guyana has "ratified" the CERD statement, it has not yet been converted into law in the country so that Amerindians continue to be disenfranchised. The letter points to the structural inequality built into the discourse of nation. Amerindians are continually denied the "claims" to land that blacks and Indians have been able to make precisely because they are constructed as and choose to call themselves "indigenous." They are at once always linked to the teleology that says they had no real concept of land ownership and further marginalized precisely because they are indigenous. Since "prior arrival theory" can only be understood as a racial essentialist theory, they must as the original indigenes, be kept in their place in order for subsequent ethnic groups—the former minority black and Indian groups during British rule—to justify their present claims to land and power. The ways in which blacks can be considered a new indigenous group is obscured by this construction of the Amerindian, since blacks could not utilize prior arrival rights discourse in the construction of their own nationalist narrative. What the letter makes clear is that the ways in which Amerindians try to assert rights or claims through a language of "prior rights" is considered "anti-government" since power and legitimacy are tied to Afro-Creole identity. While Amerindians are too small a part of the population to get control of government, because of the potential, in theory, of "prior rights" to become a superiority doctrine, they cannot utilize it to gain some measure of "power." In fact, one letter notes that the government "has seen fit to create its own parallel indigenous outfit, one that it can own, control and manipulate to suit its own political ends" while not recognizing many preexisting and newly formed Amerindian organizations.[60] The government (and the ethnic group in power) has found a way to recognize and control this potential cultural nationalist threat.

Amerindians still struggle to have an official Amerindian Day holiday, despite the recognition of Indian Arrival Day. Their native presence, under Burnham's imagining of the cooperative state, came to function as the original element of Guyanese culture but one that works only in support of a larger Afro-Creole image of national identity. East Indian identity discourse, further, does not know how to recognize this prior belonging that is both cultural and territorial and which does not have to be invented. The Umana Yana, which lies in the center of Georgetown and which Amerindians were brought from the interior to build as the largest national symbol of their presence and cultural contribution to the nation, maintains both their cultural presence and political and economic disenfranchisement by imaginatively securing their presence and the role they must play in order to be part of the nation. They are not equally the "working people" of Guyana because their identification with the land has always been presumed. In the eyes of Guyanese, it has not been "made" like that of blacks and East Indians. Guyanese nationalism and political power have congealed around this idea of "making" the land, of productivity, and of "development" (Hintzen 1997), which does not leave room for pre-Columbian or pre-modern, Amerindian forms of belonging. The letter signed by "anonymous" speaks forcefully to their marginal position (economic and political), which is facilitated by the very fact that they were there prior to others and that ruling groups since independence have not significantly changed colonial social and economic policy toward them.

CONCLUSIONS

When speaking with some Guyanese, those who remain in Guyana and those who have migrated abroad, there is a general sense that when one ethnic group attains power, things become harder, especially financially, for other groups.[61] So focused on racial/ethnic division, lower-income blacks cannot imagine solidarity with the lower income East Indians they see daily. Nor can blacks and East Indians achieve solidarity with Amerindians who remain the most politically disenfranchised and economically disadvantaged group in the country. The ongoing questioning of ethnic identity and national loyalty that the letters reveal are complicated in and outside the Republic by a host of concerns, including the increasing commercialization of the media in the country, the immigration problems which have left many without visas, and the economic exploitation of Guyana in the global market through the expatriation of its dollars.

Despite the more decidedly class-differentiated structure of today's Guyana, as a result of the ways in which "race" continues to operate as a hierarchizing principle, economic inequality is still read as racial inequality. Regardless of their real social conditions, Guyanese still relate to each other through racialized and historically conditioned representations of each other created in the colonial period to facilitate the exploitation of their labor and to reinforce white, Western superiority. Furthermore, their attachment to these ideas was exploited in the postcolonial period by the Burnham regime, and they became firmly a part of the nationalist consciousness. Today, each ethnic/racial group in Guyana continues to try to remake the nation in its own image, battling and suffering the consequences of a colonial legacy. The country has lived out Frantz Fanon's declaration with regard to the Algerian Revolution that "when dealing with young and independent nations, the nation is passed over for the race, and the tribe is preferred to the state" (1963:248). It has done so both for the reasons Fanon suggests, such as the underdevelopment of the middle class, which seeks to further its own political and economic interest at the expense of the people. It has also done so for reasons that include, as this chapter has argued, the need for groups to preserve cultural identities, which could still tell them who they were, even as the machine of capital sought to make them into something else see Allahar 2003).

The letters to the editor considered here reveal how much is at stake for Guyanese, how much they have invested in their various ethno-national discourses. They reveal their struggle to preserve what the land means to them, what they became as they shaped it, and how each group has, historically, envisioned its sense of belonging to the nation. Guyanese have not ceased to be "working people," but the potential of that historical and economic rubric to bring them together has not been realized. Instead, what they share is a structure of inequality that continues to prevent the emergence of a transcendent cultural vision (see note 39). In seeking a new concept of "nation" that could better accommodate an identity that will always be extraterritorial, Ravi Dev's letter indicates that Guyanese must find ways to recognize all forms of belonging in the territory, to recognize the historic cultures preserved in these identities, and simultaneously to achieve true democracy.

Unfortunately, the proposed means to this are not without their problems. In an April 2004 letter to the *Stabroek News*, McDonald Granger admonishes blacks, saying, "Instead of marching and protesting which frightens our East Indian brothers and sisters . . . and before some racial conflagration descends upon us, let us try to find the kind of leaders who are prepared to open up this country to the large foreign investors, so as to give Guyanese jobs and a decent standard of living for us all."[62] Granger, a member of the All Races Congress (ARC) for which he advocates in this letter, believes that an emphasis on economic prosperity for all should trump divisive attachments to India and Africa or Indianness and Africanness. In his reasoning, which reflects the rhetoric of free market democracy, an influx of foreign capital will make this possible. In Granger's statement, which reflects a steady turn in Caribbean economic policy, we see less of an investment in the "worker" and more of one in capital, or the power of money. While Guyana does need to raise the standard of living for many of its inhabitants, Granger's letter represents a problematic shift in economic and cultural thinking within the country. It is a shift that reflects not only the change in the global economic landscape from the mid-nineteenth century when world economic forces allowed blacks and East Indians to see themselves as workers and to find solidarity with each other. It is also a shift in thinking about themselves and their organic connection to the land, which no longer recognizes the real, transformative potential of their own labor and their ability to possess the product of that labor.

Today, the "cultural resistance" articulated as national resistance at independence continues in a fragmented multiplicity of forms. Present-day cultural nationalisms have failed to significantly challenge or displace the structure and culture of power that had emerged to liberate the society in the 1960s and resist neocolonialist economic and social policies that offer false promises of development and progress on par with more powerful players in the global economy. Furthermore, the postmodern investment in the "plural" subject and the sublimation of racial difference to economic need only compounds this (mis)use of cultural identities by glossing over the exploitive potential of the nation-state in the realm of racial and ethnic identification. Yet the alternative continues to be divisive. The potential to recognize within cultures the ability to contain structures that do not readily articulate with the economic rationality of the nation-state is slowly being lost. If it is ever to emerge and be effective, a self-conscious nationalism must confront the problem of state power and identity formation, and the colonial, cultural logic upon which they rest.

NOTES

1. Chambers. "A Walk Through Georgetown." In 1997, when I began doing research on an earlier version of this chapter, Chambers's site was initially compelling in its expression of diasporic longing and invocation of national pride. Although the site no longer exits, it still remains a useful point of entry into the discussion of the complication struggle over national identity in Guyana.

2. Bhabha's concept here is useful, although his analysis is specific to visualization in written narratives.

3. See "Views Invited on Indian Arrival Day being made a public holiday," *Stabroek News*, December 22, 2003. See also "Committee Recommends Nixing Holidays Shifted to Monday," *Stabroek News*, April 29, 2004.

4. The term *none* here is deliberately controversial and it directly plays into the idea that Amerindians in Guyana today, through Spivak and Gramsci, are subaltern (see note 5). Despite Stuart Hall's claim that Amerindian's are the original American *presence* ([1990] 1996), in recent historical narratives, as blacks and East Indians rewrite the nation's history, both groups point to the fact that Amerindians migrated from "Asia." This is an often ignored positioning of Amerindian peoples but one that is significant in terms of how it continuously challenges the central tenant of Amerindian rights claims, "prior arrival."

5. The term *subaltern* is used here for two reasons. First, it is mentioned in at least two of the letters that I looked at, as some Indo-Guyanese extend the term most often used to name the missing history of the "urban poor" in India to the Indo-Guyanese situation. One letter writer uses the term to denote all Indo-Guyanese, without distinguishing between the poor, those who hold positions in government, or himself as an "intellectual." Second, the term has been linked, according to Edward Said, to the attempts of other minority groups to recover and articulate their stories

(1988). I use it here to designate the Amerindians, Indians, blacks, and Chinese in the region at particular points in the nation's history. Arguably, Amerindians are only ones who can still be considered subaltern, with respect to blacks and East Indians. What gives the term salience is the structure of racial and economic inequality in Guyanese society, which was introduced by the British and continues to reproduce itself at the level of cultural identification and of politics.

6. Stuart Hall has observed, "None of the people who now occupy the islands—black, brown, white, African, European, American, Spanish, French, East Indian, Chinese, Portuguese, Jew, Dutch—originally 'belonged' there" ([1990] 1996:118).

7. When Janet Jagan became president, the fact that a white woman, formerly American, was now head of the country was noted by the local and national press. While she is now Guyanese, she is also a symbol of those colonial and neocolonial forces that have brought the country to this present crisis. This has much less to do with her own or her party's agenda but with the way in which "whiteness" can and does act as a signifier of the history of oppression of blacks. Her acceptance by East Indians has to do with her marriage to Jagan as much as it does her deep commitment to his socialist platform.

8. Despite the fact that the Civic is a predominantly black political party that has joined with the People's Progressive Party (PPP), it is consistently eclipsed in the political debate which reinforces the image that the struggle is between blacks and East Indians and that there are not alliances being formed along the lines of class that collectively exploit both groups.

9. See: "Gov't, PNC/R still at odd on dialogue." 2002. *Stabroek News*, July 17. Continuing to claim political disenfranchisement, the current leader of the PNC/R, Robert Corbin, has recently withdrawn from talks with the Jagdeo-PPP administration. See "Corbin Withdraws from Dialogue," *Stabroek News*, April 1, 2004.

10. The *Stabroek News* is published daily by Guyana Publications Ltd. in Lacytown, Georgetown, Guyana. Despite criticism of bias on the part of the *Stabroek News*, especially by East Indians groups that question its support of Indian issues, I have chosen to use this rather than the government-owned *Chronicle* or the other weekly papers more clearly associated with particular religious or political interests like *The Catholic Standard* and *The Mirror*. The paper has a large audience and is primarily read by Guyanese both in and out of the country.

11. For a discussion of class interest, race,and the centrality of both in the struggle for the post-colonial Guyanese state, see: Hintzen 1987. For more on race and class and the social hierarchy in Guyana, see Brackette Williams 1991, chapters 7 and 8.

12. Today it can be argued that ethnic conflict in many Third World nations is the result of global economic policies and that ethno nationalism is a result of these uneven policies (Chau 2003). This must be taken into account for two reasons: (1) global economic forces help to maintain the antagonism between blacks and East Indians in Guyana, and (2) following Rodney, if global market forces initially put in place the conditions for the realization of collective class interest, it is ironic that now they are agential in keeping groups apart. (I must thank Sylvia Wynter for suggesting that I read Chau. Despite the fact that her work is about dominant minority groups, the thesis is still applicable to the situation in Guyana.)

13. For a discussion of the role of the elite, see Hintzen (1989) and Moore (1995). Brian L. Moore has written that the stereotypes that circulated among Guyanese were

"largely elite ideological rationalizations" which were "reinterpreted and reshaped by the subordinate groups" (4, 12–13). See also Fanon's "The Pitfalls of National Consciousness" in which he cautions that the middle class that assumes power in the post-colonial period is unable to recognize the needs of the people and dominates the people, both politically and economically, in much the same way as the colonial bourgeoisie (1963).

14. See "Future Over Race Book in Guyana," BBCCaribbean.com, April 24, 2004. Available at http://bbc.co.uk/caribbean/news/story/2004/04/printable/040423.

15. Kwayana later became an unrelenting critic of Burnham's administration, its nationalist policies, and British and American interference in Guyanese politics.

16. Britain, the Kennedy and Johnson administrations, and the CIA intervened in Guyanese politics in the 1950s and 1960s and in his account of U.S. involvement in Guyanese politics, Arthur Schlesinger has stated: "An independent British Guiana under Burnham (if Burnham would commit himself to a multiracial policy) would cause of many fewer problems than an independent British Guiana under Jagan." For the Kennedy administration, this was to be achieved by switching to a system of "proportional representation," according to Robert Manley (1979:56–57). Political manipulation and electoral fraud kept Burnham and the People's National Congress (PNC) in power for decades. See Hintzen (1987).

17. See the work of Raymond Smith, Harry Hoetink, Gordon K. Lewis, and Elsa Goveia.

18. My thesis here is an ontologic one and it presumes that more than simply needing to find ways to preserve their culture in the New World, which they did, blacks and East Indians were also preserving something else, something less tangible but more important and which, heretofore, has been encapsulated in their prior cultural and geographic locations. What occurred with blacks and East Indians, initially, in their need to preserve cultures is not a form of "ethnic absolutism" as defined by Paul Gilroy (1993). That, it can be argued, occurred later.

19. I thank Sylvia Wynter for suggesting the usefulness of González's work for my own study.

20. See Shona Jackson, "Subjection and Resistance in the Transformation of Guyana's Mytho-colonial Landscape." In *Caribbean Literature and the Environment: Between Nature and Culture*, ed. Elizabeth DeLoughrey et al. (Charlottesville: University of Virginia Press, forthcoming).

21. My reference to the plantation in the singular refers to the plantation as a complex labor system and to its economy.

22. The "others" here refers to East Indian and Chinese immigrants who were designated "coolies" and who both were seen as less than whites but higher than blacks within the color-class hierarchy of the plantation. Their humanity, too, was in question. For colonial writing on East Indians in which this is apparent see work by Edward Jenkins.

23. See Karl Marx, *Economic and Philosophical Manuscripts of 1844* (Moscow: Progress Publishers, [1844] 1974).

24. For more information on British policies toward Amerindians, see Menezes (1977). See also Cudjoe (2003b) on the romanticization of Amerindians in colonial narrative.

25. In many ways, the promise of return to India after indenture was a false one. Planters and immigration agents made it easier and more profitable for Indians to reindenture than to return to India. For this chapter, the fact that return could remain a possibility is what matters.

26. Although the slave trade itself was not abolished until 1807, blacks entering the colony at that time were confronted with the overwhelmingly creolized blacks that has been there for generations.

27. It is important to note here one reason for hinterland development that Rodney does not give. Following Charles Mills argument in *The Racial Contract* about the racing and norming of space, it is possible to say that since "raced space will . . . mark the geographic boundary of the state's full obligations," the Guyanese hinterland was not developed because of its presumed lack of a real political and economic identity due to its identification as an underdeveloped, native space (1997:50). Following Mills, the hinterland would have been considered a "dark space," "a region normatively discontinuous with white political space" (Ibid.: 51).

28. Although he does not discuss it specifically, Rodney may be referring here to the solidarity of Jagan and Burnham in the late 1940s and early 1950s.

29. One of the best ways of understanding the new relation to the land that had to have been envisioned by those brought to the New World to work the land itself comes from Derek Walcott. In speaking of the legacy of enslaved blacks and white slave masters, Walcott has written, "I accept this archipelago of the Americas. . . . I give the strange and bitter and yet ennobling thanks for the monumental groaning and soldering of two great worlds, like the halves of a fruit seamed by its own bitter juice, that exiled from your own Edens, you have placed me in the wonder of another, and that was my inheritance and your gift" ([1974] 1998:64). Walcott's words, though speaking specifically of the black experience in the New World, shows how Caribbean people became quintessentially Caribbean, how they came to identify with the colonial landscape and to possess it, both physically and in the imagination.

30. For more on U.S. involvement, see Hintzen (1989), specifically, "Mobilization for control of the state in Guyana and Trinidad."

31. Hintzen has discussed the economic significance of and struggle for control of the state in his 1987 work. Most specifically, the chapters, "Mobilization for control of the state in Guyana and Trinidad" and "Maintaining control of the state" (1989).

32. Of black power, Burnham is quoted in *Guyana Emergent* as saying that it would "strengthen and support the social and economic revolution that is taking place here" and that "black power to us means the consolidation of this political power and its being turned to good effect to achieve economic power" (Manley 1979:96, 97). Manley has suggested that the only reason Burnham employed the discourse of black power, especially when the PNC became "directly involved in African liberation efforts" in 1971, was to stave off accusations that his administration was proimperial/foreign capital (95). Hintzen also seems to suggest that this was one of the legitimating functions of the discourse (1987). However, he does not cite Manley.

33. References to the "small man" and "real man" are taken from Burnham's own speeches.

34. This emphasis on what it means to be human stems from courses taken with and discussions with Sylvia Wynter. At the annual conference of the PNC in 1969, Burnham stated, ironically, "In Guyana there is an opportunity of the black man be-

ing a real human being who does not use his new status to impose on others what he has suffered" (Manley 1979:96). In some ways, Burnham needed the "nation" to prove that blacks have a humanity and defensible culture, all of which were denied in order for slavery to occur and even after slavery.

35. Percy Hintzen has written that "An 'East Indian' government is incompatible with conceptualizations of an Afro-Creole nation" (1997:67).

36. In her work, Elsa Goveia has suggested that what is in fact the shared culture of the Caribbean is the structure of racial inequality to which all groups tacitly acquiesce (1970).

37. In this chapter, the "nation" is loosely a cultural "structure" that promotes attachment to the state by giving citizens "a sense of belonging and identity" (Smith 1991:200). It can be understood, following Benedict Anderson, as an "imagined community" ([1983] 1991).

38. According to a *Stabroek News* article, the parliamentary committee that reviews public holidays says that one reason arrival day was selected as a national holiday is the fact that East Indians are a majority and have made a "significant contribution" to the economic development of Guyana (see note 3 for reference).

39. See Ellis (2004).

40. Timothy Brennan writes, "The 'nation' is precisely what Foucault has called a 'discursive formation'—not simply an allegory or imaginative vision but a gestative political structure with the Third World artist is constantly building or suffering the lack of" ([1990] 1995:170). While I do no wholly agree with his labeling of "the" third world artist's project, I do find his use of Foucault important for this chapter.

41. The entire quotation from Bhabha reads, "For the nation, as a form of cultural *elaboration* (in the Gramscian sense), is an agency of *ambivalent* narration that holds culture at its most productive position, as a force for 'subordination, fracturing, diffusing, reproducing, as much as producing, creating, forcing, guiding'" (Ibid. 1990: 5–6).

42. Dev (1998). The quotations that follow are taken from Dev's letter. I begin with Dev not only because of the way that his letter complicates the debate at its outset. He is one of the most frequent and prolific letter writers and his letters can be said to attract a good deal of controversy. He is a member of Guyana Indian Foundation Trust (GIFT) and he was a member of a special committee of the National Assembly designed to solicit opinions about making Indian Arrival Day a public holiday. He is also the head of Rise, Organize, and Rebuild Guyana (ROAR).

43. Further research must be done to explore this sentiment of Dev's. How many Indo-Guyanese long for deeper cultural connection with India? Do they and others feel that such a desire conflict with their identity as Guyanese?

44. Dev assigns too much to Western thought at this point, rather than limit his argument to the manipulation of religious and cultural difference by colonial forces.

45. Dev writes, "That which defines our 'Indianness' transcends limited western concepts such as 'religion' and 'culture' or even that catch all 'way of life' and yet is no facile essentialism. 'Indianness' allows and even encourages, diversity because it is built on a principle that transcends foundationalism and essentialism."

46. Partha Chatterjee's work on nation is crucial in locating the ideologies of nationhood that postcolonial societies entertained at independence and for its critique of the "nation" (1986).

47. Gampat, Dr. Ramesh. "In Guyana politics dictates economics."

48. See González (1990) and Burton (1997: chap.1). I am also indebted to discussions with Professor Sylvia Wynter.

49. Glasgow holds the following opinion about blacks and East Indians, which, in general, supports my thesis about the importance of prior cultural systems: "The Indians, unlike the Guiana African, had an inborn sense of cultural tradition. This tradition had given the East Indian a feeling of pride and security in the vast corps of Indian culture accumulated through the centuries of Indian civilization. . . . To the East Indian, culturally at war with Creole society, ethnocentrism was psychologically satisfying" (1970:89). I do not agree that Africans did not also have this "sense of tradition."

50. Khan, "Ethnicity is breaking loose from the confines of the nation-state." Khan frequently cites Dr. Ali Mazrui as an "authority on cultural studies, third world politics, Africa and Islam." The excerpts from Mazrui are taken from a 1994 UN speech, "Ethnic Violence, Conflict Resolution, and Cultural Pluralism." Mazrui is the director of the Institute of Global Cultural Studies and the Albert Schweitzer Professor in the Humanities at Binghampton Univeristy, SUNY. There is also another article that I do not consider here: Randolph Harte. "Discussing Ethnicity Is Counterproductive," *Stabroek News*, June 20, 1998.

51. Monar (1998).

52. In an untitled letter, Lin-Jay Harry-Voglezon replies to Ravi Dev letter "Indian Arrival Day's should be a national holiday." Harry-Voglezon argues that the day would be anti-African and goes on to "remind" Dev of some key historical facts that undermine his argument not only about the holiday, but also about "Indianness." Lin-Jay Harry-Voglezon. Letter, *Stabroek News*, June 2, 1998.

53. Kersting (1998).

54. "One People" (1998).

55. See Glasgow (1970) for additional material.

56. The Hermandston Accord was formed in 1998 to address the racial and political problems in Guyana. As such, its main focus is on race relations and constitutional reform. Under the Accord, the Constitution Reform Commission has been founded. The Accord has opened a dialogue between the PPP and the PNC.

57. See Brackette Williams (1991), specifically p. 234.

58. Hackett (1998).

59. "The highest courts of many Commonwealth countries have recognized the concept of aboriginal title."

60. Atkinson (1998).

61. I am referring to discussions with family members who live in the United States and in Guyana. Many of those I spoke with lived through the period before and the period of Burnham's rule.

62. Granger (2004).

5

Black Power and Black Nationalism: Lessons from the United States for the Caribbean?

Anton L. Allahar

> Black! That word. Black! And the visions came of alligator-infested swamps arched by primordial trees with moss dripping from the limbs and out of the depths of the swamp, the mire oozing from his skin, came the black monster and fathers told their daughters to be in by nine instead of nine-thirty.
>
> —Julius Lester (1969:97)

INTRODUCTION

This chapter makes the assumption that in order to understand the Caribbean we need also to understand the United States and how over the twentieth century many of the latter's domestic political and economic concerns have shaped Caribbean politics and economics. The chapter focuses specifically on the question of black nationalism as a strategy for resisting racism and ultimately for liberating black people. It concentrates mainly on the United States in the 1960s and 1970s and the experiences of black nationalists there for three reasons: (1) the geographical proximity of the United States to the Caribbean, (2) the loud echo of the U.S. Civil Rights and Black Power movements in the Caribbean, and (3) the fact that those movements were so closely tied to the philosophy and practice of (black) nationalism. So while my proximate aim in this chapter is to understand black nationalism and Black Power in the United States, I will begin with some words about my ultimate aim, the Caribbean, in order briefly to situate the problem sociologically and historically.

The region known generally as the English-speaking Caribbean comprises a set of countries that share many similarities while at the same time possessing numerable differences. In the period following Columbus's voyages, the countries of the region were transformed according to the wishes of the various colonial powers that controlled them. For the past five-hundred-plus years, these countries were molded as dependent capitalist social formations, serving generally the economic and political interests of their various masters. The granting of political independence to the English-speaking Caribbean countries in the 1960s and 1970s came at a time when Britain felt that (1) it had sufficiently cultivated a class of local leaders that was ideologically prepared to take over and run "business as usual," and (2) the direct colonial control of the countries had become both politically anachronistic and economically burdensome. Having made the economies of these countries dependent on those of Britain and other imperialist centers, it was felt that the day-to-day running of internal affairs politically could be left up to the locals while guaranteeing minimum interference in the flow of economic benefits to the mother country.

The processes of decolonization witnessed on the African continent, the Indian subcontinent, and in the Caribbean in the 1960s and 1970s will serve as my point of departure. I will take for granted the fact of European racism and the widespread European racialization of Africans, Indians, and their Caribbean descendants. This is beyond dispute. Once implanted, however, race thinking, the racialization of popular consciousness, and the entrenchment of racial awareness took on lives of their own and came to mark relations even among the formerly oppressed descendants of Africans and Indians in the Caribbean. This was the region's heritage on the eve of its independence.

As is well known, the process of colonial capture and domination, which oversaw the virtual elimination of the bulk of the region's indigenous inhabitants, also witnessed the creation of whole new societies. Depending on the country in question, new people from Europe, Africa, India, China, the Middle East, and elsewhere brought new languages, new religions, new moral codes, and new cultural practices and institutions that, in the course of time, became fused in the creation of distinct Caribbean societies. That fusion, described by some as "creolization" (Brathwaite 1971; Burton 1997), led to an amazingly complex set of relations of domination. Building on the various European models of class domination, colonial domination added a "race" and color dimension. Unlike the dominated classes in Europe, who most often shared the same or similar phenotypical features with the dominators, the Caribbean (and other colonial regions) came to exhibit a form of domination that was both class-based and color-coded. This is partially captured in the popular local saying that "if you're white you're alright, if you're brown stick around, but if you're black stay back." For in the class-race system of domination, lighter skin color and physical features that put one closer to the European norm were more highly prized than darker skin tones and features that departed from that norm (Allahar 1993). And as we know, given the hegemonic role that racism has come to play in most societies, particularly in the Caribbean, these prejudices soon came to be internalized and practiced by the dominated themselves in their dealings with one another.

CLASS FIRST

At this point I want to stress the distinction between theory and empirical practice. It is my contention that capitalism, whether in its colonial, imperialistic, or modern globalized form, is fundamentally concerned with labor exploitation. Such exploitation is primarily a class affair, and throughout its history it has seen the class of owners of capital exploit its dialectical opposite: that class which has only its labor power to sell, and which was called into existence by the owners of capital for precisely that purpose. Theoretically speaking, that the owners of capital in the colonial period (and later) were white and European is not fundamental to the development of capitalism. For there is nothing essential in the white man or woman that makes him or her any better at exploitation than any other man or woman. Indeed, throughout history the accumulation of capital has been made possible by the exploitation of white labor, female labor, child labor, indigenous labor, black labor, Indian labor, Chinese labor, and so on.

Eric Williams was clear on this point when he wrote that "slavery was not born of racism . . . rather racism was the consequence of slavery . . . it had to do not with the color of the laborer, but with the cheapness of the labor" (1966:7, 19). Stated differently, black people were not enslaved because they were black but because they were cheaper and more effective than the available alternatives. As far as racism is concerned, then, it was not until well after the fact of enslavement, and the discovery that the black African was better suited than others to the specifically harsh conditions of plantation labor, that an elaborate ideology of racial superiority and inferiority was developed. Thus, in the practical or empirical context of the Caribbean, capitalism was developed initially via the exploitation of indigenous labor, subsequently through the exploitation of slave and indentured labor (white, black, Chinese, Indian, Portuguese), and later via the exploitation of wage labor of all colors and ages and both sexes.

One point must be emphasized, however: the history of the development of dependent capitalism in the countries of the English-speaking Caribbean cannot be understood unidimensionally. If my theoretical approach specifies class as the key unit of analysis and the key point of departure, this does not mean to say that I minimize the importance of race and sex as centrally enabling factors in that history. Careful sociological analysis requires epistemologically the specification of a point of departure. And this is where a great deal of conflict and acrimony tend to occur among various groups that are party to the debate.

What, for example, is the most basic form of oppression in the region? Some will say class, others will insist on race, while yet others will claim gender or even age. And while all of these undeniably are crucial, where does one begin to develop a critical appreciation of social inequality in the Caribbean? Also, how does the chosen beginning point condition the mood and practice of contemporary politics and struggles that define the region? Holding the sex and gender questions aside for the moment, and focusing on the race-class dynamic, I turn to C. L. R. James for some direction. James wrote: "The race question is subsidiary to the class question in politics, and to think of imperialism in terms of race is disastrous. But to neglect the racial factor as merely incidental is an error only less grave than to make it fundamental" (quoted in Gilroy 1987:15). In other words, though fundamental, the class question cannot automatically be presumed to trump race everywhere and at all times, especially given the colonial experience that served to racialize public political consciousness at all levels of Caribbean society (Allahar 1998a).

Along with the practice of colonial racism, the use of racist ideology to inferiorize the African slaves and their descendants formed an integral part of the overall system of colonial domination. However, because human beings possess agency, they have been known to show various forms of resistance to that domination. Thus, whether dealing with such diverse phenomena as slavery, concentration camps, prisons, or even abject poverty, the spirit of creativity and resilience have enabled humans to offer numerous responses to their social and physical entrapment. And in this context the racial domination of blacks that is associated with slavery and its aftermath is no exception.

Thus, the present chapter is focused on a number of political responses to racism and racialization that have been fashioned by black Americans and that have informed black resistance to neocolonial domination in the Caribbean. Looking specifically at the politics of nationalism, I outline three black nationalist strategies that have been essayed in the United States and that have found favorable reception in some Caribbean political groupings. Political ideology notwithstanding, black nationalism must be rooted in the politico-economic circumstances in any given country and must be tied in the first instance to the class bases of its participants. While this is not to deny that non-class identities are real to those who hold them, what I want to suggest is that such identities are to be situated in the broader class context of differential access to economic and political power.

THE ARGUMENT

My *ultimate aim*, on one hand, is to determine how the complex race-class question is played out in the contemporary Caribbean some four decades after the securing of formal political independence. I am particularly interested in expressions of nationalism within the various countries, especially what has been termed *black nationalism*. This is not to minimize or deny the presence of an "Indian nationalism" as articulated, for example, by advocates of *Hindutva*, but that issue will be pursued more fully in chapter 9 of this volume. In addition to the foregoing, I am also interested in understanding black nationalism as a strategy for resisting racism, or, what may be somewhat different, as a strategy for liberation from racial oppression. *Hindutva*, on the other hand, will be seen as an ideology of oppression that counsels ethno-racial violence against persons who are purportedly members of the same racial groups, as well as others in the society.

By way of framing my overall concerns, I will examine the extent to which contemporary black nationalist politics in the Caribbean are informed by the struggles of black people in the United States during the 1960s and 1970s, where I have found interesting, if not instructive, parallels. What are those parallels and what do Caribbean peoples have to learn from the U.S. example? Is the liberation from oppression that the civil rights activists pursued for American blacks the same or similar to the type of liberation that contemporary black nationalists in the Caribbean envisage and pursue? And finally, are the differences and divisions that one might detect in the civil rights movement reflected in Caribbean black nationalist movements? To begin to answer these questions, this chapter asks whether there are lessons to be learned from the U.S. experience.

Apart from the parallels I have found in the two regions, there is also the long-standing relationship between American and Caribbean peoples. Whether through the institution of slavery, through travel and migration, through the presence of American military bases and multinational corporations on Caribbean soil, through general sporting and cultural exchanges, or through political and economic collaborations between the American and Caribbean elites, the peoples of the United States and the English-speaking Caribbean have a great deal of historical and social continuity. Indeed, several of the most prominent figures in the civil rights struggles in the United States were either Caribbean-born or second-generation Americans of Caribbean parents.

What I propose to argue is the following. In the United States, the civil rights struggles generally, and the Black Power movement specifically, are best understood as attempts at combating or resisting racism. I want to look critically and analytically at the so-called Black Power movement, which at various points in the 1960s was embraced by ideologically opposed groups of black nationalists: Congress of Racial Equality (CORE), National Association for the Advancement of Colored People (NAACP), Students' Non-violent Coordination Committee (SNCC), the Black Panthers, the Nation of Islam, the Republic of New Africa, and the US Organization. Thus, my first task is to tease out the various internal, ideological strands and strains that characterized the movement. For it is my impression that the contemporary manifestation of black nationalism in the Caribbean is a reflection of the Black Power movement, and the former may have a thing or two to learn from the latter; what to avoid and what to pursue.

RACE

One of the limitations that springs immediately to mind concerns the very definition of *race* and the question of "Who or what is black?" While races have no fundamental, scientific, biological meaning, socially they do, and while such things as intelligence, morality, bravery, and civility are not biologically based, many people do believe they are and act toward human beings as if this were the case. Understood biologically, then, *race* becomes real in its consequences, regardless of the fact that it is an entirely social construction. Being black in the United States, therefore, where the *law of hypodescent* or the so-called law of one drop applies, is very different from being black in the Caribbean. So any attempt to transpose and superimpose American Black Power politics onto a Caribbean reality is likely to be fraught with great difficulty.

In other words, while black nationalism and Black Power politics may have been appropriate in the United States, it is less so in the Caribbean, but this has not prevented ethnic entrepreneurs from trying. For unlike the situation where blacks comprised a mere 10 to 12 percent of the population of the United States, not only are black people the overwhelming majority of the population in the Caribbean, but their governments are also black, as are their working and professional classes and their poor. Those who will dismiss this fact of difference and oppression, and argue that power nevertheless remains in the hands of foreign multinational corporations that are principally white-owned, serve to shift the matter from one of class to one of race. Thus, in the United States, where there are many disenfranchised whites who are working class, powerless, poor, alienated, and economically exploited, the straight race argument is flawed. In Caribbean countries such

as Trinidad, Guyana, and Suriname, conversely, there are also class considerations to be taken into account when one notes that the majority of the
black and Indian populations are property-less and working class and find
themselves at the mercy of the property owners and their political allies,
white, black, Indian, Chinese, and other.

To the extent that it is the local, national, black, and Indian political elites
and bourgeois class fractions that collaborate as junior partners with the foreign multinationals (Dupuy 1991), one has to be very careful about casting
the struggle for liberation there in racial terms. For Caribbean peoples generally do not recognize the *law of one drop* as a criterion for marking membership in a racial group. Caribbean society is biologically douglarized and
creolized. And furthermore, since none of us is biologically "pure" of blood
(whatever that means), it is important to underscore the socially constructed
nature of racial categorization, which yields such designations as red nigger,
sapodilla brown, high brown, white-by-association, locally assembled white,
and half-caste.

OPERATIONAL DEFINITIONS

Before providing operational definitions of some key terms that are used in
this chapter, and because I want to focus on black nationalisms as strategies
for resisting racism, it is important to note that those who might offer resistance to racism do not necessarily have to have a critical understanding of the
phenomenon, nor must they have necessarily developed an alternative vision of the society in question (Allahar 1998b). Yet these are the ones typically targeted by ethnic entrepreneurs bent on exciting their emotions and
channeling them in the direction of predetermined political and economic
ends. Thus, the actions or resistance of the mass must not be presumed automatically to be carefully tailored to addressing or eliminating the root
causes or sources of racism. Furthermore, caution must be taken not to homogenize or essentialize the "mass" to which I refer.

In the specific case of Black Power in the United States, for example, there
was no single or common perception of racial oppression among "whites" or
"blacks" as conventionally defined. As William Van Deburg noted, just as
there were great differences in interpretation between blacks and whites,
among blacks, too, there were "ideological variants" (1992:24). And for his
part, Richard King claimed that the concept was deliberately "left ambiguous" and although "much discussion of black power was hysterical, there
were undeniable difficulties with the idea . . . and its deployment as a rallying cry" (1992:156). Then there is Theodore Draper, who, linking the concept of Black Power to "black nationalism," wrote that it was "much easier to
be a black nationalist than to know what black nationalism is" (1970:147).

Such ambiguity is fertile soil for the flourishing of ethnic entrepreneurs who claim to speak on behalf of the mass while pursuing their own narrow class or individual agendas. Invoking the cases of both African American and Caribbean ethnic entrepreneurs, who serve as leading spokespersons of their respective "nations," Robert Carr wonders skeptically,

> whether the representatives of these nations who emerge as representatives in fact represent the "people"—or "black folks," as poor and angry African-Americans and West Indians refer to their oppressed social body—or whether they merely represent themselves and consolidate their elite status on the backs of the threat of grassroots violence. (2002:8)

Ambiguity and lack of a clear understanding of their social predicaments, however, do not mean that social actors are any less likely to engage and offer resistance to the racist oppressor. These issues will be highlighted in my assessment of the Black Power movement in the United States.

Race

To begin with "race," therefore, the first step is to separate the biological from the social definitions of the term. In biological terms, "race" refers to the categorization of the human population on the basis of certain hereditary characteristics such as blood type, genetic make-up, and phenotype or physical appearance. Because a person from one genetic group can interbreed with a person from another genetic group, such categorizations, and combinations of them, offer infinite possibilities, which might be biologically interesting but sociologically questionable. In other words, where problems arise is with those sociobiologists and their apologists, who seek to argue that biological differences can explain social differences and social inequalities in such areas as morality, intelligence, income, or even parental caring for children (Herrnstein and Murray 1994; Rushton 1995).

The nonbiological conception of "race," on the other hand, stresses the idea of social construction, and argues that although the term has no biological utility, it continues to serve political and economic interests because most people believe it to be real (Miles 1989:71; Allahar 1993:52). Thus, the politics of "race" begins where the biological and social conceptions of it intersect. As long as there are those who will want to justify social practices by resort to biological claims, disagreement and conflict will be commonplace. That is, when jobs, housing, education, marriage partners, and other social amenities are distributed along racial (biological) lines, human beings will never agree, and those who are denied or disenfranchised will always find ways of resisting, whether actively or passively.

In this context, those traditional racists who insist that *races are real* will usually have a political agenda according to which social contrivances such as poverty, intelligence, morality, powerlessness, or even class privilege are cast as *natural*. In so doing they seek to remove responsibility for many social ills entirely from the realm of human, social interaction. Theirs is an attempt to legitimize a socially produced situation of fundamental disadvantage by giving to it the veneer of a natural, biological, inflexible fact. At the same time we must note that the concept of race and associated race thinking have become so hegemonic in contemporary society that it is not only the power holders who think and act as if race were real. Among the dominated classes, for example, those ethnic entrepreneurs who advance the primordialist claim (Allahar 1994b; 2001c) are also seen to be acting quite opportunistically. In other words, ethnic entrepreneurs of the dominated group(s) will also have their own economic and political agendas that downplay class analysis, will also want to argue that race is real, and will resort to primordialist claims to make their points.

Racism

Racism occurs when racial categorizations are informed by negative meanings, and when those meanings serve to relegate people to subordinate positions in a system of hierarchical social rankings. For along with its ideological message, racism is the practice of including and excluding individuals and groups from participating fully in the social economy on the basis of some imputed claims to racial (biological) similarities or differences. Racism also involves the use of these claims to deny targeted individuals and groups access to certain services and resources on these same bases. Through the process of labeling some are consigned to the supposedly inferior "races," thereby raising the questions of power and legitimacy: those with power are able to label others and have those labels stick.

The concepts of power and legitimacy are thus seen as intrinsic aspects of racism, for it is in the acting out of racially negative feelings that the practice of racism becomes manifest. And it is in this sense that ethnic entrepreneurs are cast in the role of opportunistic racists. They claim a biological distinctiveness rooted in an ancestral land and culture, socially contrive or imagine a primordial group identity, and prescribe courses of political action consistent with their goals. Though discussed more concretely in the case of Afrocentrism and the racialization of political consciousness in Trinidad (Allahar 1998a), the present argument will be developed further in the context of *Hindutva* or Hindu racism in chapter 9.

Ethnicity

If races or racial groups are supposed to speak to the biological aspects of human populations, ethnic groups speak to the sociocultural composition and practices of those populations. Depending on the social climate or environment in which they exist, ethnic groups in multiethnic societies will face differing degrees of pressure to assimilate or conform to the dominant culture. Among certain European migrants to the United States, for example, where those to be assimilated resemble the dominant group culturally and physically, that pressure is not likely to be perceived or interpreted negatively. Conversely, however, in those cases where the ethnic group in question has less in common with the dominant group(s) or culture (e.g., Afro-descended Americans), pressure to assimilate is likely to be met with varying degrees resistance, especially in the modern world where political correctness, Black Power, civil rights, and other similar social movements have served to empower formerly marginalized groups.

Resistance

Resistance in this context is defined as any action, whether physical, verbal, or psychological, and whether individual or collective, that seeks to undo the negative consequences of being categorized for racial reasons (Allahar 1998b). Thus, unlike those approaches that seek to portray the victims of racial and other types of oppression as unwitting pawns and passive recipients of the dominant ideology and practice and as lacking agency,[1] this chapter will seek to understand some ways in which such concepts as race and négritude can be used or manipulated by the oppressed to resist or mollify the deleterious consequences of racism. Resistance will be seen as a political act that is intimately tied to the wider cultural forces that frame it, conducing in the United States (and elsewhere) to the Black Power movement and black nationalism.

NATIONALISM

As noted earlier, the reaction to institutional racism in the United States was Black Power. Though unified at the affective or emotional level, the movement as a whole contained many divisive strains and tendencies that conditioned its ultimate demise and that are to be found among the black nationalists in the Caribbean today. Part of the explanation of that demise concerns what I see as common in similar movements of oppressed peoples. It is related to such movements' emphasis on descriptive sloganeering to the neglect of analytical understanding. The resulting mobilization is thus characteristically long on rhetoric and short on analysis. Especially in the formative stages of such movements, leaders are keen to cast their membership nets as widely as possible to swell their ranks and to command loyalty to the cause, while followers are often content just to follow. It is a time when serious internal criticism of the movement is discouraged and a sort of "group-think" mentality takes hold. As Richard King writes:

> When black people—or any people—conceive of themselves as a unified oppressed group, private activities or feelings are scarcely tolerated and disagreement, should it arise, is easily branded as betrayal. A conformist cast of mind easily emerges. (1992:164)[2]

As discussed in chapter 1, the idea of nationalism is best conveyed as a *sentiment of oneness*. As an ideology it speaks to the uniting of people, almost with the tightness of primordial, family bonds, and assumes an ineffable or unquestioned unity (Shils 1957; Geertz 1973) based on appeals to common birthplace, common soil, common blood: the *home* in "homeland," the *father* in "fatherland," or the *mother* in "motherland." As Steven Grosby argues,

> we attribute the properties which we see as constitutive of the family to the larger collectivity . . . use of terms like home in "homeland," father in "fatherland," or mother in "motherland." Primordial properties are seen as fundamental in the larger collectivity as well as in the family. (1994:165)

In other words, it's a family matter defined by country of origin and constitutes a call to all brothers and sisters to rally behind the cause: justice, freedom, honor, dignity, and brotherhood. The forces of opposition, the oppressors, are "otherized" and seen to be the embodiment of all that is not in the best interests of the "nation" or the "family" thus construed.

By extension, if the foregoing describes "nationalism," how does one define "black nationalism"? Is it simply that people, the country, the community, or the family in question are black? And if so, what is the definition of black? As we know in the United States, this was resolved quite expeditiously: the law of one drop; but as already noted, even if this worked in the United States, it certainly cannot apply to the Caribbean. And just as important, since along with the supposedly objective biological measure (a drop of blood), "black" also has a subjective component, which suggests that there are different degrees of blackness. This leads to cumbersome questions such as: Is the "blacker" one is the more loyal one is? How black is black? And is this not the mere inversion of white racism, whereby one uses the same racist criteria (purity of blood) of the oppressor to determine membership in the nation? And at the base of it all is the virtually impossible task of finding "pure" blood that is shared only by a discrete "nation," population, or family, and then using this to explain learned social behavior.

BLACK POWER AND BLACK NATIONALISM

The situation facing black people in what is perhaps the most racially fractured society in the modern world was confusing in the 1960s (and continues to be confusing today). As Harold Cruse noted more than thirty years
ago, "The national character of the Negro has little to do with what part of
the country he lives in. Wherever he lives, he is restricted. His national
boundaries are the color of his skin, his racial characteristics, and the social
conditions within his sub-cultural world" (1970:350). In all of this two facts
were (and continue to be) indisputable: (1) being black in America was/is
costly to black people, many of whom have paid the price of blackness with
their lives, while others have paid socially, economically, and politically; and
(2) instead of standing still or getting better, the situation has grown worse.
What strategy of (re)action or resistance should or could they pursue?

In seeking answers to these questions I borrow from William Van Deburg's
comprehensive study titled *New Day in Babylon* (1992), where, under the
umbrella of Black Power and black nationalism, there are three principal responses that have been identified. Though separable for analytical purposes,
in actuality these often shaded into one another. The first, which I label a
timid nationalism, was a combination of pluralist and integrationist ideas,
which were basically reformist and targeted integration or assimilation into
the wider society as the solution to the problems that beset black people in
America. The route to be pursued here was one of a peaceful, nonviolent resistance to racism. It is the passive resistance model made popular by India's
Mahatma Gandhi and later adopted by Rev. Martin Luther King, Jr. As a black
nationalist movement it advocated a temporary or *strategic separation* from
"white" society. This would be a period of withdrawal during which the human and other resources of the black community are consolidated, developed, and sharpened to the point where they would eventually seek to reen-
gage the wider society from a position of economic strength, political
organization, and community unity. Known by such names as pluralism,
multiculturalism, or accommodation, the advocates of this strategy of black
nationalism see racism and not capitalism as the source of black disenfranchisement. In the United States it was most associated with the NAACP,
CORE, and the SCLC.

However, where integration is a more reformist-conservative strategy for
resisting racism, a second tendency was far more radical in the right-wing
sense of the term. These were the *territorial black nationalists* who gave up
on white America and its racist practices and sought not temporary but total
separation. Their solution was either to partition certain southern states for
black people alone (South Carolina, Georgia, Alabama, Mississippi, and
Louisiana) or to leave America altogether and return to Africa. Though finding echoes in other black nationalisms, Afrocentricity is most at home in this

tendency. Like the timid nationalists, whose politics are those of short-term strategic separation with a long-term goal of assimilation or integration, total separatists did not have a critique of capitalism and presumed that the problems of black people began and ended with race. Theirs was thus a primordialist appeal, complete with the racist assumptions of all primordialisms and founded on the so-called myth of "merrie (merry) Africa" as a place where all black people lived together in harmony before the "white" man came and upset the society (Hopkins 1973; Cohen 1979). This point is further developed in chapter 9 of this volume.

A third black nationalist strategy, what has been called *revolutionary nationalism*, was also radical in tone but was different in that it had a left or socialist orientation and saw the predicament of black Americans as bound up with American capitalism and the exploitation of black labor as cheap labor. Represented principally by the Black Panthers and, to a lesser extent, by the Student Nonviolent Coordinating Committee (SNCC), this strategy embraced armed resistance of the racist oppressor and targeted the latter's agents of repression, whether local sheriffs, big city police forces, or the FBI itself. Their goal was the mobilization and education of black Americans to take pride in themselves, to have confidence in their abilities, and to assume control of their own destinies; and, as implausible as it might appear, in the long run to have a socialist revolution in America.

TIMID NATIONALISM

In the United States the pluralists represented a group of ethnic entrepreneurs who focused on the black neighborhoods and communities and reasoned that the depressed conditions facing black people were due to the fact that whites controlled the economic and political lives of those communities. Although he was no pluralist or integrationist, Malcolm X phrased their question well when he asked in 1964: "Why should white people be running all the stores in our community? Why should white people be running the banks in our community? Why should the economy of our community be in the hands of the white man?" (*Malcolm X Speaks* and *By Any Means Necessary*). Having defined the problem in straight race terms, community activists and various ethnic entrepreneurs had clear goals: to have the society's central institutions (e.g., schools, hospitals, and government agencies) pay closer attention to the needs of the people (Van Deburg 1992:15). According to the pluralists, their agenda was pro-black but not anti-white. Their leading organizations such as the National Urban League and the NAACP, which adopted strong community control resolutions in their 1969 national conventions, vigorously resisted the label of "separatists." The formation of the National Economic Growth Reconstruction Organization (NEGRO) in the early

1960s was aimed at promoting self-help within the community and in a few years it had registered significant successes owning and operating chemical, paint, and metal fabricating plants; bus companies in Watts and Harlem; a textile firm; more than six hundred housing units refurbished by its own Spartacus Construction Company; mobile stores; and a farmer's market. Arguing that slavery, exploitation, and racism had made many blacks fatalistic and welfare-dependent and had cultivated negative attitudes toward work, NEGRO went into the community and worked with the hard-core unemployed; they conducted clinics and sought generally to develop a sense of hope in the population (Ibid.:117).

One of the leaders, Dr. Thomas Matthew, was keen to distinguish between the philosophy and ideology of NEGRO and that of the total separatists, a different group of ethnic entrepreneurs with different goals, "who were laying plans to withdraw from American society, form a separate black state, or return to Africa" (Ibid.). In many respects NEGRO embodied all the positive aspects of a strong civic nationalism. To the extent that it was separatist it was a *strategic separatism* that would afford the black community a period of consolidation during which time it would be able to build up its strength only to reenter the wider society at a later date on more equitable terms. Strategic separatism, in other words, was a stepping stone to ultimate integration and cultural and finally biological amalgamation. Its community focus, which stressed civic pride, was unmistakable and within that its commitment to working with and in the schools was its hallmark. Apart from addressing pressing matters of neighborhood rot and physical deterioration of school buildings and facilities, the idea was to make the curriculum more relevant to young blacks by teaching about the positive accomplishments of black people in the fields of history, art, culture, politics, and so on. It was felt that one of the reasons for poor school performance among black children was their low self-esteem, which was directly related to the systemic denigration of all things black in the curriculum and in the society at large: in the media, history books, popular films, police reports, and even in the speeches of politicians.

One of the main foci of attention concerned economic development of the black community and the encouragement of something called "black capitalism." Pluralists and integrationists felt that one of the reasons why black people were disenfranchised did not have to do with capitalism per se but with the fact that there were not enough black capitalists. But unlike an approach that stressed the class bases of black dispossession, this focus on race was so non-threatening to the authorities that even the Republican Party and President Richard Nixon jumped on the bandwagon:

I will begin a new program to get private enterprise into the ghetto and the ghetto into private enterprise . . . it is no longer enough that white-owned enterprises employ greater numbers of Negroes . . . this is needed yes—but it has to be accompanied by an expansion of black ownership, of black capitalism (quoted in Van Deburg 1992:119).

And Nixon goes on to co-opt the very language of the movement suggesting that these initiatives would lead to "black pride, black jobs, black opportunity and, yes, black power in the best, the constructive sense of that often misapplied term" (Ibid.). Realizing the futility of permanent economic and political separatism, pluralist and integrationist black leaders embraced these promises of the government and embarked on a path of black capitalist engagement. Opting for a description of the black condition instead of an analytical understanding of it, black leaders uncritically assumed that in some magical way black capitalists would be kinder to black workers than would white capitalists. Thus, among other things, they worked through the Office of Minority Business Enterprise and the Minority Enterprise Small Business Investment Companies in pursuit of the American dream.

Recognizing that economic strength was shaky without political say, leaders also sought to raise the profile of black political representation all within America's (flawed) liberal democratic framework (Allahar and Côté 1998:9–21). Traditional black support for the Democratic Party meant that when the Republicans were in power blacks could expect to lose ground, and this led the reformist black leaders to seek accommodations within the framework of the Democratic Party. In other words, these black ethnic entrepreneurs believed in a pragmatic solution and reasoned that since they could not defeat the whites, they might as well just join them. So the early 1970s saw black politics expressed through such newly founded organizations as the Black Legislators' Association, the National Conference of Black Mayors, the National Black Caucus of Local Elected Officials, and the Congressional Black Caucus. Under the auspices of such organizations as the Southern Christian Leadership Conference (SCLC), headed by the likes of Martin Luther King and Roy Wilkins, and the Congress of Racial Equality (CORE) where Floyd McKissick and Roy Innis provided leadership, integrationist politics were alive and well.

As members of the revolutionary nationalist Black Panther–SNCC alliance would later point out, however, integrationist politics served largely to legitimize the overall political structures and processes that remained most sensitive to white business and white community concerns, while failing simultaneously to acknowledge the root causes of black disenfranchisement. In this sense integrationist politics were also a politics of distraction that gave to black leaders like King, McKissick, and Innis the illusion of participation. In the words of Stokely Carmichael:

Integration as a goal today speaks to the problem of blackness not only in an unrealistic way but also in a despicable way. . . . Integration also means that

black people must give up their identity, deny their heritage. . . . No person can
be healthy, complete and mature if he must deny a part of himself; this is what
integration has required thus far. (Carmichael and Hamilton 1967:54–55)

In sum, then, from the ideological point of view, the pluralist-integrationist
strategy for resisting racism was both reformist and conservative. Revealing
their leaders' clear ethnic entrepreneurial interests, capitalism was defined
and accepted as the only game in town, which appeased all concerned; politically those black leaders felt good about having a say (however minor that
may have been), while white political leaders (both Democrats and Republicans) and their corporate allies retained the power to define the agenda. In
the process the status quo was legitimized and the public order preserved.
By these black ethnic entrepreneurs failing to realize that capital has no race,
color, sex, or nationality; that it will exploit anywhere, anytime, and anyone,
just so long as it is able to secure the average rate of profit; that given the
logic of accumulation, black capitalism cannot be kinder to black workers
than white capitalism, this particular brand of black nationalism was not
emancipatory then and is not now.

TERRITORIAL NATIONALISM

While the pluralists pursued strategic separatism as a temporary measure that
was meant to lead ultimately to integration through black capitalism and
greater black political representation, there was another group of black ethnic entrepreneurs making their presence felt. I am referring here to the more
ideologically radical posturing of the *territorial nationalists*. As the conditions of black life in America worsened, as rising unemployment and drug
and crime rates kept pace with one another, as statistics claiming that there
were more college-aged black males in prison than in college, as divorce and
domestic violence in black families grew, and as another generation of black
youth appeared poised to self-destruct, some black nationalists came to reason that the problem with black people in America was white people in
America. And if white people would not go away, then perhaps black people should.

For many of the *total separatists*, white America and black America were
fundamentally culturally incompatible. To rescue their individuality and distinctiveness, black Americans were exhorted to rediscover their authentic
African cultural roots, for only in that rediscovery would they gain the
strength to withstand the white attempts to smother Africa's children and to
secure their true liberation. Under this separatist rubric ethnic entrepreneurs
from among the black Muslims were some of the most radical and outspo-
ken. They made religion and culture synonymous and agreed that political

liberation could not be achieved without first being racially and culturally liberated. For Elijah Muhammad, the leader of the Nation of Islam, whites were guilty of stealing and plundering the Native civilizations, and through the trials of slavery, blacks had earned a much larger share of the nation's assets than they were presently accorded. He was thus convinced that separatism met with Allah's approval, and that it was "far more important to teach separation of the blacks and whites in America than prayer" (quoted in Van Deburg 1992:140–41).

This kind of thinking among the territorial nationalists, whose agenda led them to paint all whites with the same brush, also exposed them for being just as racist as the racists they opposed. This is best exemplified in the Los Angeles–based organization called *US Organization* under the leadership of Maulana Ron Karenga. Focusing on cultural uniqueness and separation, Karenga and his followers were explicitly anti-Jewish in their pronouncements (Van Deburg 1992:171, 173) and militant about cultural separation from the mainstream. By concentrating on such things as "black" clothing, language, and hairstyles, along with "black" theater and dance, "black" art and literature, *US Organization* sought to create a "black" value system *(Nguzo Saba)* that embodied seven key elements or principles.[3] In addition, the value system encompassed the teaching of Swahili in the schools and celebrating black holidays such as Uhuru Day (August 11, commemorating the Watts riots), Kuzaliwa (May 19, Malcolm X's birthday), and Kwanzaa as an alternative to the commercialized white celebration of Christmas. It also exhorted followers generally to live the teachings of *Kawaida*, a uniquely "African" theory and practice of cultural change (Karenga 1977; Halisi 1967). Summarizing the position of this group of ethnic entrepreneurs, Van Deburg writes:

> Black Americans needed to carry out a cultural revolution before they could mount a successful political campaign to seize and reorder established institutions of power and wealth. . . . According to Karenga and his followers, black liberation was impossible, by definition unthinkable, without breaking the white culture's domination of black minds. (1992:172–73)

The idea of separatism was also endorsed by Malcolm X when he suggested that the only solution to the dilemma facing black people in America was "complete separation on some land that we can call our own" (Malcolm X 1971). This declaration was warmly received by a black nationalist organization known as the Republic of New Africa (RNA). On a trip to Africa with Malcolm, RNA's cofounder, a Yale-educated Detroit lawyer called Milton Henry, was struck by the fact that Africans who had been at college with him in the United States had returned home to assume important jobs in key economic and political sectors of their various countries. It then dawned on him that American blacks, as a group, could in no way aspire to similar levels in America. He then agreed with Malcolm that blacks in the United States comprised a separate nation and the only solution to their problems was complete independence.

By 1968 Malcolm X, Milton Henry, and his brother Richard, along with several hundred other black nationalists who had adopted African names, began to draw up plans for black statehood. Identifying the states of South Carolina, Georgia, Alabama, Mississippi, and Louisiana as a future black homeland, the leaders of the Republic of New Africa considered themselves a government in exile. Their aim was to create a space in which black people could work, live, develop community, and celebrate their Africanness with pride. In the words of the RNA minister of Culture and Education, they were after: "A completely separate nation mentally, spiritually, politically, and even in ways of marriage and burials" (Imari Obadele, quoted in Van Deburg 1992:148). They even demanded of the federal government a payoff of $400 billion, which they saw as a down payment on reparations for slavery and several hundred years of racist oppression.

Fully expecting the federal government to refuse their request, the leaders of RNA also drafted plans for self-defense that included the creation of an army, the New African Security Force. While defensively they were prepared to *resist* all "invaders" (American troops) who entered the homeland, offensively they planned a variety of terrorist attacks on America: poisoning water supplies, blowing up gasoline stations, and exploding bridges, buildings, and monuments. Once the war was sparked off they expected that northern blacks would come on board, form urban guerrilla cells, and unleash urban guerrilla warfare on cities and towns in the north. They reasoned that if the Vietnamese could defeat the American army and force it to retreat without ever dropping a bomb on American soil, they were far more advantageously placed being already inside the country. William Van Deburg wrote: "Prepared for indefinite combat through training in the RNA's peacetime police corps, the Black Legion, southern blacks would prove formidable opponents in a struggle for control of the homeland" (1992:147).

As we know, however, none of this ever came to pass. The federal government ignored both the reparations issue and the idea of cession of any territory to the RNA, black statehood was never debated in the white seats of power, there were no northern guerrilla cells formed, and no terrorist attacks of any significance. The only major change was to be seen in the stepped-up surveillance of black organizations by white police. This then paved the way for the appearance of another separatist group of ethnic entrepreneurs, the *pan-Africanists*.

Whereas the Republic of New Africa envisaged a homeland for black people *within* the United States, and celebrated a philosophical and cultural bond with their continental African brothers and sisters, another more Afrocentric strain of thinking characterized the *emigrationists*, or those who wanted to give up on America altogether and return *physically* to the African continent. Among the emigrationists it was felt that black Americans were really Africans who had lived abroad, albeit for a very long time, but who were now prepared to return "home" and reassume their rightful places in their ancestral land. The difficulty here was that the emigrationists, who were politically, culturally, and ideologically products of America and whose conceptions of Africa were formed largely by the cultural chauvinism and racism of Hollywood and the popular media, did not really have a clear idea of what Africa was like and what was at stake in pan-Africanism.

In the thinking of Benedict Anderson, theirs was an Afro-American imagined Africa! Indeed, for those who actually traveled to Africa, there were two great awakenings as they discovered that: (1) they were unfamiliar with the languages, histories, cultures, and institutions of African societies, and (2) the real Africans were not generally enthusiastic about receiving them. Beyond the color of their skins there appeared little that united these black peoples who had been separated by hundreds of years, thousands of miles of ocean, and many lifetimes of lived experiences. Paraphrasing Tom Mboya, Kenya's minister for economic planning and development, Van Deburg writes:

> Realistically the black expatriates were the African's nieces, nephews, and cousins—of Africa, but not fully African. Culturally, they could be categorized as "sub-American, and extremely little African." Indeed, said the harshest critics, they were Americans born and bred. They talked, thought, and behaved like Americans. Typically, they assumed too much and were very "brash." (1992:151)

In sum, then, as a strategy for resisting racism, total separation, whether within America or leaving for Africa, did not prove very viable. The dream of the great ethnic entrepreneur, Marcus Garvey, who himself died before ever setting foot on African soil, never materialized. And summing up the position of the total separatists, Richard King wrote:

> Clearly literal secession from the United States and establishment of a black state either in the continental United States or elsewhere were chimerae, fantasies substituting for political and social projects. Secessionist positions were usually amalgams of Garveyite dreams, biblical visions of deliverance and Nation of Islam–type social discipline. (1992:157)

Sure, there were the African Nationalist Pioneer Movement and the African-American Repatriation Association, which mounted educational tours and exchanges between Africans and black Americans, but they seemed to appeal more to individuals here and there and never led to a mass return migration movement. Ideologically the movement was both reformist and conservative.

The ethnic entrepreneurs at the head of it had no vision for black people be-yond capitalism, and in those cases where they spoke of building black com-munity and black unity, whether in the United States or Africa, the vision wa-vered between extreme idealism and utopianism and seemed to make the assumption either that color and class divisions or differentiation among black people were nonexistent, or that they were of no relevance.

Focusing on race or color, Harold Cruse noted that "within the Negro com-munity, prejudice about lighter and darker skin coloring also served as a ba-sis for class stratification." And on the question of class, he went on to pose a series of questions aimed specifically at the black ethnic entrepreneurs, whom he labeled the "Negro bourgeoisie": "Why is there such a lack of real unity among different Negro classes towards one objective? . . . We must con-sider why the interests of the Negro bourgeoisie have become separated from those of the Negro working classes" (1970:359, 361). Although Cruse does not specify what the interests of the latter are, he is correct in his basic thrust as once more territorial nationalism and its call for total separation seemed to play into the hands of the oppressors by distracting the mass of its black followers with its empty rhetoric and flawed analysis of the "black" condition in the United States.

REVOLUTIONARY NATIONALISM

The revolutionary black nationalist movement in the United States is best known as the Black Power movement. Following the teachings of Frantz Fanon, the revolutionary nationalists saw blacks in America as constituting an *internal colony*, and like all colonized people, they were subjected to capitalist exploitation, racism, and extreme violence (physical, cultural, psy-chological). Because colonization was a system of entrenched violence, vio-lence was integral to the process of decolonization and the winning of black freedom. Unlike reform-minded and conservative pluralists, who favored strategic separation, and the territorial nationalists, who pursued total sepa-ration, the revolutionary nationalists advocated a socialist alternative for America. Convinced that flight to Africa was not the solution, this fraction of black nationalists felt that black nationalism should be subordinated to so-cialism. As ethnic entrepreneurs, the leaders of this movement had alterna-tive political designs that could not be accommodated by black capitalism or Afrocentrism.

Given the overwhelming odds against them, the vast powers of control and surveillance available to the authorities, and the willingness of the latter to use illegal tactics and massive force even against American citizens, the revolutionary nationalists in retrospect appear just as idealistic as the territo-rial nationalists. In fact, their vision of the New Black Man had favorable echo with the pan-African émigrés who hoped to "find their spirits rejuvenated through association with the free-spirited, uncorrupted Africans" (Van Deburg 1992:150). As part of socialist America, the New Black Man would have a superior morality, a devotion to community, selflessness, justice, and freedom for all oppressed peoples whether within or without America. The Afrocentric content of this sentiment is unmistakable in its uncritical and mythical recasting of "merrie Africa."

The revolutionary nationalists criticized the reformism of the territorial nationalists, who, instead of opposing capitalism, seemed merely to oppose the "white" manifestation of it. Hence the latter's anger at whites but their simultaneous silence on the oppressive nature of the economic system. Acknowledging the reality of racial oppression in America, the revolutionaries were under no illusions that it was possible to abolish racism while retaining capitalism. Indeed, because racism in America was the special product of capitalism in America, they felt it was important to struggle against both racism and capitalism at the same time. And apart from embracing the then-young socialist experiment in Cuba, these ethnic entrepreneurs had no long-term, concrete program for a post-capitalist, post-racist America.

The Black Panther Party

Among the revolutionary nationalists it was the Black Panthers who most clearly articulated the vision (albeit idealistic) of a post-racist, socialist America. In the words of the chairman of the party, Bobby Seale,

> We do not fight racism with racism. We fight racism with solidarity. We do not fight exploitative capitalism with black capitalism. We fight capitalism with basic socialism. And we do not fight imperialism with more imperialism. We fight imperialism with proletarian internationalism. (1970:71)

This preparedness to look beyond the black condition as if it were an isolated case, and to embrace the struggle of all oppressed peoples, was first revealed by Seale in an open confession that some black nationalists today might find embarrassing. Growing up as a child in Oakland, California, he reflects on his early radicalization in his teen years and confesses that during those years preceding the full birth of African consciousness: "We were opposed to the white man for taking the land away from the Indians, and we identified with the Indians because our parents had Indian in them. We didn't know about Africa yet" (1970:7).

The Black Panthers, a California-based organization, represented the political vanguard of the revolutionary black nationalist movement; the philosophical, intellectual, and military arm of the black revolutionary nationalists. By the late 1960s, after forming an alliance with the SNCC that was based in New York, the Black Panther Party came to integrate the most outstanding

black revolutionaries in the entire country. Before long these leaders, themselves ethnic entrepreneurs, became household names in both black and
white America: Huey P. Newton, Bobby Seale, Eldridge Cleaver, Stokely
Carmichael, H. Rap Brown, and James Forman, among others. As noted
above, the Panthers saw nationalism as a stepping stone to internationalism
and solidarity among all oppressed people, not just black people. They resisted racism in all forms, even the black racism of the territorial and cultural
nationalists, whom they derisively called "bourgeois" and "pork chop" nationalists.

Criticizing their primordialist convictions, Bobby Seale noted that the latter make no distinction between racist whites and non-racist whites. They
say that "a black man cannot be an enemy of the black people, while the
Panthers believe that black capitalists are exploiters and oppressors"
(1970:23). For Seale and his comrades in the Party, the territorial nationalists
were black racists and "you're not going to end racism by perpetuating more
racism" (Ibid.:218). Thus, in articulating the program of the Black Panthers,
their chairman was clear: "In our view it is a class struggle between the massive proletarian working class and the small, minority ruling class. Working-
class people of all colors must unite against the exploitative, oppressive ruling class. So let me emphasize again—we believe our fight is a class struggle
and not a race struggle" (Ibid.:72).

Whereas the pluralists saw black nationalism as a means to the end of
eventual integration and assimilation, and the territorial nationalists saw it
as an end in itself, the revolutionary nationalists saw black nationalism as
a means to the construction of a non-racist, socialist America. But as
Carmichael is clear to point out, there is no getting around the fact that
American society is a racially fractured one and that it is the black man and
woman, not as individuals but as a politically united force, who must be the
first to address the situation of black people (1967:54). And anticipating the
charge that he is advocating black exceptionalism or reverse racism, he is
quick to point out: "This is not to say that there are no white people who
see things as I do, but that it is black people I must speak to first. . . . This
does not mean we do not welcome help, or friends" but "only black people
can convey the revolutionary idea that black people can do things themselves" (1968:68).

As might be expected, there were serious differences between the Afrocentrists under the leadership of Karenga, Amiri Baraka (formerly LeRoi
Jones) and other black cultural nationalists, on one hand, and the revolutionary nationalists, on the other hand. Thus, when Karenga embarked on
his mission of leading America down a path of race-first blackness and declared that US Organization members "do not accept the idea of a class struggle" (Halisi 1967:9; 23–24), they immediately ran afoul of the Panthers, who
dismissed the Afrocentric rantings and ravings of US Organization as mad-

ness, and who described Karenga himself as an "afro-cosmic lunatic" (quoted in Van Deburg 1992:174). At the same time, and reflecting their own uncritical acceptance of Hollywood's portrayal of Africans as primitive, tribal, bongo-beating simpletons, his devoted followers were derisively characterized by the Panthers as "those niggers with the bongos in their ears" (Anthony 1970:75). To this Amiri Baraka responded by charging the Panthers with being starry-eyed leftists clad in "some dead 1930s white ideology as a freedom suit" (Baraka 1972:130–31). The reference to "white ideology" was obviously aimed at the Panther version of Marxism and socialism adapted to American conditions. Soon the name calling gave way to serious physical confrontations and by early 1969 led to the declaration of open "war" between the Black Panthers and the US Organization. Several shoot-outs took place within west coast black communities, and by the time it was all over both organizations were the poorer for it.

CONCLUSION

While all parties were in agreement that full black liberation was impossible without first developing a positive black self-concept and the appreciation of black artistic and cultural achievements, they differed on the primacy that was to be accorded to the cultural dimension of the struggle. In other words, in attempting to combat anti-black racism, several questions of strategy and tactics bedeviled the efforts of the black nationalists, and had clear parallels with nationalist struggles in the Caribbean: Was a gradualist, Afro-Saxon approach aimed at the integration of blacks into white society the most realistic option? Or should a more radical, Garvey-like insistence on the establishment and promotion of a separate homeland complete with a black culture and value system be given priority? And what about those more socialist-minded types who felt that the cultural and racial struggles were all wrapped up in the larger class struggle against capitalist oppression and exploitation?

In the struggle for black liberation these are the questions on which there was no agreement and which proved to be the undoing of all concerned. Black Power and the elevation of black culture and black pride, for which everyone claimed to be fighting, became associated with bungling, in-fighting, and self-destruction. Thus, Richard King, who charged that the "nationalist position was a form of ethnic politics with an overlay of radical racial rhetoric, pluralist politics plus soul food," would go on to add that "Black Power in a political sense was . . . just ethnic, interest-group politics with a bite. Even at that it seemed questionable to call it a form of nationalism" (1992:155, 157).

Without using the term, King also sees the various leaders in question as ethnic entrepreneurs, and by the time it was over all sides in the struggle

seemed to have lost sight of the common enemy; white America felt vindi-
cated and, if anything, the overall black condition may have worsened. What
the different struggles did achieve, however, was (1) a new, heightened
black awareness; (2) a popular commitment to social activism of a racial sort;
and (3) an aggressive, in-your-face assertion that black people had "arrived"
in America. After this, America could never go back to its pre–civil rights and
pre–Black Power ways. The key question, however, was: Could it go forward? And depending on the answer, what lessons can contemporary black
nationalists in the Caribbean learn from this history? The world of the early
twenty-first century is vastly different from that of the 1960s and 1970s in the
United States, and one cannot say with certainty if the gains of the civil rights
movement could have been achieved without the black nationalist mobi-
lizations of that era. What is certain, however, is that in the current climate of
globalization, economic displacement and the uprooting of traditional communities worldwide, struggles for "national" self-determination in post-colonial regions such as the Caribbean are likely to assume increasingly ethnic
and racial dimensions.

The foregoing analysis of black nationalisms as forms of resistance to the
white power structure in the United States assumes the racialization of capitalist exploitation. And while the principal focus is on blacks in a white majority society, it does offer insights to the Caribbean where blacks are in the
majority, but where, as a differentiated group subordinated to outside imperialist forces, three distinct political strategies of national self-determination
could be discerned. The first, timid nationalism, can be seen in the politics
of decolonization that characterized the 1960s and early 1970s. The "black
intellectuals who came to power" after the British withdrew were convinced
that the true route to the emancipation of their countries and their people lay
in capitalism. Economically they were content to play the role of junior partners of foreign capital and politically they embraced the values and institutions of liberal democracy. Their nationalism really was limited to securing a
restricted degree of autonomy within a very local sphere of operations. They
rocked the boat only when it was safe to do so (e.g., Eric Williams and the
U.S. military base in Chaguaramus), and essentially sought integration into
the wider market of capitalist relations.

The territorial and separatist nationalists are to be found among the Afrocentric and Hindu nationalists discussed in chapter 9. Both these groups reject integration and opt for a form of cultural isolation that emphasizes myth,
history, and ethno-racial distinctiveness. Like the above group, they too embrace capitalism and uncritically assume that class and economic divisions
within their respective groups would be trumped by the stronger allure of
primordialism. Thus, the politics of Afrocentric and Hindu nationalism
amount to a politics of race that is engineered by astute ethnic entrepreneurs,
who eschew any vision of Trinidadian, Jamaican, Guyanese, and so forth,

civic nationalism, in favor of a retreat into the supposedly safer confines of ethnic nationalisms.

Whether at the level of rhetoric or action, the revolutionary nationalists in the Caribbean have been few. Like the Black Panthers in the 1960s, the former were inspired by the Cuban revolution of 1959. They felt that independence and national sovereignty in the Caribbean could only be secured by breaking free from the imperialist center described by Dependency Theorists (Allahar 1995:107–22). Unlike the first two groups, then, the revolutionary nationalists rejected both the politics of integration to dependent capitalism and the politics of race. In varying degrees this was evidenced in Cheddi Jagan's aspirations for Guyana, in Michael Manley's first government in Jamaica, in Maurice Bishop's Grenada (Allahar 2001a), and in Walter Rodney's vision for a socialist Caribbean. As the Cubans have learned, however, a revolutionary socialist nationalism in America's backyard is no simple matter. For where the various American administrations are never threatened by movements for economic nationalism within capitalism, or even by impassioned cries of black nationalists, the class claims of revolutionary nationalism are taken very seriously and forcefully combated at every turn.

NOTES

1. I am thinking here of traditional black nationalist and feminist politics, which, in spite of their radical posturing, unwittingly paint a picture of blacks and women as helpless victims of racists and sexists. Patriarchy in this view is hegemonic and all-pervasive, and its victims are fated forever to be victims.

2. In a somewhat different, though relevant context, I see the response of U.S. political leaders to September 11, 2001, as mirroring these very sentiments. Such things as the Patriot Act, the passage of legislation giving authorities permission to tap private phones and read people's mail, all in the name of fighting terrorism, have resulted in a jingoistic form of "patriotic correctness" that is similarly intolerant of any criticism or opposition. The idea is that while America remains a country of free speech, true patriots know that this is not the time to exercise it.

3. Umoja (unity), Kujichagulia (self-determination), Ujima (collective work and responsibility), Ujamaa (cooperative economics), Nia (puropse), Kuumba (creativity), and Imani (faith).

6

Black Power and Puerto Rican Ethno-Nationalism in the United States, 1966–1972

Jeffrey O. G. Ogbar

INTRODUCTION: POWER *A LA GENTE*

In this chapter I continue the discussion of black nationalism as a form of resistance to white racism within the United States. I focus on the struggles of Puerto Ricans in the United States during the period of the Civil Rights movement and the extent to which Black Power politics served to define and inform the ethno-national identity of the former. For in the same way that Black Power impacted certain political movements in the Caribbean, it also had a decided influence on the confusingly positioned Puerto Rican citizens in the United States. Given the complex, subjective dimensions of racial identification, most Puerto Ricans are considered "white" in Puerto Rico. But once in the United States, where the "law of hypodescent" (see chapter 1) obtains, and which specifies that "one drop of black blood" renders one black, these same individuals suffer a bewildering decline in racial status. Thus, during the late 1960s and early 1970s, many Puerto Rican immigrants and their second-generation offspring came to embrace a politicized ethno-national identity that was tempered in the fires of civil rights and Black Power. And unlike the more conservative black nationalists (timid and separatist) discussed in chapter 5, Puerto Rican nationalists embraced the radicalism of the Black Panthers and other progressive groups that abounded at the time and played an important part in defining the class-race debate of the day.

Though by no means reflecting the majority opinions of their generation, American baby boomer activists of the late 1960s and early 1970s were the central agents of militant discourse of their time. They were raised in an era of new media with immediate national and international dimensions that connected them to the struggles of young people fighting against oppression from California and Mississippi to Mexico, Peru, and South Africa. African American boomers, in particular, were inspirational to young activists worldwide. Cold war rhetoric coupled with sophisticated technological and media apparatus highlighted the black freedom movement in the United States to a global audience. As discussed in chapter 5, the American Black Power movement raised the bar of black resistance and significantly influenced the symbolism, rhetoric, and tactics of radical activism of the New Left in the late 1960s. More specifically, the Black Panther Party had some of the most visible influences on the radical activist struggles of Latinos, Asians, and Native Americans, giving rise to a visible movement of radical ethnic nationalism. Though the earliest Black Panther alliances emerged among Chicanos in California (as well as whites and Asians), none had as intimate ties with the Black Panther Party or the Black Power movement as the largely Puerto Rican *Young Lords.*

Beyond the cultural and psychological effects that radical ethnic nationalism introduced to the New Left of the late 1960s and early 1970s, the movement was truly a unique phenomenon. There are no major examples of ethnic nationalist struggles that have established alliances, as had young radicals of the Black Power era. African American, white, Puerto Rican, Chicano, Asian, and Native American radicals merged ethnic nationalist rhetoric with a struggle that emphasized class conflict and interracial coalitions. When the Black Panther Party coined the slogan *all power to the people*, it was attempting to broaden the call for Black Power by transcending race. Unique among political movements anywhere, this was an example of a radicalism that adapted to the highly racialized climate of the United States, while adhering to the fundamental principles of leftist theories that generally criticized nationalism as bourgeois efforts to subvert true radicalism (see chapter 1).

At the center of all this was the Black Power movement that provided the earliest examples of cultural nationalism and political organization around ethnic nationalist causes. More specifically, the Black Panther Party served as a paradigm of radical ethnic nationalism and a vanguard party for the revolutionary nationalist movement. The Panthers provided an appeal that was unprecedented in the annals of radical struggle, and had a determining influence on the radicalization of Puerto Rican youth in the United States. The Young Lords, for example, a violent Puerto Rican street gang in the 1960s, came under the influence of the Panthers, abandoned its violent ways, and reorganized itself politically as the Young Lords Party (YLP). Eschewing racist politics, the YLP was an inclusive organization that was increasingly radicalized and openly embraced class struggle as the vehicle for liberation within America. By the early 1970s the YLP changed its name to the Puerto Rican Revolutionary Workers Organization (PRRWO) but soon fell victim to internal factionalism and the politics of repression that is characteristic of the wider society.

PUERTO RICAN NATIONALISM

The approach to nationalism that will be employed in this chapter is consistent with that defined by Anton L. Allahar (see chapter 1). It speaks to nationalism as (1) a movement for independence or sovereignty over a territorial space and (2) a sentiment of ethnic distinctiveness and commonality that informs the movement in question. The sentiment is best expressed as a yearning for recognition or respect of minority ethnic rights, in this case Puerto Ricans in the United States. Given the history of Spanish colonialism and American neocolonialism in Puerto Rico, and the fact that the United States today is arguably the most racially fractured country in the world, many Puerto Ricans have long struggled on two fronts. The first has been directed at securing the political independence of their homeland, while the second focuses on those Puerto Ricans who live in the United States and must also struggle for ethno-national recognition and social justice.

The widespread racialization of public consciousness in American society has made for a complex challenge to independence-minded Puerto Ricans. For part of the struggle for ethnic self-determination is bedeviled by the so-called race question. Puerto Ricans come is all colors (races), and while on the island the lighter skinned ones enjoy the many privileges that come with their color, their reception in America is not unproblematic. For in a social economy where color is currency and where socioeconomic opportunities are color-coded, even the lighter skinned are stigmatized in America by their "mixed" racial appearance and their obvious language and accent differences.[1]

Puerto Rican nationalism is rooted in the late nineteenth century, when Puerto Ricans joined with Cubans in the common fight against Spanish imperialism. The United States won Puerto Rico, which had been a colony of Spain for four hundred years, after the former's defeat of Spain in the Spanish-Cuban-American War of 1898. Unlike the other possessions procured in the war, such as Cuba and the Philippines, Puerto Rico (and Guam) never received independence from the United States. Puerto Rican nationalism would ebb and flow between 1900 and the 1950s, during which time the Nationalist Party was the major expression of this nationalism. In 1930 Don Pedro Albizu Campos was elected president of the Nationalist Party of Puerto Rico, which was considered a terrorist organization by the federal authorities after a series of violent confrontations with colonial authorities. The Nationalist Party was soon repressed, Albizu was imprisoned from 1936 to 1948, and following the nationalist uprising in October 1950, Albizu was sentenced to a further seventy-two years in prison (though he was released in 1965 several weeks before he died).

The 1950 uprising fomented extensive political repression of Puerto Ricans on the island and on the mainland. The 1954 shooting of five members of the U.S. Congress by Puerto Rican nationalists only hardened this repression. Leftist radicalism among Puerto Ricans in the United States was limited mostly to white organizations, such as the Socialist Workers Party or the Communist Party USA from the late 1950s into the 1960s. These organizations addressed the question of Puerto Rican sovereignty as part of a general denunciation of imperialism, and despite increased marginalization, Puerto Rican nationalist organizations did not completely disappear.

Although the Puerto Rican Independence Movement (MPI), founded in 1959, and its New York City offshoot, the Vito Marcantonio Mission, advocated radical politics, they were chiefly concerned with Puerto Rican independence and island issues. The same can be said of the Puerto Rican Independence Party (PIP). Island-born Puerto Ricans who tended to be middle class and older than twenty-five years of age chiefly ran these organizations, but it was not until the late 1960s that Puerto Rican radical activism would develop around both mainland and island issues, while also generating a broader class appeal. Several factors precipitated the development of popular grassroots Puerto Rican nationalism, including larger anti-imperialist struggles, cold war politics, and the civil rights movement in the United States. The new Puerto Rican nationalism of the late 1960s developed simultaneously among baby boomers in two different cities, converging and giving rise to the most celebrated Puerto Rican organization of the era, the Young Lords.

By the 1940s, as a result of labor scouts who recruited for low-skilled and low-waged manufacturing and agricultural positions, large communities of Puerto Ricans were established in New York City and a few other cities (Grosfoguel and Georas 1996:193–94). New York had been a point of entry for many European newcomers who also struggled to find their footing upon arrival. Puerto Ricans, however, experienced the limitations of not only being a largely unskilled immigrant group but of not being white. White supremacy allowed economic mobility, social intercourse, and political opportunities for Jews, Irish, Italians, and other whites while simultaneously denying Puerto Ricans the same opportunities. Largely a mixture of Spanish, African, and native peoples, Puerto Ricans found discrimination pervasive, and although they were officially recognized as "white" by the federal government, de facto discrimination pervaded employment patterns as early as the 1920s.

By 1929 Puerto Ricans and African Americans earned between $8 and $13 per week while Jewish and Italian Americans earned between $26 and $44 a week, a difference of up to 500 percent in weekly wages (Ibid.:194). Like other economically marginalized groups, poor Puerto Ricans soon experienced the pathologies that typically develop in circumstances of concentrated urban poverty, material deprivation, and oppression. By 1968 Puerto Rican high school dropout rates were higher than that of African Americans,

Irish, Italians, or any other major ethnic group in New York City, and by 1970 the median family income of Puerto Ricans was lower than whites and blacks. In fact, the gap had widened between Puerto Ricans and African Americans since 1960 (Torres 1995:63). Unemployment and underemployment, police brutality, and gangs provided a backdrop to Spanish Harlem, where the first radical Puerto Rican organizations emerged.

PUERTO RICAN NATIONALISM AND BLACK NATIONALISM

In reaction to the unfavorable conditions in which Puerto Ricans lived, some Puerto Rican activists initially found space in established organizations such as the Communist Party, which had Puerto Rican cells. Others joined the efforts of civil rights organizations like the Student Nonviolent Coordinating Committee (SNCC) or the Congress of Racial Equality (CORE) in the early and middle 1960s (Serrano 1998:124–25; Martell 1998:175). But as the Black Power movement took root, the charisma of black nationalist leaders resonated among other people of color as no radicalism had heretofore. Some Puerto Ricans, particularly those who were darker skinned, identified as black, since most Americans viewed them as such. As Pablo "Yoruba" Guzmán once explained, "Before people called me a spic, they called me a nigger" (Young Lords Party and Abramson 1971:73). Small numbers of Puerto Ricans joined the largely insular, though respected, Nation of Islam (NOI). The NOI had long embraced all people of color as "black," though the message had a special meaning for African Americans.

Latinos and Asians had been members of the organization or attended the many mosques across the country. Temple #7 in Harlem was the Nation's largest mosque and was under the leadership of Malcolm X in the early 1960s. Thousands of Harlemites—African American and Puerto Rican—listened as Malcolm discussed the black freedom struggle in a global context and inveighed against white supremacy. Malcolm stressed the common humanity and common enemy of the Congolese, Algerians, Cubans, and the American "so-called Negro." Post-NOI Malcolm X transcended the confines of his earlier narrow definition of struggle, which did not see whites as potential allies. After his assassination in 1965 he became an iconic figure of revolutionary thought and revered by the American Left. By 1968 the Black Panther Party (one of many that claimed to be Malcolm's heirs) had established branches in New York and expanded arenas of leftist discourse and praxis.

Through a media savvy leadership, the Panthers spread rapidly in 1968, bolstered by a "Free Huey" movement that highlighted the efforts of black militants to challenge police terror while also offering a powerful, broader gesture of defiance to white supremacy, capitalism, and imperialism. Though it was particularly oriented toward the exigencies in the African American community, the Party was not an exclusively African American organization, for Asian Americans and Latinos had been active in the organization from the beginning.[2] And as Black Panthers spread, some Puerto Ricans gravitated to its discourse and politics. Pablo Guzmán notes that "at first the only model [of revolutionary nationalism] we had to go on in this country was the Black Panther Party. Besides that, we were all a bunch of readers" (Ibid.:74). Several Puerto Ricans became active in the New York chapter of the Panther Party from the earliest days. In fact, there were at least two members of the famous Panther 21 case of 1969, Raymond Quiñones and Albert Nieves, who were Puerto Rican.[3] Despite the clear participation of Puerto Ricans in leftist activities by 1969, with the exception of Puerto Rican college-based groups, there was no organization that simultaneously focused on Puerto Rican radical ethnic nationalism, whether on the island or on the mainland. The only exceptions were Puerto Rican college-based groups.

African American student activism and the Black Student Union (BSU) movement had inspired Puerto Ricans by the mid-1960s and although SNCC was most active in the South, it had established northern bases by 1962. Largely concerned with broader off-campus issues, small African American student groups began to address campus concerns when James Garrett and others established the first BSU in 1966 at San Francisco State College. BSUs (or their campus proximates) quickly spread across the country and attracted several Puerto Rican students. The militancy and activist program of these organizations were early models for Puerto Rican students. At City College in New York, for example, Iris Morales joined ONYX, an African American group, and studied Malcolm X as well as other black icons. Years before Morales would become a prominent member of the Young Lords, she was involved with SNCC and the NAACP. Her involvement with ONYX was a reflection of her political trajectory and affinity with the black freedom movement. At base, however, she was a radical Puerto Rican activist and nationalist.

When more Puerto Rican students arrived on campus, Morales helped form City College's first Puerto Rican organization, Puerto Ricans in Student Activities (PRISA). In 1968 PRISA members Eduardo "Pancho" Cruz, Tom Soto, Henry Arce, and others established alliances with ONYX and other black groups and by spring 1969 launched an ambitious effort in collaboration with other city college campuses for a citywide strike. The Black and Puerto Rican Student Community (BPRSC) formed the strike leadership, which was almost identical to the Third World Liberation Front of the California Bay Area, and which began with activities initiated by black students for a black studies department, more black faculty, and increased black students enrollments. Demanding a broader set of changes, including open admission for Puerto Rican and black students, the CCNY insurgents occupied buildings, renaming them after famous black and Latino leaders. That fall

Puerto Rican students formed the Puerto Rican Student Union (PRSU), which combined the campus-based concerns of PRISA and BPRSC with those of the larger Puerto Rican community in the mainland and in Puerto Rico. This development occurred after the arrival of Young Lords into NYC (Morales 1998:213–14; Serrano 1998:124–25). By the end of the 1969 spring semester, Puerto Rican nationalists in New York were eager to expand their scope of struggle.

NATIONALISM FROM THE STREETS

A different type of bottom-up politicization was developing among Puerto Ricans in the country's second largest city. Owing to the deterioration of inner-city conditions, Chicago, like New York and other major U.S. cities, suffered from a pervasive and destructive gang problem. And while gangs were generally composed along racial and ethnic lines, they were most likely to engage in criminal behavior against people of the same ethnicity. At the same time, gang rivalry was also known to transcend ethnic lines (Short and Strodtbeck 1974; Downes 1966; Vigil 1988). The politically charged climate of the late 1960s, the ubiquitous influence of the Black Power movement, and the nature of urban rebellions forced many black gang members to reconsider their activities. Many abandoned gang life and joined the Nation of Islam, the Black Panther Party, or any of the scores of largely local nationalist and Black Power organizations in cities across the country. For Puerto Ricans, the process of politicization was similar. But unlike any major Black Power organization in the country, the leading Puerto Rican radical organization of the era would have its roots in gang culture.

Puerto Ricans migrated to Chicago in substantial numbers after World War II. Lured by the new Commonwealth Office in Puerto Rico and the Point Four Program,[4] many first arrived in New York, but disaffected with conditions there moved to Chicago to work in manufacturing jobs and as migrant farm laborers. Initially, because African Americans readily fit the bill as convenient scapegoats, whites did not racialize Puerto Ricans as a distinct and organic "Other." As noted above, this was generally congruent with how most Puerto Ricans saw themselves. In fact, in 1950 79.7 percent of Puerto Ricans on the island and 92 percent of those on the mainland were classified as white on the U.S. Census.

In 1960 a full 96 percent of Puerto Ricans in the United States were classified as white (Duany 2002:248, 255). This was a result of complex policies rooted in U.S. colonial policies with the island. In the early twentieth century some government agents, as well as scholars, assuaged white American racial anxiety of absorbing a "colored" population by depicting Puerto Rico as the "whitest of the Antilles" (Ibid.:246–47). Additionally, the categorization reflected Puerto Ricans' own sense of identity, which rejected the American notion of white "purity" and hypodescent (the "one-drop rule") and simultaneously stigmatized blackness. But while the federal government recognized Puerto Ricans as whites "unless they were definitely Negro, Indian, or some other race," colloquial policy was a different matter (Ibid.:253). As mentioned earlier, unlike Puerto Ricans in New York who were racialized early and relegated to the social, political, and economic margins reserved for people of color in a white supremacist country, Chicago was a somewhat different story.

By 1960 because there had not yet been an identifiable geographically contiguous Puerto Rican community in New York, Puerto Ricans were commonly found in white areas. However, unlike those in New York, the Puerto Rican migrants to Chicago did not have a particularly close geographic relationship with African Americans. Moreover, as the most black-white residentially segregated city in the United States, Chicago provided not only significant social intercourse between whites and Puerto Ricans, it circumscribed contact with African Americans and helped extend the virulently anti-black sentiment common among white Chicagoans. Much to the dismay of many Puerto Ricans, however, they became non-white in the popular consciousness of white Americans as their numbers increased. Uptown, Humboldt Park, and Lincoln Park emerged as communities with high concentrations of Puerto Ricans on the city's white Northside.

In these areas, clashes between white gangs and Puerto Rican youth gave rise to Puerto Rican gangs as well as an inchoate political and racial/ethnic consciousness. Bouts with job and housing discrimination as well as police brutality exploded on June 12, 1966. For four days urban unrest shook Division Street in Lincoln Park and Uptown. Though Puerto Rican leadership complained of discrimination, most were loathe to be lumped together with African Americans, largely seen as more marginalized and despised than they. In fact, when Martin Luther King, Jr., offered to assist in negotiations between the community and the city, Puerto Rican leaders turned down his offer.[5] Despite the relatively tepid leadership of the Spanish Action Committee, largely invested in being recognized as a variant of European [white] ethnicity, the Black Power movement took root and Puerto Rican street youth proved central to deconstructing traditional notions of community, racial, and ethnic identity. In this process, no group was as important as the Young Lords.

ETHNIC NATIONALISM GANGLAND STYLE

Formed in 1959 by seven Chicago Puerto Rican youth, the Young Lords aimed to defend themselves against attacks from surrounding gangs. Largely engaged in battles with Italians, "Billigans" (Appalachian whites), and other Latinos, the Lords continued to grow into the early 1960s when José "Cha Cha" Jiménez was elected chairman of the organization. The Division Street Unrest as well as the spread of Black Power forced Young Lords leaders to reevaluate their organization by the late 1960s. A major catalyst for this politicization was the transformation among African American gangs in the city.[6]

In 1966 members from various black nationalist organizations fanned across the Southside and Westside to meet with and court various street gangs, such as the Stomp Lords, Comanches, Imperial Chaplins, and Black Cobras. Members of the Deacons for Defense, the Revolutionary Action Movement, SNCC, the Nation of Islam, and others directed gangs to cease attacks on black people and prepare to be agents for black people's liberation. One of the early manifestations of the influence of Black Power on street youth was the defiance to white racist attacks in the city. In the early 1960s public buses en route to the Southside's white Rainbow Beach were filled with whites who hurled cigarettes, bottles, batteries, and spit at black pedestrians. Being called "nigger" was the least of worries for black people caught in racists' path. By 1966 black gangs such as the Stomp Lords and Black Stone Rangers boarded the buses and attacked white assailants. Other black youth threw firecrackers and rocks into bus windows. Trips to Rainbow Beach on the public bus proved dangerous for many racists, and the attacks on pedestrians became very infrequent.[7]

BLACK CIVIC NATIONALISM

One gangster explained that "the militants came in and say [*sic*] why be a gangbanger and kill each other when you can kill the honkey and we began to see that the enemy was not black." The new militancy inherently rejected fear of white power, and black youth were the first to react. Elzy, a twenty-year-old Vice Lord, stated, "We were scared of the honkies but this awareness thing has kicked all that bullshit aside" (Dawley 1973:113; 118–19). By 1967 the three largest gangs, the Vice Lords, Black Stone Rangers, and the Gangster Disciples, established the LSD (Lords, Stones, and Disciples) peace treaty and began investing in civic pride and stressed self-owned commercial endeavors, including cafés, pool halls, and even a bookstore. Cha Cha Jiménez, who served a year in prison and was exposed to black nationalism, insisted that the Young Lords should similarly engage in constructive activities aimed at building community and a strong civic sense (Ibid.:111–15).[8]

In 1967 Young Lords opened a café, Uptight #2, where they talked about the general political and cultural upheaval in the country, as well as more mundane topics. Lords established service programs including a community summer picnic, a drug education program, and a Christmas giveaway of food and toys for impoverished people in the Puerto Rican community. The Lords even began dialogue with the largest street gang in the country, the notorious Black Stone Rangers, and co-sponsored a "Month of Soul Dances" with them.[9] While these efforts impressed many liberals, the Illinois deputy chairman of the Black Panther Party, Fred Hampton, and the local Panthers hoped to make the Lords into revolutionaries. In December 1968 Fred Hampton initiated a meeting with Jiménez.

REVOLUTIONARY NATIONALISM: CLASS NOT RACE

Unlike typical Black Power advocates, the Panthers considered effective political struggle to be intrinsically related to class and race simultaneously. Rejecting the rigid nationalism of the Nation of Islam or various cultural nationalists, the Panthers were particularly sensitive to how class exploitation and oppression can vigorously occur in all-black contexts. They also recognized the potential for white allies. More specific, the Panthers rejected the traditional Marxist disregard for the lumpenproletariat (Allahar 2003). In fact, they considered the lumpen the vanguard class of the revolution. In accordance with the Party's theories of class, the Panthers viewed the politicization of street gangs (lumpen) as an essential process in the political transformation of the country's "internal colonies." In their estimation, the urban rebellions that often included the poorest and most maligned elements in the community were the precursor to revolution.

The lumpenproletariat had guns and were not afraid to use them. Unfortunately, as the Panthers explained, they were not yet politically sophisticated enough to aim in the direction of the "pig power structure" more frequently. These rebellions, insisted Party leader Huey Newton, were "sporadic, short-lived, and costly in violence against the people." The task of the Panthers was clear: "The Vanguard Party must provide leadership for the people. It must teach correct strategic methods of prolonged resistance through literature and activities. If the activities of the Party are respected by the people, the people will follow the example" (1967:11). To the Panthers, the efforts of the Lords and the Rangers had been indicative of the political transformation that would make inadvertent agents of oppression into agents of liberation. Thus, the Lords, Rangers, and other street gangs could be made into harbingers of freedom, justice, and power for the people.

As Hampton began dialogue with Jiménez he also met with Jeff Fort, the leader of the Black Stone Rangers, who was less warm to the idea of revolution and radical politics than had been Jiménez. Impressed with the bold and brash militancy that characterized the Panthers, Jiménez envisioned a Puerto Rican revolutionary organization to realize liberation for Puerto Ricans on the island and in the mainland. Lords began to realize that they had been acting more like social workers by only addressing the symptoms and not the cause of social illness. "Giving gifts wasn't going to help their people," Jiménez said of the Lords. "They had to deal with the system that was messing them over."[10] Additionally, Jiménez adopted a new critique of the "empowerment" politics of grassroots capitalism. Gangs like the Vice Lords and Disciples ventured into partnerships with white businessmen, procuring resources from such stalwarts of capitalism and white power as the Rockefeller Foundation and Chicago millionaire W. Clement Stone.

Though these ventures employed many poor youth, the Panthers and Lords viewed them as insidious attempts to undermine revolutionary consciousness through capitalist cooption. For Jiménez, liberation of the Puerto Rican nation was inextricably tied to the demise of capitalism, not capitalism's accommodation of a Puerto Rican elite or bourgeoisie.

By mid-1968 Lords initiated peace treaties with virtually all of their former enemies and advised them to cease the fighting against each other but address rage "against the capitalist institutions that are oppressing us." The Latin Kings, the city's largest Latino gang, began to politically organize as well, even opening a breakfast program for children. By May 1969, the Lords had officially joined a pact with the Panthers and the Young Patriots, a gang of poor white youth with Southern roots.[11]

In this new "Rainbow Coalition," the Lords and Patriots dutifully modeled themselves after the Black Panther Party, believed to be the revolutionary vanguard. The Chairman of the Lords explained that "as we read and study other organizations . . . we see and we recognize the Black Panther Party as a revolutionary vanguard. And we feel that as revolutionaries we should follow the vanguard party."[12] In their respective communities, the Lords and Patriots held political education classes, free breakfast programs for poor children, and monitored police activities in an attempt to end police brutality. They created an organizational structure that reflected Panther influence, which included Ministers of Information, Defense, Education, and a Central Committee with field marshals. The Patriots developed an 11-Point Program and Platform that borrowed heavily from the Panthers, as did the Lords' 13-Point Program and Platform.[13] All three organizations sponsored events together, providing joint speakers and joint security.

By mid-1969, the Young Patriots and Young Lords were becoming nationally known through their Rainbow Coalition, which was featured in articles in the *Black Panther* and *Guardian* newspapers and other alternative presses. Also that year, the Coalition sent representatives to the annual convention of the Students for a Democratic Society (SDS), where José Martínez, an SDS member from Florida, met with Young Lord founders and was granted permission to start a branch in New York where Puerto Rican nationalism was still growing (Guzmán 1998:156). Amid the militant student protests, some students at New York's City College formed the Sociedad de

Albizu Campos (SAC) to bring together the militancy of college radicals with that of *El Barrio* in early 1969. Named after the Puerto Rican nationalist Pedro Albizu Campos who, as "El Maestro," inspired Puerto Ricans with calls for independence and national pride, SAC reflected the spirit of the *independentistas*. There were, however, other concerns about the plight of Puerto Ricans in the mainland.

In a struggle to bridge the chasm between unorganized street militancy and that of the college campus, community-based activists Pablo "Yoruba" Guzmán and David Pérez joined SAC and became the links to *El Barrio* that the organization desired. Yoruba, who was named after a major ethnic group in Nigeria, had a strong affinity to Africa, as well as Puerto Rico. Pérez, who was born in Puerto Rico and raised in Chicago, had involved himself in radical politics before moving to New York. Simultaneously, SAC members were reading the *Black Panther* newspaper regularly and learned of the Rainbow Coalition established by Fred Hampton. After merging with other local Puerto Rican activist organizations, SAC met with Martínez and on July 26, 1969, a coalition was formed in New York that became the New York State Chapter of the Young Lords Organization (YLO).[14]

GRASSROOTS PUERTO RICAN CIVIC NATIONALISM

Within weeks, the Lords captured headlines. In agreement with the Panther dictum to serve the people by meeting the people's basic needs, Lords asked local residents what they wanted. When informed that they wanted cleaner streets, the Lords swept streets in Spanish Harlem and put trash in piles in the middle of the street, demanding that the city pay more attention to the barrio. The images of radicals working for the people impressed many who eagerly joined the fledgling organization.[15] Lords organized against police brutality, slum housing, and poor education, and occupied a Methodist church on 111th and Lexington Avenue in December 1969, declaring it the "People's Church." For ten days the Lords held off police as the church became a center for free breakfast, clothes, health care, political education, and cultural events.

In an era of incredible contest over the "law and order" conservatism of President Nixon's "silent majority" and the rising tide of baby boomer leftist activism, events like the occupation were sensational news. The media attention was crucial in popularizing the organization to millions. From New York the YLO spread to several cities along the east coast, including Philadelphia, Newark, and Bridgeport, Connecticut. Several months later Young Lords activities extended into the Lincoln Hospital, where a group of one hundred men and women took it over on July 17, 1970, to protest inadequate health care for the poor and neglect from the city government. Though expelled by the police, the act brought attention to insufficient medical care in poor communities. The mayor of New York, John Lindsay, promised community activists that the city would build a new hospital on East 149th street to replace the dilapidated Lincoln. The new hospital opened in 1976 (Morales 1998:213–14; Guzmán 1998:159–60; Young Lords Party and Abramson 1971:69–70).[16]

Adherents of Puerto Rican independence and revolutionary nationalists, the Lords denounced the cardinal "three evils" of capitalism, racism, and imperialism. They sponsored free breakfast, drug detoxification, and garbage clean-up programs in chapters in several states. They brought attention to police brutality, worked closely with students on college and high school campuses, and even found success organizing in prisons. During the Attica Prison uprising in September 1971, insurgents issued a list of more than twenty demands to prison officials that included a request for the presence of the Young Lords and the Black Panther Party to serve as observers and advisors. In many cities Lords worked in alliances with Black Power advocates and helped realize more community control of police, political reform, and political mobilization for poor and working-class people. The Young Lords were able to work with organizations that were openly hostile to the Black Panthers, despite their official alliance with the Party. In the early 1970s the Young Lords in Newark, New Jersey, established an alliance with the Committee for a Unified Newark, led by Amiri Baraka, a leading cultural nationalist and ally of Maulana Karenga (Woodard 1999:138–40).[17]

For the Young Lords and other revolutionary nationalist organizations, various communities of color in the United States provided cheap labor and resources for capitalists, who, in people of color, found cheap, expendable labor that provided for increased quality of life for whites by enriching the white middle class considerably. Increased numbers of people of color in urban areas allowed working-class whites to assume higher socioeconomic status. But since racism was very real, working-class whites, often beholden to white supremacy, out of ignorance and cultural tradition, were intolerant of considering the affinities that they shared with working-class people of color. The Young Patriots hoped to demonstrate, however, that working-class and poor whites could be mobilized and, indeed, follow a revolutionary program led by a black organization. Preacher Man, field secretary for the Young Patriots, explained that many poor whites in Chicago's Uptown felt "forgotten" by the radical discourse of the New Left "until we met the Illinois chapter of the Black Panther Party."[18] But while white groups like the Patriots, Rising Up Angry, and White Panther Party modeled themselves after the Black Panther Party, the Panthers and Black Power had a special resonance for radicals of color.

Class exploitation was a major concern for leftists; however, the highly racialized climate of the United States made interracial political organization difficult, particularly with poor and working-class whites, considered by

many to be a more overt and crude group of racists than the middle and upper classes. Moreover, the U.S. tradition of class exploitation was significantly bolstered by white supremacy, which had profound political ramifications. Apart from the psychological comfort of knowing that one is not at
the bottom of the social ladder, poor whites were keenly aware that the capitalist structure of the society did not allow them to derive much by way of
material benefits, and this made them more potentially susceptible to a class
understanding of their position (Roediger 1991; Ignatiev 1995). People of
color who were involved in leftist liberation movements of the era were
committed to liberate themselves along class and cultural lines simultaneously. For Puerto Ricans the trappings of white supremacy were deep
rooted, despite the myth of racial tolerance on the island. From folk songs,
sayings such as *pelo malo* ("bad hair") for kinky hair, to the concept of *mejo-
rar la raza* ("bettering the race") by whitening, white supremacy was ubiquitous, though different from its U.S. variant. The Puerto Rican color hierarchy was fundamentally porous and allowed darker Puerto Ricans considered
"negros" or "mulattos" to "ascend" to whiteness with economic success. But
the ramifications of being dark were nonetheless insidious and widespread
(Santiago-Valles 1996:46).[19]

RACE, NATIONALISM, AND IDENTITY

Puerto Rican baby boomers in the United States began critically to adjust
their own notions of ethnicity, race, and identity. They increasingly challenged traditional notions of race, and explicitly addressed their own history
of racism. These shifts were a result of the peculiar American racial landscape and a history of codified white supremacy that chiefly rested on a
white/black binary. Despite the special attention given African Americans in
their fight against white supremacy, Puerto Ricans could not deny their own
depressed circumstances and the effects of racism with which they were
confronted. They were also exposed to the rhetoric of the Black Power
movement, which stressed the need to resist the cultural and psychological
entrapments of whiteness. Black Power advocates not only celebrated black
peoples' history and beauty, but many also openly vilified whites, calling
them "honkies," "crackers," "ofays," and "devils." Some publicly joked about
the way whites smelled, danced, and lacked hygiene or morality.

Though not monolithic in their attention to whites, Black Power proponents depedestalized whiteness in ways not seen in the civil rights movement.
Generations of self-hate and internalization of white supremacy were being
addressed in what many would consider a collective and profound moment
of group catharsis. Young Puerto Ricans took notice. They, too, had to affirm
themselves in ways not seen heretofore, while addressing the complicated

racial politics of their time. Puerto Rican radical ethnic nationalists initiated systematic efforts to make the psychic break from whiteness (as it was popularly understood in the United States). Moreover, there was a conspicuous celebration of Puerto Rican culture and identity that was "third world," and, in effect, not white. This was a fundamental departure from the Puerto Rican nationalism and consciousness of earlier leaders and movements.

As the first Puerto Rican radical ethnic nationalist group with a national appeal, the Young Lords denounced racism while simultaneously calling for greater emphasis on their African and Taíno histories, which had been ignored by Spanish and American imperialists. Juán González, minister of information for the Young Lords, explained the history of Puerto Rico, where the earliest census records show that blacks and Indians comprised the majority while "whites were always the smallest part of the population" (Young Lords Party and Abramson 1971:60). This message was intended to offer a somewhat cultural nationalist challenge to how Puerto Ricans viewed themselves, while adhering to the fundamental tenets of revolutionary nationalism.

Despite the fact that more than 90 percent of Puerto Ricans on the mainland classified themselves as white at this time, Young Lords made common references to whites and Puerto Ricans as separate and distinct. Cha Cha Jiménez and other Lords were careful to refer to the range of colors among Puerto Ricans as an instructive tool to inveigh against race-only discourse, while celebrating an identity that was not white. Jiménez, for example, would not make reference to the lightest Puerto Ricans as "white," but simply "light-skinned." In discussing the importance of class struggle he stated that "we relate to the class struggle because there's Puerto Ricans that are real black, then there's Puerto Ricans that are light-skinned like myself." Though he would refer to Puerto Ricans as "black," "red," and "yellow," the lightest were "light-skinned." He also insisted that it was inefficacious to insist on more "Puerto Rican" police to replace "white" police, when the fundamental job of the police (of any ethnicity or race) was to operate as "bodyguards for the capitalists."[20] Here, Jiménez implies that unlike Poles, Italians, or Irish in Chicago, Puerto Ricans as a group are distinct from European (read as "white") ethnic groups. He acknowledges that the ramifications of race are real, yet race is itself a social construct that, with its slippery contours, includes yet rejects Puerto Ricans as "others" in American racial politics.

It must be noted here that though virtually all Puerto Ricans in the United States were classified as "white" in 1970, many of them, particularly in large contiguous Puerto Rican communities on the East Coast, saw themselves as distinct from white Americans in a colloquial sense. Despite the history of prestige that many Puerto Ricans may have associated with being considered white, there is ample evidence that many, if not most, saw themselves as more than just a variant of whiteness. On the census, for example, there was no option for "Hispanic" until 1980. Once the choice was given, the percentage of Puerto Ricans who reported being white dropped from 92.9 in 1970 to 48.3 (Duany 2002:253–57).

Young Lords and other Puerto Rican militants unequivocally celebrated their Puerto Rican identity with great zeal. And though they were nationalists, they were careful to transcend the debilitating xenophobia that often typifies nationalist movements. Alliances with other people of color as well as whites were central to the YLO. Even in the context of showcasing Puerto Rican culture and history, Lords tended to be broad. In reference to the creation of a Puerto Rican cultural center, Cha Cha Jiménez noted that the center must "include some black culture, cause we got some blacks; we want to include some Chicano culture too, cause we want to include all Latins. We want to invite the people from the white community. We'll educate them." Unable to embrace a narrow form of nationalism, the Chairman of the YLO explained that "we feel that we are revolutionaries and revolutionaries have no race."[21]

What is particularly interesting about the formation and ethnic/national emphasis of the Young Lords is that the organization was never homogenous. Though mostly Puerto Rican, the Lords had Chicano members from its earliest years as a street gang, and when it evolved into a radical ethnic nationalist organization, many non–Puerto Ricans adopted its special attention to Puerto Rican independence. In fact, Omar López, a Chicano member, coined the Lords's slogan "*Tengo Puerto Rico en mi Corazón*" ("I have Puerto Rico in my heart") (Guzmán 1998:157). On the East Coast the Young Lords had members who were Cuban, Dominican, Panamanian, and Colombian. An estimated 25 percent of the Young Lords membership was African American. Despite the explicit emphasis on Puerto Rican politics and welfare, the organization was broad enough to include serious support for "power to all oppressed people," which included all "Third World people." Some non–Puerto Ricans in the organization held prominent positions, including Denise Oliver, an African American who was the first woman on the Central Committee and the Minister of Economic Development, 1970–1971 (Rivera 1996:208; Whalen 1998:121; Morales 1998:215).

Although Puerto Rican identity reflected a protean quality, it was not entirely unique in its mutability. Chicanos were similarly shifting identities and engaged in their own civil rights movement in this time. And the Young Lords were not the only radical ethnic nationalist group with a heterogeneous membership. But as much as the Young Lords helped rearticulate ethnic identity, they were also addressing deep-seated psychological issues related to hegemony and resistance and Puerto Ricans. On several occasions, Young Lords leaders indicated that they were rejecting notions of Puerto Rican passivity. Cha Cha Jiménez was careful to anchor YLO radicalism in a tradition of Puerto Rican struggle, not a departure from obsequiousness. "People consider Puerto Ricans as passive . . . but as recently as 1950 there was a revolution in Puerto Rico. Lots of revolutionaries have come out of Puerto Rico." Despite the "Uncle Toms" that oppress the people of Puerto Rico, Puerto Ricans are not unfamiliar with resistance, he explained.[22]

Notwithstanding Jiménez's insistence that Puerto Rican radicalism was not entirely aberrant, many Puerto Ricans found the Lords to be truly unique. According to Pablo Guzmán, "Puerto Ricans had been psyched into believing this myth about being docile," and "a lot of Puerto Ricans really thought that the man in blue was the baddest thing going." Guzman was shocked to first learn about the militancy of the Lords in the Black Panther newspaper:

> Jiménez was talking about revolution and socialism and the liberation of Puerto Rico and the right to self-determination and all this stuff that I ain't *never* heard a spic say. I mean, I hadn't never heard no Puerto Rican talking this—just black people were talking this way, you know. And I said, "damn! Check this out." That's what really got United States started. (quoted in The Young Lord Party 1971:75)

After numerous public demonstrations of courage, militancy, and discipline, Young Lords, according to Guzmán, were obvious models of revolutionary strength to the people in *El Barrio*. There were palpable changes in the self-awareness among Puerto Rican youth, as well as the police who were assigned the task of controlling them. "Before the Young Lords Party began people used to walk with their heads down . . . and the pigs would walk through the colonies, man, like they owned the block. They'd come in here with no kind of respect in their eyes." But after revolutionary examples, the people have been psychologically empowered, Lords claimed. They were shedding the fear that Frantz Fanon said was crippling to the colonized. Police officers, no longer taking Puerto Rican deference for granted, treaded with greater caution. The people are "fighting toe to toe [with the oppressor] and know [that the people] can take his best." Guzman stated that "the people now have hope" (Ibid.:82).

GENDER AND NATIONALIST DISCOURSE

By 1970 the Young Lords Organization experienced a fissure between its New York chapter and Chicago. The east coast chapters, under the direction of the New York leadership, became the Young Lords Party (YLP) and launched its bilingual paper, *Palante!* in May 1970. *Palante!* reflected the hyper-masculinity of the Puerto Rican nationalist movement, with acclamations that "machismo must be revolutionary." Moreover, the organization relegated women to peripheral roles in leadership, despite a general policy that granted all members access to all organizational activities. As a reaction to the widespread nature of machismo in the YLP, women offered their own challenges as early as 1969 when several female members formed a women's caucus. Caucus members shared stories of confronting the sexism of their comrades on a regular basis, forcing the male leadership to respond. Denise Oliver explains that equality for women is revolutionary. The caucus opposed machismo and the hegemonic hold that it had on men and women.

Not only were the "brothers off the street" unaccustomed to gender equality, many women had been similarly convinced of their sole role as helpers to men. "In Puerto Rican society," Oliver states, "the woman is taught to cater to the . . . demands of her father or husband. She is taught that she is inferior in her own ways" (Ibid.:50–52). The women's caucus issued demands to the Central Committee of the organization for an end to sexual discrimination and full inclusion of women into the leadership of the Lords. The all-male leadership reacted swiftly by promoting Denise Oliver and Gloria Fontañez to the Central Committee. The Lords also adopted a new slogan, "Abajo con Machismo!" (Down with Machismo!), which appeared in the newspaper and other official releases from the YLP, and made changes to the 13-point program of the Party to include denouncing sexism as point number five. "Puerto Rican women," Young Lords stated, "will be neither behind nor in front of their brothers but always alongside them in mutual respect and love."[23]

For many members of the Lords, the effort to denounce sexism was an inevitable step in the movement toward liberation. Indeed, men even formed a male caucus to discuss patriarchy and ways to resist it. Some men who considered themselves open-minded and progressive realized just how ubiquitous sexism was in the society at large. Pablo Guzmán insisted that sexism was "impractical" to revolutionary struggle and welcomed the agenda of women's liberation, though the struggle of "Third World women" was different from that of white women, who "have been put on a pedestal," while white men raped and otherwise exploited women of color (The Young Lords Party and Abramson 1971:46, 54). Others agreed that there were fundamentally different concerns between women of color and white women in the women's liberation movement. Iris Morales, a Central Committee member, noted that "we were critical of that movement for purporting to speak for all women when it represented primarily white, middle-class women. It never successfully addressed the concerns of women of color and poor women" (1998:219).

There is no doubt that many progressive groups and movements at the time, including the Black Power Movement, struggled with patriarchal policies. The movement clearly lionized black men as hyper-macho leaders, fighters, and defenders of black people. The bravado, militant rhetoric, and general character of Black Power were decidedly male-oriented. But while Black Power advocates and Puerto Rican ethnic nationalists used hyperbolic language to express their politics, the movement was not monolithic. The Black Panther Party that was the first major black organization to align itself with the Women's Liberation Movement as well as the Gay Liberation Movement. The Panthers also denounced sexism on several occasions and appointed women to key positions of leadership throughout the country. Minister of Information Eldridge Cleaver explained to men that their freedom couldn't be achieved at the expense of women's liberation. "The women are our half. They're not our weaker half; they're not our stronger half. They are our other half." Several articles written by women Panthers appeared in the *Black Panther* extolling Cleaver's position, while calling recalcitrant male members to task.[24] This progress, however, cannot overlook bouts with sexism fought by Huey Newton and others, even as the Party moved into alliances with feminists. But by 1973 the Chairman of the Party was a woman, Elaine Brown, who effectively led the organization for four years.

The Young Lords similarly accepted the challenge to transcend the narrow confines of patriarchy and made substantive changes to their organization's rhetoric and style. Clearly, the liberation of a "nation" could not tolerate the oppression of its half. There was no particular formula or model for ethnic nationalists to respond to sexism. Latino, white, and black Americans all lived in a patriarchal culture at large that openly endorsed male domination. Mainstream African American and Latino organizations reflected patriarchal traditions without considerable challenges and upheaval. The national leadership of the NAACP and Democratic and Republican parties were more male dominated than either the Panthers or Lords. But it was the passion for total liberation that raised the expectations of struggle for many radical ethnic nationalists. Despite their criticism of the white-oriented women's movement, radical ethnic nationalists were aware that women's liberation was intrinsic to national (in all senses of the term) liberation.

Similar to the process of psychological oppression experienced by African Americans who lived in a virulently antiblack world, Puerto Ricans had to resist the culturally hegemonic forces of white supremacy as well as the de facto policies that discriminated against them. In this rejection of the cultural orthodoxy there emerged the opportunity to openly criticize and change traditional gender roles. Of course, all ethnic nationalist organizations were not as responsive to the challenges of patriarchy as the Panthers and Lords, who were not fully successful in realizing their goals to destroy sexism within their organizations. But the efforts to confront sexism in a very explicit way reflected the ability of the organizations to adapt, grow, and evolve in ways that many so-called mainstream organizations had not. It was their willingness to consider new challenges and ideas that made these radical ethnic nationalist organizations attractive to young people. In addition, it was the new militant ethnic pride that drew many young people into the movement.

CONCLUSION

The politics of the Panthers and Lords reflected a conscious effort to affirm culturally a people who languished under a dehumanizing system of racial oppression, while it also refused to pander to the convenient race-only discourse that attracted many. These proponents of radical ethnic nationalism glorified their ethnicity while they eagerly embraced a polysemic nationalist framework that drew on insights from Fanon, Marx, Ché, and Mao. Too, the YLP was significantly influenced by the political analysis and teachings of the Black Panther Party and its thesis of revolutionary struggle. But as seen above, Black Power's influence on non–African Americans altered the popular discourse and public discussion of identity and equality in the United States in interesting ways. Outside and inside of the radical ethnic nationalist communities were militants who rebuked whiteness and the implications of whiteness such as status dependent on the subjugation of nonwhites. In this contextual framework, many militants sought to "humanize" whites by stripping them of any trappings of cultural prestige or supremacy.

Radical ethnic nationalists, by example, demonstrated the humanity of white people in ways that Martin L. King, Jr., and nonviolent integrationists did not. Whites were criticized in ways that they had never been. While this may appear anathema to the ideals of YLP and Panther trans-racialism, the ridicule of whites by some ethnic nationalists was an attempt to reconcile the new self-love in the midst of generations of self-hate. Whites were virtually pushed off their pedestal of whiteness and all the implied honor, prestige, and respect that skin-privilege conveyed. Black Power and radical ethnic nationalism revealed the vulnerability of whiteness. It was no longer sacrosanct or without flaw but revealed the same human frailties and shortcomings that define human beings of all colors everywhere.

There was a particular appeal that made Black Power a model for many young people of color longing for an end to the racial oppression they had endured. It allowed many to affirm themselves without concern for white scrutiny or hostility. Puerto Rican baby boomers on the mainland grew Afros, celebrated African and Taíno ancestry, and identified less as white, but still locked into the illogic of "race" and color, preferring to refer to themselves as "brown" people.

Ideological shifts changed the YLP into the Puerto Rican Revolutionary Workers Organization (PRRWO) in 1972. Like other radical ethnic-nationalist groups, such as the Black Panthers and Brown Berets,[25] the PRRWO was burdened with the customary debilitating dogmatism, which later led to factionalism and internal conflict that resulted in beatings and expulsions of its membership. By 1976 the organization was moribund.

Nevertheless, radical ethnic-nationalism in Puerto Rican communities was not solely dependent on Black Power for symbolism, political direction, or motivation. In fact, the various movements mutually influenced each other in alliances, networks, conferences, and general dialogue. They even served as pallbearers for each other when members fell during confrontations with the state, providing important emotional comfort and camaraderie. To paraphrase black integrationists who stressed the need to work with progressive whites, black people could not go it alone. Neither could Puerto Rican, Chicano, Asian, or Native American allies who were essential to each other in forming a broad-based and effective movement to realize the liberation they envisioned.

Also, the international dynamics that influenced Black Power were also felt by those involved in the Puerto Rican struggle for "national" recognition within the United States. The symbiotic relations were undeniable, although the Black Power movement was the defining one. It shaped and conditioned a period of social and cultural transformation that would have major effects on the cultural and political landscape of the country. In this the Puerto Rican community was not untouched. The Young Lords in particular extended the realm of Puerto Rican radicalism and helped popularize efforts to shift ethnic and racial identity and politics. They initiated direct challenges to the institutionalized discrimination faced by Puerto Ricans and in the process demonstrated the malleability of racial identity in a country where race has long determined one's access to the most essential human needs, even life itself. And though they did not destroy racism, they unequivocally revealed its vulnerabilities and illogic and provided a foundation upon which activists would build for decades. Unlike the Cubans in the United States, who are generally "whiter" and who are ideologically more welcome because they are fleeing America's enemy, Puerto Ricans are viewed as "darker skinned" and generally perceived by Americans as ungrateful burdens on the social system. This is especially the case with those (1) who internally resist assimilation and continue to assert a Puerto Rican national and cultural identity, and (2) who continue to speak out for national liberation of the island from U.S. neo-colonial domination.

NOTES

1. While I do not share the assumptions of those who see "race" as a real biological category, with corresponding moral, intelligence, and other social attributes, the general racialization of consciousness in the American society means that most people define "race" as real and it thus becomes real in its consequences: black people are among the least educated, they have the highest unemployment and incarceration rates, are among the lowest income earners, and so forth. In other words, while discrete biological "races" do not exist, most people believe that they do, they act on that belief, and that has serious consequences for daily lived experiences of all concerned.

2. Though some have argued that Japanese American Richard Aoki was a co-founder of the Party, official Panther history from the beginning only includes Huey P. Newton and Bobby Seale as co-founders. Aoki is acknowledged, however, as a "consultant" and close comrade to the Party. In Seattle, however, Guy Kuruse was one of the first Asian Americans to become an official member of the Black Panther Party. See "Yellow Power," *Giant Robot* 10 (spring 1998):76. Bobby Seale, conversation with author, April 2002, Washington, D.C.

3. The Panther 21, also known as the New York 21, was the infamous trial of 21 Black Panthers for conspiracy charges to bomb various parts of the city. After serving over a year in prison, all were acquitted.

4. President Harry S. Truman initiated the Point Four Program in 1949 as tool to extend industrial capitalism into underdeveloped countries. Puerto Rico was used as a model of this industrialization. Incentives, such as lower fares to the mainland, were offered to impoverished Puerto Ricans who had been courted by labor scouts.

5. Earlier in 1966 King moved into a Chicago slum in an attempt to demonstrate the Northern varieties of white supremacy. The particular virulence of Chicago racism and its rigid housing policies informed his decision to relocate to that city. Though his focus was African Americans, he had been increasingly sensitive to how racism affected other people of color. See also www.gangresearch.net/latinkings/lkhistory.html (accessed May 25, 2003).

6. "Interview with Cha Cha Jiménez," *Black Panther*, June 7, 1969, p. 17.

7. Ahmed Rahman, telephone interview with author November 20, 2002, and Washington, D.C., April 18, 2002.

8. Dawley (1973:113–15); David Dawley, interview with author May 16, 2003.

9. Flyer, n.d., UCBSPC, Box 18, folder 33, Young Lord Organization.

10. "Interview with Cha Cha Jiménez," *Black Panther*, June 7, 1969, p. 17.

11. "From Rumble to Revolution: The Young Lords," *Ramparts*, October 1970; Flyer, n.d., UCBSPC, Box 18, folder 33, Young Lord Organization; see also Hilliard and Cole (1993:229).

12. "Interview with Cha Cha Jiménez," *Black Panther*, June 7, 1969, p. 17.

13. "From Rumble to Revolution: The Young Lords," *Ramparts,* October 1970; Flyer, n.d., UCBSPC, Box 18, folder 33, Young Lord Organization.

14. Ibid., 156–57; The Young Lords Party and Abramson (1971:75–77); "Palante Siempre Palante! A Look Back at the Young Lords." Available at http://netdial.caribe.net/dfreedma/beginnin.htm (accessed July 30, 1999).

15. Felipe Luciano, speech, St. Lawrence University, April 1997.

16. Available at http://netdial.caribe.net/~dfreedma/itsupou.htm July 30, 1999).

17. The Panther Party leadership officially condemned cultural nationalism as politically innocuous and counterrevolutionary. Karenga's organization, US Organization, the leading cultural nationalist group, and the Party viciously attacked each other in speeches, writings and physically.

18. "Young Patriots at U.F.A.F. Conference," *Black Panther*, July 26, 1969, p. 8.

19. The Puerto Rican Civil Rights Commission in 1959 and 1972 found explicit discrimination against darker skinned Puerto Ricans pervasive on the island.

20. "Interview with Cha Cha Jiménez," *Black Panther*, June 7, 1969, p. 17.

21. "We're Fighting for Freedom Together. There Is No Other Way," *Black Panther*, August 2, 1969.

22. "We're Fighting for Freedom Together. There Is No Other Way," *Black Panther*, August 2, 1969.

23. "Palante Siempre Palante: The Young Lords," written, produced, and directed by Iris Morales (1966).

24. "Roberta Alexander at Conference," *Black Panther*, August 2, 1969, p. 7; "The Role of Revolutionary Women," *Black Panther*, May 4, 1969, p. 9.

25. *Brown Berets* was a Chicano organization based in Los Angeles. It was formed in 1967 and had a close relationship with the Black Panthers.

7

Politics of Ethno-National Identity in a Postcolonial Communal Democracy: The Case of Fiji

Steven Ratuva

One of the salient features of Fiji's post-colonial political configuration is the uneasy yet dynamic interplay between political identity and distinctive ethnic identity. This seemingly contradictory yet accommodating tendency is a product of the communal engineering process, which has been a significant feature of Fiji's communal democracy since independence in 1970. Political identity here refers to "civic" rights and values of individuals or groups in relation to the state (see chapter 1), and these rights and values are usually embedded in national doctrines and constitutions. Ethnic identity, on the other hand, refers to communal values, cultural symbolisms, and collective consciousness associated with a group. This distinction will be elaborated later.

I use the term *communal democracy* here to refer to the way in which liberal democratic institutions, ideology, and practices (see Allahar and Côté 1998:8–21) have been remolded to accommodate distinctive communal concerns. Thus, notions of constitutionally constructed political rights and universal suffrage, for instance, are reconfigured to facilitate the perceived interests and demands of particular communities. So on one hand is the need for a national political identity and on the other hand is the desire to maintain distinctive communal rights, thus reconfiguring the bounds of constitutional democracy in order to capture communal diversity. Recognition of both communal identity and individual democratic rights takes place simultaneously and is institutionalized as part of the state ideology and dominant political discourse. The result is a symbiotic synthesis of sorts, which simultaneously embodies tension between and accommodation of universal political rights and ethnic concerns in a dynamic way. This is what I propose to call communal democracy.

Very much like the cases of Trinidad, Guyana, and Suriname, Fiji's communal democracy is "syncretic" in nature. In other words, there is a complex interrelationship of opposition and accommodation taking place simultaneously between political and cultural discourses. While there may be contradiction between sociopolitical and socioeconomic dichotomies, there is also accommodation and in some cases synthesis of divergent discourses. Some pertinent examples of these "dichotomies" are multiracialism and communal distinctiveness, neoliberal development policies and state interventionism through affirmative action, and modernization and preservation of traditional values (Ratuva 2002a). These dichotomies are seen to go hand in hand with government policies, or as part of the broader dynamics of social change.

Similar to the question of the Kurdish minority in Turkey discussed by Cenk Saraçoğlu (see chapter 8), this chapter is concerned with the dialectical relationship between political identity and ethnic identity in Fiji and how they exist side by side and define and shape each other. This tense yet mutual relationship has helped to maintain a fragile yet self-sustaining continuity in a country recently beset by political instability.[1] Paradoxically, tension and instability are part of the same dynamic equation where, depending on the empirical circumstances, one would be more dominant than the other, but both are required for the social situation to persist. In other words, because the two variables do not exist independently of each other, the state becomes the site for both contradiction and accommodation as different communal identities compete, negotiate, compromise, or sometimes converge.[2]

POST-COLONIAL DEMOCRACY IN FIJI

The South Pacific state of Fiji is a classic example of a post-colonial communal democracy. It became independent from Britain in 1970 after ninety-six years of colonial rule. The total population is about 800,000 and of these, 51 percent are indigenous Fijians, 44 percent Indo-Fijians, and 5 percent constitute minorities such as those of European descent, Chinese descent, and other Pacific Islanders.[3] British colonial policy dictated the formal and political separation and distinctive communal development of these ethnic groups through a series of political changes and legislations under the native policy (Ratuva 1999). And like any other colonial situation, the economic and political institutions and structures of Fijian society were entirely controlled by the British colonial masters. Under the native policy, indigenous Fijians remained locked into a rigid communal and subsistence way of life, which kept them distant from mainstream national politics and economic development. Indo-Fijians, who were brought in as indentured laborers in the late 1800s and early 1900s, were confined to the regimented life of the sugar cane plantations, while Europeans largely ran the civil service, government, and business. The indigenous Fijians' main asset was land, which was leased out for commercial farming, and Indo-Fijians provided labor and Europeans provided capital, technology, expertise, and managerial control. Profits were largely siphoned back to Australia by the Colonial Sugar Refining Company (CSR) (France 1969).

There was minimal social interaction among the three ethnic groups, as their relationship was defined largely by the colonial policy of divide and rule and division of labor under the agrarian colonial capitalist economy (Sutherland 1994). At the political level, separation was institutionalized through separate ethnic representation to the law-making Legislative Council. Colonial "democracy" was largely a European affair, where only Europeans had voting rights. It was only after years of agitation that Indo-Fijians were granted universal suffrage in 1929. Indigenous Fijian representation was through a paternalistic nomination process where the chiefs nominated representatives from their own ranks. It was not until 1965, only five years before independence and thirty-five years after the Indo-Fijians, that indigenous Fijians finally gained universal suffrage.[4]

Upon independence in 1970, Fiji's indigenous Fijian elites, groomed for leadership by the colonial state (see discussion of Fanon in Allahar 2003: 44–53), took over the reigns of power through the Alliance Party. The Alliance Party, under the leadership of Oxford-educated and high chief Ratu Sir Kamisese Mara, led Fiji for seventeen years before it was defeated in the 1987 general election by Dr. Timoci Bavadra's Fiji Labour Party–National Federation Party Coalition. This led to widespread political agitation by nationalist Fijians who feared political usurpation by Indo-Fijians, who dominated the new ruling coalition. Bavadra's victory was a threat to the powerful "historical bloc"[5] consisting of indigenous Fijian chiefly authority, the largely indigenous Fijian Methodist Church, and European-Indo-Fijian big business, which have been part of Fiji's ruling stratum since independence. The largely indigenous Fijian military under then Lt. Colonel Sitiveni Rabuka intervened in support of Fijian ethno-nationalism, overthrew the Bavadra government in a coup d'état, abrogated the 1970 Independence Constitution, and put in place a series of interim political arrangements, including the promulgation of a new indigenous-favored 1990 Constitution.

The first postcoup election was won by Rabuka's political party, the *Soqosoqo ni Vakavulewa ni Lewe ni Vanua* (SVT), which ruled the country until 1999 when its electoral fortunes waned, allowing the Fiji Labour Party, under Mahendra Chaudhry, who became the first Indo-Fijian Prime Minister, to ascend to political leadership. This led to further ethno-nationalist mobilization, leading to the May 2000 coup,[6] when a group of elite soldiers with their civilian supporters held the prime minister and ministers hostage for more than thirty days. After the release of the hostages, the military arrested the leader of the coup, George Speight, a failed businessman, and his followers.

The first election after the 2000 coup took place in August 2001 and Laisenia Qarase, a banker by profession, was elected prime minister. While this brief historical snapshot is by no means comprehensive, it does provide a backdrop against which an analysis of the dynamics of ethnic and national identity construction and reproduction in Fiji may be undertaken.

THEORIZING COMMUNAL AND ETHNIC IDENTITY

The concepts "communal" and "ethnic" in Fiji are often used interchangeably. However, their precise meaning is best grasped via an excursion into the relevant theoretical literature. To begin, the term *communal* is used to designate various forms of "social relationships, which take place within geographically defined areas . . . or to relationships which are not locally operative but exist at a more abstract, ideological level" (Jary and Jary 1991:72). There is no given (or primordial) and objectively defined social "boundary" for a community, as Cohen suggests. Rather, it is based on simultaneous symbolic construction of similarities and differences:

> "Community" thus seems to imply simultaneously both similarity and difference.
> The word thus expressed a *relational* idea: the opposition of one community to
> others or to other social entities. . . . The use of the word is only occasioned by
> the desire or need to express such a distinction. It seems appropriate, therefore,
> to focus our examination of the nature of community on the element which embodies this sense of discrimination, namely, the *boundary*. (Cohen 1974:12)

In this sense (of being "relational" and having a constructed "boundary"), the social category "community" has parallel, if not similar, features as the terms *ethnicity* or *ethnic group*, the same way that the adjectival form *communal* is used interchangeably with *ethnic* (as in communal segregation or ethnic segregation). This is a significant aspect of the social constructionist approach originally elaborated by Barth (1969), who, using the social anthropology framework, argued that communities are products of social construction and reproduction. Cohen's emphasis on the role of symbolism in the social construction of community boundaries is, with slight modification, "a powerful contribution to our understanding of ethnicity" (Jenkins 1997:42). Thus, while community is a broader category that could be based on varied forms of mobilization and organization like religion, professions, neighborhood, and so forth, ethnicity is more specific and socioculturally defined. But my concern here is their area of convergence, where ethnicity becomes the mobilizing force for communalism. What, then, are the defining characteristics of ethnicity? This is where the primordial versus social constructionist debate becomes significant in illuminating the dynamics of communal relations in Fiji.

PRIMORDIALISM VERSUS SOCIAL CONSTRUCTIONISM

One of the most influential exponents of the primodialist approach is Geertz (1973), who defined ethnicity in relation to "primordial attachments" or innate and a priori characteristics such as personalities and kinship.[7] Geertz tried to understand primordial attachments in the context of the development of the modern political sentiment of citizenship in the emerging postcolonial states:

> [The] crystallization of a direct conflict between primordial and civil sentiments— this "longing not to belong to any other group"— . . . gives to the problems variously called tribalism, parochialism, communalism, and so on, a more ominous and deeply threatening quality than most of the other, also very serious and intractable, problems the new states face. (1973:261)

Nevertheless, Geertz was also aware of the fluidity and relative nature of primordial bonds. He argued that the "strength of such primordial bonds and the types of them are important, differ from person to person, from society to society, and from time to time" (1973:259). However, the primordialist approach has been widely criticized because "ethnicity tends to be conceived by this school of thought as an essentially innate disposition" (Cohen 1974:xii), and as such tends to purvey "a picture of underived and socially unconstructed emotions that are un-analysable and overpowering. . . . A more un-intelligible and un-sociological concept would be hard to imagine" (Eller and Coughlan 1993:187). However, primordialism fails to explain the changing patterns of social organization, identity, and culture, and tends toward a static and almost biologically deterministic view of human society.

The social constructionist discourse, on the other hand, challenges the assumed naturalistic tendency of the primordialists and could be summarized in the following four aspects: ethnicity involves cultural *differentiation* (although identity is always a dialectic between similarity and difference); ethnicity is *cultural*—it is based on shared meanings—but it is produced and reproduced in *social* interaction; ethnicity is to some extent *variable* and *manipulable*, not definitively fixed or unchanging; and ethnicity as a social identity is both *collective* and *individual, externalized* and *internalized* (Jenkins 1997:40).[8] Because it is manipulable, ethnicity remains a politically explosive identity marker, and is fraught with intellectual and political prejudice and controversy, as Horowitz wrote: "Ethnicity has fought and bled and burned its way into public and scholarly consciousness" (1985:xi).

Following this, Allahar (1996) spoke of the "soft" understanding of primordial attachment as preferable to a "hard" understanding. Rationality is the key here mainly because class affiliation, which is tied to occupation, income, and economic position, clearly addresses compelling and immediate requirements of survival in modern society. But to the extent that ethnicity and race can influence class position and the structure of opportunity in society, individuals can be expected, to the extent it is possible, to emphasize or de-emphasize their ethno-racial attributes. This is why, in contrasting class and ethnic identities under contemporary circumstances, Daniel Bell noted that "ethnicity has become more salient because it can combine an interest with an affective tie" (1975:169).

One of the earliest sociological references to "ethnic" groups was by Max Weber, who argued that "ethnic membership does not constitute a group; it only facilitates group formation of any kind, particularly in the political sphere. On the other hand, it is primarily the political community, no matter how artificially organized, that inspires the belief in common ethnicity" (1978:389). Weber's argument is that people's consciousness of common ancestry or collective belonging is a result of common action. The idea later influenced Chicago sociologist Everett Hughes, who suggested that identity is a result of the way in which the groups of "ins" and "outs" define each other's space and "act as if it is a separate group" (1994:91). In a way, Weber and Hughes influenced the later social constructionist model of ethnicity, which argues that "ethnic groups are what people believe or think them to be; cultural differences mark group-ness, they do not cause it (or indelibly characterize it); ethnic identification arises out of, and within, interaction between groups" (Jenkins 1997:11).

It was not until the 1960s, however, that the notion of ethnicity became widespread in sociological and anthropological studies where there was a shift in discourse from "race" to "culture" to "ethnicity." As Ratcliffe suggests, "the significance of ethnicity lies in its salience for group consciousness and collective action" (1994:6). This approach recognizes the importance of the "in-group" definition of ethnic space but does not include "external" imposition of ethnic boundaries and labels. Bulmer's definition seems to incorporate most of the variables generally accepted as part of the ethnicity discourse; he says that ethnicity is a more inclusive concept than that of race. For an ethnic group is a collectivity within a larger society having real or putative common ancestry, memories of a shared past, and cultural focus on one or more symbolic elements which define the group's identity: kinship, religion, language, shared territory, nationality, or physical appearance (1986:54). This definition is still problematic because it is too loose and allows for a limitless number of ethnic categories without any definitive and recognizable delineating factors. On the other hand, if it is applied uncritically, it would conceptualize ethnicity as being static and rigid, thus undermining the historical possibility of ethnicity as a "shifting" and "imaginary" construction (Ratcliffe 1994:7). Nevertheless, despite the diversity in conceptual approaches, there is a more or less general consensus that ethnicity refers to a collective identification based on certain historical and cultural characteristics, and the reasons for identification vary anywhere from defensive mobilization to hostile political engagement.

ETHNICITY AS TRANSACTION

In other words, ethnicity is seen as transactional in two ways: first are the processes of *internal definition*, where members of a group collectively define their own individual and group identity in relation to some recognizable culturally specific practices; and second is the *external definition*, where individuals and groups are collectively defined by "Others." External definition could either entail validation of others' internal definition of themselves or the imposition and characterization by others, which may significantly affect the social experiences of the categorized (Eriksen 1993). The processes of internal and external definition are, in the complex encounters of day-to-day social life, interrelated in a dialectical way. External definition takes place within an active social relationship between individuals and groups, and intervention in other people's lives implies the power (competitive access to and control over resources) or the authority (deployment of "legitimate means") to do so. Power and authority are strongly embedded in active social relationships, whether formal or informal (Hughes 1994).

Whether in the Caribbean, in the societies of advanced capitalism in the West, or in Fiji, where ethnic politics are sharply defined, the social construction of the ethnic "other" is key. In other words, the "us" and "them" or "in group" and "out group" definitions are fundamental to the process of ethnicity formation, which involves the interrelated processes of production, reproduction, and transformation of the "groupness" of culturally differentiated collectivities.[9] External definition could be a mirror for internal definition; it has an impact on conceptualization of the self. Group solidarity and resistance could also result from perceived threats from external definition to established internal definitions. Defense of threatened identities could be a basis for political mobilization, around either certain culturally specific or historically reinvented primordial symbols.

Moreover, according to Jenkins (1997:90), external categorization may be "internalized" by the categorized group under at least five possible scenarios. First, the imposed definition may complement and externally validate the existing internal definition; second, external definitions may induce incremental cultural changes over time; third, the external category may be produced by those who are seen to have legitimate authority to do so; fourth, external categorization may involve the deployment of force to impose culturally symbolic categories of the oppressor; and finally, the rejection of externally imposed boundaries and definitions may become an expression of autonomy and self-identification. Though instructive, Jenkins's schema is weak on the grounds that it assumes a distinctive duality between the internal and external. In everyday interaction, there is a more complex process taking place where cultural reproduction becomes a complex synthesis of both internalization and externalization. As in the case of Fiji, external definitions by the colonial state were modified by indigenous Fijians and redeployed as a new identity, rather than being accepted wholesale and indiscriminately.

The social constructionist approach emphasizes the question of agency of actors. Its focus, however, is the social group and in the process it undermines the importance of individual psyche and other presumed, in-born factors that may influence people's behavior. It also challenges the conception of identity as rooted in such biological features as skin color and genetics. This approach also tends to generalize about the universality of social behavior, without taking into consideration the limitations of particular social reproduction and engineering.

SOCIAL CONSTRUCTION OF PRIMORDIALITY AND PRIMORDIALIZATION OF SOCIAL CONSTRUCTION

I wish to advance the argument that the complex expanse of the ethnic phenomenon deserves a more flexible and encompassing framework, which synthesizes relevant aspects of the primordial and social constructionist approaches that Allahar (1994b) sees as "more than an oxymoron." While ethnic boundaries and phenomenological characteristics of ethnic symbolisms such as language, religion, values, and norms are by and large social constructions, there are also important cultural markers such as kinship and emotional attachments, which result from an interplay between primordial and socially constructed tendencies. Add to this the fact that, for whatever reasons, physical features (skin color, hair texture, facial structure, body type, etc.) are assigned social meanings that in turn inform human behavior and social and political interaction.

In Fiji, for instance, ethnic identity is continually defined and redefined by particular shared cultural expressions and identifiable physical characteristics. Indigenous Fijians define themselves and are defined by others in relation to a common Fijian language (although with minor regional variations), ceremonial practices, communal norms, religion (Christianity), and particular eating and social habits. These social factors are complemented by primordial assumptions about being the original children of the land. Indo-Fijians speak Hindi (a local diaspora variation) and are defined by their cultural ceremonies, food, and other specifically "Indian" practices. There are physical characteristics associated with certain groups that also help define their group identity. These include widely held images of the "thin, weak, but brainy Indian" in comparison to the "big, muscular, and brainless Fijian." While some of these features are based on observable physical characteristics, they are all invested with interpretive and prejudicial social meaning.

At one level, especially from "external" lenses, it may be argued that nationalism is based on historically constructed assumptions and myths about racial genesis and immemoriality (see chapter 1). However, within the group itself, there is a subjective "internal" cosmological "reality," which is collectively shared and reproduced over generations. Nationalism is usually associated with primordial links to these cosmological realities such as an ancestral homeland. This is very true of indigenous Fijian nationalism, encapsulated in the term *Taukei* (original owner of the land). Ethnic identification can be understood in terms of social collectivity as well as individual subjective consciousness and interaction with the society. Individual consciousness and collective will impact on each other in a symbiotic way. Ethnic boundaries are not always a result of collective consensus, as they are often subverted from within and from outside. Definition of ethnic boundaries in a modern state usually takes place in a situation of relativity between competing groups.

The group itself defines its own boundary, which is often contested or agreed to by other groups. Sometimes the state may impose its own definition, even determining the extent of the ethnic boundary. In Fiji, everyone is officially designated as belonging to either "Fijian," "Indian," or "Others." Indigenous Fijians define themselves as *Taukei* and define Indo-Fijians as *Vulagi* (visitor). On the other hand, Indo-Fijians define themselves as "Fijians" just as much as indigenous Fijians. As a compromise, the 1997 Constitution defines everyone as "Fiji Islanders" and the major ethnic groups as Fijians and Indo-Fijians. But nationalist Fijians reject this, saying that since Indo-Fijians are "Indians" and not Fijians, they should be called "Indians."[10]

DEFINING THE REAL FIJIAN

The 1990 nationalist constitution employed a biological line of reasoning and attempted to define who an indigenous Fijian really was by suggesting that only those whose patrilineal parental line was Fijian were legitimately indigenous Fijians. When one was deemed indigenous Fijian through this, then the name would appear in the *Vola ni Kawabula*, the living record of all born indigenous Fijians and their land ownership titles, kept by the Fijian Lands Commission. According to the formula, if the mother was European and the father was indigenous Fijian, then the child was considered "Fijian"; but if the father was European and the mother indigenous Fijian, then the child was not

Fijian. The purpose of the exclusivist exercise was to deliberately create a smaller circle of claimants to native land to "protect Fijian land." This experiment was later discarded after controversies arose; among the latter were the potential deregistration of a number of prominent indigenous Fijians and public charges of racism and sexism against the government.

These examples show the highly contested nature of ethnic boundaries in Fiji. Ethic definitions and boundaries can be redefined to serve external as well as internal political interests. The imposition of an external category by a more powerful other is more than simply a process of categorization, as it entails intervening into and changing a social world and its accompanying experiences. These scenarios represent the dilemma related to the imposition of ethnic identity by others where on one hand is the internalization of the imposed ethnic identity and on the other hand is the resistance to the external definition. As we will see later, this dilemma manifests itself in a contradictory political and ethnic nationalism where on one hand, there is the need to create a unifying identity for diverse ethnic groups, and on the other hand, there is the clamor by these groups to maintain their own separate identity.

However, while ethnicity is a social construct, claims to primordial links are still significant since "primordial characteristics" could actually be "constructed" to justify certain claims (Allahar 1996). As an ideology and social organizing principle, ethnicity is occasionally linked to claims of primordialism (thus providing it with a primary and permanent sense of identity and relative resilience) and is influenced by more pragmatic situational factors. The primordial claim has an inherently psychological dimension to it. This involves the invoking of the kinship myth about an imagined cultural community as a "family," complete with myths of common ancestry and history. These serve as a basis for constructing an ethnic ideology, as the ideological consciousness arising from such identification could remain embedded in the communal psyche for a long time. And when necessary it could also be deployed in various forms as a justification underscoring demands for various political and economic rights and nationalistic causes (see chapter 1). Thus, ethnic solidarity tends to intensify as the struggle over scarce resources escalates (Stavenhagen 1996). The ethnic myths reproduced over time define the moral and political character of the "us" in relation to "them." An important component of these ethnic myths are ethnic stereotypes that collectively embody the identity, not of real individuals with actual and affective ties, but of strangers in an "imagined community" (Anderson [1983] 1991).

The interface between primordialism and social constructionism is a dynamic one. Primordial characteristics can be socially (re)constructed and socially constructed symbols can be deemed primordial and immemorial. There is a constant engagement where social constructions are primordialized and primordial factors are socially constructed (Allahar 1994b).

CONSTRUCTION OF ETHNIC IDENTITIES:
A COMPARATIVE SYNOPSIS

Modern indigenous Fijian identity must be understood at three levels. The first is the formal bureaucratic level, which consists of neo-colonial "traditional" institutions such as the Great Council of Chiefs, the Fijian Affairs Board, the Native Land Trust Board, the Provincial Councils, and the Ministry of Fijian Affairs, which were part of the British colonial strategy of keeping indigenous Fijians in a centralized, cohesive, and separate system under the British policy of indirect rule. These institutions became part of the indigenous Fijian social structure in a permanent way. Recommendations to restructure these institutions in 2002 by a government-commissioned committee were outrightly rejected by the indigenous Fijian political elites, who wanted to maintain the neo-colonial order.[11] The second level concerns the ideological realm and relates to political norms, religion (Christianity), symbols, and practices such as kinship, the chiefly system, and its traditional authority, mythology, land, machismo, patriarchy, and the paramountcy of Fijian interests. These social and ideological forms provide the justification and legitimacy for the existence of the various neocolonial institutional processes. The third level deals with everyday cultural symbols and practices such as language, dress, food, dances, and sports (rugby). Over time, a great number of these have been readapted and reinvented to meet emerging needs and circumstances, although there is still the claim that these are traditional pursuits (see Keesing 1989; Lawson 1996).

These three processes constitute a complex but mutually engaging and interlocked synthesis of political and ethnic identity, which make up the Fijian communal identity. It is powered by the synergy between structural norms, political ideology, cultural mythology, and everyday cultural engagement. Recontextualizing Gramsci, I have used the term *communal hegemony* to refer to this institutional, political, ideological, and cultural complex, which mobilizes indigenous Fijians and generates collective consent to chiefly authority and communal values. But this consent is not total because of what Gramsci referred to as "dual consciousness," or the contradicting values which lead to "counter-hegemony." In other words, tension within the indigenous Fijian community does exist in various forms such as tribal and regional loyalty, land disputes, kinship ties, political ideology, religion, and so on. And as is well known, these often come to the surface during times of social upheaval (Ratuva 1999; 2002a). Chiefly authority is often contested and certain aspects of traditional ideologies are constantly subverted, transformed, and deliberately recontextualized. These are some of the internal dynamics, which give indigenous Fijian communal identity an adaptive, transformational, and thus durable character.

The lines between these three modes of identity are often blurred by the dynamic relationship between them. The indigenous Fijian institutions are usually linked to ideological justifications and cultural mythology and are often subsumed under chiefly authority. This complex interplay gives them a coherent, dynamic, and changing character and also makes it difficult to distinguish between political and ethnic identity. There are, however, two contesting discourses on the nature of indigenous Fijian identity. The first is what may be termed the "traditionalist school," which conceives of neo-colonial institutions such as the Great Council of Chiefs as indispensable and immemorial (Bole 1992:3). The second is the "politics of tradition school," which argues that Fijian tradition is deliberately invented to serve political purposes (Keesing 1989; Lawson 1996).

Both arguments, however, have their own drawbacks but, they do indeed provide some interesting insight into the dynamics of culture and their reproductive potential. Traditional identity in the indigenous Fijian context is a mixture of both pre-colonial, colonial, and post-colonial practices and symbolism. Culture is neither static as the traditionalists argue, nor is it just a product of opportunistic ethnic entrepreneurs (see chapters 1, 5, and 9) who are given to deliberate manipulation and mystification of emotionally charged ethnic symbols, as the politics of tradition school would argue. Cultural reproduction is an ongoing dynamic process, which constitutes incorporating the new, modifying the old, and creating a different synthesis. It can be either deliberate or subconscious. The process can be reversed. The use of the term *traditional* is relative to situations and conditions; thus, it is important to note that whatever their origins, the multiplicity of institutional, cultural, and political factors continue to define indigenous Fijian identity in a dynamic way.

Indo-Fijian identity is far more difficult to define because of the complex and heterogeneous make-up of both horizontal and vertical sub-cultural categories. The first speaks to the existence of divisions along lines of ethnic exclusiveness as characterize Punjabis, Gujeratis, Muslims, Hindus, South Indian, North Indian, and so forth, while the second speaks to caste stratification. Through lenses of "outsiders," Indo-Fijian identity is generally defined by cultural characteristics such as language, dance, food, and other cultural practices, as well as the common historical diaspora status with continental Indian origin. The Indo-Fijian communal identity has been shaped by the new cultural context and the political and socioeconomic conditions associated with global transmigration.

The caste system has largely disappeared and new egalitarian conceptions of social structure based on fragmented but coherent modes of cultural expressions and practices have come to replace them. While these are specifically adapted to the new historical conditions, they have taken shape and evolved in a unique way. While traces of old continental Indian values still exist, newly constructed versions of culture such as food, language, music and entertainment, and sense of identity have evolved in a distinctively Fijian way. The new cultural regrowth has become the basis of a new homeland and a new diaspora identity, what in the Caribbean has been called "creolization" (Allahar 1994a).

But as discussed in chapter 9, the new and the old continue to engage each other. Reference to a mythological ancestral past, rooted in grand ancient Indian civilizations, is sometimes invoked through literature to provide a sense of place in the past, continuity, and primordiality (see Nandan 2001). The emotional links with the grand civilizations of the past, together with qualities of thrift and hard work, are often articulated subconsciously and sometimes consciously as evidence of a more superior culture than that of the native *jungalis* (bushmen). This largely underpins Indo-Fijian stereotypes of indigenous Fijians as we will later examine in detail. Interestingly, indigenous Fijians also reinforce the belief that Indo-Fijian culture, by way of its more elaborate technology and commercially oriented nature, are more superior than their own "simple" culture. However, the feeling of Indo-Fijian cultural superiority is counteracted by the notion of indigenous Fijian political superiority. The former is an expression of cultural superiority and the latter is an expression of political superiority.[12]

The persistent demand for political rights and representation by Indo-Fijians during the colonial period provided the conditions for a new political identity. Indo-Fijians were granted the franchise in 1929 and with it a new political disposition and role within the colonial political space and discourse. Indo-Fijian politicians became the effective, unofficial opposition to the British colonial politicians who were patronizing to indigenous Fijians but resentful of Indo-Fijians (Ali 1980). Separate ethnic representation became the institutional embodiment of the convergence between ethnic and political identities.

ARTICULATION OF COMMUNAL CONSCIOUSNESS: A DIALECTICAL PROCESS

By communal consciousness, I refer to culturally embedded perceptions and awareness that form the basis for ethnic perception in everyday societal transactions and even in political relationships. In a multiethnic society, communal consciousness is largely a construction of a group about itself in relation to others, or of others about another group. It is a synthesis of diverse forces such as the perception of a group of its own assumed primordial self, the projection of this perception of self to construct others, or the assimilation of others' perceptions to construct a self-identity. The contradictions, accommodations, and synthesis of these dynamic processes continuously define group identity. Thus, group identity is not static but transactional, reinventable, and transformational (Jenkins 1997).

Years of separate development under the colonial native policy and institutionalized communalism in Fiji helped to create and culturally institutionalize separate but dynamically engaging communal perceptions, which are still prevalent today. These perceptions are based on assumptions regarding inter- and intra-ethnic characteristics and constitute both identifiable cultural norms and generalized stereotypes. Indigenous Fijians stereotype Indo-Fijians as greedy, selfish, and cunning. Indo-Fijians are referred to as *Kaidia*, a term that conjures images of a manipulative and untrustworthy character bent on conspiring to usurp indigenous Fijian rights. On the other hand, indigenous Fijians are portrayed by Indo-Fijians as lazy, stupid, and careless. They are generally perceived as intellectually inferior, prone to criminality, and without commercial and political sophistry to engage with the modern world (Ratuva 2002b).

However, on the other side of same coin are "positive" imaginings. For instance, while indigenous Fijians cast Indo-Fijians as selfish, they are also seen as hardworking and ambitious. Indigenous Fijian parents increasingly send their children to Indo-Fijian–run committee schools for "better" education and encourage their children to emulate Indo-Fijian children's educational ambitions. At the same time, indigenous Fijians would be perceived by Indo-Fijians as friendly and accommodating. Paradoxically, an observed or assumed behavioral characteristic is defined in two diametrically opposite ways. Again this reflects the syncretic nature of Fiji's cultural relations (Ratuva 2002a). In addition, the externally constructed stereotypic conceptions are often assimilated and internalized by the respective groups. Indigenous Fijians often use the dictum *Kaiviti ga sa Kaiviti*, meaning "typical of Fijians" or "a Fijian is always a Fijian" to explain their own business or educational inability and failure. They also see themselves as friendly, accommodating, and tolerant. Indo-Fijians often accept certain behavioral characteristics such as being miserly as "typical" of their own cultural disposition.

Thus, the dialectics of communal consciousness involve a syncretic relationship of simultaneous negation and accommodation, of internalization and externalization of communal perceptions. This complex process entails the internalization of externalities and externalization of internalities and renders communal identity fluid and adaptable yet permanent and immemorial simultaneously. For a communally politicized society such as Fiji, accommodation of various aspects of other's communal identity helps to absorb and ameliorate tension.

Culturally negative imageries are sometimes publicly articulated at the level of political or parliamentary discourse. In August 2002, the Minister for Social Welfare and Women said in a parliamentary speech that "Indians are like weeds which take up space" (*Fijilive* 2002). These words were uttered in the heat of the moment at a time when parliamentary debate had taken an ethnic twist while debating an issue. The minister was publicly condemned by Indo-Fijian and indigenous Fijian civil society groups and was asked to withdraw the statement but refused. But the fact that cultural imageries, which are normally articulated in private, reach the realm of parliamentary debate shows that the line between private and public discourses in ethnic and political debates is readily transgressed. Imageries, which are assumed to be primordially ethnic in nature, are represented as political identity at the level of political discourse. This also shows the extent to which cultural and political identities are continually being redefined and invoked to project political sentiments under certain given conditions. The image of "weeds" is associated with assumed cultural and primordial characteristics of selfishness, being manipulative, and being parasitic.

In another case the leader of the Labour Party and deposed Prime Minister, Mahendra Chaudhry, remarked that indigenous Fijians were a confused lot trying to preserve the past and present at the same time and suggested that "reform will have to be brought into Fijian society to free them from this communal and cultural obligation" (*Fijilive* 2002). This statement had a stereotypic undercurrent, which reinforced the perception that indigenous Fijians were still backward *jungalis,* or bushmen (the term Indo-Fijians is often used to refer to indigenous Fijians). Reaction to this statement was more subdued because the negative expressions were more subtle than the weeds analogy, but it does raise questions about the role of ethnic stereotypes in political discourse. One of the "safest" ways Fiji citizens locally and overseas publicly articulate private ethnic prejudice is the use of Internet discussion forums where racist comments are directed generally to a particular ethnic group without the fear of being identified.[13]

Public articulation of private ethnic imageries in Fiji can provoke negative reaction and often they are silently endorsed by people with established prejudices, either in a humorous or serious way. Paradoxically, rejection and acceptance may be contradictory, yet they ensure a kind of "equilibrium," which helps to absorb tension and conflict. Public articulation of communal prejudice may sometimes take away the political heat, which would otherwise be implosively locked within. At the same time it is a mechanism whereby private prejudice is made transparent and subjected to open scrutiny through inter- and intracommunal evaluation of communal psyche and ethnic identity.

ETHNO-NATIONALISM AND COMMUNAL RELATIONS

In Fiji, tension between two notions of nationalism dominate the political landscape, shape each other, and constitute the broader dynamics of communal politics and ethnic relations generally. The first is the highly contested civic nationalism based on the clamor for common identity and citizenship under the constitutionally prescribed common label of "Fiji Islander." The second is ethno-nationalism, based on the notion of separate communal identity, demands, and mobilization along ethnic lines. The two contending modes of ethno-nationalism revolve around the two major ethnic groups, the indigenous Fijians and Indo-Fijians. The two modes of ethno-nationalism are based on exertion of legitimacy but are expressed in different ways. Indigenous Fijian ethno-nationalism is based on the notion of being the indigenous group and the need for the paramountcy of Fijian interests as a given imperative. The British native policy facilitated and institutionalized this in a politically and culturally embedded way.

The earliest form of indigenous ethno-nationalism was anti-colonial in nature and, needless to say, this was systematically suppressed by the British through their pacification policy. Later anti-British indigenous nationalism was kept at bay through the process of political assimilation and co-option, which underpinned the native policies. These included the restructuring of the traditional institutions to meet British governance interests, adoption of a universal land-owning system, and declaration of land as inalienable. Furthermore, there was the cooption of a class of British-educated comprador chiefs, ideologically nurtured within the paradigm of the colonizers, as mediating agents between the British and the indigenous Fijian population at large (see chapter 1). These basic reforms nurtured a culture and system of protectionism, patronage, and dependency between indigenous Fijians and the British, thus effectively neutralized political dissent.

The arrival and presence of the Indo-Fijians in Fiji as sugarcane plantation laborers further took the political heat off the British as Indo-Fijians were deliberately vilified as "the enemy." The Indo-Fijian demand for greater political representation, refusal to join the army during the Second World War, and demand for common roll (as opposed to the communal roll) were some of the incidents that reinforced indigenous Fijian distrust of Indo-Fijians and the former's feelings of insecurity. The distrust and insecurity were further heightened by the Indo-Fijian commercial, educational, and professional ambitions; visible material possessions; and the perception by indigenous Fijians that they were viewed as culturally inferior by Indo-Fijians. Accompanying this was the fear that both indigenous Fijian land and culture were threatened by the more ambitious, disciplined, and hardworking Indo-Fijians.

These concerns were effectively contained by the Alliance Party after independence in 1970 through its multiracial yet pro-indigenous policies. But after the party lost the 1987 election to the indigenous Fijian-led but predominantly Indo-Fijian Fiji Labour Party, senior members of the party began mobilizing indigenous Fijian nationalist support, including the predominantly indigenous Fijian military. As noted earlier, this culminated in two military coups in May and September 1987 led by Colonel Sitiveni Rabuka to oust the newly elected government and reaffirm indigenous political supremacy. Another coup took place in May 2000 when a unit in the military joined forces with nationalist conspirators to take over the government after Mahendra Chaudhry, the first Indo-Fijian Prime Minister, was voted into power. The coup plot was later foiled by the military, which moved in to arrest the coup makers and put in place a civilian government and later new elections.

The important point here is that since 1987, indigenous nationalism has incorporated political violence in the form of coups as a potential instrument of regime change. While indigenous ethno-nationalism has a strong political expression, it also has a culturally embedded form in the shape of identity construction, norms, mythology, and communal consciousness. The political and cultural discourses inform and shape each other in a dynamic way. Protection of culture is sometimes used to justify political expressions of ethno-nationalism and cultural expressions sometimes embody deeply political discourses.

Indo-Fijian ethno-nationalism is largely reactive and a form of resistance to indigenous ethno-nationalism. This is expressed through communal solidarity in the form of bloc voting, especially for politicians like Mahendra Chaudhry, who promise them political salvation and invoke ethnic sentiments to mobilize Indo-Fijians against indigenous Fijians.[14] Indo-Fijian ethno-nationalism does not have the same violent streak as indigenous ethno-nationalism but the two have mutually defined each other and provided the other with the justification for their existence. Both are deliberately and systematically invoked by politicians from both sides of the political polarity for purposes of communal mobilization when important national issues are discussed in parliament or in other public fora. They are also the main mobilization tools during election campaigns to win voters. Invoking ethno-nationalist sentiments is regarded as an accepted political norm to which individuals and groups uncritically subscribe.

ETHNIC IDENTITY, POLITICAL IDENTITY, AND THE STATE: PARADOX OF COMMUNAL DEMOCRACY

As stated earlier, ethnic identity in Fiji is associated with various cultural values, collective experiences, and symbolisms associated with a particular ethnic group, whether "Fijian" or "Indian." These could be either internally defined by the group itself or externally defined by others as a result of years of restricted interaction during the colonial and post-colonial periods. Political identity, on the other hand, refers to the political and civic rights and consciousness of the different communities within the state as a political community, which transcends communal boundaries. These civic rights are accorded to citizens and enshrined in the Bill of Rights of the 1997 constitution (see 1997 Republic of Fiji Constitution).

Oscillation between ethnic and political identity is a dynamic process wherein the distinction between ethnic and political identities often disappears as people tend to mistake one for the other. In Fiji's ethnically charged political climate, political identities become the basis for political expression, whether Indo-Fijians demanding equal political rights or indigenous Fijians clamoring for political paramountcy. The preponderance of the communal discourse in Fiji has rendered ethnic and political identity inseparable. Political relations and political ideology are largely perceived and defined in unreservedly ethnic terms. Consequently, political identity assumes an ethnic character and ethnic identity becomes a political construct. However, the historical process of state-sponsored communal engineering in Fiji has blurred the distinction between political and ethnic identity. As a result, ethnic characteristics and values are used as a basis for constructing one's political space, place, and status within the political community at large. This was done through official categorization of ethnic groups in constitutions and other state institutions, separate ethnic representation to the colonial Legislative Council (and later Parliament), and nurturing and reproduction of a communalistic state ideology to justify political separation and keep people within their defined political orbits.

Over time, the synergy between political and ethnic identity came to define communal boundaries and perceptions. Consequently, various forms of political behavior and institutions came to be associated with particular ethnic communities. For instance, notions of individual rights, state constitutionalism, and civil service integrity and honesty came to be associated with European political identity. Fijian political identity came to be associated with the Great Council of Chiefs, chiefly respect, political consensus, and even paramountcy of Fijian interest.[15] Dissent and individualism were considered "un-Fijian." On two occasions (during the 1987 and 2000 coups) there were attempts to redefine the state political identity as an indigenous identity. Indian political identity came to be associated with agitation for equal rights, individualism, and collective conspiracy. Because these political identities are based on assumed cultural characteristics, they have been socially crystallized as part of communal stereotypes. To some indigenous Fijians, the current leader of the Indo-Fijian community, Mahendra Chaudhry, is the embodiment of Indian power hunger, selfishness, and arrogance. To some Indo-Fijians, Laisenia Qarase, the indigenous Fijian prime minister, represents Fijian incompetence and lack of sophistry. Collective stereotypes are embedded in individual personalities and vice versa.

Ethnic identity is mostly invoked in everyday discourse within the private domain and sometimes by extremist nationalists. The 2000 coup leader

George Speight once said that his nationalist beliefs were not against Indian culture but for protection of indigenous political rights and identity from being undermined by Indo-Fijians. The fear of being politically dominated by Indo-Fijians has always been a powerful undercurrent which helps drive indigenous nationalism. Similarly, ethnic identity is also invoked in times of national celebrations and when there is talk of national reconciliation and unity, where notions of multiculturalism and cultural tolerance become dominant themes. Often ethnic identity is eclipsed by political identity.

Fijian people have come to take ethnic identity for granted because it is always there and will not be taken away, even if one's political identity is perceived to be usurped. Sometimes protection of political identity in the form of rights and privileges would come before protection of basic cultural values and ethnic identity. This is often the case with the indigenous Fijian nationalist discourse, where demand for political rights interfaces with ethnic domination. Often political rights may refer to political "protection," as in the colonial days, and sometimes it may refer to political domination, a view that became prevalent since the nationalist military coup in 1987.

THE POST-COLONIAL CHALLENGE: UNITY IN DIVERSITY

The demarcated political space created by the British divide and rule policy spawned the separate development of the two communal identities, which became crystallized and reproduced over the years as part of Fiji's dominant ethnic discourse (Ratuva 2002b). The communal discourses, institutions, and political culture Fiji inherited at independence were products of the colonial communal engineering process, where politics were deliberately configured along communal lines. The major post-colonial challenge was to construct a new discourse, which synthesized different communal identities into a common national identity yet maintained communal distinctiveness. This experiment accounted for the syncretic nature of Fiji's post-colonial political configuration, where multiple communal identities were accommodated in a broader national political identity.

The dominant political discourse under Mara's postcolonial Alliance government since independence in 1970 was "multiracialism" (Mara 1997). Fiji's multi-racial model was based on the Alliance Party structure itself, which consisted of three arms. These were the Fijian Association, whose membership was by indigenous Fijians; the Indian Alliance, which was for Indo-Fijians; and the General Electors Association, which was for Europeans, Part-Europeans, Chinese, Pacific Islanders, and other minorities. This model was based on the post-colonial Malaysian consociationalist arrangement, where various ethnic-based political parties such as the United Malays National Organization (for indigenous Malays), Malaysian Chinese Association (for Chinese), and Malaysian Indian Congress (for Indians) constituted the umbrella Malaysian Alliance (Ratuva 1999). Fiji was on the verge of replicating the Malaysian consociationalist model at independence, but after the ethnic riots in Malaysia in 1969 this ambition was promptly shelved.

Nevertheless, although the Alliance Party model was not replicated within the state political structure, the party philosophy still provided the ideological fulcrum on which the multi-racialist discourse of the postcolonial state was launched. This multi-racialist discourse was to embody the political identity of the state. But there was a fundamental contradiction within this state identity. On one hand was the assumption that the state was the ultimate embodiment of a political synthesis of diverse political identities, and on the other hand, there was the conscious attempt to preserve communal distinctiveness through separate political representation and encouragement of separate cultural identities.

Another significant characteristic was that multi-racialism only involved convergence of political identities, not ethnic or cultural identities. Ethnic identities were considered too sacred to be shared with others. Thus, the multi-racialist state identity existed independently of ethnic and cultural identity. Multi-racial interaction became a purely symbolic exercise in the form of official observance of each community's religious holidays[16] and everyday accommodation of selected aspects of each other's cultural products, such as food. Curry became the most popular dish among all communities.

Political identity was very much crystallized by the constitution itself. For instance, of the fifty-two parliamentary seats under the 1970 independence constitution, indigenous Fijians were allocated twenty-two, Indo-Fijian twenty-two, and other minorities eight (Fiji Government 1970). The seat distribution was meant to serve two purposes simultaneously: first, to maintain a sense of ethnic balance and accommodation and thus create an impression of a unified national identity; and second, to preserve distinctive communal interests. The 1990 and 1997 constitutions also provided similar formulae for ethnic representation but in varying communal proportions. And while political balance and communal accommodation were fundamentally dichotomous, they remained the primary variables for sustaining the syncretic post-colonial political formula.

The political identity of the state was assumed to be the sum of the distinctive political identities of different communities. In operational terms, the identity of the state was only viable and legitimate if the distinctive political identities of ethnic groups remained mutually balanced, both numerically and in terms of political power. But as we saw during the 1987 and 2000 coups, this uneasy formula was sustainable only if political power rested with the indigenous Fijian elites. This dilemma symbolizes the central paradox of Fiji's communal democracy.

Since independence in 1970, the center of political gravity for this power balance lay with the indigenous Fijian chiefly system and indigenous bureaucratic elite and intelligentsia. Chiefs in particular provided the main symbolic and functional power behind the Alliance Party. Chiefly identity (*vakaturaga*) was the symbolic force used to legitimize indigenous Fijian political identity and legitimacy (Ratuva 1999). The state's multi-racial identity was actively articulated through political rhetoric, national celebration of ethnic and religious holidays, multicultural celebrations during the Fiji national day (October 10), and political propaganda through the press and tourism marketing overseas. The Air Pacific (Fiji's international airline) marketing slogan was "Fiji: The way the world should be." The Fiji multi-racial model was seen as one of the most successful in the world. On his visit to Fiji in 1986, Pope John Paul II commented that Fiji's multi-racial society was an exemplary one for the rest of the world.

This delicate imagery projection was important for the Alliance Party's legitimacy, and it hoped that the propagated multi-racial identity of the state would have political spin-offs and would be beneficial for its international and local image-making and political campaigns. This would give it the uncontested status as the only legitimate party to rule a multi-ethnic Fiji society. The claim was perfectly justified given that the other two major parties were monoethnic in nature: the predominantly Indo-Fijian National Federation Party and the predominantly indigenous Fijian Nationalist Party. The Alliance's multi-racial appeal helped to consolidate its national hegemony by linking up various communities, socio-economic classes, religions, ethnic groups, political persuasions, and state institutions such as the military into a "national consensus" of sorts. The power gravity of this consensus revolved around Fijian chiefly authority, Indo-Fijian business acumen, and European capital.

The resilience of the Alliance Party hegemony was first tested in 1977 when it lost the general election to the predominantly Indo-Fijian National Federation Party (NFP). The loss was due to the 25 percent swing of indigenous Fijian votes to the extremist Fijian Nationalist Party and a 16 percent swing of Indo-Fijian votes to the National Federation Party. But because the NFP could not form a government on time, the Governor General, Sir George Cakobau, himself a high chief, appointed Ratu Sir Kamisese Mara (another high chief and relative) prime minister until the next election later the same year. The election was historically significant because it manifested the uneasy relationship between multi-racialism and indigenous Fijian political identity. The Alliance's claim to have a monopoly over indigenous Fijian political identity and loyalty was proven wrong by the Fijian Nationalist Party, which sought to undermine the Alliance's multiracial discourse. Playing on the fear of "an Indian takeover," they managed to push the notion of indigenous Fijian political paramountcy to the forefront. The nationalists were angered by what they saw as Mara's close liaison with Indo-Fijian business and his manipulation of the chiefly authority to maintain his personal power and wealth.

Since 1977, the struggle over who legitimately represented indigenous Fijian political identity and interests became part of intraindigenous Fijian communal conflict. This was further compounded by the formation of the Western United Front (WUF), a political party, which claimed to represent the interests of the indigenous Fijians in the western part of Fiji. "Westerners," as they are affectionately called, have always maintained a sense of autonomy relative to other parts of Fiji (Durutalo 1986). The Alliance Party ruled for another ten years before once again losing the 1987 general election, this time to the multi-racial but predominantly Indo-Fijian Fiji Labour Party–NFP coalition. The defeat of the Alliance Party shifted the center of political gravity away from the mainstream indigenous Fijian power bloc, and this caused an imbalance in the original political equation. This seismic shift shook the very foundation of the Alliance establishment and, as a result, the multi-racial façade, which was once projected as state identity, crumbled and gave way to indigenous Fijian ethno-nationalism. The Alliance's defeat was interpreted by many indigenous Fijians as a direct threat to indigenous political identity. For example, indigenous Fijians in the Labour Party such as Dr. Timoci Bavadra, party leader and deposed prime minister, were branded as "traitors" and "Indian lovers" by nationalist propagandists (Ravuvu 1991).

ETHNIC IDENTITY TRUMPS CLASS

Moreover, the Fiji Labour Party itself suffered from an identity crisis in that while it prided itself as a multi-racial, working-class party, most of its elected politicians were Indo-Fijians. Ignoring the class basis of the party's political thrust, to the nationalists, this became visible "evidence" of Indian takeover. The electoral victory of the Labour-led coalition posed a threat not only to the indigenous Fijian chiefly establishment but also to the Indo-Fijian and European business community, who were loyal to the Alliance and saw a trade unionist–led government as a threat to their business-class interests. A number of big businesses were alleged to have been involved in the destabilization campaigns after Dr. Bavadra came to power (Bain 1994).

On May 14 the coup took place. The indigenous Fijian political identity, nurtured and finely balanced with multi-racialism during the early postcolonial era, exerted itself in an unprecedented violent way. The military, a powerful arm of the chiefly establishment and Alliance consensus, intervened to shift the center of gravity back to where it once was (Sanday 1991;

Ratuva 1999). The Alliance consensus had collapsed and in its place grew an extremely nationalistic indigenous movement whose ideas converged with those of the Fijian Nationalist Party. This movement, which called itself the *Taukei* Movement, initiated the nationalist protests, which preceded the coup. The multi-racial identity of the Alliance Party, which it bestowed ceremoniously on the state as national identity, became a façade that only held up when there was indigenous Fijian political rule. The outwardly expressed multi-racial identity was not congruent with the underlying dynamics of political reality. Nowhere, however, was a class appreciation of the social divisions apparent. This testifies to the deep racialization of public political consciousness.

Upon taking political power in 1987, Lt. Colonel Sitiveni Rabuka abrogated the 1970 Constitution and later promulgated the 1990 Constitution, which institutionalized indigenous Fijian control of the state and created an ethnocratic state of sorts. Among other things, it prescribed an ethnic quota of fifty percent or more in the civil service and political dominance of indigenous Fijians. But the ethnocratic state did not last long. The indigenous Fijian identity of the state slowly subsided as a result of increased internal and external pressure on the regime. The prime minister, Sitiveni Rabuka, coup leader and self-styled biblical Moses of the indigenous Fijians, succumbed to these pressures and agreed to constitutional reform in the direction of a multiracial constitution. That constitution (of 1997) aimed to reestablish multiculturalism as the state political identity. It was different from the 1970 Constitution because it was the product of nationwide and international consultation. The 1970 Constitution was the product of closed-doors consociationalist negotiation and compromise between indigenous Fijian and Indo-Fijian leaders in London. Thus, in terms of process, the 1997 Constitution had greater democratic legitimacy.

However, both constitutions were the same in that each attempted to define the state identity as multicultural yet accommodated separate political identities for different ethnic communities. The 1997 Constitution attempted to provide greater space for inter-ethnic engagement through an increase in the number of common roll or cross-ethnic seats. It was hailed as one of the "best" constitutions in the world. It provided for affirmative action, a bill of rights, proportional ethnic representation to parliament, and a relatively equitable democratic electoral process through the Alternative Vote (AV) preferential system. But one of the fundamental problems was that indigenous Fijian nationalists saw it as posing a threat to indigenous interests. A significant number of Fijian provinces (eight out of fourteen) rejected the *Reeves Report* produced by the Constitutional Review Commission (CRC) as the basis for the new constitution, which was a form of social engineering, and which attempted to "force" political parties and ethnic groups to work together through the AV electoral system and multi-party cabinet.

The first election after the 1997 Constitution took place in 1999 and saw the victory of the Fiji Labour Party. The Labour victory swept aside the political middle-ground alliance of coup leader Rabuka and Jai Ram Reddy, the leader of the NFP. Rabuka had been transformed from a fiery nationalist demagogue to a moderate multi-racialist. He articulated his reconciliatory politics by joining hands with Reddy's NFP and initiating institutional reform towards multi-racialism. However, Indo-Fijian voters voted overwhelmingly for the Labour Party, which swept through all Indo-Fijian seats. The NFP did not win a single seat. Even Reddy, a well-respected politician of statesman-like status and champion of the Indo-Fijian rights for decades, copped the brunt of the humiliation by losing his own seat.

The Fiji Labour Party under Mahendra Chaudhry effectively manipulated the racial card and, ironically, fear of indigenous Fijian domination to mobilize support by masquerading as the only defender of Indo-Fijian interests. Still oblivious to the class interests of their political leaders, the Indo-Fijian voters had rejected the middle-ground reconciliatory politics overwhelmingly and opted to maintain communal, ethnic solidarity. The multi-ethnic spirit of the 1997 Constitution had minimal impact on the Indo-Fijian political psychology. Because of its social engineering mechanics and moderate ideological focus, the 1999 Constitution was only workable in the context of middle-ground politics.

THE POLITICS OF ETHNIC DISTRACTION

Just like fifteen years before, the Labour victory frighteningly shifted the center of political gravity once more. Although Chaudhry, the first Indo-Fijian prime minister, decided to co-opt two major indigenous Fijian political parties, the Fijian Association Party (FAP) and Veitokani ni Lewenilotu Vakarisito (VLV), into the ruling equation, this was seen by many indigenous Fijians as a form of multi-racial tokenism by a man who had earlier rejected the Rabuka-Reddy multi-ethnic experiment in the first place. To win universal acceptance Chaudhry tried to appease indigenous Fijians through provision of senior cabinet positions to indigenous Fijians, building alliances with chiefs and articulating pro-indigenous development initiatives. Chaudhry's antics did not work as nationalists saw him as an untrustworthy political manipulator and a symbol of *Kaidia* (Indian) domination.

The shift in the political center of gravity toward Indo-Fijian communalism was to have drastic consequences for political stability. The indigenous Fijian ethno-nationalists interpreted it as a direct affront to their political and cultural interests, in particular what they saw as their right as perpetual rulers of their ancestral land, under the "paramountcy of Fijian interest" principle. On May 19, 2000, a group of elite soldiers and nationalist politicians and civilians, led by George Speight, a businessman and alleged conman, staged a coup that toppled Chaudhry's government. The members of the deposed government were held hostage for more than a month. The military, the last bastion of state authority, intervened to save the state from being taken over by the nationalist rebels after the unarmed police were ineffective against Speight's armed thugs and after the president's life had been threatened. The military abrogated the constitution and declared martial law and put in place an interim government, which governed Fiji until new elections in August 2001. That election was won by the *Soqosoqo Duavata ni Lewe ni Vanua* (SDL), roughly translated as Association for People's Unity, under current Prime Minister Laisenia Qarase.

The military was the last bastion of state authority and intervened to salvage the state from domination by extremist nationalists. This was a change in political stance by the military compared to its intervention in 1987. The military had by now identified itself as a national institution rather than simply an arm of the indigenous Fijian establishment. This identity transformation had been going on for a number of years as a result of the new leadership after the departure from the military of Rabuka, who had politicized the Fiji military in a blatantly ethnicist way. The military did not back the coup because a number of senior officers insisted that the military was not going to be used by the rebels to serve their political interests. They did not want to go through the same futile and humiliating process as 1987. This change of stance by the military was symbolic because, unlike in 1987, the military leadership no longer saw the military as an indigenous Fijian institution intervening on behalf of indigenous Fijian ethno-nationalism but as a state institution to serve the national interest. Part of the process of redefining its identity included reprofessionalization and depoliticization of the military organizational structure and ideology.

The 2000 coup brought the shift of the state's political identity full circle: from multi-racialism (1970–1987) to indigenous nationalism (1987–1997), from indigenous nationalism to multi-racialism (1997–1999), and from multi-racialism to indigenous nationalism (2000–2003). The victory by the SDL during the August 2001 election consolidated indigenous Fijian control once more as the post-2000 coup state was dominated largely by indigenous Fijian actors. The new prime minister, Laisenia Qarase, who came into power in the 2001 general election, saw himself having to balance between keeping his indigenous Fijian constituency happy and providing a national political appeal to maintain a sense of trust, confidence, and security among Indo-Fijians. This has not been easy given Qarase's openly pro-indigenous policies.

The tension between national and ethnic interests again came to the fore when in July 2003 the Supreme Court ruled that in accordance with the 1997 Constitutional provision, Qarase was to reserve a number of cabinet positions for Chaudhry's Indo-Fijian dominated Labour Party. Interestingly, both

Qarase and Chaudhry won elections through ethnic appeal, but the Supreme Court ruled in favor of a multi-party, multi-ethnic cabinet. At the time of writing the two parties were still negotiating the number of seats each would have. Already, however, the more nationalist indigenous Fijians are not happy with the court's decision and are blaming the multi-racial constitution for the crisis. They are still adamant that the cabinet and government, for that matter, must always be in the hands of the indigenous Fijians. But government has agreed to the multiparty formula. The question, however, is how much ethnic accommodation will it allow?

CONCLUSION

The construction and reproduction of communal identity in Fiji is a complex phenomenon. While there are primordial factors associated with such identity, there are also interrelated social, cultural, and political considerations that shape communal relations and perceptions. Furthermore, as discussed in chapter 1, given the nature of colonial domination, questions of identity are also complicated by the manipulation of race and ethnic markers that are used to divide and distract colonial subjects. This notwithstanding, the government's take on communal identity steered clear of any hint of class politics, for the latter is far too politically and socially destabilizing and not easy to accommodate within a colonial capitalist project. The reproduction and institutionalization of ethnic and political identity in Fiji was fundamental to the British colonial policy of divide and rule.

Ethnic identity was used as the basis for constructing and articulating political identity in both its institutional and ideological manifestations. Contestation over state power then became and still continues to be based on ethnic and political identification and consciousness. Essentially, ethnic and political identities are not identical, but through years of evolution they have been molded into inseparable components of communal politics. One defines the other in an almost symbiotic relationship. While there is clamor for a political identity at the national level, there is also demand for distinctive ethnic identity. These tendencies exist "mutually" side by side, revealing the clear syncretic nature of Fiji's communal democracy.

In sum, then, Fiji's communal democracy has a complex dynamics of its own that changes as a result of shifts in the political and ethnic center of gravity. The search for political equilibrium in Fiji's communal democracy has been constantly subverted by indigenous ethno-nationalism, justified by the ideology of paramountcy of Fijian interests. Ironically, indigenous nationalism is itself a product of communal democracy, which encourages and reproduces civic political identity and distinctive communal identity simultaneously. The 2000 coup brought to the surface a lot of the contradictions of communal democracy. The military intervened and thwarted the indigenous civilian takeover of the state; but the state system has not in itself changed, despite the change in the ideological and professional focus of the military away from being an institution of indigenous rights to one that serves national interests. The political interplay between ethnic identity and national identity has caused tensions that have provided the environment for greater accommodation but remains a salient feature of Fiji's communal democracy.

NOTES

1. States with similar ethnic configuration as Fiji, such as Malaysia, have been referred to as syncretic states. See Jesudason (1996).

2. Joel Migdal's "state in society theory" becomes instructive here. For him, the state consists of societal forces in a state of perpetual competition and contestation over state power. This is very similar to the dynamics of ethnic competition in Fiji, where ethnic groups contend for control of the state (Migdal 2001).

3. In Fiji the officially designated ethnic groups are Fijians, Indians, and Others (those categorized as neither Fijian nor Indian). This categorization is problematic and has been criticized because it assumes a given set of ethnic characteristics that are universally agreed upon. Given the racial paralysis of Western society that stems from the history of African slavery and its aftermath, and owing to their gross phenotypical features, Fijians would appear to the Western eye as "blacks." The latter, however, is a Western political concept that makes no sense to the Fijian. Indeed, in Fiji, the closest term in the language is *Melanesian* (from melanin), which is very differently politically charged than "black."

4. Indigenous Fijians felt comfortable under the paternalistic atmosphere of the native policy, and over time they had come to accept British hegemony as the most "natural" political condition.

5. The term *historical bloc* is used here in the Gramscian sense to refer to the alliances forged between fractions of power holders to maintain hegemony or rule by consent (Gramsci [1971] 1997).

6. This coup d'état was most reminiscent of the Muslimeen coup and momentary take over of the Trinidad government in 1990.

7. Perhaps one of the earliest exponents of the primordial approach was the American sociologist Edward Shils, who in 1957 referred to it as "a state of intense and comprehensive solidarity" (quoted in McKay 1982:398).

8. The social constructionist view has been called different things by different scholars. For example, there is the "situational approach," which stresses the flexibility of the concept (Ratcliffe 1994). McKay, on the other hand, describes it as "mobilizational" because ethnicity can be used for purposes of political mobilization.

9. The distinction between "groups" and "categories" must be drawn. A "group," as in an ethnic group, represents a collectivity as meaningfully conceptualized and defined by its members who are self-aware of their distinctiveness. A "category," alternatively, is a collectivity defined in relation to criteria formulated by social researchers (sociologists, anthropologists, etc.).

10. This situation is virtually identical to that of the Indo-Trinidadian as discussed by Allahar (1998a) and Ryan (1999b).

11. In 2001 a committee was set up to review the system of Fijian Administration. It recommended a number of changes aimed at making indigenous Fijians adapt better to modern changes, but the recommendations were rejected on the grounds that they would lead to a breakdown in Fijian culture. See *Fijilive.com* and *Daily Post*, Friday September 20, 2002.

12. Once more, the parallels with Indo-Trinidadians are most compelling.

13. For instance, see the *Fijilive* website discussion forum. This of course is not unique to Fijians abroad, for a cursory surfing of the web will reveal that similar fora abound among Trinidadians and Guyanese.

14. The similarities with Basdeo Panday in Trinidad, particularly in the 1990s, are striking and compelling. Both Chaudry and Panday were the first Indian prime ministers of their respective countries, and both employed the rhetoric of ethnic solidarity and communalism to appeal to Indian voters (Allahar 1998a). And although Cheddi Jagan was the first Indian prime minister of Guyana, his socialist philosophy and ideology led him to privilege the class question over the race and ethnic one.

15. The term *paramountcy of Fijian interest* originally referred to provision of special favors for indigenous Fijians. Over the years, however, especially after the nationalist-inspired 1987 military coup, it took on a more aggressive posture and was driven by the demand for indigenous Fijian political domination.

16. In Fiji the main religious holidays observed apart from the Christian ones are Prophet Mohammed's birthday and the Hindu Divali (festival of light) celebration.

8

Theoretical Reflections on Ethnicity and Nationalism: The Kurdish Question in Turkey, 1923–1980

Cenk Saraçoğlu

The recent rise of ethnic movements and ethnic conflicts all around the world constitutes an anomaly for liberal ideology since it anticipated the demise of ethnic attachments following the development of industrial capitalism (Hutchinson and Smith 1996:v). Most of the liberal ideologues expected that the liberation of market forces from social and political control would give birth to the emancipation of all people, who would in turn inhabit a prosperous world free of social conflict. Industrialization, they felt, would remove the bases for ethnic and racial identification, which were assumed to be "pre-modern" forms of attachment. Consequently, the conflicts stemming from these "pre-modern" ties were expected to vanish. The idea of individualism, which was supposed to be a general norm in industrial capitalist societies, was assumed to transcend and trivialize "pre-modern" forms of collective identification:

> Racial and ethnic forms of identification and social organization, though historically important, were *unnatural* and represented archaic or pre-modern forms of social organization. In a modern industrial society (of which the United States was the supreme example) in which social positions are allocated on the basis of achieved criteria such as education, learned skills, and personal qualities, racial and ethnic criteria were both inappropriate and a hindrance to social functioning. Racial and ethnic criteria were thus incompatible with a modern form of society that required meritocracy for its proper development and could be expected, over time, to disappear. (Thompson 1989:73)

Today's reality, however, contradicts all of these expectations (see chapter 1). The persistence and renewal of conflictual forms of social identification

such as religious fundamentalism, ethnic nationalism, and racism indicate
that the promises of liberalism are far from being realized.

But liberals were not alone in this optimistic view, for among orthodox
Marxists an assimilative power was attributed to industrial capitalism, according to which ethnic or tribal ties would be replaced by class-consciousness
and class identities. The class-based identifications were expected to transcend all other pre-capitalist or feudal forms of social identification. This expectation inevitably led orthodox Marxism to ignore the significance of ethnicity and ethnic conflict in capitalist social formations. Because "class" was
held to be the only relevant form of identification in capitalist societies, the relationship between the class and ethnicity or ethnic nationalism was not thoroughly theorized.

Nevertheless, I will argue that this problem is not inherent in Marxism's
general theoretical framework and its essential propositions. Rather, this is a
problem of the orthodox interpretation of Marxism, which is generally silent
on the relationship between capitalism and ethnicity. In this chapter I argue
that by preserving the essential premises of dialectical materialism, it is still
possible to interpret and theorize the relationship between the phenomena of
class and ethnic consciousness. However, to develop an alternative interpretation of Marxism primarily entails a critique of the orthodox Marxist understanding of dialectical materialism. Therefore, after the critique of orthodox
Marxism I will suggest that it is best to adopt a dialectical understanding of the
relationship between the capitalist relations of production or class relations
and the development of ethnic consciousness or ethnic mobilization. The
theoretical assumptions involved in this approach will then be applied to the
historical development of the Kurdish question in Turkish capitalism. This
will enable a better critical understanding of ethnic conflict in a capitalist society. My investigation will comprise three (concrete-abstract-concrete) dialectically related steps. The first step is to show why the assumptions of orthodox Marxism are not helpful in providing an understanding or explanation
of those concrete cases in which capitalism is directly responsible for ethnic
mobilization. The second is an abstract or theoretical rethinking of Marxism
based on these empirical manifestations, to which orthodox Marxism could
not develop a comprehensive theoretical explanation. The third and final step
is the interpretation and analysis of the development of capitalism in Turkey
and its relationship to the so-called Kurdish Question. To begin I will offer
some definitions of key terms such as *ethnicity* and *nationalism*.

CONCEPTUAL DEFINITIONS

In dialectical materialism, the fact that "how things happen" is taken as a part
of "what they are" (Ollman 1993) makes it analytically impossible to provide

time- and context-independent definitions for any social phenomenon. This holds true for the notions of ethnicity and nationalism, which take different forms in different times and in different social contexts (Davis 1978:4). Therefore, my conceptualization of ethnicity and nationalism here will reflect the particularity of the empirical situation under examination. But this is not to deny the fact that the sentiments of ethnicity and nationalism in their general forms have persisted in industrial capitalism. The point is that, depending on the empirical context, these sentiments have been incorporated to different social elements in different times and places.

I take ethnicity as a form of social relation between people who regard themselves as being *culturally* distinct from others (Eriksen 2002:4). This is to say that for ethnicity to come about, a group of people should have a sentiment of "we-ness," and hence should be able to perceive the people outside their group as "others." Because this consciousness is constituted and prolonged through social relations and interaction, it becomes necessary to reproduce these relations for the maintenance of ethnic identities. Thus, individuals in an ethnic group should be in contact with or aware of the members in their own group in order to prolong their ethnic consciousness or ethnic identities. In other words, there should be certain social practices among the members of an ethnic group that enable them to define themselves in relation to the members of other groups.

Ethnicity could be created from a variety of social bases. The social commonalities of religion, language, and culture can all constitute the basis for ethnic identity formation. However, it is undeniable that the concrete form of ethnic identities might vary according to what constitutes the basis for the sentiment of "we-ness" (Oomen 1997:17). The important thing to note is that the *real* existence of these commonalities is neither necessary nor sufficient for ethnicity to come about. Rather, what is significant is whether the members of an ethnic group consider these commonalities real, or whether there are strong social mechanisms that would make the individuals of an ethnic group believe that these commonalities really exist. As Anton Allahar puts it:

> To argue that some aspect of behaviour is irrational is not to say that it does not exist or is not real, since the consequences are quite real for those whom they touch, whether or not the latter accept the definition of the situation adopted by those who initiate the behaviour in question. Thus, whether or not a blood tie actually exists between a given person and his or her community, is less important than the fact that he or she *believes* it does and acts in accordance with such belief. (1996:7)

Furthermore, because the social significance and power of ethnic identities in shaping group action and social activity may vary according to location and time, the following questions suggest themselves: Under what social conditions do ethnic attachments become important? What kind of social factors are important in influencing the political behaviors of an ethnic group? How does a change in the political behaviors of a certain ethnic group affect the general organization of society? Answers to these questions will be pursued in the investigation of the relationship between ethnic identities and capitalist relations of production in Turkey.

Like ethnicity, nationalism is a form of social relation through which members of a social group construct a sense of "we-ness" and define the non-members as outsiders. Also, like ethnic identities, national identities can be constructed on the basis of any social commonality that is continuously reproduced in daily practice. However, the essential character of the nation, which distinguishes it from the category of ethnicity, is that nations can only be defined according to their relationship to an existing state or a state to be imagined by the members of that nation. Then we can argue that a nation *might* be an ethnic group that links its commonalities with an idea of a state. This is the case with ethnic nationalism as discussed in chapter 1. At the same time, a nation can be composed of more than one ethnic group, giving rise to a civic nationalism, where ethnic groups identify themselves not only in ethnic terms but also in accordance with their civic identities (Eriksen 2002:119). Certain forms of nationalism, therefore, may not have a dominant ethnic character. An important point that will be developed later is that nationalism and national identity can be employed ideologically to conceal existing class differences within a *nation*.

Ethnic nationalism, on the other hand, is an ideal that holds that a defined territory should be governed by a state whose structure is shaped according to values of one dominant ethnic group. This is to say that ethnic nationalism is a form of ethnic consciousness that is tied to the idea of a state. Thus, as will be seen, the notion of "Turkish ethnic nationalism" refers to the idea that all social and political relations in Turkey should be organized according to cultural values of Turkish ethnicity. Kurdish ethnic nationalism, on the other hand, implies that it is necessary to form a separate state in the Kurdish areas of Turkey, which is to be constituted on the basis of Kurdish ethnicity. For according to my particular conceptualization, Kurdish and Turkish ethnic nationalism are necessarily irreconcilable sentiments.

DIALECTICAL MATERIALISM AND ETHNIC STUDIES

The issues of nationality and ethnicity have always been a source of friction for orthodox Marxist interpretations of capitalist societies (Doane 1996:176). In particular, two key theoretical understandings of orthodox Marxist interpretations close the doors to any possible theorization of the relationship between capitalist relations of production and the sentiments of nationalism or ethnicity. The first is the idea that the fundamental contradiction between labor and capital in a capitalist society shapes all superstructural institutions like the state, law, politics, ideology, and culture. According to this idea, any form of social relationship in a capitalist society is taken as a direct reflection of class relations (Berberoglu 1994:20), which in turn renders concerns with nation and ethnicity as secondary (Davis 1978:3). Stated differently, because the fundamental division in a capitalist society is assumed to take place between the working class and the capitalists, all other forms of political self-identification are simply taken to be irrelevant for orthodox Marxist analysis, also known as "reductionist economism" (Kellner 1989:11).

Another theoretical difficulty with orthodox Marxist interpretations on the national and ethnic question is its presupposition that ethnicity, race, and kinship—as precapitalist sentiments—would be *spontaneously* dissolved with the emergence of industrial capitalist societies. This dissolution occurs because of the ostensible fact that capitalism homogenizes all nonclass groups and divisions. It is felt that modern, industrial society would create a convenient social milieu for social groups to organize themselves only according to their class interests. As an extension of this theoretical position, orthodox Marxist interpretations maintain that because ethnicity and ethnic conflict characterize precapitalist social formations, they are not relevant for analyzing capitalist relations of production. I call this logic, which inevitably pushes the notion of ethnicity outside the realm of Marxian social theory, the "mechanistic understanding of Marxism." Both the reductionist economism and mechanistic understanding of Marxism can easily be seen in the writings of Hilferding, Kautsky, and Plekenhov (Kellner 1989; Merleau-Ponty 1973).

While there are certain assumptions in Marxist theoretical frameworks that might encourage the above theoretical conclusions, I argue that an alternative reading of Marx is possible. This alternative reading might provide significant conceptual and theoretical tools for us to understand the formation and the transformation of ethnic identities and the relationship between the reality of ethnic mobilization and the general organization of capitalist society. However, before showing the possibility of Marxist theorization of the notions of ethnicity and nationalism, a critique of the two above-mentioned theoretical premises of orthodox Marxism is necessary. At this point it is important to note that my criticism will target not only the orthodox Marxists but also some non-Marxist scholars who criticized Marx or Marxist theory—rather than a specific interpretation of Marxism—for being inherently reductionist. The latter is also an orthodox interpretation of Marxism because by using some vulgar interpretations of dialectical materialism, they abstain from thinking of an alternative interpretation of Marxism and criticize Marxist theory on the basis of their oversimplified or orthodox understanding of Marxist methodology.

A CRITIQUE OF REDUCTIONIST ECONOMISM

Reductionist economism refers to a theoretical position arguing that the labor-capital contradiction in capitalist societies directly determines the superstructural institutions of those societies.[1] In Kellner's words:

> Orthodox Marxism at the time tended toward a reductionistic "economism," which interpreted the dynamics of history primarily in terms of economic development in the "base" that supposedly controlled developments within the "superstructure." This version of Marxism was deterministic in two dimensions: the economic base determined the superstructure, and laws of history, rooted in the economy, determined the trajectory of all social life. (1989:11)

When the labor-capital contradiction is taken as a universal abstraction—regardless of specific social contexts and in spite of problems that surround unilateral deterministic arguments—we can expect that all capitalist societies will take the same form, whatever their specific conditions and characteristics. However, historical evidence shows us that although the labor-capital contradiction becomes an essential element of all capitalist societies, in each society the capitalist social formation exhibits context-specific variability. In other words, each capitalist society conveys some historical and contextual specificity. The reason for this situation is that in capitalist societies the base or the labor-capital contradiction reflects on superstructural institutions through existing contextually and historically specific media.

In addition to this, the superstructural institutions—shaped by the economic base—in turn influence the essential labor-capital production in capitalist societies. Therefore, in opposition to the orthodox Marxist formulation, we can argue that the economic base and social superstructure are not in a directly deterministic relationship but rather a dialectical one in which both evolve together and reinforce one another. This is quite explicitly expressed in Engels's writings:

> According to the materialist conception of history the determining element in history is *ultimately* the production and reproduction in real life. More than this neither Marx nor I have ever asserted. If therefore somebody twists this into the statement that the economic element is the *only* determining one, he transforms it into a meaningless, abstract and absurd phrase. The economic situation is the basis, but the various elements of the superstructure . . . also exercise their influence upon the course of the historical struggles and in many cases preponderate in determining their *form*. There is an interaction of all these elements, in which, amid all endless *host* of accidents (i.e., of things and events whose inner connection is so remote or so impossible to prove that we regard it as absent and can neglect it), the economic movement finally asserts itself as necessary. ([1890] 1977:487)

It is necessary, therefore, to understand not only the relations in the economic realm but also in the political, ideological, and cultural realms in order to comprehensively analyze the dynamics of change in a capitalist society. Most important, it becomes vital to unravel the interconnections of social life. This implies that class struggle is not limited to the economic sphere where exploitation actually occurs, but "it expands from economic and social spheres into the spheres of politics and ideology" (Berberoglu 1994:27).

Engels's clarification notwithstanding, some commentators continue to criticize Marxist theory for being inherently reductionist because of the alleged deterministic power of the dynamic base over the passive superstructure. On this basis writers like Ernest Gellner (1983:94, 115) and Liah Greenfeld (1992:489) argue that Marxism is unable to take account of the notions of nationalism and ethnicity and remains locked in an economic determinist logic. Gellner, for example, states that "crucial superstructural features (the state and literacy) do not correlate with the appearance of the really decisive infrastructure change" (1983:115), thus repeating an earlier criticism (Ibid:94). And for his part, James Kellas finds Marxist theory irrelevant for the study of ethnic and national mobilization when he charges that:

> Marxists and other economic determinists believe that social and political behaviour can be reduced to economic interests, particularly those of economic classes, sections, groups and so on. Thus nationalism is seen as either a disguised economic interest or in Marxist terms as "false consciousness" which has misled people and stopped them pursuing their "true" class interests. (1991:45)

Not only the critics of Marx but also some proponents of Marxist theory interpret the origin and formation of nationalism through the same unilateral relationship between the base and superstructure. Micheal Hechter (1975), for instance, explains the development of ethnic nationalism in the Celtic region entirely as the result of early British capitalism's exploitation of the region. From this perspective ethnic mobilization in Celtic territories is taken strictly as a response to exploitation of the British bourgeoisie, and Hechter is of course unable to account for the changing political tendencies of Celtic nationalism in history and for Celtic nationalism's reproduction of the dominant social relations of production in that specific social formation (Calhoun 1993:227).

While I do not deny that a specific form of nation or nationalism is tied to a specific mode of production, the rigid, one-way base/superstructure relationship is not *sufficient* to understand the role of the sentiments of nation and nationalism as possibly occurring independently at the superstructural level. This claim permits me to make the theoretical observation that in an

ethnically divided capitalist society, even while ethno-political mobilization
and ethnic conflicts are largely affected by the specific form of class relations
in this society, class relations might also be shaped by ethno-national sentiments. Since the base and superstructural entities are inextricably inter-
woven, ethnic conflicts might be a very important component of the capitalist establishment in a society. The best example of this situation is the
apartheid regime in South Africa, where it became very difficult to separate
ethnic divisions from class divisions and to think of racism independent of
capitalism.

CRITIQUE OF THE MECHANISTIC INTERPRETATION OF MARXISM

Another orthodox assumption open for question is that during the industrialization process all pre-modern attachments, such as ethnicity and kinship,
will be dissolved. Supposedly, this occurs because with the advent of capitalist relations of production people would be denationalized (Townshend
1996:34) and automatically identify more with their class positions.[2] Here,
the formations of class-consciousness and class identity are taken as necessary, mechanistic consequences of the emergence of capitalism, and as a
consequence the role of human agency within the historical and political
process is denied. Such an understanding of Marxism reduces historical materialism to a deterministic, scientific theoretical framework and conceals its
"humanistic" essence that emphasizes praxis. From this mechanistic understanding, Clive Christie, for instance, implies that Marx expects a spontaneous demise of the sentiments of the nation, ethnicity, and nationalism with
the internationalization of capitalism (1998:227).

This mechanistic reading of Marx is the result of an insufficient distinction
between class and class *consciousness*. Although it is undeniable that the
emergence of the bourgeoisie and working class is an integral and necessary
condition for capitalist relations to exist, it does not mean that this will automatically give birth to a subjective construction of class-consciousness and
class identity. Classes and class-consciousness are, in fact, analytically separable constructs (Berberoglu 1994:22). While class-consciousness cannot appear before the emergence of social classes, the classes themselves can have
an independent character. In other words, despite the fact that the presence
of a working class is a necessary component of the capitalist mode of production, development of a class identity would be the result of a political and
social process within which workers become aware of their class position in
a certain capitalist social context. Stated differently, the presence of the capitalist mode of production and of classes is a necessary but not a sufficient
condition for "class identity" and "class consciousness" to form.

This interpretation of the Marxist theoretical framework does not necessitate the transposition of the general Marxian framework but requires a better elaboration and delineation of Marx's ideas. In fact, the above described "objective" and "subjective" understanding of class is embedded in the Marxian conceptions of "class in itself" and "class for itself" (see chapter 1). Marx understands and conceptualizes class and its many related ideas (e.g., alienation, exploitation, relations of production) at different levels of abstraction. Therefore, in order to understand what class means in a certain theoretical context one should take into consideration the level of abstraction that Marx employs (Ollman 1977).

We should distinguish here the *structural* understanding of the working class, which is constructed according to the place of social groups within existing relations of production, and a subjective and more *humanist*[3] understanding of class that accentuates the formation of class-consciousness through certain social and political processes.[4] Marx himself clarifies this distinction:

> Economic conditions had first transformed the mass of the people of the country into workers. The combination of capital has created for this mass a common situation, common interests. This mass is thus already a class as against capital, but not yet for itself. In the struggle, of which we have noted only a few phases, this mass becomes united, and constitutes itself as a class for itself. The interest it defends becomes class interests. But struggle of class against class is a political struggle. (1963:73)

This discussion of the conceptions of class-in-itself and class-for-itself signifies the fact that, as opposed to the orthodox interpretations of Marxism, the abandonment of "pre-capitalist" forms of social identification is not a structural result of the emergence of industrial capitalism. Rather, it is a possibility that can only be realized through certain social and political processes within which workers interact, develop commonalities, unravel bourgeois ideology, and thereby realize where their historical interests lie. In order to create an obstacle to the formation of class identities, the dominant classes always put forward some alternative identities that would override class struggle and class identity. Therefore, when we take into consideration that the bourgeoisie aims to define national identity and its concomitant ideology as hegemonic,[5] in order to blanket class contradictions and prevent a working-class consciousness from developing, social identities themselves become areas of class struggle. In Szymanski's words,

> Nationalism is the advocacy of ethnic or "national" solidarity and action over class-consciousness and action. It is, thus, the opposite of class-consciousness that argues solidarity should occur and political alliances be formed primarily along class lines (even against the relatively privileged groups within one's subordinate

ethnic group). Nationalism and class-consciousness are, thus, alternative strategies of political action for gaining improvement in one's life. (1983:430)

However, in certain historical moments the ideology of nationalism and
national identity might be a constitutive element of working-class consciousness and identity. The relationship between nationalism and class
identity can take different forms according to the specific trajectory of class
struggle in specific social contexts. Class struggle sometimes might include a
struggle for being able to represent national identity and national interests,
which would interpellate people as national subjects against the dominant
classes. This "interpellation" might be *realized through* the formation of a
power bloc, composed of different class factions, under the hegemony of
working-class interests but *based upon* the ideology of nationalism and its
associated identity (Laclau 1977).

In general, however, the labor-capital contradiction—in certain historical moments—can take the form of a contradiction between class identity
and national identity, which indicates to us that issues of ethnic nationalism become vital to understanding the trajectory of class struggles in certain capitalist societies. Ethnic nationalism, in these societies, can function
as an ideological tool of the bourgeoisie to overshadow class identity and
class-consciousness. At this point, one can imagine that the national bourgeoisie will not welcome the appearance of alternative or rival forms of
self-identification, for instance, the emergence of another, potentially
strong and united ethnic movement. As the bourgeoisie aims to hegemo-
nize its own nationalistic ideology, it cannot tolerate the spread of an alternative nationalist system of thought. In this respect, and if only in theory, an ethnic conflict or a counterethnic movement can be perceived as
an aspect of class relations at certain historical moments.

This shows us that the sentiment of ethnicity and nationalism might become a very constitutive element of capitalist societies, contrary to what is
expected by orthodox Marxists. In the particular case of the Kurdish people
in Turkey, I will show that Turkish nationalism has become a constitutive element for the formation of the capitalist relations of production in Turkey. I
also claim that the emergence of a rival Kurdish ethnic mobilization affected
the ideological strategies of the Turkish bourgeoisie, and that this situation
affected the structure of Turkish capitalism in general.

This critique of orthodox Marxism and my alternative theoretical position
necessitate my asking the following preliminary questions in order to analyze the particular case of the Kurds in Turkey: How do the specific characteristics of Turkish capitalism and the changing ideological strategies of the
Turkish bourgeoisie influence the development of a Kurdish ethnic nationalism and a Kurdish political movement? In turn, how do the emergence and
the transformation of Kurdish ethnic nationalism shape the structure of the

capitalist social formation in Turkey, including its ideological, political, and legal structure? By answering these questions I will contextualize the development of Turkish capitalism within the evolution of its Kurdish question, and vice versa. The answers to these questions and the theoretical framework developed above will be embedded in my treatment of the historical development of capitalism and specifically the so-called Kurdish question in Turkey.

THE KURDISH QUESTION IN TURKEY (1923-1980)

"The Kurdish question" is a way of describing the problems that Kurdish people experienced in Turkey and the political and social repercussions of their problems for the entire Turkish society. However, this is not an empty concept used to define this particular problem; rather, it is an indication of a specific political perspective on the situation of Kurds in Turkey. In Turkish political discourse, anyone who uses the term "the Kurdish question" to define the uneasy situation of the Kurds will fall into the camp of those who understand the problems facing the Kurds as stemming fundamentally from the historical suppression of their identities and the denial of their cultural rights in Turkey. In official Turkish discourse, two other concepts are used to describe the same situation, which show the reluctance of the official Turkish to recognize the presence of a particular Kurdish identity. One of these concepts is "the Southeastern Problem," which holds that the problem of the Kurdish people is due mainly to regional economic backwardness, and that this problem can be transcended simply by making new economic investments in that specific area where Kurdish people live. In other words, this means that the problem is not a Kurdish one per se but a regional one. This is actually an ideological distortion of the *space* of the Kurdish question. The other concept is "the terror problem," which implies that the problems of the people in the Southeastern Anatolia are due to the terrorist activities of the PKK (Kurdistan Workers' Party) organization that provoked the Kurdish people to rebel against the Turkish state. When we consider the fact that PKK intensified their activities in the region after 1985, the discourse of "the terror problem" is seen as an ideological distortion of the *history* of the Kurdish question.

WHO ARE THE KURDS?

Before analyzing the relationship between the structure of Turkish capitalism and the evolution of the Kurdish conflict it is necessary to understand what "Kurd" and "Kurdish identity" mean. While clarifying the general characteristics of Kurdish ethnicity I will use the conceptualizations of ethnicity, identity, and nationalism outlined above. As argued before, the existence of the group members' belief that they share certain commonalities is more important than a supposedly real existence of these commonalities. Therefore, while speaking about several constructed and reproduced commonalities among the Kurdish population, the discussion will center on what Kurds believe to be common and unique among them, and how Kurds reproduce these commonalities through certain social practices.

To begin, the geographic concentration of Kurds in the eastern and southeastern parts of the Anatolia is one of the common bases for Kurdish identification. Kurds are settled in a very inaccessible mountainous area that is far from the administrative center of Turkey. This situation has protected the Kurdish people from other external cultural influences and has enabled them to develop strong endogenous relationships. The other significant characteristic of Kurds is that they have always had a belief that they were the indigenous people of Anatolia before Turks migrated to the region in the tenth century (Cornell 2001:34). This belief has long been a significant element in Kurdish ethnic nationalism. The other important commonality is that Kurds, despite having considerably different dialects across Anatolia, have a common language. Some Kurdish nationalists believed that the Kurdish language has its roots in the ancient Medes civilization (Van Bruinessen 1994:15).

Today, the Kurdish regions include eastern and southeastern Anatolia, northeastern Syria, northern Iraq, northwestern Iran, and southern Armenia and Azerbaijan. They do not have a state and are subject to the external authority of other countries, most notably Turkey, Iran, and Iraq. An important point to mention here is that due to the specific characteristics of the capitalist social formations in each of these countries, Kurdish groups in the various countries have developed distinctive features. This was augmented after the 1950s, when the differences in the economic and social conditions of the countries in which Kurds constituted a minority become more marked, and it became very difficult for Kurdish people to develop a transnational social and political community. Therefore, the Kurdish question in Turkey can be analyzed independently of the Kurdish conflict in Iraq and Iran, each of which has its own specific social dynamics.

There are no reliable demographic statistics on the Kurds in any of these countries because of the reluctance of the Middle Eastern governments to conduct a systematic census on the ethnic composition of their people (Ibid.:13). However, most research on the Kurdish question gives a range of between 24 and 27 million Kurdish people in the region. According to this research, almost half of the Kurdish people in the Middle East live in Anatolia, namely within the borders of the Turkish Republic (McDowall 2000:4).

KURDS IN THE OTTOMAN EMPIRE

Before analyzing the relationship between the Turkish capitalist social formation and the Kurdish ethnic movement, I will briefly describe the conditions of the Kurds in the Ottoman Empire. This is necessary to understand the seeds of Turkish capitalism, the accompanying ideology of Turkish nationalism, and the sources of the Kurdish nationalist movement. However, it is not easy to find evidence of significant Kurdish social mobilization during Ottoman times, owing to the nature and structure of Ottoman social organization and the specific features of the Kurdish ethnic group. The Ottoman Empire was a pre-capitalist social formation in which relations of production and economic transactions were cardinally shaped by the efficient exploitation of the land (McCarthy 1997:107). The Sultan, whose position was preserved by an Islamic religious ideology, was assumed to own all the lands within the Ottoman borders on behalf of the state, and the land was temporarily distributed to state officials in exchange for military service. The size and quality of these lands varied according to the significance of the positions held by the state officials (Quataert 2000:28). In exchange for these land grants, state officials had to sustain a specified number of soldiers, which varied according to amount of land ownership. In this system only Muslim people were granted rights to hold certain political positions, directly corresponding to the size of land owned. Again, only Muslims were obliged to work on these lands owned by the state. The non-Muslim subjects were exempt from military and agricultural duties; they instead were required to pay an extra tax, called *cizye*. While paying an extra tax, however, Christian subjects were allowed to partake in the trade activities of the Empire, which put them in an economically superior position vis-à-vis Muslim peasants.

In this system, ethno-linguistic and racial[6] hierarchy was absent. However, the existence of a religion-based stratification was explicit. In this hierarchy, Muslims occupied politically superior positions regardless of their ethnic background (Lewis 1965:329). To be Muslim in the Ottoman Empire functioned as a unifying identity, and encompassed ethno-linguistic groups such as Circussians, Bosnians, Turks, Slavs, Arabs, and Kurds. At this time, the idea of ethno-linguistic stratification was anathema to the logic of Ottoman administration because as long as different ethnic and cultural groups belonged to the Muslim community, they were treated equally as "Ottoman citizens" (McDowall 2000:91). Muslims, then, depending on their political and social abilities, had access to all political and social institutions except the Sultanate, which was a hereditary position. As a result, the idea of "intraethnic" differences among Muslim communities remained "thin" (Cornell and Hartman 1998:83), that is, these differences could not go beyond minimally organizing daily social practice. Under the terms of "Ottoman citizenship," Kurds were viewed ethnically like any other Islamic group, for example, the Turks and Arabs, and "were simply called *ra'yat* (i.e., subjects), without any ethnic label attached" (Van Bruinessen 1992:46).

However, these social balances underwent a profound change towards the end of nineteenth century when Young Turks ("Jeunne Turks")—as the military and bureaucratic elite of the society—acquired a politically powerful position in the Ottoman administration at the expense of the Sultan's power. This newly rising elite upheld the idea of Turkish nationalism, which was designed to justify their rising economic and military positions in the Ottoman Empire at the expense of the Sultan's position. The ultimate aim of the nascent elite was to create a national economy within which they might be able to realize their economic interests. The construction of a national economy primarily necessitated an end to European control over the stagnating Ottoman economy and abolished the economically privileged status of the non-Muslim minorities like Greeks, Jews, and Armenians, who historically had the power to shape the economic balances in the Ottoman Empire by controlling national and international trade activities.[7]

IDEOLOGY OF TURKISH NATIONALISM

Turkish nationalism and the Turkish identity were at this moment in history employed as the ideological justification of the policies toward creating a national economy under the rising bureaucratic military elite. Turkish nationalism was also a challenge to the traditional Sultan's ideology of Ottomanism, which aimed to preserve the status quo. The status quo in the last analysis would favor the interests of European capital and non-Muslim merchants. However, the idea of "Turkishness," which was a created by this bureaucratic-military elite, ran contrary to the longstanding Ottoman organization of society, which followed Islamic prescriptions. As a result, Arabs in the Ottoman territories were alienated from the Ottoman administration and when circumstances demanded their political mobilization, this was done on the basis of their (natural) primordial ethnic ties.

In the nineteenth century, we still cannot find any serious nationalistic mobilization among Kurds, even if the ideology of Turkish nationalism did not involve them. This is because of both the specific intragroup characteristics of Kurds themselves and the inability of the Jeunne Turks to establish a complete hegemony of Turkish nationalism over the Ottoman society, leading to the persistence of Islamic identities as an alternative to "Turkishness." First of all, unlike Arabs and Turks, Kurds lacked an established civic, urban culture and an established literature because they were situated in mountainous areas that presented an obstacle to developing communication and political mobilization. This situation, at the end of the nineteenth century, prevented Kurds from developing an ethnic or nationalist identity in the short run. In addition to this, although the Jeunne Turks were in power after 1908, they were unable to break the persistence of Muslim identity and its Islamist ideology.

Kurds, therefore, challenged Turkish nationalism not with an ethnic Kurdish nationalism but with an Islamist ideology, which unified the pro-Sultan powers in Ottoman society. For all these reasons, during the nineteenth century and the early years of the twentieth century, one cannot see a strong Kurdish ethnic mobilization as Kurdish reaction melted in the larger pot of Islamic movements. This does not mean that there was not a Kurdish identity in these years. Rather, the point is that the Kurdish people considered themselves as distinct from other ethnic groups in Ottoman society because of their linguistic commonalities and geographic concentration; but this identity was "thin" and less important than their Islamic identity. In other words, Kurdish identity was not developed enough to fuel an ethno-political mobilization (McDowall 2000).

The situation of the Kurds in the Ottoman Empire shows us that even if there appeared large-scale social transformations, each ethnic group was unevenly influenced by this transformation. When Turkish nationalism became the ideological instrument of the new bureaucratic elite to challenge the authority of the Sultan, Kurds and Arabs exhibited different reactions to this situation. As opposed to the orthodox Marxist expectation, social and economic transformations do not directly reflect on all ethnic groups equally; instead, their reflections vary according to the specific characteristics of ethnic groups, even if they share the same class position.

This critique of the orthodox interpretation of Marxism and my own theoretical position will become clearer during the discussion of the relationship between the Turkish capitalist social formation and Kurdish ethnic mobilization, spanning the period between 1923 and 1980. I will divide this period into two segments: first, I will discuss the early period of the republic, which followed the demise of the Ottoman Empire and included a rapid and radical modernization and nation-building process that alienated Kurds from the existing system and Turkish state; the second period extends from 1950 to 1980, during which the Kurdish political movement incorporated itself with the Turkish left.

THE DEVELOPMENT OF TURKISH CAPITALISM (1923–1950)

After the demise of the Ottoman Empire following the First World War and the consequent fall of the Ottoman Sultanate, a particular segment of the bureaucratic-military elite in the Ottoman administration acquired political power in the new Turkish Republic. In terms of my theoretical framework, which is to be applied to the Kurdish conflict in Turkey, the most important thing is to unravel the dynamics of Kurdish ethnic nationalism within the context of capitalism in Turkey and to explain how the changes in Kurdish ethnic mobilization, in turn, affected the structure of Turkish capitalism. Therefore, I should first describe the relations of production in Turkey in the early period of the republic (1923–1950), when the social and economic conditions that facilitated a strong capitalist economy were absent, when agricultural production was overwhelmingly dominant, and when there were a few state-owned industrial establishments.[8]

The ultimate objective of the governing elite of the Republic of Turkey, however, was the establishment of industrial capitalism. In order to realize this project, they had to strengthen their political and economic position, which necessitated the establishment of a strong national state through which they would (1) legitimize and exercise their authority and (2) undertake the development of large-scale capitalism. This, of course, entailed cleansing all alternative power sources in the society from Anatolia, including the remnants of the Ottoman institutions and the Ottoman Islamic ideological patterns and any other ideological element. As a result, a top-down and authoritarian nation-state building and secularization process became the necessary component of the elite's attempts to prepare the necessary infrastructure for Turkish capitalism.

The modernization and secularization project of the bureaucratic elite or the embryonic bourgeoisie[9] was in its essence a bourgeois project of constructing a capitalist social formation in Turkey. The entire legal and political framework was reorganized according to the interests of this inchoate bourgeoisie (Berik and Bilginsoy 1996:39), which were tied in with the acceleration of capitalist development in Turkey:

> The laws to encourage industry passed in 1927 and 1929 offered generous incentives to Turkey's capitalists. They were offered free state land for the construction or expansion of industry, exemption from certain taxes and customs duties for the import of industrial plants. (Ahmad 1995:87)

However, because of the lack of a strong individual capitalist class in the early period of the Turkish Republic, the main investor became the Turkish state. Not surprisingly, the necessary resources for these state investments were extracted from poor Anatolian peasants and workers.

In this respect, we can argue that in contradistinction to the development of capitalism in Europe, the industrial capitalist and working class were largely products of the state in Turkey (Akkaya 2002:129). Even when the state was not able to undertake certain large-scale industrial projects, foreign capital was assigned to build the necessary infrastructure for the formation of capitalism in Turkey. This situation, inevitably, further increased the economic burden on Anatolian peasants, because access to foreign capital entailed the transfer of agricultural resources and raw materials of Turkey to more developed centers of Western Europe (Keyder 1981:3). In the end, the deepening poverty of Anatolian peasants and increasingly unequal distribution of resources across Turkey rendered it necessary for the newly formed Turkish bourgeoisie to intensify its repressive measures and ideological mechanisms to be able to counter any possible challenge coming from the poor Anatolian population. This is, in fact, a situation that is typical of all late-industrializing capitalist societies:

> As the dominant classes in these societies have found it necessary to legitimize their increasingly unpopular rule to maintain law and order, to protect private property, and to prevent a revolution against the prevailing social system, the state has adopted a technocratic approach with a focus on capital accumulation and economic growth, combined with severe repression of the working class and other labouring segments of the society. (Berberoglu 1994:63–64)

Yet as I argued in my critique of economist reductionism, we must problematize the idea that the form of these repressive and ideological mechanisms is the same in every society. As an alternative approach I argue that these mechanisms are necessarily influenced by specific contextual and historical characteristics of any society within which they operate. The same situation is also very relevant for the development of capitalism in the Turkish Republic, where, in the early years, the ideological appeals of the bourgeoisie reflected certain specific features of Turkish society that should be taken into consideration before drawing conclusions about the evolution of capitalism in Turkey.

The existence of a large population of Kurds, for instance, is one of the most significant specific characteristics of the capitalist social formation. Therefore, while the economic strategies and the ideological mechanisms adopted by the Turkish bourgeoisie influenced the social conditions of the Kurdish people in Turkey, Kurds' reaction to these changes have become very influential in shaping the policies of the Turkish bourgeoisie. I will begin the analysis of these relationships by first describing the nature of Turkish nationalism as the ideology of the embryonic Turkish bourgeoisie in the early period of the republic.

As I argued before, the formation of capitalism under the control of a nascent bourgeoisie, which was the bureaucratic-military elite, made it necessary to form a strong nation-state. This nation-state had to render itself the prevailing power in the society to be able to repress any possible challenge to the modernization and capitalism project of the Turkish bourgeoisie. This necessitated cleansing existing centrifugal Ottoman elements and its Islamic ideology from public life. However, when "Islam was cleansed from the public sphere" (Yavuz 2000:22), the Turkish bourgeoisie had to confront a difficult political situation, since after the elimination of Islamic values it lacked a unifying ideology for managing its economically and ethnically divided society (Ahmad 1995:75). At this point in history, Turkish nationalism, which was also very compatible with the aim of creating a national bourgeoisie, was designed to replace Islam as an ideology. According to Karpat,

> theoretically, the state represented the entire nation, even though the population had not yet become fully aware of its own national identity. In fact it was the state which strove to create a Turkish nationalist ethos according to a secularist-nationalist philosophy that was alien to the folk culture. This was the nationalist ideology of the period; it had limited relevance to social realities. (1973:319)

The underlying political purpose of Turkish nationalism was the prevention of the development of class consciousness and class ideology, both of which serve to ignite class struggle (Akkaya 2002:130–31). Turkish nationality was presented as a common bond for all people in Turkey, regardless of their class position, and while it sought to transcend class and ethnic differences, class-based associations and labor unions were prohibited under the provisions of labor law. This eventually prepared a secure context for unfettered exploitation and the undisturbed accumulation of capital. The pressure over the labor movement, in the end, impeded the development of any institutional channels for constructing working-class consciousness and identity (Ibid.:132).

The ideology of Turkish nationalism favored the values of rationality, positivism, and individualism at the expense of the Ottoman values of religion and communalism. Therefore, contrary to the social organization in the Ottoman Empire, the new Turkish state introduced Turkishness and modernity as central elements of the new society. Given that there had not been any politically mature Turkish nationalism in Ottoman times due to the *millet* system, it became very challenging for the new Turkish state to manufacture a Turkish nationalism as a transcendent bond (Kirisci and Winrow 1997:23).

In order to deconstruct the prevailing Islamic identity and to produce and promote a Turkish national identity, very complex ideological mechanisms were instilled. Accordingly, as discussed in chapter 1, many myths and symbols were created to form a material basis for the construction of Turkish nationalism. Moreover, Turkish history was reinterpreted in a way to provide "evidence" for the imagined superior characteristics of the Turkish nation and for the denial or the inferiorization of the other ethnic groups in Anatolia, including Kurds. On the way toward establishing a homogeneous state, expressions of Kurdish language and culture were banned; there also emerged many legal regulations ensuring the exile of the Kurds from their traditional areas to the other parts of the country, a gerrymandering-like policy that aimed to break their majority position in certain regions of Anatolia. The following remarks of Ismet Inonu, the successor of Mustafa Kemal as president, provide a good summary of the official ideology of the Turkish state in the early days of republic: "We are frankly nationalists . . . and nationalism is our factor of cohesion. In the face of a Turkish majority, other elements have no kind of influence. We must Turkify the inhabitants of our land at any price, and we will annihilate those who oppose the Turks or 'le Turquisme'" (quoted in Barkey and Fuller 1998:10).

In promoting and hegemonizing the values of Turkish nationalism, "the state used the army, schools, media and art . . . to break away from Islam and the Ottoman legacy" (Yavuz 2000:23). As a result, the "unknown" cultural traditions of Turkish ethnicity came to the surface and the forgotten historical myths of Turks[10] were revitalized by the state in every sphere of life. Without the repressive and centralist undertakings of the Turkish state, the reproduction and hegemonization of Turkish nationalism across Anatolia were unthinkable.

The emphasis put on the development of the Turkish language was one of the most significant manifestations of Turkish nationalism. The introduction of the officially created and promoted "Sun-Language Theses" and "Turkish History Theses" mainly constituted ideological justification for the superiority of Turkish ethnicity. In the Sun Language Theses (*Gunes Dil Teorisi*), it was argued that all existing languages were derived from old Turkish, which implies the claim that all nations were derived from Turkish origin in their essence. In the Turkish History Theses, which was very complementary, it was assumed that from ancient times, droughts and economic seasons forced migrations from Central Asia to the East, West, and South:

> These migrants were Turkish-speaking. . . . They brought to the regions they settled developed civilizations. It was they who founded civilizations in Mesopotamia, Egypt, Anatolia, China, Crete, India, and Aegean regions and Rome. They were Turks. These Turkish speaking people had the major role in founding and developing civilizations and in spreading them to the world. (Besikci, quoted in Hirschler 2001:2)

When the formation of capitalism went hand in hand with a Turkish ethnic nationalism, Turkish identity and Turkish citizenship were emphasized and the presence of the Kurdish culture and Kurdish ethnicity in Anatolia was denied. In this respect, Turkish ethnic nationalism and the denial of the Kurds became a typical feature of Turkish capitalism. Ergil explains that:

> The root of this intolerance is to be found not in the character of the Turkish people or their political leaders but in the very nature of the Turkish state. This state is based on a conception of "nation-building" that calls for standardizing

the citizenry to make them Turkish in language and nationality, secular in orientation, and obedient to the state. Such a conception naturally leads to the denial of diversity and repression of any other expression of group identity. The Turkish official mentality invariably confuses unity with uniformity. (2000:123)

Turkish nationalism had an inherent flexibility to present itself as both a civic nationalism, which would emphasize the idea of being a Turkish citizen, and an ethno-cultural nationalism, which would promote the idea of the supremeness of Turkish ethnicity. Here, the "civic" dimension of the nationalist discourse made it possible for assimilated Kurds to rise in political and economic ranks as long as they adopted the values of Turkish nationalism. This enabled the Turkish state to adopt the stand that "there is no barrier to the advancement" of any person within the state and that "everyone living within the borders of the Turkish Republic who considers themselves Turkish is Turkish" (Robbins 1993:661), both of which were designed to assimilate other ethnic groups. On the other hand, the "ethnic nationalist dimension" of Turkish nationalism that denied the existence of any other ethnic group in Anatolia formed the basis of hegemonic control and repression of the Kurds, who rejected the values of Turkish capitalism and Turkish nationalism. In fact, the civic and ethnic dimensions of Turkish nationalism reinforced each other. In terms of co-opting assimilated Kurdish people by allowing them to occupy the military, political, and bureaucratic ranks, civic nationalism secured the persistence of Turkish ethnic nationalism and its hegemonic control. This was because assimilation and co-optation partly prevented the emergence of any strong Kurdish centrifugal leadership, which would threaten the Turkish bourgeoisie and its capitalist project.

When having economic capital and political power in the society entailed the adoption of the values of not only Turkish capitalism but also Turkish nationalism, this situation expectedly gave birth to a situation that members of the entire bourgeoisie necessarily carried a Turkish identity. To have a Kurdish ethnic identity and consciousness and to have a bourgeois identity and consciousness became mutually exclusive sentiments. Under these conditions class differences and ethnic differences began to overlap.

Then, in the early period of the republic, the worsening economic conditions of Kurds—the result of the embryonic bourgeoisie's capitalism project—accompanied the official denial of Kurdish identity. This situation inevitably alienated the Kurdish population from the Turkish state. Ironically, we can argue that the Kurdish ethnic awareness was accelerated by the Turkish state's official denial of the Kurdish presence in Anatolia (Hirschler 2001:27). In other words, Kurdish nationalism started to flourish as a reaction to Turkish nationalism. However, it was still undeveloped because of the aforementioned ongoing rural character of Turkish society and especially of those regions where Kurds were concentrated. This rural character posed an obstacle to the organization of the Kurdish people and prevented the emergence of an urban Kurdish nationalist movement as a rival to the very well-organized ideology of Turkish nationalism.

While the weak Kurdish nationalism in the early period of the Republic was politically mobilized and reinforced by several rebellions, the "religious fundamentalist" nature of those rebellions was more pronounced than their ethno-nationalist character (Atacan 2000:73) since, in the first place, they emerged as a reaction to the secularist reforms of the Turkish state. This is not to say that these rebellions conveyed solely an Islamic element rather than an ethno-nationalist one, but the strong presence of the former overshadowed the latter. Of the eighteen rebellions that took place between 1924 and 1928, the Sheikh Said Rebellion (1925), as the first large-scale nationalist uprising by the Kurds (Kirisci and Winrow 1997:100), is most worth analyzing in order to paint a clearer picture of how the Turkish state utilized both coercive and ideological measures to paralyze any challenge to its capitalist project. Sheikh Said Rebellion's leadership was undertaken by the Kurdish religious leaders, who were very discontented with the Turkish state's radical secularist reforms. Therefore, although the rebellion conveyed certain significant national characteristics and its ultimate aim was the establishment of an independent Kurdistan, "its mobilization, propaganda, and symbols were those of a religious rebellion" (Olson 1989:153).

The predominance of the religious character of the rebellion over its ethno-nationalist nature, in fact, created a justification for the Turkish bourgeoisie to suppress it by strict coercive measures (Poulton 1997:96). When the "national interest" was defined as the continuation and preservation of the radical modernist and secularist reforms, the religious and Kurdish nationalist values represented by the Sheikh Said Rebellion were comprehended as a direct challenge to the Turkish modernism's progressive rationale. In this sense, the ethnic nationalist character of the rebellion was ignored by the Turkish state when it intentionally treated it not as an ethnic but as a primitive religious rebellion (Yegen 1999:561). Therefore, the Sheikh Said Rebellion and the subsequent Kurdish rebels were understood and presented not as an ethno-nationalist uprising but as an extension of the resistance of the old values of the Ottoman times to the Turkish modernism.

THEORETICAL REFLECTIONS

These complex relationships between the development of capitalism in Turkey and the political behaviors of the Kurdish population show us, above all else, that the labor-capital contradiction in Turkey had a very specific form and was accompanied by its specific ideological justifications. The impact of class relations on the superstructural institutions was not direct but rather was mediated by certain historical characteristics of Turkish society. As a result, the embryonic Turkish bourgeoisie developed a nationalist ideology unique to its class. But make no mistake, in the early period of the Republic the economic base and superstructural institutions were not in a one-sided relationship where the economic base determined the superstructure. Rather, both evolved together and reinforced one another.

Another important consideration is that nationalism, which was considered irrelevant by the orthodox interpretation of Marxism, emerged as an essential ideological component of the capitalist social formation in Turkey. And reciprocally, Turkish nationalism also prepared the conditions for the emergence of Kurdish nationalism, which in turn gave Turkish capitalism its unique features. Orthodox interpretations of Marxism here would expect that during the development of capitalism in Turkey the exploited Anatolian workers and peasants would develop class-consciousness and class identity, which would iron out their "precapitalist" ethnic and cultural differences. However, what we see in our case is that because of the hegemony of Turkish nationalism and accompanying state repression, and because of the rural character of the country, it became very difficult for the poor, exploited population to develop a class-consciousness in opposition to the Turkish bourgeoisie. The latter's reactions, then, were one of two types: either they were assimilated to the culture and values of Turkish nationalism, or they developed their own Kurdish nationalism as a defense (Cornell 2001:19).

Class-consciousness and class identities, then, are not structural and mechanistic outcomes of the emergence of capitalist relations of production but a probable consequence of a political and social struggle within which an exploited population politically interacts and communicates. In the early period of the republic, and because strong state promotion of Turkish national identity served to suppress the appearance of class-consciousness, we can argue that class, ethnic, and national identities themselves became an area of class struggle and hegemony. As the consolidation of Turkish nationalism was vital for the Turkish bourgeoisie to realize their objective class interests, the appearance of Kurdish nationalism, as an alternative to Turkish nationalism, threatened the security of the bourgeoisie and influenced its political maneuvers. These observations suggest that under specific circumstances nationalism and ethnicity might become essential components of capitalist relations of production.

URBANIZATION, PROLETARIANIZATION, AND THE KURDISH MOVEMENT (1950–1970)

The full impact of these political developments would become more observable during the 1950s, which witnessed the rapid urbanization of the Kurdish population. The transformation of money-capital and commercial capital into productive capital accelerated after the construction of the necessary social and economic infrastructure in the early period of the republic (Ercan 2002:21). However, state intervention and foreign capital involvement still constituted the bulk of industrial initiative. The ongoing state investments in this period aimed to convert the domestic merchant into an industrial bourgeois, which resulted in the emergence of some particular capitalist groups, who were able to make limited private investments and undertake commercial activities by themselves (Karpat 1973:124). Within a relatively short space of time the increasing pace of industrialization accelerated the rate of urbanization, which brought attractive employment opportunities to the rural population, and between 1927 and 1963 the urban population increased almost threefold (Ibid.:73). This also facilitated the emergence of an urban proletariat and a student movement in such industrial areas Istanbul, Izmir, and Adana (McDowall 2000:402), where the number of industrial workers grew from 35,000 in 1923 to more than 1.5 million in 1962 (Karpat 1973:270).

With this state-sponsored project, which was called the inward-oriented capital accumulation strategy (also known as Import Substitution Industrialization), production, growth,[11] and profits increased greatly in the short run. However, the continuity of this situation depended largely on the increasing technology imports from advanced capitalist countries to be used in the production of some intermediate and industrial goods (Ercan 2002:24). This, in the end, put Turkish capitalism in an international debt cycle, which eventually led Turkish capitalists to increase the level of exploitation of the working class and to the appearance of a working-class opposition. The increasing working-class militancy—especially in urban areas—forced the Turkish state to allow labor unions and some socialist political parties to operate freely in Turkey (Karpat 1973:273). However, this in essence aimed more to police working-class action by encouraging them to organize in controllable, state-sponsored labor unions rather than in politically oppositional organizations. Turk-Is was one of these unions, whose leadership set up close relations with the Turkish bourgeoisie and Turkish state (Akkaya 2002:133). However, worsening conditions could not prevent some alternative left-wing organizations from becoming very influential, and under unions like DİSK[12] and socialist parties like TİP[13] there emerged a strong leftist workers' movement, which was also fuelled by the rise of international left-wing movements (Bozarslan 1992:100).

With the founding of DİSK and TİP, there was a noticeable increase in the number of working-class actions and strikes (Akkaya 2002:135), which began seriously to threaten the import substitution industrialization strategy of the Turkish bourgeoisie. This, in turn, led the bourgeoisie to exert pressure on the state institutions to address the radicalization of the working class, leading ultimately to increased repressive actions against the workers and left-wing political organizations. After the 1950s, and as a reaction to the rise of organized working-class politics and its socialist ideology, Turkish nationalism adopted a strong anti-communist stand, presenting itself as the protector of the Turkish nation from the rising "communist threat" emerging from the Soviet Union. Following this Turkish nationalism had two main enemies after the 1950s: on the outside, the Soviet Union; and on the inside, the socialist movement.

It is relevant here to examine the kinds of influences these developments had on Kurdish identity and Kurdish nationalism. For given the industrial development of the country and the rapid process of urbanization, Kurds were no longer limited to their original geographic area. Along with this, as they moved into the traditional Turkish areas in the towns and cities, they began to compete with Turkish workers for jobs and other economic opportunities. Nevertheless, while the ethnic and cultural differences of the Kurds set them apart from the Turks, this did not automatically lead to the former's development of group solidarity. What did happen, however, was that the mere fact of urban living and industrial employment brought the Kurdish migrants together, facilitated communication and interaction among them, enabled them to experience their common condition as an ethnic group whose identity is denied, and this is what created the possibility for their ethnic self-awareness to develop.

After the 1950s, however, Kurdish nationalism exhibited very different characteristics from the Kurdish movement that emerged in the early period of the Turkish Republic. It had become less of a religion-oriented movement that reacted against the secularist reforms of the Turkish state and openly embraced a political stance. Thus, rather than solely organizing themselves according to their ethnic identities, and rather than reacting simply against the nationalist ideology of the Turks, the Kurdish people came proactively to constitute a significant part of the left-wing and working-class movement in Turkey. Generally speaking, they avoided state-sponsored labor unions like Turk-Is and opted instead for socialist labor unions and political parties that were critical of Turkish nationalism and its suppression of the Kurdish people.

Following this, in the Fourth Congress of Workers' Party of Turkey (1969), the Kurdish question was evaluated in class terms as follows:

> There is a Kurdish people in the East of Turkey. . . . The fascist authorities representing the ruling classes have subjected the Kurdish people to a policy of assimilations and intimidation which has often become a bloody repression. . . .
> To consider "Eastern question" as merely a matter of economic development is, therefore, nothing but an extension of the nationalistic, and chauvinistic approach adopted by the ruling classes. (Kendal 1993:87)

In the urban setting, then, Kurds carried not only an ethnic but a class identity as well, and these were accentuated because of the increasing rates of eco-

nomic exploitation that they experienced. And as they embraced more of a socialist political stance, the nationalists responded with a clear anti-Kurdish,
racist discourse in 1960s and 1970s. As McDowall explains:

> To be Kurdish was, as being Turkish had been a century earlier, to be a primi-
> tive rustic or, worse, a Caliban. . . . One journal Otuken stated "Kurds do not
> have the faces of human beings" and advocated their migration to Africa to join
> the half-human half-animals who lived there. It went on to warn "They can learn
> by asking their racial fellows, the Armenians, that the Turks are very patient, but
> when angry no one can stand in their way." (2000:407)

The position was summed up even more blatantly by the well-known Turkish conservative commentator Nihal Atsiz, who states that "one who does not
have Turkish blood is not Turkish even though he does not speak any other
language except Turkish while communists are people who are racially de-
generate, villains, whose origins are not known and who are not Turkish"
(quoted in McDowall 2000:411).

As the Turkish bourgeoisie intensified its nationalist appeals they were
able to win the support of a considerable part of the Turkish population
(Poulton 1997:133–50). And as the further entrenchment of capitalism deepened the level of exploitation and poverty within the country, the Turkish
urban-poor openly blamed the Kurdish migrants in the cities, who com-
peted with them for scarce jobs and who were seen to be responsible for
the depression of wages. Edna Bonacich (1980) argues that in a split labor
market in which the wages are divided according to ethnic lines, we can expect ethnic antagonisms and the potential for ethnic mobilization and conflict. This is precisely what occurred in Turkey as the working class became
ethnically divided and the development of class-consciousness was seriously impaired.

CONCLUSIONS

These developments in Turkey after the 1950s provide very strong empirical
support for my argument and my critique of orthodox Marxism. The expression of Kurdish identity and Kurdish nationalism in the 1960s and 1970s can
be seen as a resonance of the class struggle in Turkey, since it posed a challenge against the dominant Turkish nationalist ideology of the Turkish bourgeoisie. Therefore, we can argue here that in some respect in the 1950s and
1960s the expressions of Turkish ethnic nationalism and Kurdish ethnic nationalism were in the service of different class ideologies. However, because
the political and class features of these nationalisms were very different from
one another, their ideological content was also fundamentally incompatible.
While Turkish ethnic nationalism, at certain times, carried assimilative and

racist features by claiming the superiority of Turkish ethnicity, Kurdish ethnic nationalism was more focused on acquiring some cultural and economic
rights minus the racist discourse. In other words, while serving to divide the
working-class movement, Turkish nationalism can also be seen as one of the
most important factors that shaped the trajectory of class struggle in Turkey,
proving the dialectical interaction between the economic base and superstructural institutions.

The rise of Kurdish nationalism in the urban setting and Turkish nationalism's continual manipulative power over the Turkish urban-poor also indicate that the ideology of nationalism is not an irrelevant but rather a constitutive element of industrial capitalism in certain social contexts. In our
particular case, we saw that rather than eradicating their ethnic ties, urbanization and industrialization in Turkey after the 1950s reinforced and transformed Kurdish ethnic nationalism. The incorporation of Kurdish nationalism into the working-class movement and the strict adherence of the
Turkish bourgeoisie to Turkish nationalism showed that *nationalism* can
also serve as an important component of class ideologies and class struggle.
In addition, the fact that Turkish nationalist identity posed an obstacle to the
emergence of a unified working-class movement once more signified that
developing a class-consciousness and class identity are not inevitable consequences of the emergence of industrial capitalism but a matter of political
and social struggle.

In sum, then, in this chapter I criticized two interrelated assumptions of orthodox Marxist theory. The first one was its economist reductionism, which
attributed a one-sided deterministic power to economic relations in forming
the superstructural institutions in a capitalist society. The other was a mechanistic understanding of historical materialism, which thought of the emergence of class identities and the disappearance of ethnic ties as the necessary
result of the emergence of industrial capitalism. When Marxism is interpreted
in these two ways, it becomes very difficult to gain insight into the relationship between the realities of ethnic nationalism and capitalist relations of
production. Because economic reductionism considers the relations in the
economic sphere the only significant variable to analyze, it removes the possibility of understanding the role of ethnic identity and ethnic politics in capitalist societies. The mechanistic understanding of historical materialism, on
the other hand, expects that class identities, which will be the automatic consequence of the emergence of industrial capitalism, will sooner or later iron
out the precapitalist ethnic ties. Hence, according to this, there is no need to
theorize the relationship between ethnicity and capitalism.

I argued that an alternative reading of Marx can provide valuable insights
into the role of ethnicity in capitalist societies. As opposed to the orthodox,
I suggested that the relationship between the economic base and the manifested superstructures in Marxism is not one-sided and deterministic but re-

ciprocal and dialectical. The dialectical relationship between infrastructure and superstructure conveys the characteristics of the historical and contextual specificities of a given social setting. Therefore, in an ethnically divided society, class relations might carry the characteristics of these ethnic divisions. In addition, I proposed that class-consciousness and class identities are not automatic results of the emergence of capitalist relations of production. Rather, a political and social struggle is necessary for them to come about since bourgeois ideology will always produce some other alternative identities to prevent class identities from being constructed. I claimed that nationalist ideology and national identity have historically been the most common of these alternative identities in capitalist societies, particularly in Turkey. This shows us that nationalism, rather than being eradicated, remains an important constitutive element of capitalist societies. In this sense class struggle has always been a struggle for identity and extended toward all parts of social life rather than being limited to the economic realm.

NOTES

1. Of course, it is not possible to find any scholar who claims that he or she is a reductionist economist or who presents his or her theoretical framework in such a simplistic manner. However, both the reductionist economism and the mechanistic understanding of Marxism are embedded in many social analyses. The weakness of some Marxist interpretations in analyzing the question of ethnicity and nationalism is indeed due to this embeddedness of orthodox Marxist tendencies in some theoretical frameworks.

2. I do not deny that there are some excerpts in Marx's writings that open the way for such an interpretation. For instance, when Marx and Engels state that "national differences and antagonisms between peoples are daily more vanishing, owing to the development of the bourgeoisie, to freedom of commerce, to the world-market, to uniformity in the mode of production and in the conditions of life corresponding to thereto" (from Karl Marx and Frederic Engels, *Communist Manifesto*, 1955:29). This provides a justification for an orthodox Marxist reading. However, when we think of the unity of the Marxist philosophy, I still maintain that an alternative reading is possible to theorize the central role that nationalism plays in capitalist societies.

3. Here, "humanist" refers to the perspective that sees sensuous human action as necessary for and central to social change. This differs from a "structuralist" point of view.

4. This subjective conceptualization of the class is embedded in the early writings of Marx, while the structural and objective is put forward in later writings, especially in *Capital*.

5. The hegemony of bourgeois ideology or hegemonic bourgeois ideology here refers to "the successful attempts of the dominant class to use its political, moral and intellectual leadership to establish its view of the world as all-inclusive and universal, and to shape the interests and needs of subordinate groups" (Carnoy 1984:70).

6. "Race" here refers to a social group having a sentiment of "we-ness" with imagined common blood ties and with an imagined common ancestry (Allahar 1996:6–10).

7. In 1915 the ethnic distribution of the capital in the Ottoman Empire was as follows: Greek, 60 percent; Armenian, 20 percent; Muslim (regardless of the ethno-linguistic divisions), 15 percent; Jewish, 5 percent; and foreign, 10 percent (Kazgan 1999:52).

8. According to Karpat (1973:54), "A national census of industry taken in 1927 counted a total of 65,245 manufacturing and business sites employing a total of 256,855 people or roughly 2 percent of the population."

9. Embryonic bourgeoisie, here, refers to those people who had money-capital in their hands but were unable to circulate this money-capital according to capitalist market conditions due to the lack of convenient social and economic infrastructure.

10. The myths that they were Turks who founded the early Anatolian civilizations and who made the primary technological inventions in the history of science were embedded in the Turkish nationalist discourse.

11. While in 1929 the population of Turkey was 14,200,000 and the Gross National Product was 1.8 million, in 1967 the population was 33,044,000 and the GNP was 103.780. In the seven years between 1960 and 1967 the GNP increased almost twofold as a result of import substitution industrialization (Karpat 1973:70).

12. The Confederation of Revolutionary Workers' Union.

13. Workers' Party of Turkey.

9

Class, "Race," and Ethnic Nationalism in Trinidad

Anton L. Allahar

> The Negro has a deep contempt . . . for all that is not white; his values are
> the values of white imperialism at its most bigoted. The Indian despises the
> Negro for not being an Indian; he has, in addition, taken over all the white
> prejudices against the Negro and with the convert's zeal regards as Negro
> everyone who has any tincture of Negro blood. . . . Like monkeys pleading
> for evolution, each claiming to be whiter than the other, Indians and Ne-
> groes appeal to the unacknowledged white audience to see how much they
> despise one another. They despise one another by reference to whites.
>
> —Naipaul (1962:84)

INTRODUCTION: THE SLEDGE HAMMER AND THE MOSQUITO

Whereas orthodox Marxist treatments of inequality privileged class over
"race," chapter 1 began with a neo-Marxist appreciation of class theories of
ethnicity and attempted to articulate the links among "race," class, and nationalism. In recent years, however, there has been a reaction to the neo-
Marxist articulation that has come from ethnic political entrepreneurs, who
seek to reverse the order and to privilege "race" over class. The latter thus
appear to be unmindful of the advice of C. L. R. James, who wrote that:

> The race question is subsidiary to the class question in politics, and to think of
> imperialism in terms of race is disastrous. But to neglect the racial factor as
> merely incidental is an error only less grave than to make it fundamental. (cited
> in Gilroy 1987:15)

Among those who promote the "race first" argument, those black nationalists known as Afrocentrists are the best known, but they are not
alone. Thus, along with the Afrocentrists who address the situation of diasporic Africans, this chapter will also discuss Indian nationalists or those
who advance the idea that diasporic Hindus must look to mother India for
unity (see chapters 2 and 4), inspiration, and protection (*Hindutva*). Both
these movements, Afrocentrism and *Hindutva*, will be unpacked and analyzed, and later examined in light of the contemporary Trinidad political
experience.

To the "race first" activists, the class approach, which is principally associated with Marx, is seen as a white, European approach, and hence invalid.
While Afrocentrists are politically defensive and intellectually conservative,
not all their members are willing to admit to this. Thus, at a conference of
Caribbean academics and scholars in 2002, I presented a paper that was
highly critical of a book edited by two Afrocentric academics (Smart and Nehusi 2000). I described the seven contributors to this book as Afrocentric and
racist, and challenged their assertion that Trinidad was an African country
with an African culture (carnival, calypso, and steelband), in which other
ethnic groups were marginal cultural interlopers. During the question period
one colleague, who wanted to distance herself from Afrocentrism but to retain the critique of racism, accused me of "using a sledge hammer to kill a
mosquito."

The implication was that the Afrocentric racist position was such a minority position (the mosquito) that it did not warrant the detailed critical scrutiny
to which I subjected it in a twenty-five-page paper (the sledge hammer). Following this, another colleague at the same panel discussion charged me with
writing a "lazy man paper," again implying that I chose an easy target, or a
target that was easily assailable and did not really merit a sustained critique
of the sort I offered. Both charges suggested that mine was an intellectual
overreaction, for although there was racism in the Afrocentric position, it was
deemed to be minimal and best dealt with by ignoring it. Hence my "lazi-
ness" resided in the fact no great intellectual perspicacity was needed in order to refute the racist implications of Afrocentrism.

I disagreed with both critics and suggested as Afrocentric sympathizers
they were in denial over the social and political implications of this philosophy. The denial has two related aspects, one emotional and the other political. The emotional aspect of Afrocentrism is linked to contemporary concerns with political correctness and the fact that groups that have been
traditionally downtrodden must now be empowered and given their fair
due. In this logic, to criticize Afrocentrism is to be insensitive at best and
racist at worst. The political aspect of Afrocentrism speaks to the fact that
there are many academic ethnic entrepreneurs, who, though uncomfortable
with the intellectual and historical claims of this philosophy, nevertheless

opportunistically embrace and defend it. There are professorships, academic tenure, research grants, and careers to be made.

In this context, it is interesting to read what Wim van Binsbergen has to say about Afrocentrism as an academic enterprise in general. For in spite of the fact that he is one of the strongest supporters of the Afrocentric position, he is upfront in acknowledging the serious problems inherent in this school of thought. In fact, his comments are so accurate and simultaneously damning that one wonders how he and other Afrocentrists can justify their embrace of this tradition of scholarship. He writes:

> If one is familiar with current Afrocentrist writings one cannot help being aware of the deficiencies which are endemic to that genre: the poor scholarship; the amateurish and autodidactic approach to grand historical and comparative themes without systematic use of obvious sources and obvious methods; the Afrocentrist authors' manifest and deliberate isolation from current debates and current advances in the fields of scholarship they touch on; and the tendency towards Black racism. (2003:¶3)

Like my above-mentioned critics, Binsbergen's defense of Afrocentrism is that it is useful as a consciousness-raising exercise. But as was argued in chapter 1, it is best seen as a *false* consciousness-raising exercise that borders on blind faith and the acceptance of revealed truths that one usually associates with religious belief.

What is crucial to bear in mind is the fact that history, particularly revisionist versions of it, are replete with myth. Not that anything is wrong with myth per se, for much of daily living depends on the willingness of people to construct myths, to believe in them and even to live by them. Whether one is discussing the myth of God (religion), of race (biology), of the nation (primordial unity), or of market democracy (capitalism), human beings have shown tremendous inventiveness and an equal preparedness to engage in self-delusion. In the human search for meaning and belonging, whether to a clan, a tribe, a race, or a nation, the species has shown itself to be remarkably adept at creating myths of belonging and rootedness. As Anthony Smith has written: "No national movement and no persisting ethnic identity can emerge without a bedrock of shared meanings and ideals" for all such rootedness "must come to terms with the basic myths and symbols which endow popular perceptions of ethnic boundaries and identities with meanings and sentiments" (1984:95). Often these are myths of a pristine, heroic past when their leaders or elders were brave and virtuous, and when their ethnic or tribal communities were politically and socially undifferentiated and united in peace. Once more Smith writes: "The community, according to this mode of myth-making, is descended from a noble and heroic ancestor, and for that reason is entitled to privilege and prestige in its own and other peoples' estimations" (Ibid.:96).

MYTH AND MAKE-BELIEVE

The point is that even if imagined or invented, the political consequences of identities thus constructed are very real. And in the context of the present argument the myths propagated by the Afrocentrists and Hindu nationalists are no less instructive. But apologists notwithstanding, it is important to point out that as ethnic entrepreneurs, the motives of Afrocentrists and Hindu nationalists must not be confused with the responsibilities of serious intellectuals or scholars, even if some of the former do indeed believe that theirs is the correct view of history and that what they are claiming is proper. If an Afrocentric approach to the world were to "have positive confidence-building or identity affirming functions," Stephen Howe writes, that would be "if it were true, the strongest defence of the movement" (1998:5). Unfortunately, however, as the prominent black historian Wilson J. Moses has argued, "Like most mythologies, it is only half believed and simply represents an attempt on the part of respectable, *honest people* to create a positive folk mythology" (quoted in Thomas 1995:27 [my emphasis]). This much is clear and noncontentious, but Howe's critique of this aspect of Afrocentric thinking is powerful:

> One can certainly accept that more-or-less honest people, in their capacity as political activists, might seek to build a positive folk mythology which encourages those they wish to mobilize—even if they do not wholly believe in the propositions they advance. It is less clear whether honest *intellectuals* can properly behave in such a way, using their university posts, editorships, classroom or media access and apparatus of scholarship to do so. . . . I do not think that the faith in the political or psychological benefits of false "folk mythologies" is justified. (1998:5)

Religion is premised on such things as faith, trust, and make-believe. It is about accepting as "true" things for which there is no compelling scientific or empirical proof. In this regard, belief is the opposite of knowledge, but within the general lay community it is common to see them treated as synonyms. Nevertheless, make-believe cannot be dismissed as irrelevant and inconsequential, for as will be shown with Afrocentrism and *Hindutva*, so much of the human being's philosophical take on the world, so much of his or her daily living involves make-believe that it cannot simply be deemed unreal and hence irrelevant. The importance of this is best captured in the classic statement of W. I. Thomas to the effect that "if men define the situations as real they are real in their consequences" (Thomas and Thomas 1928:572), for human social actions are based on many different things, including their beliefs, and even if those beliefs are not based in science and empiricism, the actions they drive and the consequences they produce can be very real.

Consider a religious belief such as Christianity, which historically led to the Crusades and deaths of hundreds of thousands of non-Christians. The same applies to those extremist Hindus who have created *Hindutva* or the Hindu nationalist movement. Thousands of dead Indian Muslims and Indian Christians are offered as proof. But make-believe does not only concern religion. In the modern world it attaches to and informs the politically charged notions of "race," ethnicity, and identity. Thus, in the context of Trinidad, Selwyn Ryan could write that a great deal of what today passes for Indian, Hindu, or African culture or identity amount to no more than "half forgotten or barely remembered collective memories or myths manufactured by *political and cultural warriors and entrepreneurs* who are seeking to use them to augment their stock of political, social or economic capital for purposes of resource mobilization" (1999b:24 [my emphasis]). There is no clearer example of this than the person of Selwyn Cudjoe, who unabashedly asserts that "although few of us may be able to say from what part of Africa we came; to what ethnic group we belonged; and the language our forefathers used, it remains true that we were shaped by our Africanness even though we had to adapt to the vagaries of the New World" (2001e:¶22).

Make-believe and myth are closely related phenomena that have very real meaning for the believers. This is where all manner of political, cultural, and ethnic entrepreneurs skillfully play upon the insecurities of the mass of believers in order to mobilize them toward some concrete political, economic, or cultural goal. This said, it is important to note that whether dealing with racial, national, ethnic, or cultural identities, these are not totally fictitious and without historical referent, for as Ryan continues: "Both the Indian and African communities brought with them their 'ethnic ghosts,' memories of economic, religious, and cultural practices, values and ways of doing things which were learnt in their homelands and embedded in their subconscious" (1999b:24). And though long removed from their original homelands, the ghosts in question can have a decided impact on the lives and behaviors of individuals and groups within those communities.

Within the academy, then, there are those who have not yet worked out the intellectual details and implications of the Afrocentric and *Hindutva* claims and who want to continue to privilege the race argument but who at the same time are uncomfortable with openly declaring their opposition to class analysis. So among adherents of Afrocentrism, for example, not all are alike or equal; there are varying degrees of embrace of the Afrocentric position. At one extreme one finds the timid or soft Afrocentrists, whose political identities are situational and fluid and who will move back and forth as the situation demands, while at the other extreme are the hard or Afrocentric racists, whose political identities are quite fixed. My accusers in the above anecdote are thus more opportunistic and closer to the first variety, while those who follow the ideas of Molefi Kete Asante are closer to the second.

As outrageous as the extremist claims of racists may appear, they must not be casually dismissed as was suggested in the exchange involving "the sledge hammer and the mosquito." For it is my contention that in the minds of the general populace such claims can have very favorable echo and can produce disastrous consequences for ordinary citizens. As is well known, for example, although the powers attributed to witches and witchcraft are not scientifically verified, many people believe they are real and the legal authorities in many countries have tried and executed persons accused of practicing witchcraft. Similarly, if the Afrocentrists are simply extremists who are not to be taken seriously, the same must be said of religious entrepreneurs of every variety and the millions who hang on their every word, who make huge financial contributions to their "churches" and who are often prepared to carry out acts of violence, even mass suicide as in the case of Jim Jones and the Peoples' Temple in Guyana, when commanded by their leaders.

Focusing specifically on ethnic political mobilization, most human beings are basically followers in search of leaders whom they will "charismatize" and who in turn will define and give purpose to their lives and dictate their courses of action (Shils 1965:202). Out of this circumstance ethnic entrepreneurs are born. Ronald Glassman describes the followers in question as willingly allowing "themselves to be carried away by the charismatic experience" (1975:617), while Irvine Schiffer sees them as "a rescue-hungry people" who, "in time of crisis or distress" will "invest a leader with charisma" (1973:11). Schiffer also goes on to add that the masses in any given society are most vulnerable to unscrupulous leaders since they "have not in the main been equipped with insight and comprehension into the sociocultural and economic forces of their time" (1973:8).

Especially in an age of globalization, displacement, rootlessness, and widespread alienation, many ordinary people will be susceptible to the appeals of self-appointed leaders. Eager to root themselves in a sense of community, whether religious, political, sexual, recreational, or racial, individuals attempt to combat the generalized sense of meaninglessness and social dislocation, and this is where ethnic entrepreneurs emerge to cast their emotional appeals that often find very receptive ears. Given the combined histories of colonialism, slavery, indentureship, and racism, whether dealing with an advanced capitalist country such as the United States, or a dependent capitalist country like Trinidad, the emotionally charged racial appeals of ethnic entrepreneurs are not to be taken lightly. For as will be shown, among the alienated and angry black and Indian working classes, and increasingly even among the more comfortable classes who feel threatened by the ravages of globalization (deindustrialization, deskilling, displacement, downsizing), it is often comforting to be able to point fingers at a general, ill-defined, racial enemy in whom all one's fears may be concentrated.

ASANTE AND AFROCENTRISM

There are a few core themes around which hard Afrocentrists construct their ideas. Central to these is the assertion by Molefi Kete Asante (formerly known as Arthur Lee Smith), who is arguably the leading exponent of Afrocentricity: "To be Afrocentric is to place Africans and the interest of Africa at the center of our approach to problem solving" (1987:198). Asante is a black nationalist whose main focus is on the African Americans in the United States. He is not advocating a return to Africa but rather a historical and psychological corrective in the lives of African Americans specifically, and all Americans generally. Asante feels that, as a worldview, Eurocentricity is fatally flawed. Because human civilization began in Africa, it is necessary to return Africa to the center of the human story and not to privilege the distorted, hegemonic European view that dwarfs black accomplishments and relegates black people to the periphery of history and civilization.

The concern with African origins is premised on the search for authenticity or purity of descent. Owing to slavery, racism, exploitation, and alienation, African Americans are said to have been given a distorted understanding of themselves, and if they are to be made whole again, if their self-esteem is to be restored, they must recapture the glory of their past: "There is neither recognition of African classical thought nor of the African classical past in the Eurocentric formulations. We are essentially left with a discontinuous history and an uncertain future" (Asante 1987:9). That recapture is a massive project that is simultaneously intellectual and political. The first speaks to the rewriting or correction of the historical record, and the second involves black community self-awareness and self-promotion. Because the black experience is unique, Afrocentrists maintain that only black people could truly understand it, write about it, and propose remedies to its debilitating legacy. Reflecting on what may be termed "black exceptionalism," Selwyn Cudjoe has written: "As well-intentioned as others might be, they cannot understand the complexities of our desires, the nuances of our behaviour, and the ethos of our-being-in-this-place" (2001d:¶12).

To this extent Afrocentrists are not interested in "white" (especially European) theories and theorists, for even the progressive ones among the latter are so trapped in their own "white" world of hegemonic thought that they are unable to deal objectively with the black experience. As observed in chapter 5, this is where Marx as a white European is seen as having nothing to say to the African: "Marxism oversimplifies the significance of our history. . . . Marxism's Eurocentric foundation makes it antagonistic to our worldview; its confrontational nature does not provide the spiritual satisfaction we have found in our history of harmony" (Asante 1988:79–80). And while extolling the virtues of the négritude movement that "set out to write literature with African sensibilities," Asante noted that "nothing transforms our self-concept like authentic confrontation" (1988:70).

This said, he goes on to equate what he calls Marxism, on one hand, with capitalism, on the other hand, when he writes that:

> Operating on the European values of confrontation developed from the adventures of Europeans during the terrible White Ages, both of these systems believe in utter destruction of aliens. This, of course, is contradictory to the Afrocentric value which respects difference and applauds pluralism. . . . In economics therefore, Marxism's base is antithetical to the African concept of society. Life for the Afrocentric person is organic, harmonious, and cultural because it is integrated with African history. However, the Marxist view of life is as competitive as that of the capitalist, since both are rooted in Eurocentric materialism. (1988:79–80)

Although the tenor of his writing is absolutist (one is either African or non-African, either black or white), Asante addresses the question of "racial mixing" and the consequences for an Afrocentric consciousness. He acknowledges that in America many blacks will likely have what he calls English blood, but in spite of that a true Afrocentric consciousness will transcend the biological and cultural limitations of Englishness, for

> the core of our collective being is African, that is, our awareness of separateness from the Anglo-American experience is a function of our historical memory, the memory we have frequently denied or distorted. Such experiences are rooted in our ancestral home and defined by social and legal sanctions of four hundred years in America. Regardless to [sic] our various complexions and degrees of consciousness we are by virtue of commitments, history, and convictions an African people. (1988:27)

This invoking of an uncritical, primordial, idyllic, African solidarity is based on pure myth and make-believe and leads Asante to make the outlandish charge that "only in traditional Western societies are there conflicts between classes; such is not the case when we operate from our traditional base of harmony" (1988:18). The direct implication, then, is quite simplistic and holds that Europeans are bad while Africans are good. But that's not all for he goes on boldly to assert that "there is no such thing as black racism against whites; racism is based on fantasy; black views of whites are based on fact" (1988:32). What comes to mind in all of this is the notion of "the myth of Merrie Africa" as discussed by A. G. Hopkins:

> On this view the pre-colonial era was a Golden Age, in which generations of Africans enjoyed congenial lives in well-integrated, smoothly-functioning societies. The means of livelihood came easily to hand, for foodstuffs grew wild and in abundance, and this good fortune enabled the inhabitants to concentrate on leisure pursuits . . . of interminable drumming and dancing. (1973:10)

PRIMORDIALISM AND ETHNIC NATIONALISM

An instructive example of nationalism as false consciousness within the working-class movement in the Caribbean can be seen in the idea of black cultural nationalism in the context of Black Power and the specific link to an Afrocentric consciousness. The term *Black Power* brings to mind the civil rights movement of the 1960s in the United States and the loud echo of that movement in the Caribbean region. Recall, for example, the concern with black nationalism and the popular disaffection following the 1968 refusal of the government of Jamaica to permit Walter Rodney's return to the country, the Black Power fallout in the Caribbean from the Sir George Williams University (Montréal, Canada) incident in 1969, the 1970 Black Power challenge to the managerial bourgeoisie in charge of the state in Trinidad and Tobago, and the promulgation in 1970 of the anti–Black Power Public Order Act in Barbados, among others.

To begin, however, I want to revisit the definition of the term *nationalism*, with a view to clarifying its relevance to the debate over false consciousness, race, and class. Among commentators, one of the central elements of the definition concerns the "origins" of nationalism. There are those, for example, who see nationalism as an extension of ethnicity, a sentimental survival or a primordial carryover from traditional or premodern times (Shils 1957; Geertz 1973). This interpretation, what I have called *soft primordialism*, eschews the biological tie of blood and opts instead for a more cultural understanding of primordialism (Allahar 1996:6–10). In the words of Anthony Smith:

> What counts here are not blood ties, real or alleged, but a spiritual kinship, proclaimed in ideals that are allegedly derived from some ancient exemplars in remote eras. The aim is to recreate the heroic spirit (and the heros) that animated "our ancestors" in some past golden age." (1984:96)

It is not accidental, therefore, that human beings should feel ties to their parents, siblings, relatives, community, place of birth, or even country of birth. Such ties are a complex mix of myth, belief, emotion, and the realities of physical existence (Grosby 1994:165).

Known generally as primordial ties, such attachments are the stuff of life as humans go about their daily affairs and seek to impart *meaning* to what they do. Such meaning, which is largely symbolic, is seldom explicitly articulated but is nonetheless shared by all members of a given community, and simultaneously serves as a kind of social cement that binds the community together. And this is where the notions of racial belonging and common biological origins are introduced by ethnic entrepreneurs, who are bent on promoting a nonclass consciousness among the popular masses. At a certain level those people, places, and things that are closest to one, that resemble one another and that sustain physical and emotional life, come symbolically to mark off an in-group from an out-group, and in the process imputed differences among competing ethnic groups are easily politicized by ethnic entrepreneurs in pursuit of their own ends. The often unquestioning devotion that coethnics, who comprise some kind of an imagined, extended family, are said to feel for one another is thus seen to be based on the primordial attraction explained by the clichéd claim that "blood is thicker than water." Thus, Edward Shils wrote earlier of the prominence and ubiquity of self-identification "by kinship connection and territorial location"; but, he charges, such self-identification must be related to "man's need to be in contact with the point and moment of his origin and to experience a sense of affinity with those who share that origin" (1968:4). And Grosby echoes these exact sentiments when he wrote: "One's parents give one life. The locality in which one is born and in which one lives nurtures one; it provides the food necessary for one's life" (1994:169).

This said, one of my principal concerns is to understand the conditions under which nationalist sentiments are portrayed in primordialist terms and how they come to play a central role in class-divided societies. My concerns also speak to how those sentiments are able to spark and regulate conflicts between and among ethnic groups in postcolonial, third world countries. To this extent the politics of nationalism and nationhood in these areas are quite different from the politics that attended the formation of European nation-states such as Greece, whether in the period of antiquity or of early modernity. Stated differently, I am interested in territorially based nation states that house multiple ethnic groups. Thus, as noted earlier, a nationalist movement, *cum movement*, may comprise a group with a clearly defined, political sense of self that is in search of a territorial space it can call home (Africa for the Afrocentrists and India for the Hindu nationalists). When that sense of self informs the actions of a group which claims myths of common descent; shared historical memory; linguistic, religious, and cultural sameness; and so on, we are able to speak of an ethnic nationalist movement.

This being the case, it is possible to identify ethnic-nationalist movements *within* nation states. For example, a nation state such as Trinidad may house rival "nationalist" movements linked to specific class fractions, or groups seeking recognition, autonomy, and jurisdiction over their own affairs. Such groups and movements are likely to be separatist and will understandably engage in the wider competition among ethnic groups for national autonomy or national dominance over the other(s). In multiethnic states such movements are also fuelled economically by competition over scarce resources: jobs, housing, land, education, credit, and bank loans, among other things. And in a racialized social situation, where class concerns are politically submerged or downplayed, the competitive encounters between members of different ethnic groups will assume an ethnic character, and members may be expected to advance both ethnic claims to entitlement and ethnic explanations of their disenfranchisement.

Rationality is the key here mainly because class affiliation, which is tied to occupation, income, and economic position, clearly addresses compelling and immediate requirements of survival in modern society. But to the extent that ethnicity and race can influence class position and the structure of opportunity in society, individuals can be expected, to the extent it is possible, to emphasize or de-emphasize their ethno-racial attributes. This is why in contrasting class and ethnic identities under contemporary circumstances, Daniel Bell wrote that "ethnicity has become more salient because it can combine an interest with an affective tie" (1975:169). This is what is involved in the social construction of ethno-nationalist primordial identities, for where there is keen competition over goods that are both scarce and needed, various individuals and groups can be expected to choose *rationally* to embrace or even invent attachments to such groups; in other words, to play the ethnic card.

In the Caribbean (as elsewhere), the source of such political contestations was the period of European colonization of the so-called New World, which served to superimpose European political forms, economic practices, and cultural values onto the new world countries that they conquered and reshaped. In the process the European powers redefined the countries and peoples (indigenous or imported) in question in accordance with bourgeois European interests and values. And while colonial rule was in place, the masters sought, generally successfully, to promote the more or less stable political acceptance of the status quo by all groups concerned. Once colonization ended, however, and the Europeans withdrew from the colonies, new opportunities were created for the formerly colonized to come to the fore and to assert a new political identity.

CULTURAL NATIONALISM

The nationalism in question is more properly understood as *cultural nationalism*, and extols the virtues of tradition and of adhering to the cultural and institutional practices of one's (supposed) ancestors. Cultural nationalists romanticize the idea that each people had a golden age that was infinitely better than the present, and argue that those time-honored and culture-bound practices (marriage, family, religion, economics, politics) that worked in the past ought to be retained.

Nationalism is not the awakening and assertion of these mythical, supposedly natural and given units. It is, on the contrary, the crystallization of new units, suitable for the conditions now prevailing, though admittedly using as their raw material the cultural, historical and other inheritances from the pre-nationalist world. (Gellner 1983:49)

For primordialists and cultural nationalists, then, there is something almost magical in the notion that "birds of a feather stick together"; that primordial attachments or what at the wider group level have been called those larger "family resemblances" (Calhoun 1993:215) have a compelling attraction for many primary groups, communities, and societies around the world.

According to Edward Shils, the intense attachment to a primary group, for example, one's kinship group, is neither a function of simple interaction among members nor merely a matter of affect or emotion. Indeed, the attachment is not easily explicable in words for it embraces a unique type of deep bonding that fellows do not deem necessary to articulate consciously. It is seen to comprise: "especially 'significant relational' qualities which could only be described as primordial. . . . It is because a certain ineffable significance is attributed to the tie of blood" (1957:142). Following Shils, Clifford Geertz attempts to systematize the treatment of the concept—primordialism—and to elaborate its meaning. He speaks of "a corporate sentiment of oneness" and "a consciousness of kind" (1973:260, 307), which can be seen to stem from the sharing of a common geographical space, common ancestors, common culture, language, and religion, and which in turn produce "congruities of blood, speech and custom." Such congruities, Geertz argues:

> are seen to have an ineffable, and at times overpowering, coerciveness in and of themselves. One is bound to one's kinsman, one's neighbour, one's fellow believer, *ipso facto*; as a result not merely of personal affection, practical necessity, common interest, or incurred obligation, but at least in general part by virtue of some unaccountable absolute import attributed to the tie itself. (1973:259)

But what is more, the tie itself assumes a sacred quality so that members of the same group also feel a spiritual communion, an extreme "we-consciousness," with their fellows, even if they do not know them directly; even if they do not particularly care for each other personally. This clearly fits Benedict Anderson's ([1983] 1991) notion of the nation as an *imagined community*, particularly in the context of the modern nation where tens and hundreds of thousands, if not millions, of people in ethnically differentiated groups can comprise a single civic nation. It is just not possible for all members to know one another, to experience and feel what the other experiences and feels, or to have the same values and interests as the other: "It is *imagined* because the members of even the smallest nation will never know most of their fellow-members, meet them or even hear of them, yet in the minds of each lives the image of their communion" ([1983] 1991:15). Quite simply, all are said to be bound together in a common nation, and in times of external threats, of international tensions and conflict, there are numerous examples of how the ideology of nationalism has been manipulated successfully to demand that "adherents be willing both to kill and to die for their nation" (Calhoun 1993:212).

That their willingness to kill and die for countless others whom they do not and most likely will never know seems secondary to what appears as the compelling duty to defend the homeland, or what is often emotionally invested in familial terms as "the motherland" and "the fatherland." This is what led Anderson to write that: "In fact, all communities larger than primordial villages of face-to-face contact (and perhaps even these) are imagined" ([1983] 1991:15). But to say that such communities and their attendant traditions are imagined is not to imply that they are fraudulent or false, as is suggested by the term "invention of tradition" coined by Eric Hobsbawm and Terrence Ranger (1983). For in the minds of believers, they are very real and have very real consequences for social action (Allahar 1993:46–48).

A HOSTILE AND RECALCITRANT MINORITY

In the years leading up to political independence in Trinidad, the volatile ideas of decolonization, freedom, and black self-rule filled the political air. In Trinidad at the time, the Afro-dominated People's National Movement (PNM) party was the best-organized and most disciplined of the political parties in the country. Furthermore, in a land where residential patterns followed distinct ethnic and class lines, the charismatic leader of the PNM, Eric Williams, was able to use clear ethno-racial appeals in reaching out to black voters in the more economically depressed areas. Given the numeric majority of the blacks at the time, he was confident that he could count on his Afro-Trinidadian constituencies to give him the political support he needed to lead the country to independence. However, the late 1950s was also a time of federal politics, a time when many hoped for a West Indian federation of the various English-speaking countries. This notwithstanding, it was not long before political in-fighting, personality clashes among leaders, and petty insular jealousies dashed all such hopes.

Speaking generally, West Indian federal politicking also had a decided impact on national politics, and it was during this time that the Indian-dominated Democratic Labour Party (DLP) emerged on the Trinidad political scene. In Eric Williams's estimation, the prime role of the DLP was that of a political spoiler. He was proved correct in the elections of the West Indian Federal Parliament (March 25, 1958), when Trinidad was divided into ten seats and the DLP was able to defeat the PNM by winning six of those seats. Williams was incensed and felt betrayed by a group he thought he had decisively silenced in the 1956 General Elections. And this was when he was moved to utter that infamous indictment of Indians as "a hostile and recalcitrant minority" (*PNM*

Weekly, April 21, 1958) that has served to condition the ethnic dimension of Trinidad's political evolution ever since. As we will see, the indictment has also served to energize a whole generation of Afrocentric ethnic entrepreneurs.

NATIONAL ASSOCIATION FOR THE EMPOWERMENT OF AFRICAN PEOPLE

If we feel that we are Trinbagonians first, it is clear that we can have little sympathy for Afro-Trinbagonians who wish to proclaim their Africanness, worship within an African framework of belief and feel that charity should begin at home. (Cudjoe 2000:¶20)

A clear case of ethnic entrepreneurship of the Afrocentric variety can be had in the person of Selwyn Cudjoe, a Trinidadian who teaches at Wellesley College (Massachusetts). He is very much like two other Caribbean ethnic entrepreneurs based outside of the region: Ian Smart, a Trinidadian who teaches at Howard University; and Kimani Nehusi, a Guyanese based at the University of East London. As argued by Amanda Zavitz and Anton Allahar (2002), Smart and Nehusi (2000) exhibit the classic features of ethnic entrepreneurs who operate within the academy. Like so many others of their ilk, in building their academic careers they openly traffic in blackness and seem untroubled by the tall claims they make: that civilization was invented by Africans; that all black people, regardless of where they are born, are African; that the African mind is one and undifferentiated; and that, as evidenced by its Carnival, Trinidad is an African country.

In similar vein, Cudjoe is bent on rallying black Trinidadians to the cause of Africa. In 1998 he founded the National Association for the Empowerment of African People (NAEAP), which is directed at all black Trinidadians but especially at the young black males and females in the society. In his words, the NAEAP is created "to address and redress effectively the various problems and issues which Africans face in Trinidad and Tobago" (Cudjoe 2001c:¶1). And with respect to those who accuse him of (black) racism he is quick to point out that "recent genome studies" show that "there is no scientific basis for the concept of race" (2000:¶5). This notwithstanding, he goes on to write as if "races" were real and exhorts black youth "to be morally responsible young people with a view to committing themselves towards the enhancement of their *race* and their community" (Ibid.:¶4 [my emphasis]). To this end, the NAEAP's motto is "Taking care of our people's business" (Cudjoe 2000:¶1) and has six main objectives (Ibid.:¶2):

1. to act as a representative body for Africans in Trinidad and Tobago and throughout the Caribbean;

2. to collaborate with other groups in the promotion of African unity;
3. to set up educational, commercial, and social infrastructure for the enhancement of the socioeconomic growth of Afro-Trinbagonians;
4. to act as an advocate for the legitimate interests of Afro-Trinbagonians in the private and public spheres;
5. to empower and to uplift Afro-Trinbagonians; and
6. to perform all other actions that will enhance the total well being of Africans in Trinidad and Tobago and throughout the Caribbean.

A major incentive for forming the NAEAP was undoubtedly the 1995 electoral victory of the United National Congress (UNC) and the swearing in of Trinidad's first Indian prime minister. Immediately thereafter fear and apprehension were widely felt in several sectors of the black population, and at that point, in the guise of calypsonians, ethnic entrepreneurs in the entertainment business came to the fore to channel the fears of the black people and to racialize even further the public's political consciousness. Allahar (1998a) identified several of the calypsonians in question and highlighted the contributions of two in particular: Cro Cro (Weston Rawlins) and Sugar Aloes (Michael Osuna). In the estimations of the latter, the Indians of Trinidad were poised for revenge, and the blacks, whose own ethno-political confidence and arrogance led them to stay away from the polls in November 1995, would be made to pay. Cro Cro and Sugar Aloes attacked the UNC's theme of "national unity" and berated as traitors all black Trinidadians who endorsed that theme.

The political mood was and continues to be fed by heightened individual insecurity, national disunity, and ethnic mistrust. In the field of education, one of NAEAP's main foci, this mistrust is clearly captured by Cudjoe's suspicions concerning how Indian teachers might relate to African students. Because he does not trust Indians, he is led rhetorically to ask: "do Indian teachers teach African children with the same fervour and commitment they devote to teaching Indian children" (2001d: ¶11)? The implication is that in such a racially divided society it is best to have African teachers teach African children. The logistical problems presented by such a limited understanding of the society and its educational system are too numerous to mention.

The insecurity and mistrust also embrace the cultural realm of the calypso, as was evidenced in 2004 when Cro Cro stepped once more into the limelight of controversy with his calypso titled "Face Reality." Along with the leaders of drug rings, the calypso targets allegedly corrupt politicians and well-placed individuals suspected of white-collar crimes (fraud) and invites the bandits to "kidnap dem." It is a volatile time when desperate, undereducated and unemployed black youth, who are indeed living through a "time of crisis and distress" as described by Schiffer (1973:11), have responded to

Cro Cro's call and have unleashed a spate of kidnappings and murders where the victims are disproportionately Indian. Along with the repeated refrain of "kidnap dem," the calypso avers:

Dey dress with jacket and tie,
Dey thief and living a lie,
Dey better pay back all the wrong things dey do,
Or the bandits coming for you.

While the kidnappings were initially drug-related, now they are directed increasingly at Indian politicians and their families, with a recent (May 2004) kidnap and murder victim being Ashmead Baksh, the son of an opposition parliamentarian. For Selwyn Cudjoe, however, "the calypso establishes its moral position by affirming what can be called Old Testament justice" (2004b:¶3). Cudjoe feels that as a visionary and an artist, Cro Cro "might well be a voice in the wilderness, trying to say that the small man must receive justice" (2004b:¶12). In his ethnic entrepreneurial and populist view the "small man" is the poor black man, but in characteristic contradictory style he makes no mention of the justice for those scores of innocent victims of the small man's justice.

Though generally ignorant of Indian history, culture, and values, Cudjoe is intent on speaking about these matters with a view to scoring political points among his followers. Thus, in his verbal sparring with the equally extremist Indians in the Maha Sabha, he affirms that "in a system where the demarcation of people is based on the color of their skins—the Brahmins being the fairest color whereas those at the lowest caste are dark in color—it is understandable how the leader of the Maha Sabha could see African people as being genetically inferior" (Cudjoe 2003b:¶23). While Hindus are definitely color-conscious and equally capable of racism, Cudjoe's characterization of them is quite simplistic. His venom, though, is not reserved for Indians alone, for those blacks who oppose his racial views are also targeted for failing to see the reality of Indian (Hindu) racism. Speaking of two Afro-Trinbagonians (Wade Mark and Morgan Job), who are members of the Indian-dominated UNC, Cudjoe affirms that: "What the Wade Marks and Morgan Jobs cannot know is that the contempt Panday and his kind feel for them is imbricated within a Hindu world view that holds blackness in utter contempt" (2000:¶14). And, he continues, "Blackness is associated with and is the place reserved for the Sudra or the untouchables, the lowest caste that stand [*sic*] at the bottom of the Hindu pecking order" (2000:¶15).

In his ongoing battle with the UNC and its Indo-Trinidadian leader, Cudjoe charges Panday with having a plan for the triumph of Indians over the blacks. Putting words into Panday's mouth, he attributes to the latter the claim that "the only way to triumph over the Negro is to join him and make him feel important. In our analysis, we realised that the Negro mind gives in easily to other races simple [*sic*] because they like to depend on the fortunes of others. After all, Creoles are simple fools" (Cudjoe 2000:¶11). In other words, "'The Negro,' as some of them calls [*sic*] us, likes to be flattered and made to feel important" (Cudjoe 2000:¶14). Curiously, Cudjoe may very well have fallen prey to the Negro weakness he identifies when he relates a story of an unnamed Indian (from India) scholar who had visited his house: "When he was leaving my home he bent and touched the slippers I was wearing with his fingers and then brought it [*sic*] to his heart. He then informed me that this was how Indians honored their gurus" (2000:¶49). In a moment of self-aggrandizement, Cudjoe thus arrogates unto himself a guru-like status. One is thus left to wonder who Cudjoe had in mind when he declared that "the stupidity that fools utter always seem to outlive them and leave their traces on the sober discourses of serious people" (2001c:¶23).

Of interest also is the way in which NAEAP gives an African identity priority over a Trinidadian identity. Arguing that Trinidadian nationalism was and is an impediment to the development of African consciousness and unity, Cudjoe writes that the disunity among African Trinidadians "resulted from a nationalist perspective that subjugated the interest of Africans to the national interest" (2000:¶19). Thus, lamentably, "Afro-Trinidadians have seen themselves as Trinidadians and Tobagonians first; and Africans second or third," whereas "Indo-Trinbagonians have always seen themselves as Indians first and Trinbagonians second or even third" (2000:¶16–17). In an ironic sense, he seems to applaud the Indians for their loyalty to India, but elsewhere that same loyalty is turned against the Indians, who are accused of disloyalty to Trinidad (Persad and Maharaj 1993:xxvii; Maharaj 2002:ii; Ramharrack n.d.:¶2). As a consequence, those Trinidad blacks who place their Trinidadian national identity over their primordial African origins are very misguided and feel no loyalty to their racial group (Cudjoe 2000:¶18).

Interestingly, Cudjoe's political hero, Eric Williams, would have disagreed with him, for it was Williams himself who wrote about the type of unity needed to nourish Trinidad and Tobago in its independence era: "There can be no Mother Africa for those of African origin, and the Trinidad and Tobago society is living a lie and heading for trouble if it seeks to create the impression or to allow others to act under the delusion that Trinidad and Tobago is an African society" (1962:281). Williams even went on to affirm that there can be no Mother England, Mother China, Mother Syria, and so forth, which would demand dual loyalties, since in this country "the only Mother we recognise is Mother Trinidad and Tobago, and a Mother cannot discriminate between her children" (Ibid.).

Cudjoe's "entrepreneurship" can also be seen in the way he introduces religious imagery when addressing his followers. Sounding much like a TV evangelist (religious entrepreneur) who manipulates feelings of guilt among the faithful, Cudjoe tells an audience of NAEAP members that they have a duty and responsibility to ensure the success of the Association. Then he makes a strong plea for tithes in excess of 10 percent along with other financial and material contributions: "If you do not tithe and if you do not support us, how can you expect us to exist in the kingdom of this world?" (2000:¶38). And sounding just like a Jim Baker or Jimmy Swaggart, shortly after the impassioned plea he announces that "today, I feel a love breeze blowing into this room" (2000:¶50); the more the love, the stronger the breeze and the bigger the contribution.

As the self-appointed voice of the African-Trinidadians, NAEAP finds itself constantly at odds with the self-appointed voice of Indo-Trinidadians, the Maha Sabha. Both organizations are headed by ethnic entrepreneurs bent on presenting their positions and claims in extreme terms, and in the process, while cementing their own political positions, they talk past one another and do more to divide the society than to bring it together. Thus, reflecting on the advances made by Indians in the areas of religious unity, the ownership of television programs and radio broadcasts, economic prosperity, and political victory in the form of the UNC, Cudjoe, the president of the NAEAP, was moved to declare that the "the Indianization of the society is taking place in front of our eyes" (2004a:¶14).

Curiously, one of the areas of Indianization he singles out for attention is the disproportionate visibility of Indians on television and the fact that there are six Indian-owned radio stations (Ibid.:¶1). For its part, one of the Maha Sabha's leading spokespersons (Kamal Persad) argues that the mistrust of Indians is firmly based on the virtual exclusion of Indians and Indian points of view from the national media. Persad is convinced that the national press is a "creole vehicle to maintain, protect and defend their order of things. . . . Today, the so-called national daily and weekly press carry no Indian viewpoint of things but allow and tolerate many anti-Indian articles, and writers with a clear creole and black perspective are allowed free reign" (1996:49).

HINDU NATIONALISM OR *HINDUTVA*[1]

Thus, while Africa is a continent and Afrocentrism is based on the myth of Africa as a single, unified country or nation, India is a de facto country that makes possible the claim for a Hindu nationalism or *Hindutva*, which is tied to the political and religious beliefs and practices of Hindus in India. As Chetan Bhatt and Parita Mukta note, "Diaspora Hindu nationalism has been important for the ideological and political shape of Hindu nationalism in India" (2000:409). While the blending of politics and religion is by no means a new phenomenon, once in the hands of ethnic entrepreneurs, it is given a special twist in diasporic politics. Some of this will be highlighted in the case of Trinidad, where an aggressive diasporic form of Hindu nationalism has come to serve as a defense against an equally insipid black nationalism or Afrocentricity. My charge is that both forms of nationalism promote false consciousness and serve the purpose of ideological distraction. This is then skillfully used by ethnic entrepreneurs to foster ethnic awareness among their followers, to sow ethnic divisions between the latter and members of rival ethnic groups, and in the process to minimize the development of class awareness among all. This amounts to what I call false consciousness or a non-class appreciation of social inequalities.

Understanding the genesis of *Hindutva* politics is not too complicated. In the so-called prescientific age, when religion exerted a firm hold on peoples' beliefs, imaginations, and behaviors, fear, superstition, intolerance, and bigotry were usually the order of the day. It was also a time of great individual insecurity as the mysteries of the universe and God's directing of it were accepted entirely as matters of faith and fate. Those religious leaders who claimed to be directly or indirectly in touch with the word of God were able to convince a vulnerable population that they were rightfully entitled to rule and to intercede with God on behalf of the wider society. Thus construed, religion was a decidedly political undertaking. It played on the fears and ignorance of unsophisticated or ordinary people, and was manipulated by the more literate classes to ensure the latters' positions of privilege.

Nevertheless, with the rise of science and modernity it was generally expected that widespread ignorance would be conquered and that the sources of superstition and human insecurity would be demystified. In other words, the religious card would be lost to ethnic entrepreneurs, who would then have to look more widely at various elements of secular culture for their political ammunition. But this did not entirely come to pass, for as was discussed in the case of Cudjoe and the NAEAP, the rise and spread of capitalism, colonialism, imperialism, and globalization (Rajagopal 2000:467), along with physical displacement, cultural alienation, economic exploitation, and racial oppression, proved fertile ground for entrepreneurs of all sorts. Insecurities created among the formerly enslaved and indentured populations brought to the New World were politically manipulated by ethnic entrepreneurs of the various groups, and a revived interest in religiously based ethnic identification was harnessed and molded to suit the prevailing conditions.

Similar to the primordialist claims of the Afrocentric ethnic entrepreneurs (Smith 1984:96), Indian political activists make great use of the mythical and pristine past from which the proud ancestors are said to have derived; they lament the loss of that past and stress the need to recapture it. Thus, recognizing the opportunism of Hindu nationalists and their ethnic entrepreneurial designs, Romila Thapar noted that "their presentation of the Indian past, the Hindu past, as a great golden age that began in the 5th millennium or 4th millennium B.C. and continued unabated until the Muslims arrived on the scene, becomes nonsensical, because it is unreal" (2000:606). To this Bhatt and Mukta paraphrase the nationalists as saying that "India was not only a Hindu nation and a Hindu civilization, but its Hindu origins were primordial, existing from time immemorial" (2000:412), and Mary Searle-Chatterjee rounds out this type of thinking when she says that for this group, "being 'Hindu' is a primordial identity, rooted in a homogeneous and continuing culture" (2000:498).

At this point it is important to note that not all politics involving Hinduism is given to the charge of ethnic political entrepreneurship; for *Hindutva* is different from Hinduism. The former is a political ideology and movement and the latter is a religion. As a political ideology Hindu nationalism was first articulated by Vinayak Damodar Savarkar in 1923 and was "based on the primacy of blood belonging, religious identity and territorial nationhood" (Mukta and Bhatt 2000:402–3). To this extent the ideology fits well with the description of nationalism as a territorially based movement (see chapter 1) informed by primordial appeals. The words of Savarkar, author of the founding text of the Hindu nationalist movement (*Hindutva—or who is a Hindu?*), are most instructive as they invoke once more the idea of identity as rooted in family and place of origin: "A Hindu is a person who looks upon the land that extends . . . from the Indus to the sea as his Fatherland, his Motherland and his Holyland" ([1923] 1989:3). Savarkar's primordialist sympathies are unmistakable. For him the supposed blood bond among all Hindus meant that they constituted a separate and pure "race" that "was defined by the blood that Hindus share and which has flowed down from the ancient Vedic fathers" (Bhatt and Mukta 2000:413).

By taking liberties with history and biology as the Afrocentrists and black nationalists have done, Savarkar and others had a view of "race" that was purportedly biological, but when pressed, they could slide into a more social, hereditarian definition: "This conception of 'race' is very slippery indeed and could use the epistemic resources of culture and civilization or spirituality and religion or 'blood' and nation without necessarily having any epistemic responsibility for the use of any of these ideas" (Bhatt and Mukta 2000:414). This observation is key to understanding today's Hindu nationalism, for Savarkar's politics "cannot be conceived as an ethnic, religious, 'racial' or nationalist ideology, but can float in an indeterminate way across all these ideas" (Ibid.).

Savarkar proved to be a great influence on Keshav Baliram Hedgewar, an activist for Indian independence, who in 1924 founded the most important Hindu nationalist organization in the country: the Rashtriya Swayamsevak Sang (RSS, the National Volunteers' Corps). The ideology of the RSS is *Hindutva*, which informs the thinking of the powerful former ruling party of India, the Bharatiya Janata Party (BJP). The RSS is a highly organized and disciplined, militant, and semi-paramilitary organization dedicated to the recruitment and training of young, preadolescent males for the defense of Hindu India. The idea is to combat the traditional stereotypical Gandhian image of the passive, weak, apologetic, emasculated, and effeminate Indian (Mukta 2000:448) and to cultivate in its place a picture of a proud, strong, and assertive Hindu, who is not afraid to defend his roots and his homeland. Hedgewar was convinced that the weakness of India was due to the fact that the country had been invaded and conquered, first by the Turkish-Afghan Muslims and later by the British, and in the process the philosophy, culture, and practice of Hinduism were diluted.

To restore the historic and pre-invasion glory of Hindus and the Hindu nation (Hindu Rashtra) it was necessary to shatter the stereotype of the weak Indian and to militantly oppose two of its most serious adversaries: Islam and Christianity. To this end the activities of the Vishwa Hindu Parishad (VHP or World Hindu Council) are focused on strengthening the community, even if it means using extreme force and violence against perceived enemies. This includes vicious attacks against Muslims and Christians (Indian and Western) in India (Rajagopal 2000:468), the rape of Indian nuns (Thapar 2000:615), and the burning to death of an Australian missionary in Orissa in 1999 (Mukta 2000:442–43). As is known, however, the violence has not been confined to the mother country alone but has spilled over into the Indian diasporas all over the world, Trinidad included.

A prime strategy of the VHP has been the "'reconversion' to Hinduism of those who have left the 'Hindu fold' and adopted Islamic or Christian faiths" (Bhatt and Mukta 2000:421), for whereas Islam and Christianity are viewed merely as religions, Hinduism is seen as a more all-encompassing "primordial way of life revealed for all humanity" (Ibid.). The Islamic threat that began with the Turkish-Afghan invasion came full circle in 1947 with the partition of India and the formation of the independent Muslim state of Pakistan. Hindus saw this as a further raid on their lands and resources and relations between both countries have always been troubled. To this end the mobilization of Hindu nationalists in the name of what Dhooleka Sarhadi Raj calls "interest group politics" whereby "religion comes to serve as the handmaiden of political gain" (Raj 2000:538) fits well with my discussion of ethnic entrepreneurship. And in the above example the political agenda of the ethnic entrepreneurs is informed by the desire to reclaim Pakistan, Bangladesh, and Kashmir and to restore the Akhand Bharat (undivided homeland of India). The ethnic entrepreneurs who head the organization are men of substance from the upper and middle castes: "teachers, government bureaucrats, soldiers and merchants. The leadership and officers of the RSS were, however, from Maharashtrian Brahmin castes" (Bhatt and Mukta 2000:415).

HINDUTVA IN TRINIDAD

Dr. D. P. Pandia was one of the principal exponents of Hindu nationalism during the 1930s and right into the period of the Second World War. As a member of the Indian National Congress party, he visited Trinidad in 1941 and had a decisive influence on Hari Prashad Singh, the so-called Father of Indian Nationalism in Trinidad. Even before arriving in Trinidad Pandia "had been on a sort of unofficial ambassadorial mission, traveling throughout the world where Indians were settled, carrying the Indian nationalist message and taking up issues affecting the Indians Overseas" (Persad and Maharaj 1993:xxv). He was also responsible for organizing the Hindustani Sevak Sangha (also known as the Hindu Swayamsevak Sangh [HSS]) in Fyzabad, Trinidad (Ibid.). Outside of India, the HSS is the main name used by the RSS, which, as noted earlier, is a semi-paramilitary organization created in the mid-nineteen-twenties to inculcate Hindu supremacist ideology and promote disciplined physical training among young Hindu men charged with defending the Hindu religion, philosophy, and way of life (Mukta and Bhatt 2000:404). And as we have seen, this is the very organization that, in the name of *Hindutva*, is also responsible for the persecution and murders of thousands of Indian Muslims and Christians in India.

Energized by the efforts of expatriates like Pandia and Pandit N. Khuzru, local ethnic entrepreneurs like M. J. Kirpalani, Adrian Cola Rienzi, Mitra Sinanan, and H. P. Singh were able to nurture an incipient Indian nationalism in Trinidad as far back as the latter years of the nineteenth century; sometimes those efforts were more successful than others. By the 1940s, however, Persad and Maharaj tell us that in much of the island there were organizations devoted to social, cultural, and religious matters of the Indian community: "The dominant principle of organization was race, Indian, and even religious groups viewed themselves as being Indian first" (Persad and Maharaj 1993:XXVll; Indian Review Committee 1991c:13).

Following the echo of *Hindutva* in Trinidad, it was felt by Hindu activists over the years that far too many of their group had become converted to Christianity and Islam. These gains were realized largely among the illiterate, rural Hindus, who were initially targeted by the Canadian Presbyterian missionaries and later by all variety of Christian Protestant religions. Christian philosophy and teaching are very different from Hindu philosophy and teaching because the latter incorporates the idea reincarnation and speaks of *dharma* (natural law, order, duty) and *karma*, or the fact that one's actions in this life will have consequences in one's future life. Christianity offers the possibility of forgiveness and absolution from sins in this life, and this proves extremely attractive to many poor, rural Hindus, especially those who are not schooled in the philosophy of their religion and who are living in a country (Trinidad) whose reality is far removed from that of the mother country (India).

So great is the perceived threat posed by Christian missionaries that Trinidad Hindus have issued warnings and guidelines to members of their community informing them of how best to deal with the Christians. The invoking of external threat as a ploy for building internal unity was addressed by Thapar in the Indian context when she spoke of *Hindutva* ideologues (ethnic entrepreneurs) using ethno-religious "identity to mobilize politically" and swell the ranks of membership, for "not only do more and more people have to be recruited, but this recruitment requires that the group be said to be threatened by another. Thereby the mobilization becomes more intense" (2000:607). The following is an excerpt from a pamphlet that was publicly circulated in Trinidad. It was titled *Hindus Defend Our Dharma! A Call to Action* (n.d.).

> This is a call to action for Hindus in Trinidad. Hindu Dharma is under attack! Enemies of our religion are on the streets, radio, television and even in our homes. They are openly working to destroy Hinduism and convert us to Christianity. We Hindus must stand up to preserve our Dharma from destruction by these Ravans [evil doers]. It is our duty! We must all become warriors for Sanatan Dharma [the eternal religion] or else be guilty of betrayal of our faith. If we protect our dharma it will protect us!

The three-page statement is a practical, step-by-step guide for Trinidadian Hindus to deal with attempts to infiltrate their religion and poison the religious beliefs of Hindus. As noted, the concern is that Christian missionaries (Pentecostals, Jehovah Witnesses, Open Bible, Mormons, Seventh Day Adventists, etc.) are on the move and seeking to convert Hindus, young and old. It asks, "What are we [Hindus] doing?" in response to the Christian missionary offensive, and the answer is:

> Some Hindus are "putting them in their place" and driving them off, but most are tolerating these religious scavengers. We do not have an organized campaign to defend against their attack, to put all Hindus on guard against these missionaries. That is why a large number of Hindus are converting and becoming vicious enemies of Hinduism.

Together with the Christian offensive, there are also the threats posed by Islam. According to *Hindutva* fundamentalists, Islam continued to make inroads into the Hindu community by giving to Indian Muslims an identity that stressed Islam at the expense of their Indian-ness. This echoes the comments of Biju Mathew and Vijay Prashad, who, writing in the context of Indians in the United States, said that for those who are Muslim, their "Muslim identity is more important than their Indian identity" (2000:527–28). In other words, their religious identity took precedence over their national origin or their "racial" identification as Indian (Searle-Chatterjee 2000:499).

HINDU-MUSLIM MISTRUST

Given the political entrenchment of Afro-Trinidadians and their dominant presence in the cultural life of the nation, Hindus see the conversion of Indians to Islam and Christianity as a net loss for the Indian "race." To the extent that it is possible, then, Hindu ethnic entrepreneurs seek to utilize "race" (Indian-ness) to make appeals for group solidarity among all Indian-descended Trinidadians with a view to promoting unity within the Indian community where Hindus constitute the religious (and political) majority. Two such entrepreneurs write:

> The experience of leaving India, the long journey to the Caribbean, the experience of living and working in a foreign environment which at times was hostile to the Indian presence, bonded all Indians together and created a strong sense of Indianness, and in time, resulted in the founding of Indian religious and secular organizations. (Persad and Maharaj 1993:xxvii)

These two authors advance the primordialist argument like their fellow colleagues on the Indian Review Committee, who also see the Muslim Indians in Trinidad as rejecting their Indian history and cultural survivals, and as constituting a threat to the *Hindutva* movement: "the Indian fundamentalist Muslim experience is one of denial of his Indianness and destruction of his Indian consciousness" (Indian Review Committee 1990a:1; 1990b:11).

In developing the argument that Trinidadian Indians were Trinidadian first and not traitors to the cause of Trinidadian independence and sovereignty, Persad and Maharaj seem to contradict themselves when they wrote that "after five years of black domination, living under the British *raj* was a far more tolerable and preferable option" (1993:xi). And not too much later they also go on to state categorically that "clearly the Indian community viewed itself as a distinct and separate community, one nation living in a common space with other nations. It was clear also that there was to be retention or links with India" (xxiv). Thus, it is not clear just how these authors would square their own separatist feelings with the more Trinidadian nationalist sentiments of H. P. Singh, whom they so revere and celebrate. For H. P. Singh was not a separatist at heart. However, following the early PNM electoral victories that were widely rumored to be fraudulent, he did demand that the rigged voting machines be eliminated and that new elections be held. Failing that, he called for a system of proportionate representation, since in his estimation, the Indians would have won if the election were fair in the first place. If neither of these two were granted, he saw no alternative but to call for separation under the slogan: *parity or partition* (Singh 1993a:6–7).

This idea of separation has found favorable echo in the Indesh Freedom Party, which is seeking the establishment of an Indian homeland in Trinidad (Persad 1993:117–19; Ryan 1996:46–47). But much like Asante, ethnic entrepreneurs like Kamal Persad and Ashram Maharaj seem not to be bothered by contradiction. Therefore, when they write that Indian-Trinidadian nationalism "never expressed itself in terms of superiority over other communities in Trinidad," they seem willfully ignorant of the basic claims of *Hindutva*, or the supremacist ideology that has attended the movement from its inception.

Returning to the question Hindu-Muslim mistrust and the division it brought to the Indian community, the editors of *The Indian Review*, who sound exactly like Cudjoe, are best left to speak for themselves. In an editorial titled "Muslim or Indian First?" (1991c), it was written: "Of course, Indian-Muslim unity could only strengthen the Indian community if Indian Muslims identify with their self and do not negate their Indian-ness." It was felt that Indian Muslims in Trinidad were confused about their identity and torn between being Indian Muslims and Indians: "In being Islamic one must deny Indian and everything Indian even to the point of rejecting Indian music. It amounts to a total self-denial, and its replacement with Arabism or African Islam" (1991c:13). The politicization of Islam is also a concern since Indian Muslims would likely be more dominated by the black Muslim political and ideological agenda (Indian Review Committee 1990b:11), and more concerned "with the Palestinian problem and Arab unity and not with discrimination against *Indian* Muslims in Fiji, Barbados, Guyana" and Trinidad, or with the larger issue of "*Indian* unity" (1991c:13 [my emphasis]).

Finally, on the question of "race" and ethnic identity, the editorial in question came down squarely on the side of "race" and cautioned against those who wish to "debunk race" and promote the wishy-washy Islamic notion of the "the brotherhood of man." For that mistake had been made before. In their words, to follow the Islamic teaching "is to make the mistake of the communists in believing that class and class position could bring about unity. It is in fact to engage in *false consciousness*" (Ibid.:13 [my emphasis]).

What is interesting here is the way in which the Hindu ethnic entrepreneurs of the Indian Review Committee directly reverse the argument concerning false consciousness (see chapter 1). In the classical use of the term, those who either ignore or deny class and promote the distractions of "race" and ethnic awareness are precisely the ones guilty of false consciousness. Here, however, echoing the sentiments of Asante and the Afrocentrists, the charge is that "race" is real while "class," as an invention of the communists, had clearly shown itself to be irrelevant to the struggles of oppressed peoples. There could be no clearer example of ethnic entrepreneurship. And this is also why someone like Niala Maharaj, commenting on the debate over the celebration of Indian Arrival Day in Trinidad, could correctly accuse the editors of *The Indian Review* of political opportunism: "this new celebration of an event which Indians have largely forgotten has no *raison d'être* except in the minds of would-be Indian leaders wishing to shepherd Indian thinking in certain directions" (Indian Review Committee 1991a:15). The "would-be" leaders are the ethnic entrepreneurs, and the "shepherding of thinking" is the use of ethnic and religious ideology to convince Indians to follow a certain ethno-political path.

In the same way that poor and working-class blacks can be manipulated and lured into a falsely conscious "race" awareness by Afrocentric ethnic entrepreneurs, poor, lower caste, and working-class Indians are also vulnerable to the appeals of Hindu ethnic entrepreneurs, who are "predominantly upper caste Hindu men" (Rajagopal 2000:470). Led by skilful ethnic entrepreneurs of the upper castes and classes, many poor and working-class Hindus are encouraged to adopt the latters' definitions of what Hinduism means and to commit grave acts of violence against non-Hindus in defense of those definitions:

> The strength of the *Hindutva* movement lies in its ability to draw in large numbers of people who are not upper caste or middle class, both in India and the diaspora. . . . In India for, example, very poor migrant workers have been implicated in violence against Muslim communities. In Britain, there is evidence that working-class individuals from a traditional leather-working [a very low caste occupation] community in Leeds became leading members of the Hindu Swayamsevak Sangh. (Bhatt and Mukta 2000:426)

And while in the Caribbean the violent excesses of Indian *Hindutva* have not been felt, the philosophy has been well received by politically ambitious individuals in the Maha Sabha and their erstwhile colleagues on the Indian Review Committee. In the words of Kamal Persad: "The present political situation of Indians and Hindus in this region and the emerging new geo-political possibility must be on our agenda for serious consideration and debate. The ideology of *Hindutva* can provide the guide" (1997:7).

The favorable reception of *Hindutva* ideology by certain segments of the Trinidad Indian population was carefully engineered by the ethnic entrepreneurs in the Maha Sabha and on the Indian Review Committee. This reception was conditioned by the fact that by 1945, after one hundred years of living in Trinidad, the majority of Indians no longer entertained any idea of returning to India and had come to see themselves as constituting an overseas Indian community: "that there would be no return to the ancient and ancestral motherland of India." Once exposed to the New World environment in the Caribbean and the Americas, however, "white colonial rule followed by African domination has contributed to the yearning by Indians for the creation of an Indian homeland—Bharatiyadesh/Industan" (Indian Review Committee 1991b:3).

Within Trinidad's diasporic Hindu community there developed strong relations with their continental brethren. And on the occasion of the visit to Trinidad by one of the greatest and most venerable contemporary Hindu personages, Ravi-ji wrote: "We invite the HH Shankaracharya Swami Divyananda Saraswatti of Bhanupur Peetha to form a special bond with the Hindu Caribbean." That primordial bond, established over centuries of common, spiritual Hindu experience and ancestry, is much like the historic bonds invoked by Afrocentrists to rally their supporters under the banner of historical and cultural purity, and to lament the loss of a bygone era of greatness. The original Shankaracharya, Ravi-ji notes, was born in the late eighth century and in the many millennia that have followed since:

> the Hindu civilization witnessed varying fortunes. Glorious empire-building, cultural and intellectual developments took place. India also saw waves of explorers and plunderers attracted to India's wealth, fertile lands, and culture. India also saw the period of decadence, loss of virility and psychological fear. (2000:24)

As a journalist and leading spokesperson of the Hindu community, Ravi-ji reported on the World Hindu Conference 2000 held in Trinidad (August 17–20, 2000) and wrote that the conference "comes at a time when Hindus are severely challenged in the Caribbean. This is so too for all Hindus wherever they are domiciled, even in India. For the Caribbean Jahaajis (brothers) and their descendants, we have lived with this challenge throughout our history as we set about to gather our spirits and reconstruct our heritage and society" (2000:8). The "challenge" of which he speaks is one of religious and cultural survival, and though not a follower of *Hindutva* Ravi-ji does aid the cause by emphasizing the Indian over the Caribbean cultural identity. This uncritical and unconditional endorsement of anything Indian can be seen in the primordial identification of Siddharta with Trinidad-born V. S. Naipaul:

> Because of Naipaul's greatness the Indians in Trinidad, in particular, have a readymade situation to establish under his name a literary foundation for emerging Indian writers, who by evidence of their potential, seem destined to bring further glory to the Indian diaspora. Everywhere Indians vicariously glory in Naipaul's name. (Siddharta 1996:4)

The point, however, is that given the racialization of Trinidad's political consciousness, Naipaul is seen (and sees himself) mainly as an Indian writer, as opposed to a Trinidadian. But to what extent is this celebration of India and Indian-ness a response to Afrocentrism? In other words, is Afrocentrism the cause or the consequence of the positive reception of the *Hindutva* message in Trinidad? It is best to let Naipaul speak for himself and the tradition from which he comes.

Thus, as he is about to leave Oxford University in 1953, and the question of returning to Trinidad arises, Naipaul writes to his father: "Trinidad as you know has nothing to offer me" (1999:221). And not much has changed in the fifty years ensuing, for after winning the Nobel Prize for Literature in 2001 he affirmed that while he happened to live in England, his roots were in India. He gives no positive acknowledgement to Trinidad as his country of birth. Particularly instructive is another exchange with his father, Seepersad, who writes to Naipaul about three of his Trinidadian cousins (Deo, Phoolo, and Tara), who were living temporarily with the Naipauls. They were young women who were just beginning to date: "These girls have become so ultra modern," Seepersad writes, "they make no distinction between Negroes, Mussulmans or other people." And he goes on:

> Deo says, without the semblance of a blush, there's nothing bad or ugly in a Hindu girl marrying a Negro boy. Her actual words: "What does it matter as long as you can be happy?" As to Muslims: "Why, they are only human." They have not merely expressed these things as mere opinion. They are nostril-deep in the thing. A week or so ago Phoolo brought in a young black-as-coal (I assure you I do not exaggerate) dougla. She wanted to know what I thought of her marrying this man. (Naipaul 1999:134–35)

And speaking once more of Deo: "She is openly contemptuous of the Indian way of life" (Ibid.:136). Then Seepersad laments that in spite of all "my begging and scolding that she give up the company of low people," Deo was intransigent. Reacting to this, Naipaul writes to his sister Kamla, who at the time was studying in India. "Home affairs. Sad isn't it? Just in case you haven't, you must hear now that Deo is chasing penniless men, Phoolo niggers, and Tara douglas. So there!" (1999:144).

Obviously Naipaul's racism (and that of his father) antedates the arrival of Afrocentrism *per se* and goes back to the xenophobic feelings shared by both blacks and Indians from the days of their earliest encounters. According to Kamal Persad, a local Hindu nationalist, the mistrust of Indians continues to the present and is fully realized in the various national media outlets where Indians and Indian points of view are still muted. "One must recognise what is the national press: a creole vehicle to maintain, protect and defend their order of things, their sacred 'calypso land,' their view of what is national." And, he continues, "The media men and women are simply not prepared to tolerate alternative views and perspectives. Today, the so-called national daily and weekly press carry no Indian viewpoint of things but allow and tolerate many anti-Indian articles, and writers with a clear creole and black perspective are allowed free reign" (1996:49).

In support of this charge, and writing in 1996, shortly after the defeat of the PNM and the coming to power of Trinidad's first prime minister of visible East Indian descent, Ashram B. Maharaj was concerned that three decades of black PNM rule has resulted in a racially stacked public service. The new Indian-headed government of Basdeo Panday, he feared, would encounter major problems from the mostly black civil service when it came to the implementation of new legislation, new economic, political, and social policies, and new attempts to redistribute more equitably the resources of the state (Maharaj 1996:5–8).

The assumption that all Indians are united (Chandraji 1996) and share a common point of view is challenged by Joy Mahabir, who puts forward more of a creole Trinidadian position: "One does not have to look to India to find 'Hindu fundamentalism.' We have it right here in the rhetoric of 'purity' advanced by the Maha Sabha and several organizations who wish to forget our history of indentureship, and our active part in Trinidadian culture" (Mahabir 1998). And Mahabir is not alone, for on the question of primordialism and Hindu nationalism, the columnist Indira Maharaj wrote in the *Express* on Friday March 2, 2001:

> Whenever I write a column in which I am critical of the Maha Sabha, one of the criticisms levelled at me in public and private is that I am being disloyal to Hindus. And, frequently this is followed by one of the following remarks: "we are one family," "what about Hindu unity?" "the Hindu community is too vulnerable," "we cutting down we own," "we should not wash [our] dirty laundry in public." (2001:17)

But Maharaj is mindful of the racial politics in the wider society and is convinced that before losing the elections "the UNC's tenure in office has had the effect of making Indos better Trinidadians." The ill-defined sense of a national identity among many Indos she sees as the expected outcome of Indian "marginalisation, alienation and cultural peripheralisation" under the PNM government. The coming to power of the UNC represented a new chapter in which Indian exclusion had "given way to a greater sense of belonging, a sense of being an equal, of not being a second-class citizen, of being 'genuinely Trinidadian' among Indos in the landscape" (Maharaj, 2001:17). For both Mahabir and Maharaj, then, the response to the racist exclusion of Indians by the PNM government is not Hindu racism or *Hindutva*, and "name calling across the racial fence" (Rother 1997), but the effective engagement of all the racist forces within the society.

Like the Afrocentrists who denounce Eurocentrism and embrace Afrocentrism, the Hindu nationalists also seem to subscribe to the idea that two wrongs do somehow make a right. Reflecting on the black pride movement, which saw t-shirts with various popular symbols of Africana, the faces of prominent black leaders et cetera on them, an article supplied by the Maha

Sabha to the *Express* noted that "the Africans here blatantly promote Afro-centric behaviour. They wear the map of Africa on their clothes. They wear jerseys painted with Malcolm X, Garvey, Mandela, Luther King, and Haile Selassie." While the tone of the article suggests that this is wrong, it does nevertheless state that: "Perhaps it's time for Indo Trinidadians to start wearing jerseys printed with a map of India saying: 'I am Hindu and proud; am Indian and proud'; with pictures of Nehru, Gandhi, Bhadase Maraj, and Lord Ganesh printed on their chests" (1998).

CONCLUSION

As peoples' political consciousness in multiethnic states such as the Caribbean becomes increasingly ethnicized, it seems as though the sense of civic nationalism has begun to give way to the earlier ethno-cultural claims to identity and distinctiveness. This is the point at which myth comes to play a crucial role in a people's sense of identity, for in the Caribbean as elsewhere, though imagined or invented, that idea of a lost ancestral home is very real to the believers, and it serves to inform their social engagements in their worlds in very tangible ways. In other words, modern or civic nationalism, which was born of an earlier ethnic or cultural nationalism, is not quite divorced from the latter. Indeed, the two appear to reinforce each other as "the civic concept of a modern nation . . . to become truly a 'nation,' requires the unifying myths, symbols and memories of pre-modern *ethnie*" (Smith 1988:11). And in the process, where "the ethnic concept of the nation and the ethnic model of national organization" appear to have seized the day, they curiously force "even groups which defined themselves in civic terms to regard themselves increasingly as ethnic nations" (Smith 1988:12).

This is where the examples of Afrocentrism and *Hindutva* in the Caribbean become relevant. For it is the bourgeois and petty-bourgeois nationalist intellectuals of the region who have come to serve as ethnic entrepreneurs and who seek deliberately to fashion myths of the "nation" with a view to mobilizing popular political support for one or another political project. Such intellectuals and ethnic entrepreneurs "select the historical memories and elaborate the myths of descent of the relevant *ethnie*" and are usually quite clear to name which elements of culture will be emphasized and which will be ignored in the mythical reconstruction of the "nation." Anything that in their estimation will unify the "nation" and set it apart from others is deemed politically useful. So the process is not left to chance for these:

> nationalist intellectuals do not make their selections and elaborations in a purely arbitrary manner. Typically, they find already to hand various folk-tales, ballads,

epics, customs and rituals, which they then seek to weave into a continuous, dramatic narrative of the "rediscovered nation." (Smith 1988:13)

The aim is to present a clear and compelling history of the group, even if largely invented, with a view psychologically and emotionally to mobilizing coethnics for political ends. In an Orwellian sense this is all about politically rewriting history so that it accords better with the understanding that the ethnic entrepreneurs, who emerge as leaders of ethnic movements, wish to impart. Paraphrasing the ideas of Marx and Engels's concerning the relationship between the ruling class and the ruling ideas of every age (1947:39), Ashley Doane wrote of those leaders the following: "To the extent that an elite or bourgeoisie of an ethnic group or nation controls the means of ideological production, they will play a key role in the construction and reconstruction of group identity" (1996:183).

In sum, focusing on the Caribbean I charge that the region as a whole is creolized, while Trinidad itself is a douglarized nation (i.e., in racial terminology, a nation that is defined predominantly by the mixing of African- and Indian-descended people). The various political cultures of the region were all forged in the fires of colonization, slavery, racism, indentureship, and dependent capitalism. As a consequence they betray the scars of these historical processes. There is certainly no democracy of races anywhere in the Caribbean, just as there is no class democracy, if by democracy one understands an equal access to, and sharing of, the social fruits. Indeed, what one finds is liberal democracy, which enshrines the inequalities of dependent capitalism. The various political cultures, including black cultural nationalism, thus exist in the service of those foreign and locally dominant capitalist classes and the protectors of the dependent capitalist order—the postcolonial state (Dupuy 1991). To this extent the politics of nationalism linked to "race," ethnicity, religion, and other social divisions will serve very clear class interests and condition the political cultures of the region and its various member countries. But one must not be distracted, for even though divisions may appear on the surface to be ethnic or racial, they remain fundamentally of a classed economic and political nature.

NOTE

1. I wish to acknowledge the generosity of Burton Sankerelli and Selwyn Ryan, who made their private files and notes on Hindu nationalism available to me.

References

Ahmad, Feroz. 1995. "The Development of Class Consciousness in Republican Turkey: 1923–1945." Pp. 75–94 in *Workers and the Working Class in the Ottoman Empire and the Turkish Republic: 1839–1950*, edited by Donald Quataert and Eric Zurcher. London: Tauris Publishers.

Akkaya, Yuksel. 2002. "The Working Class and Unionism in Turkey Under the Shackles of the System and Developmentalism." Pp. 129–44 in *The Ravages of Neo-Liberalism: Economy, Society and Gender in Turkey*, edited by Nesecan Balkan and Sungur Savran. New York: Nova.

Ali, A. 1980. *Plantation to Politics: Studies on Fiji Indians*. Suva: University of the South Pacific and Fiji Times.

Allahar, Anton L. 1990. "The Evolution of the Latin American Bourgeoisie: An Historical-Comparative Study." *International Journal of Comparative Sociology* 31, nos. 3–4 (September–December): 222–36.

———. 1993. "When Black First Became Worth Less." *International Journal of Comparative Sociology* 34, nos. 1–2: 39–55.

———. 1994a. "Differential Creolisation: East Indians in Trinidad and Guyana." *Indo Caribbean Review* 1, no. 2: 123–39.

———. 1994b. "More than an Oxymoron: Ethnicity and the Social Construction of Primordial Attachment." *Canadian Ethnic Studies* 26, no. 3: 18–33.

———. 1995. *Sociology and the Periphery: Theories and Issues*, 2nd ed. Toronto: Garamond Press.

———. 1996. "Primordialism and Ethnic Political Mobilization in Modern Society." *New Community* 22, no. 1: 5–21.

———. 1997. "History and the Genesis of Fragmented Caribbean Identities." *Journal of Social Sciences* 4, no. 2: 3–31.

———. 1998a. "Popular Culture and the Racialisation of Political Consciousness in Trinidad." *Wadabagei: Journal of the Caribbean and Its Diaspora* 1, no. 2: 1–41.

———. 1998b. "Race and Racism: Strategies of Resistance." Pp. 335–54 in *Racism and Social Inequality in Canada: Concepts, Controversies and Strategies of Resistance*, edited by Vic Satzewich. Toronto: Thompson Educational Publishing.

———, ed. 2001a. *Caribbean Charisma: Reflections on Leadership, Legitimacy and Populist Politics*. London: Lynne Rienner.

———. 2001b. "Framing of Political Culture in the English-Speaking Caribbean: Cuban Socialism vs. US Imperialism." *Canadian Journal of Latin American and Caribbean Studies* 26, no. 52: 223–43.

———. 2001c. "The Politics of Ethnic Identity Construction." *Identity: An International Journal of Theory and Research* 1, no. 3: 197–208.

———. 2001d. "'Race' and Class in the Making of Caribbean Political Culture." *Transforming Anthropology* 10, no. 2: 13–29.

———. 2003. "'Racing' Caribbean Political Culture: Afrocentrism, Black Nationalism and Fanonism." Pp. 21–58 in *Modern Political Culture in the Caribbean*, edited by Holger Henke and Fred Reno. Jamaica: University of the West Indies Press.

Allahar, Anton L., and James E. Côté. 1998. *Richer and Poorer: The Structure of Inequality in Canada*. Toronto: James Lorimer.

Amin, Samir. 1987. "Nationalism." *The New Palgrave: A Dictionary of Economics*, vol. 3. London: Palgrave.

Anderson, Benedict. [1983] 1991. *Imagined Communities: Reflections on the Origin and Spread of Nationalism*. New York: Verso.

Anonymous. "The Highest Courts of Many Commonwealth Countries Have Recognized the Concept of Aboriginal Title." *Stabroek News*, December 25.

Anthony, Earl. 1970. *Picking Up the Gun: A Report on the Black Panthers*. New York: Dial.

Appadurai, Arjun. 1990. "Disjuncture and Difference in the Global Cultural Economy." *Public Culture* 2, no. 2: 1–24.

———. 1996. *Modernity at Large: Cultural Dimensions of Globalization*. Minneapolis: University of Minnesota Press.

Appadurai, Arjun, and Carol Breckenridge. 1989. "Why Public Culture?" *Public Culture* 1, no. 1: 5–9.

Arun, T. G., and J. D. Turner. 2002. "Financial Sector Reforms in Developing Countries: The Indian Experience." *The World Economy* 25, no. 3 (March): 429–46.

Asante, Molefi Kete. 1987. *The Afrocentric Idea*. Philadelphia: Temple University Press.

———. 1988. *Afrocentricity*. Trenton, NJ: Africa World Press.

Atacan, Fulya. 2001. "A Kurdish Islamist Group in Modern Turkey: Shifting Identities." *Middle Eastern Studies* 37, no. 3: 111–44.

Atkinson, James. 1998. "Government Should Work with Existing Amerindian Organizations." *Stabroek News*, December 23.

Bain, A. 1994. *Labour and Gold in Fiji*. London: Oxford University Press.

Bakhtin, Mikael. 1968. "Introduction" to *Rabelais and His World*, translated by Helene Iwolsky. Cambridge, MA: MIT Press.

Barajas, Adolfo, Roberto Steiner, and Natalia Salazar. 2000. "Foreign Investment in Colombia's Financial Sector." Pp. 355–87 in *The Internationalization of Financial Services: Issues and Lessons for Developing Countries*, edited by Stijn Claessens and Marion Jansen. The Hague: Kluwer Law International.

Baraka, Imamu Amiri. 1972. *Raise, Race, Rays, Raze: Essays Since 1965*. New York: Vintage.

Barkey, Henri, and Graham Fuller. 1998. *Turkey's Kurdish Question*. Oxford: Rowman & Littlefield.

Barth, Frederick. 1969. *Ethnic Groups and Boundaries: The Social Organization of Cultural Differences*. Oslo: Universitetsforlaget.

Basch, Linda, Nina Glick Schiller, and Cristina Blanc-Szanton, eds. 1992. *Towards a Transnational Perspective on Migration: Race, Class, and Nationalism Reconsidered*. New York: New York Academy of Sciences.

———, eds. 1994. *Nations Unbound: Transnational Projects, Postcolonial Predicaments, and Deterritorialized Nation-States*. Langhorne, PA: Gordon and Breach.

Baum, Daniel Jay. 1974. *The Banks of Canada in the Commonwealth Caribbean: Economic Nationalism and Multinational Enterprises of a Medium Power*. New York: Praeger.

Beck, E. M., Patrick Horan, and Charles Tolbert. 1978. "Stratification in a Dual Economy: A Sectorial Model of Earnings Determination." *American Sociological Review* 43:704–20.

Beckles, Hilary McD., and Brian Stoddart, eds. 1995. *Liberation Cricket: West Indies Cricket Culture*. Manchester, UK: University of Manchester Press.

Beim, David O., and Charles W. Calomiris. 2001. *Emerging Financial Markets*. New York: McGraw-Hill.

Bell, Daniel. 1975. "Ethnicity and Social Change." Pp.141–74 in *Ethnicity: Theory and Experience*, edited by Nathan Glazer and Daniel P. Moynihan. Cambridge, MA: Harvard University Press.

Benítez-Rojo, Antonio. 1996. *The Repeating Island: The Caribbean and the Postmodern Perspective*, 2nd ed., translated by James E. Maraniss. Durham, NC: Duke University Press. [original Spanish, 1992]

Benjamin, Walter. [1936] 1968. "The Work of Art in the Age of Mechanical Reproduction." Pp. 217–53 in *Illuminations*, edited by Hannah Arendt, translated by Harry Zohn. New York: Schocken.

Berberoglu, Berch. 1994. *Class Structure and Social Transformation*. Westport, CT: Praeger.

Berik, Günseli, and Cihan Bilginsoy. 1996. "The Labour Movement in Turkey: Labour Pains, Maturity, Metamorphosis." Pp. 37–64 in *The Social History of Labour in the Middle East*, edited by Ellis Jay Goldberg. Boulder, CO: Westview Press.

Beşikçi, İsmail. 2001. "Türk Tarih Tezi ve Kürt Sorunu," quoted in Konrad Hirschler, "Defining the Nation: Kurdish Historiography in Turkey in the 1990s." *Middle Eastern Studies* 37, no. 3 (July 2001): 145–66.

Bhabha, Homi K. 1990a. "Dissemi-nation: Time, Narrative, and the Margins of the Modern Nation." Pp. 291–320 in *Nation and Narration*, edited by Homi K. Bhabha. London: Routledge.

———. 1990b. *Nation and Narration*. New York: Routledge.

Bhatt, Chetan. 2000. "Dharmo rakshati rakshitah: *Hindutva* Movements in the UK." *Ethnic and Racial Studies* 23, no. 3: 559–93.

Bhatt, Chetan, and Parita Mukta. 2000. "*Hindutva* in the West: Mapping the Antinomies of Nationalism." *Ethnic and Racial Studies* 23, no. 3: 407–41.

Binsbergen, Wim van. 2003. "Is There a Future for Afrocentrism Despite Stephen Howe's Dismissive 1998 Study?" Available at www.geocities.com/warriorvase/defence.htm (accessed September 9, 2003).

Birbalsingh, Frank. 1997. *From Pillar to Post: The Indo-Caribbean Diaspora.* Toronto: TSAR.

Birbalsingh, Frank, and Clem Shiwcharan. 1988. *Indo-West Indian Cricket.* London: Hansib.

Bissember, Enid E. 2003. Protocol II of the CARICOM Single Market and Economy: Implications for Banking and Finance. CARICOM Secretariat Economic Intelligence and Policy Unit.

Blauner, Robert. 1972. *Racial Oppression in America.* New York: Harper & Row.

Blejer, Mario I., and Marko Škreb. 1999. "Financial Reforms and Economic Transitions: An Overview of the Major Issues." Pp. 1–16 in *Financial Sector Transformation: Lessons from Economies in Transition,* edited by Mario I. Blejer and Marko Škreb. New York: Cambridge University Press.

Block, Fred. 1994. "The Roles of the State in the Economy." Pp. 691–710 in *The Handbook of Economic Sociology,* edited by Neil J. Smelser and Richard Swedberg. Princeton, NJ: Princeton University Press.

Bole, F. 1992. "Fiji's Chiefly System and Democracy." Pp. 10–15 in *Culture and Democracy in the Pacific,* edited by A. Ravuvu. Suva: IPS.

Bonacich, Edna. 1972. "A Theory of Ethnic Antagonism: The Split Labour Market." *American Sociological Review* 37, no. 5: 547–59.

———. 1976. "Advanced Capitalism and Black/White Race Relations in the United States: A Split Labour Market Interpretation." *American Sociological Review* 41, no. 1: 34–51.

———. 1980. "Class Approaches to Ethnicity and Race." *Insurgent Sociologist* 10, no. 2: 9–23.

Bosworth, Barry, Rudiger Dornbusch, and Raúl Labán. 1994. *The Chilean Economy: Policy Lessons and Challenges.* Washington, DC: The Brookings Institution.

Boxill, Ian. 1993. *Ideology and Caribbean Integration.* Mona, Jamaica: Consortium Graduate School of Social Sciences with Canoe Press.

Bozarslan, Hamit. 1992. "Political Aspects of the Kurdish Problem in Contemporary Turkey." Pp. 95–114 in *The Kurds,* edited by Philip G. Kreyenbroek and Stefan Sperl. London: Routledge.

Brah, Avtar. 1996. *Cartographies of Diaspora.* London: Routledge.

Brathwaite, Edward Kamau. 1971. *The Development of Creole Society in Jamaica.* Oxford: Clarendon Press.

Brennan, Timothy. 1989. "Cosmopolitans and Celebrities." *Race and Class* 31, no. 1: 1–19.

———. [1990] 1995. "The National Longing for Form." Pp. 170–75 in *The Postcolonial Studies Reader,* edited by B. Ashcroft, G. Griffiths, and H. Tiffin. New York: Routledge.

Brown, Deryck R. 1989. *History of Money and Banking in Trinidad and Tobago from 1789–1989.* Port of Spain: Central Bank of Trinidad and Tobago.

Brownbridge, Martin. 2002. "Banking Reforms in Africa: What Has Been Learnt?" *Insights* 40 (March). Available at www.id21.org/insights/insights40/insights-iss40-art01.html (accessed February 2, 2003).

Bulmer, Martin. 1986. "Race and Ethnicity." Pp. 54–75 in *Key Variables in Social Investigation*, edited by Robert G. Burgess. London: Routledge & Kegan Paul.

Burton, Richard. 1997. *Afro-Creole: Power, Opposition and Play in the Caribbean*. Ithaca, NY: Cornell University Press.

Calhoun, Craig. 1993. "Nationalism and Ethnicity." *Annual Review of Sociology* 19: 211–39.

Campbell, Ernest Q., ed. 1972. *Racial Tensions and National Identity*. Nashville, TN: Vanderbilt University Press.

Carmichael, Stokely. 1967a. "Black Power: Its Need and Substance." Pp. 34–56 in *Black Power: The Politics of Liberation in America*, edited by Stokely Carmichael and Charles V. Hamilton. New York: Vintage Books.

———. 1967b. "White Power: The Colonial Situation." Pp. 2–32 in *Black Power: The Politics of Liberation in America*, edited by Stokely Carmichael and Charles V. Hamilton. New York: Vintage Books.

———. 1968. "Power and Racism." Pp. 61–72 in *The Black Power Revolt*, edited by Floyd Barbour. Boston, MA: Extending Horizons Books.

Carnoy, Martin. 1984. *The State and Political Theory*. Princeton, NJ: Princeton University Press.

Carr, Robert. 2002. *Black Nationalism in the New World: Reading the African American and West Indian Experience*. Durham, NC: Duke University Press.

Central Statistical Office. 1996. *1990–91 Population and Housing Census of the Commonwealth Caribbean*. Collected in *Social Indicators 1985–1992*, Office of the Prime Minister, Central Statistical Office, Republic of Trinidad and Tobago, Port of Spain, Trinidad.

Chandraji. 1996. "Are You a Hindu?" Pp. 24–25 of *The Indian Review*. Couva, Trinidad: India Review Committee.

Chatterjee, Partha. 1986. *Nationalist Thought and the Colonial World: A Derivative Discourse*. London: Zed Books.

Chau, Amy. 2003. *World on Fire: How Exporting Free Market Democracy Breeds Ethnic Hatred and Global Instability*. New York: Doubleday.

Chilcote, Ronald, and Joel Edelstein. 1974. *Latin America: The Struggle with Dependency and Beyond*. New York: John Wiley.

Chirot, Daniel. 1977. *Social Change in the Twentieth Century*. New York: Harcourt, Brace, Jovanovich.

———. 1986. *Social Change in the Modern Era*. New York: Harcourt, Brace, Jovanovich.

Christie, Clive. 1998. *Race and Nation*. London: Tauris Publishers.

Claessens, Stijn, and Tom Glaessner. 1999. "Internationalization of Financial Services in Asia." Presented at the conference Investment Liberalisation and Financial Reform in the Asia-Pacific Region, August 29–31, Sydney, Australia.

Clifford, James. 1992. "Diasporas." *Cultural Anthropology* 9, no. 3: 302–38.

Cohen, A. R. 1974. *Urban Ethnicity*. London: Tavistock.

Cohen, Robin. 1979. "The Making of a West African Working Class." Pp. 5–21 in *The Politics of Africa: Dependence and Development*, edited by Timothy M. Shaw and Kenneth A. Heard. New York: Africana Publishing Co.

Coleman, William D. 1996. *Financial Services, Globalization and Domestic Policy Change*. Houndmills, UK: Macmillan Press.

Cornell, Stephen, and Douglas Hartman. 1998. *Ethnicity and Race*. London: Pine Forge Press.

Cornell, Svante. 2001. "The Kurdish Question in Turkish Politics." *Orbis* 4, no. 1: 31–46.

Cox, Oliver C. 1970. *Caste, Class and Race*. New York: Monthly Review Press.

Crowder, Kyle D., and Lucky M. Tedrow. 2001. "West Indians and the Residential Landscape of New York." Pp. 81–114 in *Islands in the City: West Indian Migration to New York City*, edited by Nancy Foner. Berkeley: University of California Press.

Cruse, Harold. 1970. "Revolutionary Nationalism and the Afro American." Pp. 345–69 in *For a New America*, edited by J. Weinstein and D. Eakins. New York: Vintage Books.

Cudjoe, Selwyn. 2000. "Afro-Trinbagonians: No Longer Blinded by Our Eyes." Available at www.trinicenter.com/cudjoe/2000/April/012000.htm.

———. 2001a. *Afro-Trinbagonians: No Longer Blinded by Our Eyes*. Wellesley, MA: Calaloux.

———. 2001b. "Black Empowerment Day." Available at www.trinicenter.com/cudjoe/2001/Mar/252001.htm

———. 2001c. "Cudjoe Answers the Critics." Available at www.trinicenter.com/cudjoe/2001/June/0462001.htm

———. 2001d. "National Association for the Empowerment of African People: A Retrospective." Available at www.trinicenter.com/cudjoe/2001/April/042001.htm

———. 2001e. "Race, Nation and Identity: The Case for the National Association for the Empowerment of African People." Available at www.trinicenter.com/cudjoe/2001/May/042001.htm

———. 2001f. "Respecting Our Culture." Available at www.trinicenter.com/cudjoe/2001/Apr/042001.htm

———. 2003a. "Afro-Trinbagonians, Racism and the Education System." Available at www.trinicenter.com/cudjoe/2003/1909.htm

———. 2003b. *Beyond Boundaries: The Intellectual Tradition of Trinidad and Tobago in the 19th Century*. Wellesley, MA: Calaloux Publications.

———. 2004a. "The Indianization of the Society." Available at www.trinicenter.com/cudjoe/2004/2601.htm

———. 2004b. "Morality and Politics." Available at www.trinicenter.com/cudjoe/2004/1502.htm

———. 2004c. "A Voice in the Wilderness." Available at www.trinicenter.com/cudjoe/2004/2201.htm

Daly, Vere T. [1966] 1975. *A Short History of the Guyanese People*. London: Macmillan.

———. 1974. *The Making of Guyana*. London: Macmillan.

Danns, Donna. 1996. "Financial Sector Development in the Caribbean 1970–1995." Paper presented at the Monetary Studies Conference, Trinidad and Tobago.

Davis, Horace. 1978. *Towards a Marxist Theory of Nationalism*. New York: Monthly Review Press.

Davison. R. B. 1962. *West Indian Migrants*. London: Institute of Race Relations, Oxford University Press.

Dawley, David. 1973. *A Nation of Lords: The Autobiography of the Vice Lords*. New York: Anchor Press.

Denizer, Cevdet. 2000. "Foreign Entry in Turkey's Banking Sector, 1980–97." *Mimeo*.

Dev, Ravi. 1998. "One People, One Nation." *Stabroek News*, June 1.

Doane, Ashley. 1996. "Rethinking the National Question: Toward a Theory of Ethnicity and Nationality in the New World Order." Pp. 175–92 in *Marxism Today: Essays on Capitalism, Socialism and Strategies for Social Change*, edited by Chronis Polychroniou and Harry Targ. London: Praeger.

Dookeran, Winston. 2002. "The Financial Liberalisation Agenda: Performance and Prospects." Pp. 429–41 in *Caribbean Survival and the Global Challenge*, edited by Ramesh Ramsaran. Kingston, Jamaica: Ian Randle Publishers.

Downes, David M. 1966. *The Delinquent Solution: A Study in Subcultural Theory*. New York: Free Press.

Draper, Theodore. 1970. *The Rediscovery of Black Nationalism*. New York: Viking.

Drummond, Lee. [1980] 1996. "The Cultural Continuum: A Theory of Intersystems." Pp. 189–214 in *Blackness in Latin America and the Caribbean*, vol. 2, edited by Arlene Torres and Norman E. Whitten, Jr. Bloomington: Indiana University Press.

Duany, Jorge. 2002. *Puerto Rican Nation on the Move: Identities on the Island and in the United States*. Chapel Hill: University of North Carolina Press.

Dupuy, Alex. 1991. "Political Intellectuals in the Third World: The Caribbean Case." Pp. 74–93 in *Intellectuals and Politics: Social Theory in a Changing World*, edited by Charles C. Lemert. London: Sage.

———. 1996. "Race and Class in the Postcolonial Caribbean: The Views of Walter Rodney." *Latin American Perspectives* 23, no. 2, issue 89 (spring): 107–29.

Durutalo, S. 1986. *The Paramountcy of Fijian Interest and Politicization of Ethnicity*. Suva: South Pacific Forum.

Eller, J., and R. Coughlan. 1993. "The Poverty of Primordialism: The Demystification of Ethnic Attachments." *Ethnic and Racial Studies* 16, no. 2: 185–202.

Ellis, Clarence F. 2004. "There Is Nothing in Indian Arrival Day for Either Race to Celebrate." *Stabroek News*, January 9.

Engels, Frederick. [1890] 1977. "Letter to Joseph Bloch." Pp. 487–89 in *K. Marx and F. Engels: Selected Works in Three Volumes*, vol. 3. Moscow: Progress Publishers.

———. [1893] 1977. "Letter to F. Mehring." Pp. 495–99 in *K. Marx and F. Engels: Selected Works in Three Volumes*, vol. 3. Moscow: Progress Publishers.

Ercan, Fuat. 2002. "The Contradictory Continuity of the Turkish Capital Accumulation Process: A Critical Perspective on the Internationalization of the Turkish Economy." Pp. 21–38 in *The Ravages of Neo-Liberalism: Economy, Society and Gender in Turkey*, edited by Neşecan Balkan and Sungur Savran. New York: Nova.

Ergil, Doğu. 2000. "The Kurdish Question in Turkey." *Journal of Democracy* 11, no. 3: 122–35.

Eriksen, T. H. 1993. *Ethnicity and Nationalism: An Anthropological Perspective*. London: Pluto.

Esperanza, Martell. 1998. "'In the Belly of the Beast': Beyond Survival" in *The Puerto Rican Movement: Voices of the Diaspora*, edited by Andrés Torres and José E. Valázquez. Philadelphia: Temple University Press.

Fanon, Frantz. 1963. *The Wretched of the Earth*, translated by Constance Farrington. New York: Grove.

Farrell, Terrence W. 1993. "Banking in a (Rapidly) Changing World." Address to Bank of Nova Scotia Management Meeting. Port of Spain, Trinidad. Mimeo.

Figueroa, Daurius. 2000. *A Spy in the Houses of Hate: The Ironies and Paradox of Black on Black Racism in Post Colonial Trinidad and Tobago.* Port of Spain, Trinidad: Daurius Figueroa.

Fiji Government. 1997. *Constitution of the Republic of Fiji.* Suva: Government Printer.

Fijilive.com and *Daily Post.* Friday, September 20.

Forrest, Raymond. 1991. "No Requiem for Workers Bank," *The Financial Gleaner,* January 18.

France, P. 1969. *The Charter of the Land: Custom and Colonization in Fiji.* Melbourne: Oxford University Press.

Frank, André Gunder. 1972. *Lumpenbourgeoisie; Lumpendevelopment: Dependence, Class and Politics in Latin America.* New York: Monthly Review Press.

Franklyn, Delano. 2001. *The Right Move: Corporate Leadership and Governance in Jamaica.* Kingston: Arawak Press.

Gampat, Ramesh. 1998. "In Guyana Politics Dictates Economics." *Stabroek News,* October 30.

Geertz, Clifford. 1973. *The Interpretation of Cultures.* New York: Basic Books.

Gellner, Ernest. 1983. *Nations and Nationalism.* Oxford: Blackwell.

Gendzier, Irene L. 1973. *Frantz Fanon: A Critical Study.* New York: Pantheon Books.

Gereffi, Gary. 1994. "The International Economy and Economic Development." Pp. 206–33 in *The Handbook of Economic Sociology,* edited by Neil J. Smelser and Richard Swedberg. Princeton, NJ: Princeton University Press.

Gereffi, Gary, and Peter Evans. 1995. "Transnational Corporations, Dependent Development, and State Policy in the Semiperiphery: A Comparison of Brazil and Mexico." Pp. 203–35 in *Latin America's Economic Development: Confronting Crisis,* edited by James L. Dietz. Boulder, CO: Lynne Rienner Publishers.

Geschwender, James. 1978. *Racial Stratification in America.* New York: William Brown & Co.

Giddens, Anthony. 1984. *The Nation State and Violence.* Berkeley: University of California Press.

Gilroy, Paul. 1987. *There Ain't no Black in the Union Jack: The Cultural Politics of Race and Nation.* London: Hutchinson.

———. 1993. *The Black Atlantic: Modernity and Double Consciousness.* Cambridge, MA: Harvard University Press.

———. 2000. *Against Race: Imagining Political Culture Beyond the Color Line.* Cambridge, MA: Harvard University Press.

Girvan, Norman. 2000. "Globalization and Counter-Globalization: The Caribbean in the Context of the South." Pp. 65–87 in *Globalization a Calculus of Inequality: Perspectives from the South,* edited by Denis Benn and Kenneth Hall. Kingston: Ian Randle Publishers.

Glasgow, Roy Arthur. 1970. *Guyana: Race and Politics among Africans and East Indians.* The Hague, the Netherlands: M. Nijhoff.

Glassman, Ronald. 1975. "Legitimacy and Manufactured Charisma." *Social Research* 42, no. 4: 615–36.

Golwalkar, Madhav S. [1939] 1944. *We, or Our Nation Defined.* Nagpur: Bharat Publications.

Gomes, Ralph. [1979] 1998. "Race, Class, and Politics in Guyana: The Role of the Power Elites." Pp. 146–59 in *Blackness in Latin America and the Caribbean,* vol.

2, edited by Arlene Torres and Norman E. Whitten, Jr. Bloomington: Indiana University Press.

González, José Luis. 1990. *Puerto Rico: The Four Storeyed Country*, translated by Gerald Guinness. Maplewood, NJ: Waterfront Press.

Goveia, Elsa. 1970. "The Social Framework." *Savacou: A Journal of the Caribbean Artists Movement* 2 (September): 7–15

Gramsci, Antonio. [1971] 1997. *Selections from the Prison Notebooks*, edited and translated by Quintin Hoare and Geoffrey Nowell Smith. New York: International Publishers.

Granger, McDonald. 2004. "Talk of 'Motherlands' Is Divisive, ARC Is the Answer." *Stabroek News*, April 3.

Greenfeld, Liah. 1992. *Nationalism: Five Roads to Modernity*. Cambridge, MA: Harvard University Press.

Grosby, Steven. 1994. "The Verdict of History: The Inexpungeable Tie of Primordiality." *Ethnic and Racial Studies* 17, no. 1: 164–71.

Grosfoguel, Ramon, and Chole S. Georas. 1996. "The Racialization of Latino Caribbean Migrants in the New York Metropolitan Area." *CENTRO: Journal of the Center for Puerto Rican Studies* 8, nos. 1–2: 190–201.

Guillén, Mauro F., and Adrian E. Tschoegl. 1999. "At Last the Internationalization of Retail Banking? The Case of the Spanish Banks in Latin America." Wharton Financial Institutions Center Working Paper Series. Available at http:// fic.wharton .upenn.edu/fic/papers/99/9941.pdf (accessed February 16, 2005).

Gupta, Akhil. 1992. "The Song of the Nonaligned World: Transnational Identities and the Reinscription of Space in Late Capitalism." *Cultural Anthropology* 7, no. 1: 63–79.

Guzmán, Pablo. 1998. "La Vida Pura: A Lord of the Barrio." Pp. 173–91 in *The Puerto Rican Movement: Voices of the Diaspora*, edited by Andrés Torres and José E. Valázquez. Philadelphia: Temple University Press.

Haas, Ernst B. 1986. "What Is Nationalism and Why Should We Study It?" *International Organization* 40, no. 3 (summer): 707–44.

Habermas, Jurgen. 1994. "Struggles for Recognition in the Democratic Constitutional State." Pp. 107–48 in *Multiculturalism: Examining the Politics of Recognition*, edited by Amy Guttman, translated by Shierry Weber Nicholson. Princeton, NJ: Princeton University Press.

Hackett, M. L. 1998. "The Conference on Race and Discrimination Was a Success." *Stabroek News*, December 24.

Haggard, Stephan, and Sylvia Maxfield. 1996. "The Political Economy of Financial Internationalization in the Developing World." Pp. 209–36 in *Internationalization and Domestic Politics,* edited by Robert O. Keohane and Helen V. Milner. Cambridge: Cambridge University Press.

Halisi, Clyde. 1967. *The Quotable Karenga*. Los Angeles: US Organization.

Hall, Stuart. 1980. "Race, Articulation, and Societies Structured in Dominance." Pp. 305–46 in *Sociological Theories: Race and Colonialism*. Paris: UNESCO.

———. [1990] 1996. "Cultural Identity and Diaspora." Pp. 110–21 in *Contemporary Postcolonial Theory: A Reader*, edited by P. Mongia. London: Arnold.

———. 1995. "Negotiating Caribbean Identities." *New Left Review* (January–February): 3–14.

Hall, Stuart, et al. 1978. *Policing the Crisis: Mugging, the State and Law and Order*. London: Macmillan.

Harney, Stefano. 1996. *Nationalism and Identity: Culture and Imagination in a Caribbean Diaspora*. London: Zed Books.

Hebdige, Dick. 1987. *Cut 'n' Mix: Culture, Identity, and Caribbean Music*. New York: Methuen.

Hechter, Micheal. 1975. *Internal Colonialism: The Celtic Fringe in British National Development 1536–1966*. Berkeley: University of California Press.

Henke, Holger. 2001. *The West Indian Americans*. Westport, CT: Greenwood Press.

Herrnstein, Richard, and Charles A. Murray. 1994. *The Bell Curve: Intelligence and the Class Structure in American Life*. New York: The Free Press.

Hill, Errol. 1972. *Trinidad Carnival: Mandate for National Theatre*. Austin: University of Texas Press.

Hilliard, David, and Lewis Cole. 1993. *This Side of Glory: The Autobiography of David Hilliard and the Story of the Black Panther Party*. Boston: Little, Brown and Company.

Hintzen, Percy. 1989. *The Costs of Regime Survival: Racial Mobilization, Elite Domination and Control of the State in Guyana and Trinidad*. Cambridge: Cambridge University Press.

———. 1997. "Reproducing Domination: Identity and Legitimacy Constructs in the West Indies." *Social Identities* 3, no. 1: 47–75.

Ho, Christine. 1991. *Salt-Water Trinnies: Afro-Trinidadian Immigrant Networks and Non-Assimilation in Los Angeles*. New York: AMS.

Hobsbawm, Eric. 1990. *Nations and Nationalism since 1780: Programme, Myth, Reality*. New York: Cambridge University Press.

Hobsbawm, Eric, and Terrence Ranger, eds. 1983. *The Invention of Tradition*. Cambridge: Cambridge University Press.

Hoffman, Susan. 2001. *Politics and Banking: Ideas, Public Policy and the Creation of Financial Institutions*. Baltimore: The Johns Hopkins University Press.

Hopkins, A. G. 1973. *An Economic History of West Africa*. London: Longman.

Horowitz, David L. 1985. *Ethnic Groups in Conflict*. Berkeley: University of California Press.

Howe, Stephen. 1998. *Afrocentrism: Mythical Pasts and Imagined Homes*. London: Verso.

Hughes, E. 1994. *On Work, Race and Sociological Imagination*. Chicago: University of Chicago Press.

Hutchinson, John, and Anthony D. Smith, eds. 1996. *Ethnicity*. Oxford: Oxford University Press.

Hylland Eriksen, Thomas. 2002. *Ethnicity and Nationalism: Anthropological Perspectives*. London: Pluto Press.

Ignatiev, Noel. 1995. *How the Irish Became White*. New York: Routledge.

Indian Review Committee. 1990a. "From Black Power to Black Muslimeen." Editorial in *The Indian Review* 4 (August–September): 1–3.

———. 1990b. "The Indian Muslim—Dilemma of Race and Religion." Editorial in *The Indian Review* 4 (August–September): 11.

———. 1990c. "An Indian Position of the African Emancipation Day Celebration." Editorial in *The Indian Review* 4 (August–September): 4–10.

———. 1991a. "Indian Arrival Day—May 1991." Editorial in *The Indian Review* 1:15.

———. 1991b. "Industan." Editorial in *The Indian Review* 1:3.

———. 1991c. "Muslim or Indian First?" Editorial in *The Indian Review* 1:13.

International Monetary Fund (IMF). 2000. *World Economic and Financial Surveys. International Capital Markets: Developments, Prospects, and Key Policy Issues.* Washington, DC: International Monetary Fund.

Isaacs, Harold R. 1975. *Idols of the Tribe: Group Identity and Political Change.* New York: Harper Colophon.

James, C. L. R. [1962] 1992. "From Toussaint L'Ouverture to Fidel Castro." Pp. 296–314 in *The C. L. R. James Reader*, edited by Anna Grimshaw. London: Blackwell.

———. 1969. *Beyond a Boundary.* London: Hutchinson.

———. 1980. *Spheres of Existence: Selected Writings.* London: Allison and Busby.

Jameson, Fredric. 1986. "Third World Literature in the Era of Multinational Capitalism." *Social Text* 15, no. 1: 65–88.

Jary, D., and J. Jary. 1991. *Collins Dictionary of Sociology.* London: HarperCollins Publishers.

Jenkins, R. 1997. *Rethinking Ethnicity: Arguments and Explorations.* London: Sage.

Jesudason, J. 1996. "The Syncretic State and the Structuring of Oppositional Politics in Malaysia." Pp. 128–60 in *Political Oppositions in Industrialising Asia*, edited by G. Rodan. New York: Routledge.

Jiménez, Cha Cha. 1969. "We're Fighting for Freedom Together. There Is No Other Way." *Black Panther*, August 2.

July, Peter. 1995. "Rise of the Formal Institution of Banking in the Community." *CARICOM Perspective* 65 (July): 91–93.

Karenga, Maulana Ron. 1977. *Kwanzaa: Origin, Concepts, Practice.* Los Angeles: Kawaida.

Karpat, Kemal. 1973. *Social Change and Politics in Turkey.* Leiden: E. J. Brill.

Kazgan, Gülten. 1999. *Tanzimattan 21.Yuzyyla Türkiye Ekonomisi.* Istanbul: Bilgi Üniversitesi Yayinlari.

Kearney, Michael. 1991. "Borders and Boundaries of the State and Self at the End of Empire." *Journal of Historical Sociology* 4, no. 1: 52–74.

Keesing, R. 1989. "Creating the Past: Custom and Identity in the Contemporary Pacific." *Contemporary Pacific* 1, nos. 2–3: 19–42.

Kellas, James. 1991. *The Politics of Nationalism and Ethnicity.* London: Macmillan Press.

Kellner, Douglas. 1989. *Critical Theory, Marxism and Modernity.* Cambridge: Polity Press.

Kendal. 1993. "The Kurds Under the Ottoman Empire." Pp. 11–37 in *A People without a Country*, edited by Gerard Chaliand. New York: Olive Branch.

Kersting, M. L. 1998. "No True Racism in Guyana." *Stabroek News*, December 24.

Kessler, Timothy. 1999. *Global Capital and National Politics: Reforming Mexico's Financial System.* Westport, CT: Praeger Publishers.

Keyder, Çağlar. 1981. *Definition of a Peripheral Economy: Turkey 1923–1929.* Cambridge: Cambridge University Press.

Khan, Bhabur M. 1998. "Ethnicity Is Breaking Loose from the Confines of the Nation-State." *Stabroek News*, December 24.

Kiernan, V. G. 1983. "Nation" and "Nationalism." Pp. 344–45 and 346–49 in *A Dictionary of Marxist Thought*, edited by Tom Bottomore. Cambridge, MA: Harvard University Press.

King, Nicole. 2001. *C. L. R. James and Creolization: Circles of Influence*. Jackson: University of Mississippi Press.

King, Richard H. 1992. *Civil Rights and the Idea of Freedom*. New York: Oxford University Press.

Kirisci, Kemal, and Gareth Winrow. 1997. *The Kurdish Question and Turkey*. Portland, OR: Frank Cass.

Klass, Morton. 1961. *East Indians in Trinidad: A Study of Cultural Persistence*. Prospect Heights, IL: Waveland Press.

———. 1991. *Singing with Sai Baba: The Politics of Revitalization in Trinidad*. Boulder: Westview Press.

Knight, Franklin. 1990. *The Caribbean: The Genesis of a Fragmented Nationalism*. New York: Oxford University Press.

Knox, Paul, and John Agnew. 1998. *The Geography of the World Economy: An Introduction to Economic Geography*, 3rd edition. London: Arnold.

Laclau, Ernesto. 1977. *Politics and Ideology in Marxist Theory*. London: Verso Books.

La Guerre, John, ed. 1974. *Calcutta to Caroni: The East Indians of Trinidad*. London: Longman Caribbean.

———. 1975. "Afro-Indian Relations in Trinidad: An Assessment." *Social and Economic Studies* 25, no. 3: 291–306.

Lamming, George. 1981. "Foreword." *A History of the Guyanese Working People, 1881–1905*, by Walter Rodney. Baltimore: The Johns Hopkins University Press.

Lawson, Stephanie. 1996. *Tradition versus Democracy in the South Pacific: Fiji, Tonga and Western Samoa*. Cambridge: Cambridge University Press.

Lenin, V. I. 1969. *What Is to Be Done?* Moscow: Progress Publishers.

Lester, Julius. 1969. *Look Out, Whitey! Black Power's Gon' Get Your Mama!* New York: Grove Press.

Lewis, Bernard. 1965. *The Emergence of Modern Turkey*. London: Oxford University Press.

Lindgren, Carl-Johan, Gillian Garcia, and Matthew I. Saal. 1996. *Bank Soundness and Macroeconomic Policy*. Washington, DC: International Monetary Fund.

Lovelace, Earl. 1988. "The On-Going Value of Our Indigenous Traditions." Collected in *The Independence Experience*, edited by Selwyn Ryan. St. Augustine, Trinidad: Institute for Social and Economic Research, University of the West Indies.

Lue Lim, Gail. 1991. *Jamaica's Financial System: Its Historical Development*. Kingston: Bank of Jamaica.

Lukács, Georg. 1971. *History and Class Consciousness*. London: Merlin Press.

Lukauskas, Arvid. 2002. "Financial Restriction and the Developmental State in East Asia: Toward a More Complex Political Economy." *Comparative Political Studies* 35, no. 4 (May): 379–412.

Maha Sabha. 1998. "An Afrocentric Racism." *Express*, February 12.

Mahabir, Joy. 1998. "Rhetoric of Hinduism Misused," *Express*, April 10.

Maharaj, Ashram B. 1996. "Representative Bureaucracy in Trinidad and Tobago." *The Indian Review*: 5–8. Couva, Trinidad: India Review Committee.

Maharaj, D. Parsuram. 2002. *Clash of Cultures: The Indian-African Competition in Trinidad*. Arima, Trinidad: The Indian Free Press.

Maharaj, Indira. 2001. "Maha Sabha." *Express*, March 2.

Makler, Harry, and Walter L. Ness, Jr. 2002. "How Financial Intermediation Challenges National Sovereignty in Emerging Markets." *Quarterly Review of Economics & Finance* 42, no. 5 (winter): 827–51.

Malcolm X. 1970. *By Any Means Necessary*. New York: Pathfinder Press.

——. 1971. *The End of White World Supremacy: Four Speeches by Malcolm X*, edited by Imam Benjamin Karim. New York: Seaver.

Malkki, Liisa H. 1992. "National Geographic: The Rooting of Peoples and the Territorialization of National Identity among Scholars and Refugees." *Cultural Anthropology* 7, no. 1: 24–44.

Mangru, Basdeo. 1999. *Indians in Guyana: A Concise History from Their Arrival to the Present*. Chicago: Adams Press.

Manley, Robert H. 1979. *Guyana Emergent: The Post-Independence Struggle for Nondependent Development*. Boston: Schenkman Publishing Co.

Mara, K. K. T. 1997. *The Pacific Way: A Memoir*. Honolulu: University of Hawaii Press.

Marichal, Carlos. 1997. "Nation Building and the Origins of Banking in Latin America, 1850–1930." Pp. 339–77 in *Banking, Trade and Industry: Europe, America and Asia from the Thirteenth to the Twentieth Century*, edited by Alice Teichova, Ginette Kurgan-Van Hentenryk, and Dieter Ziegler. Cambridge: Cambridge University Press.

Martell, Esperanza. 1998. "In the Belly of the Beast: Beyond Survival." Pp. 173–91 in *The Puerto Rican Movement: Voices of the Diaspora*, edited by Andrés Torres and José E. Valázquez. Philadelphia: Temple University Press.

Marx, Karl. 1963. *The Poverty of Philosophy*. New York: International Publishers.

——. 1974. *Economic and Philosophical Manuscripts of 1844*. Moscow: Progress Publishers.

Marx, Karl, and Frederick Engels. 1947. *The German Ideology*. New York: International Publishers.

——. 1955. *The Communist Manifesto*. New York: Appleton-Century-Crofts.

Massey, Douglas, and Nancy Denton. 1993. *American Apartheid: Segregation and the Making of the Underclass*. Cambridge, MA: Harvard University Press.

Mathew, Biju, and Vijay Prashad. 2000. "The Protean Forms of Yankee *Hindutva*." *Ethnic and Racial Studies* 23, no. 3: 516–34.

McCarthy, Justin. 1997. *The Ottoman Turks*. London: Longman.

McDowall, David. 2000. *A Modern History of the Kurds*. London: Tauris.

McKay, J. 1982. "Primordial and Mobilizationalist Approaches to Ethnic Phenomena." *Ethnic and Racial Studies* 6, no. 2: 395–420.

McKinnon, Ronald. 1973. *Money and Capital in Economic Development*. Washington, DC: Brookings Institution.

Melwani, Lavina. 1995. "What Are Over 200,000 Guyanese Hindus Doing in New York State?" *Hinduism Today*: 95–108.

Menezes, Mary Noel. 1977. *British Policy towards the Amerindians in British Guiana, 1803–1873*. Oxford: Clarendon Press.

Merleau-Ponty, Maurice. 1973. *Adventures of the Dialectic*. Evanston, IL: Northwestern University Press.

Migdal, Joel. 2001. *State-in-Society: Studying States and Society and How They Transform and Constitute One Another*. New York: Cambridge University Press.

Miles, Robert. 1989. *Racism*. London: Routledge.

Miller, Daniel. 1997. *Capitalism: An Ethnographic Approach*. Oxford: Oxford University Press.

Mills, Charles. 1997. *The Racial Contract*. Ithaca, NY: Cornell University Press.

Milner, Helen V., and Robert O. Keohane. 1996. "Introduction." Pp. 3–24 in *Internationalization and Domestic Politics*, edited by Robert O. Keohane and Helen V. Milner. Cambridge: Cambridge University Press.

Mizruchi, Mark S., and Linda Brewster Stearns. 1994. "Money, Banking and Financial Markets." Pp. 313–41 in *The Handbook of Economic Sociology*, edited by Neil J. Smelser and Richard Swedberg. Princeton, NJ: Princeton University Press.

Monar, Rooplall. 1998. "We Are Not Indians, We Are Guyanese." *Stabroek News*, October 30.

Moore, Brian L. [1987] 1995. *Cultural Power, Resistance and Pluralism: Colonial Guyana 1838–1900*. Kingston, Jamaica: The University Press of the West Indies.

Morales, Iris. 1996. "Palante Siempre Palante: The Young Lords" (documentary). New York: Latino Education Network, Inc.

———. 1998. "Palante, Siempre Palante: The Young Lords." Pp. 210–27 in *The Puerto Rican Movement: Voices of the Diaspora*, edited by Andrés Torres and José E. Valázquez. Philadelphia: Temple University Press.

Morris, Mervyn, ed. 1990. *Contemporary Caribbean Short Stories*. London: Faber & Faber.

Mukta, Parita. 2000. "The Public Face of Hindu Nationalism." *Ethnic and Racial Studies* 23, no. 3: 442–66.

Mukta, Parita, and Chetan Bhatt, eds. 2000. "*Hindutva* Movements in the West: Resurgent Hinduism and the Politics of Diaspora." Special Issue. *Ethnic and Racial Studies* 23, no. 3: 401–615.

Munck, Ronaldo. 1986. *The Difficult Dialogue: Marxism and Nationalism*. London: Zed Books.

Murinde, Victor. 2001. "Does Africa Need Foreign Banks?" Africa Online. Available at www.africanonline.com/site/Articles/1,3,46765.jsp (accessed February 2, 2003).

Nagel, Joane, and Susan Olzak. 1982. "Ethnic Mobilization in New and Old States: An Extension of the Competition Model." *Social Problems* 30:127–43.

Naipaul, V. S. 1961. *A House for Mr. Biswas*. London: Andre Deutsch.

———. 1962. *The Middle Passage: Impressions of Five Societies, British, French and Dutch in the West Indies and South America*. London: Andre Deutsch.

———. 1999. *Letters Between a Father and Son*. London: Little, Brown and Company.

Nairn, Tom. 1975. "The Modern Janus." *New Left Review* 94 (November–December): 3–29.

———. 1977. *The Break-Up of Britain*. London: New Left Books.

Nandan, N. 2001. *Requiem for a Rainbow: A Fijian Indian Story*. Canberra: Pacific Indian Publications.

Neiman Auerbach, Nancy. 2001. *States, Banks and Markets: Mexico's Path to Financial Liberalization in Comparative Perspective*. Boulder, CO: Westview Press.

Newton, Huey P. 1967. *Essays from the Minister of Defense.* Pamphlet.

Ogbu, James. 1990. "Minority Status and Literacy in Comparative Perspective." *Daedalus* 119, no. 2: 141–68.

Ollman, Bertell. 1977. *Alienation: Marx's Conception of Man in Capitalist Society.* Cambridge: Cambridge University Press.

Ollman, Bertell. 1993. *Dialectical Investigations.* New York: Routledge.

Olson, Robert. 1989. *The Emergence of Kurdish Nationalism and the Sheikh Said Rebellion: 1880–1925.* Austin: University of Texas Press.

"One People." 1998. Editorial. *Stabroek News,* December 24.

Ong, Aihwa. 1999. *Flexible Citizenship: The Cultural Logics of Transnationality.* Durham, NC: Duke University Press.

Oomen, T. K. 1997. *Citizenship and Identity: From Colonialism to Globalism.* London: Sage.

Oxaal, Ivar. 1971. *Race and Revolutionary Consciousness: A Documentary Interpretation of the 1970 Black Power Revolt in Trinidad.* Cambridge, MA: Schenkman.

Pantin, Raoul. 1990. *Black Power Day: The 1970 February Revolution, A Reporter's Story.* Santa Cruz, Trinidad: Hatuey.

Patterson, Orlando. 1973. "The Ritual of Cricket." *Jamaica Journal* 3, no. 1 (1969). Reprinted in *Caribbean Essays: An Anthology,* edited by Andrew Salkey. London: Evans Brothers.

Pearson, Hugh. 1994. *In the Shadow of the Panther.* New York: Addison-Wesley.

Pérez, Sofía A. 1997. *Banking on Privilege: The Politics of Spanish Financial Reform.* Ithaca, NY: Cornell University Press.

Persad, Kamal. 1993. "Lingering Dream of an Indian Homeland." Pp. 117–19 in *H. P. Singh: The Indian Struggle for Justice and Equality against Black Racism in Trinidad & Tobago (1956–1962),* edited by Kamal Persad and Ashram Maharaj. Chaguanas, Trinidad: Indian Review Press.

———. 1996. "The Indian Spectre or Crisis in the Media." *The Indian Review:* 45–52. Couva, Trinidad: India Review Committee.

———. 1997. *Hinduraj in the Caribbean.* Pamphlet. Couva, Trinidad: Indian Review Committee.

Persad, Kamal, and Ashram Maharaj. 1993. "Introduction: H. P. Singh and Indian Nationalism in Trinidad & Tobago." Pp. xl–lxvii in *H. P. Singh: The Indian Struggle for Justice and Equality against Black Racism in Trinidad & Tobago (1956–1962),* edited by Kamal Persad and Ashram Maharaj. Chaguanas, Trinidad: Indian Review Press.

Pomerleano, Michael, and George J. Vojta. 2001. "What Do Foreign Banks Do in Emerging Markets? An Institutional Study." Presented at the World Bank, International Monetary Fund and Brookings Institution Third Annual Financial Markets and Development Conference, Open Doors: Foreign Participation in Financial Systems in Developing Countries. April 19–21, New York.

Poulton, Hugh. 1997. *Top Hot, Grey Wolf and Crescent.* New York: New York University Press.

Prashad, Vijay. 2000. *The Karma of Brown Folk.* Minneapolis: University of Minnesota Press.

Quataert, Donald. 2000. *The Ottoman Empire 1700–1922.* Cambridge: Cambridge University Press.

Raj, Dhooleka Sarhadi. 2000. "'Who the Hell Do You Think You Are?' Promoting Religious Identity among Young Hindus in Britain." *Ethnic and Racial Studies* 23, no. 3: 535–58.

Rajagopal, Arvind. 2000. "Hindu Nationalism in the US: Changing Configurations of Political Practice." *Ethnic and Racial Studies* 23, no. 3: 467–96.

Ramharrack, Baltoram. (n.d.). "Distinguished Caribbean Hindu: Balram Singh Rai." Available at www.Caribbeanhindu.com/Rai.htm (accessed January 13, 2005).

Ramkissoon, Ronald. 2002. "Globalisation and the Caribbean Financial Sector: Toward a Strategy for Survival." Pp. 455–64 in *Caribbean Survival and the Global Challenge*, edited by Ramesh Ramsaran. Kingston, Jamaica: Ian Randle Publishers.

Ratcliffe, Peter, ed. 1994. *"Race," Ethnicity, and Nation: International Perspectives on Social Conflict*. Bristol, PA: UCL Press.

Ratuva, Sitiveni. 1999. "Ethnic Conflict, Communalism and Affirmative Action in Fiji: A Critical and Comparative Study." Unpublished Ph.D. diss., Institute of Development Studies, University of Sussex.

———. 2002a. "The Paradox of Multi-Culturalism: Managing Differences in Fiji's Syncretic State." Paper presented to international conference on Pluricultural States and Rights to Differences, University of New Caledonia, July 3–5.

———. 2002b. *Participation for Peace: A Study of Inter-ethnic and Inter-religious Perception in Fiji*. Suva: Ecumenical Center for Research, Education and Advocacy.

Ravi-ji. 2000. "Warm Welcome to a World Teacher." *Sunday Guardian*, August 6: 24.

Ravuvu, A. 1991. *The Façade of Democracy*. Suva: Reader Publishing House.

Regis, Louis. 1999. *The Political Calypso: True Opposition in Trinidad and Tobago, 1962–1987*. Gainesville: University Press of Florida.

Ritzer, George. 1992. *Classical Sociological Theory*. Toronto: McGraw-Hill.

Rivera, Raquel Z. 1996. "Boriquas from the Hip-Hop Zone: Notes on Race and Ethnic Relations in New York City." *CENTRO, Journal of the Center for Puerto Rican Studies* 8, nos. 1–2: 202–15.

Robbins, Philip. 1993. "The Overlord State: Turkish Policy and the Kurdish Issue." *International Affairs* 69, no. 4: 657–76.

Rodney, Walter. 1981. *A History of the Guyanese Working People, 1881–1905*. Baltimore: The Johns Hopkins University Press.

Roediger, David R. 1991. *Wages of Whiteness: Race and the Making of the American Working Class*. New York: Verso.

Rother, Larry. 1997. "High Level Name Calling across the Racial Fence." *Express*, August 21.

Ruhomon, Peter. [1947] 1988. *Centenary History of the East Indians of British Guiana 1838–1938*. Guyana: East Indians 150th Anniversary Committee.

Rushton, J. Philippe. 1995. *Race, Evolution and Behaviour: A Lifehistory Perspective*. New Brunswick, NJ: Transaction Publishers.

Ryan, Selwyn D. 1972. *Race and Nationalism in Trinidad and Tobago: A Study of Decolonization in a Multiracial Society*. Toronto: University of Toronto Press.

———. 1996. *Pathways to Power*. St. Augustine, Trinidad: Institute for Social and Economic Research, University of the West Indies.

———. 1999a. "East Indians, West Indians and the Quest for Caribbean Political Unity." *Social and Economic Studies* 48, no. 4: 151–84.

———. 1999b. *The Jhandi & the Cross: The Clash of Cultures in Post-Creole Trinidad and Tobago*. St. Augustine, Trinidad: Institute for Social and Economic Research, University of the West Indies.

Ryan, Selwyn D., and Taimoon Stewart, eds. 1995. *Black Power Revolution of 1970— A Retrospective*. St. Augustine, Trinidad: Institute for Social and Economic Research, University of the West Indies.

Said, Edward. 1988. "Foreword." Pp. v–x in *Selected Subaltern Studies*, edited by R. Guha and G. C. Spivak. New York: Oxford University Press.

Sanday, J. 1991. *The Military in Fiji: A Historical Development and Future Role*. Working Paper, Australian National University.

Santiago-Valles, Kelvin. 1996. "Policing the Crisis in the Whitest of All the Antilles." *CENTRO, Journal of the Center for Puerto Rican Studies* 8, nos. 1–2: 42–57.

Savarkar, Vinayak D. [1923] 1989. *Hindutva Or Who Is a Hindu?* Bombay: Veer Savarkar Prakashan.

Schiffer, Irvine. 1973. *Charisma: A Psychoanalytic Look at Mass Society*. Toronto: University of Toronto Press.

Seale, Bobby. 1970. *Seize the Time: The Story of the Black Panther Party and Huey P. Newton*. New York: Random House, 1970.

Searle-Chatterjee, Mary. 2000. "'World Religions' and 'Ethnic Groups': Do These Paradigms Lend Themselves to the Cause of Hindu Nationalism?" *Ethnic and Racial Studies* 23, no. 3: 497–515.

Searwar, Lloyd, ed. 1970. *Co-Operative Republic, Guyana 1970: A Study of Aspects of Our Way of Life*. Georgetown: Government of Guyana.

Seecharan, Clem. 1993. *India and the Shaping of the Indo-Guyanese Imagination 1890s–1920s*. Leeds, UK: Peepal Tree and the University of Warwick.

Serrano, Basilio. 1998. "'Rifle, Cañon, y Escopeta!' A Chronicle of the Puerto Rican Student Union." Pp. 124–43 in *The Puerto Rican Movement: Voices from the Diaspora*, edited by Andrés Torres and José E. Velázquez. Philadelphia: Temple University Press.

Shils, Edward. 1957. "Primordial, Personal, Sacred and Civil Ties." *British Journal of Sociology* 8, no. 2: 130–45.

———. 1965. "Charisma, Order and Status." *American Sociological Review* 30, no. 2: 199–213.

———. 1968. "Color, the Universal Intellectual Community, and the Afro-Asian Intellectual." Pp. 1–17 in *Color and Race*, edited by John H. Franklin. Boston: Houghton Mifflin.

———. 1981. *Tradition*. London: Faber & Faber.

Short, James F., and Fred L. Strodtbeck. 1974. *Group Process and Gang Delinquency*. Chicago: University of Chicago Press.

Siddharta, Orie L. 1996. "Within the Rising Sun—More Rising Sons and Daughters." *The Indian Review*: 3–4. Couva, Trinidad: India Review Committee.

Singh, Hari Prashad. 1993a. "Hour of Decision." Pp. 1–7 in *H. P. Singh: The Indian Struggle for Justice and Equality against Black Racism in Trinidad & Tobago (1956–1962)*, edited by Kamal Persad and Ashram B. Maharaj. Chaguanas, Trinidad: Indian Review Press.

———. 1993b. "The Indian Enigma." Pp. 84–104 in *H. P. Singh: The Indian Struggle for Justice and Equality against Black Racism in Trinidad & Tobago (1956–1962)*, edited by Kamal Persad and Ashram B. Maharaj. Chaguanas, Trinidad: Indian Review Press.

Smart, Ian Isidore, and Kimani S. K. Nehusi, eds. 2000. *Ah Come Back Home: Perspectives on the Trinidad and Tobago Carnival*. Washington, DC: Original World Press.

Smith, Anthony D. 1983a. *State and Nation in the Third World*. New York: St. Martin's Press.

———. 1983b. *Theories of Nationalism*, 2nd ed. New York: Holmes and Meier.

———. 1984. "National Identity and Myths of Ethnic Descent." *Research in Social Movements, Conflict and Change* 7:5–130.

———. 1988. "The Myth of the 'Modern Nation' and the Myths of Nations." *Ethnic and Racial Studies* 11, no. 1: 1–26.

———. 1991. *National Identity*. Reno, NV: University of Nevada Press.

Smith, M. G. 1965. *The Plural Society in the British West Indies*. Berkeley: University of California Press.

Smith, Roy C., and Ingo Walter. 1997. *Global Banking*. New York: Oxford University Press.

Stavenhagen, Rodolfo. 1996. *Ethnic Conflict and the Nation-State*. London: Macmillan.

Stuempfle, Stephen. 1995. *The Steelband Movement: The Forging of a National Art in Trinidad and Tobago*. Philadelphia: University of Pennsylvania Press.

Sudama, Trevor. 1983. "Class, Race and the State in Trinidad and Tobago." *Latin American Perspectives* 10, no. 4, issue 39: 75–96.

Sutherland, W. 1994. *An Alternative History of Fiji to 1992*. Canberra: Australian National University Press.

Szymanski, Albert. 1983. *Class Structure: A Critical Perspective*. New York: Praeger.

Taylor, Charles, et al. 1994. *Multiculturalism: Examining the Politics of Recognition*, edited by Amy Guttman. Princeton, NJ: Princeton University Press.

Thapar, Romila. 2000. "On Historical Scholarship and the Uses of the Past." [Interviewed by Parita Mukta]. *Ethnic and Racial Studies* 23, no. 3: 594–615.

Thomas, Clive. 1974. "Imperial Monetary Arrangements and the Caribbean" Pp. 153–58 in *Readings in the Political Economy of the Caribbean*, compiled and edited by Norman Girvan and Owen Jefferson. Kingston, Jamaica: New World Press.

Thomas, Greg. 1995. "Multiculturalism versus Afrocentricity: The Black Studies War." *Village Voice* (January 17): 23–29.

Thomas, William Isaac, and Dorothy Thomas. 1928. *The Child in America*. New York: Alfred Knopf.

Thompson, Richard. 1989. *Theories of Ethnicity: A Critical Appraisal*. New York: Greenwood Press.

Thompson, Robert Farris. 1983. *Flash of the Spirit: African and Afro-American Art and Philosophy*. New York: Vintage.

Thorburn, Diana. 1997. "Gender, Regionalism, and Caribbean Development: An Examination of CARICOM Policy." M.Sc. Thesis, Institute of International Relations, University of the West Indies, St. Augustine, Trinidad and Tobago.

———. 2000. "A Reformed Public Sector in an Integrated Caribbean in the 21st Century? Some Preliminary Results from a Project with These Goals." Paper presented at the 2000 Congress of the Latin American Studies Association, Miami, Florida.

———. 2002. "Implications of Liberalisation for Commercial Banking in the Caribbean." Pp. 442–55 in *Caribbean Survival and the Global Challenge*, edited by Ramesh Ramsaran. Kingston, Jamaica: Ian Randle Publishers.

Tölölian, Khaching. 1991. "The Nation-State and Its Others: In Lieu of a Preface." *Diaspora* 1, no. 1: 3–7.

Torres, Andres. 1995. *Between Melting Pot and Mosaic: African-Americans and Puerto Ricans in the New York Political Economy*. Philadelphia: Temple University Press.

Torres Rivas, Edelberto. 1977. "Notas Sobre la Crísis de la Dominación Burguesa en América Latina." Pp. 13–70 in *Clases Sociales y Crisis Política en América Latina*, edited by Raúl Benítez Zenteno. Mexico: Siglo Veintiuno.

Townshend, Jules. 1996. *The Politics of Marxism: The Critical Debates*. London: Leicester University Press.

Turner, Victor. 1986. "Carnaval in Rio: Dionysian Drama in Industrializing Society." Pp. 123–38 in *The Anthropology of Performance*. New York: PAJ Publications.

Van Bruinessen, Martin. 1992. "Kurdish Society, Ethnicity, Nationalism and Refugee Problems." Pp. 33–67 in *The Kurds*, edited by Philip G. Kreyenbroek and Stefan Sperl. London: Routledge.

———. 1994. "Kurdish Nationalism and Competing Ethnic Loyalties." *Peuples Méditerranéens* 68–69:11–37.

Van Deburg, William L. 1992. *New Day in Babylon: The Black Power Movement and American Culture, 1965–1975*. Chicago: University of Chicago Press.

Vigil, James Diego. 1988. *Barrio Gangs: Street Life and Identity in Southern California*. Austin: University of Texas Press.

Walcott, Derek. [1974] 1998. "The Muse of History." Pp. 36–64 in *What the Twilight Says*. New York: Farrar, Straus, and Giroux.

———. 1993. *The Antilles: Fragments of Epic Memory: The Nobel Lecture*. New York: Farrar, Straus, and Giroux.

Wallerstein, Immanuel M. 1972. "Social Conflict in Post-Independence Black Africa: The Concepts of Race and Status Group Reconsidered." Pp. 207–26 in *Racial Tensions and National Identity*, edited by Ernest Q. Campbell. Nashville, TN: Vanderbilt University Press.

———. 1979. *The Capitalist World-Economy*. Cambridge: Cambridge University Press.

Waters, Mary. 1999. *Black Identities: West Indian Immigrant Dreams and American Realities*. Cambridge, MA: Harvard University Press.

Weber, Max. 1978. *Economy and Society*. Berkeley: University of California Press.

Whalen, Carmen Teresa. 1998. "The Young Lords in Philadelphia." Pp. 107–23 in *The Puerto Rican Movement: Voices of the Diaspora*, edited by Andrés Torres and José E. Valázquez. Philadelphia: Temple University Press.

Williams, Brackette. 1991. *Stains on My Name, War in My Veins: Guyana and the Politics of Cultural Struggle*. Durham, NC: Duke University Press.

Williams, Marion V. 1996. *Liberalising a Regulated Banking System: The Caribbean Case*. Hants, UK: Avebury.

Williams, Eric. 1962. *History of the People of Trinidad and Tobago*. Port of Spain, Trinidad: PNM Publishing Co.

———. 1966. *Capitalism and Slavery*. New York: G. P. Putnam's Sons.

———. 1970. *From Columbus to Castro: The History of the Caribbean, 1492–1969.* New York: Vintage Books.

Williams, Robin M., Jr. 1994. "The Sociology of Ethnic Conflicts: Comparative International Perspectives." *Annual Review of Sociology* 20:9–79.

Wolpe, Harold. 1986. "Class Concepts, Class Struggle and Racism." Pp. 110–30 in *Theories of Race and Ethnic Relations*, edited by John Rex and David Mason. Cambridge: Cambridge University Press.

Woodard, Komozi. 1999. *A Nation within a Nation: Amiri Baraka (LeRoi Jones) and Black Power Politics.* Chapel Hill: University of North Carolina Press.

Worrell, DeLisle. 1983. "Banking in Barbados, 1960–82." Central Bank of Barbados. October. Mimeo.

Wotherspoon, Terry, and Vic Satzewich. 1993. *First Nations: Race, Class and Gender Relations.* Scarborough, Ontario: Nelson.

Wright, Winthrop R. 1974. *British-Owned Railways in Argentina: Their Effect on Economic Nationalism, 1854–1948.* Austin: University of Texas Press.

Yavuz, Hakan M. 2000. "Cleansing Islam from the Public Sphere." *Journal of International Affairs* 54, no. 1 (fall): 21–42.

Yeğen, Mesut. 1999. "The Kurdish Question in Turkish State Discourse." *Journal of Contemporary History* 34, no. 4: 555–68.

Yelvington, Kevin, ed. 1993. *Trinidad Ethnicity.* Centre for Caribbean Studies at the University of Warwick Series. Knoxville: University of Tennessee Press.

Young Lords Party and Michael Abramson. 1971. *Palante: The Young Lords Party.* New York: McGraw-Hill.

Zavitz, Amanda, and Anton L. Allahar. 2002. "Racial Politics and Cultural Identity in Trinidad's Carnival." *Identity: An International Journal of Theory and Research* 2, no. 2: 125–46.

Zysman, John. 1983. *Government, Markets and Growth: Financial Systems and the Politics of Industrial Change.* Ithaca, NY: Cornell University Press.

About the Contributors

Anton Allahar was born in Trinidad, West Indies, and moved to Canada in 1969. He completed his MA and PhD in Political and Economic Sociology at the University of Toronto and is currently Professor of Sociology at The University of Western Ontario. Dr. Allahar's principal areas of interest are economic development, the politics of liberal democracy, and nationalism and ethnic relations. He has published six books and monographs on various sociological dimensions of Cuban, Caribbean, and Canadian society. In addition, he has edited five volumes on various aspects of politics, ethnicity, and nationalism; published over fifty refereed journal articles and book chapters; and served as editor of the *International Journal of Comparative Race and Ethnic Studies,* coeditor of the *International Journal of Sociology,* and associate editor of *Identity: An International Journal of Theory and Research.*

Shona Jackson recently completed her PhD in the Modern Thought and Literature Program at Stanford University. She is also the founder and coeditor of the Caribbean Studies book series at Lexington Books. Dr. Jackson has been an instructor at George Mason University and has taught at both Stanford and Howard Universities. She is the author of "Caribbean Women Authors and Identity in Literature" (1996); "Race, Sex, and Historical Tension in the Search for the Transcendental Creole Subject" (forthcoming 2005); and "Subjection and Resistance in the Transformation of Guyana's Mytho-colonial Landscape" (forthcoming 2005). Dr. Jackson now teaches at Texas A&M in the English Department.

Joshua Jelly-Schapiro was born in the Green Mountains of Vermont and is a 2002 graduate of Yale College. Supported by a Parker Huang fellowship, he conducted participatory research on popular education and community development in Havana, Cuba. The essay that appears herein is adapted from a senior thesis in Yale's Ethnicity, Race, and Migration Program the associated students and faculty of which he would like to gratefully acknowledge for their dedication to making the links between knowledge production and social change ever more real. In addition to his work as an activist and youth soccer coach, he has published work in *The International Socialist Review* and numerous student publications, including *Continua, Glimpse,* and the *Journal of Contemporary Culture.*

Jeffrey O. G. Ogbar received his BA in History from Morehouse College and his MA and PhD (both in History) from Indiana University. He is currently Associate Professor of History and Director of the Institute for African American Studies at the University of Connecticut. His publications include *Black Power: Radical Politics and African American Identity* (2004) and an edited volume entitled *Civil Rights: Problems in American Civilization* (2003). He is also author of several scholarly articles. Dr. Ogbar's academic interests include nationalism, radical social protest, and hip-hop.

Steven Ratuva is a political sociologist and a fellow at the Department of Political and Social Change in the Research School of Pacific and Asian Studies at the Australian National University. He completed his PhD at the Institute of Development Studies, University of Sussex, United Kingdom. His areas of research interest and expertise are comparative ethnic conflict, conflict resolution, state-civil relations, the military, and affirmative action. He has taught at the University of the South Pacific in Fiji and has carried out joint research with a number of international research institutions and universities. Dr. Ratuva has also been Conflict Resolution and Democratic Governance Advisor and consultant to a number of international agencies such as the United Nations Development Programme and Asian Development Bank.

Selwyn Ryan is Professor Emeritus at the University of the West Indies. Dr. Ryan received his PhD in Political Science from Cornell University and has taught in the West Indies, Canada, Ghana, and Uganda. Dr. Ryan has also been a member of the board of two Constitutional Commissions established by the government of Trinidad and Tobago. He was also Chairman of the Public Utilities Commission of Trinidad and Tobago and Deputy Chairman of the Caribbean Press Council. Dr. Ryan is the author and editor of more than ten books and scores of articles on all aspects of Caribbean society and politics. He has served as president of the Caribbean Studies Association and as Head of the Department of Government (University of the West Indies, St. Augustine). At the time of his retirement, he held the position of University

Director of the Institute of Social and Economic Research at the University of the West Indies.

Cenk Saraçoğlu received his BA in International Relations in 2002, from Bilkent University in Ankara, Turkey. He then joined the Sociology Department at The University of Western Ontario, where he obtained his MA in Sociology. His main areas of interest are theories of ethnicity and nationalism, the Kurdish question in Turkey, women and development, and international political economy. He recently published "Nihal Atsiz: Sub-consciousness of the Ultra-Nationalist Movement in Turkey" (2004) and has worked as a teaching assistant in the History Department of Sabanci University, Istanbul. Mr. Saraçoğlu is currently a PhD candidate in the Department of Sociology at The University of Western Ontario.

Diana Thorburn was born in Jamaica and holds an MA in International Relations from the University of the West Indies, Trinidad. She recently completed her PhD in the Department of Western Hemisphere Studies at the School of Advanced International Studies, Johns Hopkins University. Her dissertation is a political economy analysis of the domestic factors involved in the expansion of multinational retail banks in Latin America in the 1990s. Dr. Thorburn is currently a lecturer in the Department of Government at the University of the West Indies, Mona, Jamaica. Her publications include "Gender, Regionalism, and Caribbean Development" (1997), "A Reformed Public Sector in an Integrated Caribbean in the 21st Century?" (2000), and "Implications of Liberalisation for Commercial Banking in the Caribbean" (2002).